Twenty-First Joyce

The Florida James Joyce Series

Florida A&M University, Tallahassee
Florida Atlantic University, Boca Raton
Florida Gulf Coast University, Ft. Myers
Florida International University, Miami
Florida State University, Tallahassee
University of Central Florida, Orlando
University of Florida, Gainesville
University of North Florida, Jacksonville
University of South Florida, Tampa
University of West Florida, Pensacola

Twenty-First Joyce

Edited by Ellen Carol Jones and Morris Beja

University Press of Florida
Gainesville/Tallahassee/Tampa/Boca Raton
Pensacola/Orlando/Miami/Jacksonville/Ft. Myers

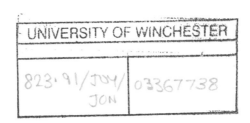
Copyright 2004 by Ellen Carol Jones and Morris Beja
Printed in the United States of America on acid-free paper

09 08 07 06 05 04   6 5 4 3 2 1

Library of Congress Cataloging-in-Publication Data
Twenty-first Joyce / edited by Ellen Carol Jones and Morris Beja.
p. cm.—(The Florida James Joyce series)
Include bibliographical references and index.
ISBN 0-8130-2760-8 (cloth : alk. paper)
1. Joyce, James, 1882–1941—Criticism and interpretation. 2. Ireland—
In literature. 1. Jones, Ellen Carol. II. Beja, Morris. III. Series.
PR6019.O9Z846 2004
823'.912—dc22   2004055479

The University Press of Florida is the scholarly publishing agency
for the State University System of Florida, comprising Florida A&M
University, Florida Atlantic University, Florida Gulf Coast University,
Florida International University, Florida State University, University
of Central Florida, University of Florida, University of North Florida,
University of South Florida, and University of West Florida.

University Press of Florida
15 Northwest 15th Street
Gainesville, FL 32611-2079
http://www.upf.com

For Zack Bowen

Contents

The Incertitude of the Void: Modernist Narrative

Foreword

The diversity of issues in this collection is more than ample testimony not only to the continuing popularity of James Joyce but also to the seemingly endless fascination he generates in novel critical ways in which his work may be profitably addressed. The continuing fertility of the ideas that are embedded in his fiction motivates generation after generation of scholars to adapt new methodologies better to address both the modern and postmodern as well as the age-old problems he so graphically depicts. Joyce demanded new interpretive ideas to address the new questions he raised and unprecedented techniques he helped generate. If Joyce studies in the twenty-first century are as diverse and rewarding as the splendid essays compiled by Ellen Carol Jones and Morris Beja, there is no end in sight as to what possibilities Joyce will offer his readers.

We became aware of the emergence of pop-culture Joyce appreciation when Dublin celebrated the centenary of his birth in 1982 amid public festivities that bought Joyce out of religious and political exile and into the warm glow of a potential Irish tourist asset. London's Joyce millennial celebration helped open up a new Gregorian age of homage and emphasized Joyce's twenty-first-century kinship to modern cultural, political, and social concerns. And about the time this volume is released, Joyceans will be gathering in Dublin and across the world to celebrate the one hundredth anniversary of Bloomsday—a modern/postmodern commemoration of a day on which a fictive journey was taken by an immortal ad salesman—and Joyceans will make their international biennial pilgrimage in celebration of the epiphanic reality of his fiction. Whatever prompts the rites that celebrate the nature of Joyce's genius also provides a living vital proof of his enormous contributions to modern society.

I would like to express my deep and sincere appreciation of my old friends and colleagues, Ellen Carol Jones and Morris Beja, whose hard work in organizing the academic program for the 2001 Miami Joyce conference ("2001: A Joyce Odyssey") led to the present volume. I am indebted to them for their generous dedication of this book and for our lifetime of friendship and mutual respect in the celebration of Joyce. I am equally thankful to my friends in Joyce studies who agreed to contribute their brilliant essays to a volume dedicated to its own series editor. I am a little embarrassed (though I'll get over it) because I feel so proud of being honored in this way by my colleagues in Joyce, the crowd that was, after all, the one I always wanted most to please.

Some substantial share of any Florida-generated laurels rightly belong to Bernard Benstock, who was the first editor of the *James Joyce Literary Supplement* and the University Press of Florida's Joyce Series, and who, along with Patrick McCarthy, formed the nucleus of what Stephen Joyce used to refer lovingly to as the "Miami Mafia."

Zack Bowen, University of Miami

Abbreviations

The following abbreviations are standard for references to Joyce's works and important secondary texts, following the conventions established by the *James Joyce Quarterly*. Where a contributor has used an alternative edition, that edition will be noted in the Works Cited at the end of the essay.

CP   Joyce, James. *Collected Poems.* New York: Viking, 1957.

CW   Joyce, James. *The Critical Writings of James Joyce*, edited by Ellsworth Mason and Richard Ellmann. New York: Viking, 1969.

D   Joyce, James. *Dubliners: Text, Criticism, and Notes*, edited by Robert Scoles and A. Walton Litz. New York: Viking, 1969.

E   Joyce, James. *Exiles.* New York: Viking, 1951.

FW   Joyce, James. *Finnegans Wake.* New York: Viking, 1939; London: Faber, 1939 and subsequent reprints. These two editions have identical pagination. Citation includes page and line number.

GJ   Joyce, James. *Giacomo Joyce*, edited by Richard Ellmann. New York: Viking, 1968; London: Faber, 1968.

JJA   Joyce, James. *The James Joyce Archive*, edited by Michael Groden et al. 63 volumes. New York, Garland: 1977–80.

JJI   Ellmann, Richard. *James Joyce.* New York: Oxford University Press, 1959.

JJII   Ellmann, Richard. *James Joyce.* Rev. ed. New York: Oxford University Press, 1982.

Letters

I, II, III Joyce, James. *Letters of James Joyce*, Vol. I, edited by Stuart Gilbert. New York: Viking, 1957; reissued with corrections 1966. Vols. II and III, edited by Richard Ellmann. New York: Viking, 1966.

P   Joyce, James. *A Portrait of the Artist as a Young Man.* The definitive text corrected from Dublin Holograph by Chester G. Anderson and edited by Richard Ellmann. New York: Viking, 1964. Joyce, James. *A Portrait of the Artist as a Young Man: Text, Criticism, and Notes*, edited by Chester G. Anderson. New York: Viking, 1968.

SH   Joyce, James. *Stephen Hero*, edited by Theodore Spencer, John J.
          Slocum, and Herbert Cahoon. New York: New Directions, 1963.
SL   Joyce, James. *Selected Letters of James Joyce*, edited by Richard
          Ellmann. New York: Viking, 1975; London: Faber, 1975.
U   Joyce, James. *Ulysses*, edited by Hans Walter Gabler, et al. New
          York and London: Garland, 1984, 1986. Editions published by
          Garland, Random House, Bodley Head, and Penguin. Citations
          include episode and line number.
U   Joyce, James. *Ulysses*, 1934; reset and corrected 1961 (New York:
          Vintage-Random, 1990). Citations include page number.

Nacheinander, Nebeneinander

The Joyce Centuries

Ellen Carol Jones and Morris Beja

We seem to be in for another Joyce century.

Cyril Connolly famously begins his *The Unquiet Grave* by saying, "The more books we read, the sooner we perceive that the true function of a writer is to produce a masterpiece and that no other task is of any consequence. Obvious though this should be, how few writers will admit it" (1). One writer who would have admitted it—who based his whole working life and career on that assumption—was James Joyce. As it turned out, Joyce produced more than one masterpiece. Even in an age in which many critics shy from aesthetic judgments of any kind, few serious readers or critics deny the term "masterpiece" to his major works: *Dubliners, Portrait, Ulysses,* and—controversial as it in particular remains—*Finnegans Wake.* That is why he continues to be read into the twenty-first century, and why it is more essential than ever to explore and study the sources of the power of his work.

Joyce is frequently cited as the outstanding literary artist of the twentieth century, and almost invariably as its most important and influential novelist. All indications are that, as the title of this volume suggests, he will remain a key figure in the twenty-first century—and beyond. For, as Richard Brown observes in the present volume, reading for example *Ulysses* "from a twenty-first-century perspective may remind us how far we have come in our cultural consciousness since the book was written and how far it has helped to construct the stages of that progress away from reductive binaries and toward something else in our present and future states. But it may also remind us of how far we still have to go." We hope and believe that the essays here collected serve as such a reminder even as they help us along our way.

The Same People in the Same Place—or Different Places: Cultural
Studies, History, Nationalism, and Transnationalism

The essays in "The Same People in the Same Place—or Different Places"
contribute to our contemporary understanding of Joyce's works through
perspectives employing cultural studies, new historicism, popular culture,
economic and political theory—and thoroughgoing scholarship.

"Joyce's Dubliners, like their real-life counterparts, and like many citizens of postcolonial nations today, reside in a transitional economy that
partakes uneasily of both the premodern and the industrial. In such circumstances, gift practices become particularly powerful markers of social
status and connection," claims Mark Osteen in "'A Regular Swindle': The
Failure of Gifts in *Dubliners.*" Osteen analyzes a "spectrum of aborted largesse": the distortions and perversions of social obligations by Joyce's
Dubliners that result in social fragmentation and alienation. "Handicapped
by poverty, duplicity, and delusions of grandeur," Joyce's characters, he
points out, "nonetheless seek to promote fellowship and status through
gift exchanges; but the results are bribery, hostility, and despair. Efforts at
displaying generosity almost inevitably metamorphose into what Little
Chandler's wife, Annie, calls a "regular swindle."

Dissecting the economic, religious, political, and sexual reasons for the
failure of gifts in colonial Dublin, Joyce contrasts the impotent idealism of
giving as a moral imperative with mercenary investments in erotic and
social capital. *Dubliners* suggests that "only those flexible enough to negotiate the transition between the realms of gift and commodity escape self-
swindling." And Osteen notes as well that the failure of largesse in Joyce's
early style may effect his own self-swindling: "After all, what is Joyce's
meticulous verbal parsimony—that vaunted 'scrupulous meanness' of
style that he described to Stanislaus . . . —but the Dublin affliction translated into the practice of composition?" By using sociological, anthropological, and economic studies to examine Joyce's world, Osteen suggests
how we may "challenge current critical commonplaces and . . . establish
new paradigms for the next century of Joyce studies, and indeed for an age
of globalization in which the last pre-industrial economies are being converted to capitalism."

Mary Lowe-Evans explores in "Joyce's Sacred Heart Attack: Exposing
the Church's Imperialist Organ" how Irish women—the gendered subaltern of British imperial rule—are also peculiarly subjected to a second
master, an alternative empire, "the holy Roman catholic and apostolic

church" (*U* 1.643–44). Through Joyce, she examines how women can collude in the consolidation of the church's will to phallocratic and imperial power—and come to represent that power—without understanding or questioning it. The Sacred Heart operates as "the silent and invisible puppeteer" behind that collusion. Lowe-Evans suggests that Irish devotion to the Sacred Heart, coming to prominence during the drive for political independence in post-Famine Ireland, provides Joyce "a specific, detailed emblem of the colonized psyches of the Irish people (one that effectively contributed to the myth of suffering Ireland) on one hand, and ecclesiastical ambition on the other." Joyce deploys that emblem, among other religious icons, "to open the way into a much larger debate involving the Irish Catholic Church, Irish independence, and sexual identity." Depicting Eveline in the final scene of the *Dubliners* story as immobilized, Joyce demonstrates, according to Lowe-Evans, how the will to live outside the bounds of the ecclesiastical patriarchal and imperial gaze is foreclosed. Such a strategy indicates Joyce's conviction "that Catholic devotional practice lends itself both to the proximate goal of developing a docile congregation and to the larger purpose of maintaining and expanding a hierarchical phallocracy" in the exercise of ecclesiastical empire-building. By exposing "the complicated ways in which the church harnessed and manipulated the forces of human desire," Lowe-Evans argues, "his works continue—in the twenty-first century—to trouble the orthodox."

Anne Fogarty reminds us that Joyce criticism "needs at once self-consciously to catalogue and take stock of the wealth of exegesis that his work has attracted; to position itself in relation to longstanding debates; inventively to formulate fresh questions and to reconnoiter new fields of inquiry; and finally to acknowledge the provisionality of all attempts to pin down the protean qualities of Joyce's fiction." Exploring the interaction between space and time in "States of Memory: Reading History in 'Wandering Rocks,'" Fogarty argues that even though this fragmented episode concentrates on the present, it registers and depicts different forms of individual, national, and collective memory and also playfully portrays and deconstructs several competing versions of Irish history. Critical reception of this section of *Ulysses* notes its experimentalism, yet Fogarty asserts that even though critics have accepted the consensus that "Wandering Rocks" diagnoses the ills and moribund nature of Irish society, they have ignored the conflicting personal, political, and historical perspectives within the episode.

In probing how current theories of cultural memory might be deployed in order to analyze the competing and elusive types of historical recall in "Wandering Rocks," Fogarty considers the extent to which Joyce's text is embedded in and helps to construct the historical contexts through which we view them. Analyzing historical allusions in the successive fragments, she demonstrates the extent to which the entire chapter is hinged upon competing versions of history: imperial and nationalist, private and public, heroic and antiheroic. The references to historical events and figures, she argues, have "a double impetus: they alert us to the inchoate and splintered nature of history in the divided collectivity of a colonial society, but they also resurrect potent memories of a buried, yet continuous, Irish counterinsurgency." Discussing the historical allusiveness of this episode of *Ulysses* and of the modes of memory on which it draws, she shows that as "the material and historical realities to which *Ulysses* alludes recede further from us, one of the chief challenges facing the twenty-first-century critic is how to prevent these contexts, on the one hand, from fading, and on the other, from solidifying into falsely reductive accounts of early twentieth-century Ireland."

Richard Brown presents a new millennial retrospect on some of the ideological implications of sport in *Ulysses* in "Cyclopean Anglophobia and Transnational Community: Re-reading the Boxing Matches in Joyce's *Ulysses.*" In "Circe," Stephen's fight with the soldiers, echoing the novel's boxing references, potentially subverts the "binary model of national conflict" itself. Issues of "cultural legitimation, of social class, of gender (especially . . . of masculinity), of ideology, of cultural identity and community" are played out in representations of sport, games, and the spectacle of sport both in popular culture and in Joyce's text. Thus the sporting references in *Ulysses* serve as more than "popular-cultural documentary"; they demonstrate, as paradigms of the dangers of binary oppositions in culture and in politics, "how Joyce's texts can draw attention to the ways in which cultures tend to make strategic monstrosities out of their 'others.'" Sport and the popular cultural spectacle of sport thus provide Joyce's audience "analogies both for Stephen's utopian but emergent model of the transnational kind of community that might be imagined as a goal of his aspiring literary production and for Bloom's sometimes transcendently pragmatic politics of the everyday."

"Jumbo, the elephant, loves Alice, the elephant" (*U* 12.1496). Exploring how Joyce compacts sociopolitical history in a throwaway, Sebastian Knowles tells us "The True Story of Jumbo the Elephant." When P. T.

Barnum in 1882 "bought English" and bought big, acquiring Jumbo from the Regent's Park Zoo, all of Britain seemed to indulge in rituals of mourning as commercialized as any Barnum himself could have scripted. Such extravagant investment in the spectacle of mourning during the Boer War and Irish Land League agitation, the London *Times* wrote, suggested that "it speaks volumes for the fundamental levity of adult nature that men have, for the last fortnight, given the first and foremost place in those of their thoughts which did not regard themselves, not to kingdoms and their destinies, but to Jumbo." As Knowles points out, this comedy, "played on a hyperbolic stage, is a distraction, as it is in 'Cyclops,' and a distraction from the same subject: the loss of a gigantic imperial dream." Tethered to that dream just as securely as Alice the Elephant was tethered to Jumbo's remains, and indulging in proleptic—and parodic—spectacles of mourning its loss, the British lamented the Empire's self-eclipse *avant la lettre*.

Storytelling as a process of de-reification, John Rocco argues in "Time Travel on Wings of Excess: 'Ithaca' and a Message in a Bottle," renders history manageable: "the processes behind the machine of history—industrialization, imperialism, colonialism, class conflict—are depicted on a level that can be grasped as a 'petty' event." Noting that Joyce wrote *Ulysses* "surrounded by the chaos of war and the destruction of that bourgeois artifact Flaubert crafted called the novel," Rocco maintains that "Ithaca" follows "Flaubert's fascination with and critique of the bourgeois 'fact'; but at the same time, the penultimate chapter of *Ulysses* excessively announces the end of history, the end of bourgeois mimesis, and the end of the novel." And the large dot at the end of this chapter of excess, Rocco suggests, signals the end of excess, the end of representation.

In a moving and personal postscript, Rocco considers not only "Joyce's impact on American culture" (especially rock music) but also a new perspective on Joyce and "the end of history" since September 11, 2001.

Dagger Definitions: Translation and Language

Through his writing, Joyce explores how culture is produced in the act of social survival and *as* an act of social and political survival. Survival—what Jacques Derrida terms *sur-vivre*, to live on the borderlines—becomes a process of negotiation between incommensurable cultural differences, signaled, often, by incommensurable linguistic differences. In such a cultural politics, translation—of language, of bodies—becomes the metaphor for the historical necessity (in our time as in Joyce's) of the colonized to bear witness, and itself bears witness to what cannot be signified, to silence, to the incommensurable.

In "Joyce *en slave* / Joyce Enclave: The Joyce of Maciej Słomczyński—A Tribute," Jolanta W. Wawrzycka investigates Derrida's point that, for Walter Benjamin, the translator ensures the original text's demand for survival: "Translation augments and modifies the original, which, insofar as it is living on, never ceases to be transformed and to grow. It modifies the original even as it also modifies the translating language. This process—transforming the original as well as the translation—is the translation contract between the original and the translating text" (Derrida 122). Such a contract, Derrida maintains, "is destined to assure a survival, not only of a corpus or a text or an author but of languages." No social contract is possible, he insists, "without a translation contract," without the mediation and reconciliation that translation enacts between languages and between cultures (122, 125). How, Wawrzycka asks, is the original text *languaged* in the target language? Maciej Słomczyński demands that "translated work should resemble a living organism," the original living on in the target language. Wawrzycka argues that Słomczyński succeeds in his task as translator of creating for his audience—and through his audience, because reading itself is an act of translation—a "Polish Joyce." In making her argument, Wawrzycka shows that "translation, the ultimate act of close reading and interpretation, partakes in a variety of late-twentieth-century postmodern and postimperial phenomena by having engendered theoretical stances that opened venues for re-reading received sociocultural milieus."

"Ah, Dedalus, the Greeks!" Mulligan urges, "You must read them in the original" (*U* 1.79–80); to do so obviously helps. Much lip service has been paid over the years, for example, to the associations between Bloom and Odysseus, but Keri Ames's knowledge of Homer in "the original," and her attention to the denotations and connotations of Homer's actual words, lead in "The Rebirth of Heroism from Homer's *Odyssey* to Joyce's *Ulysses*" to a study of Joyce's approach to "heroism"—an approach that both "revolutionizes" and "reinforces" Homer's conception of ἥρως. We always knew that the "hero" of the *Odyssey* had reconceived the heroism of the *Iliad*; Ames details how that revolution works itself out within the *Odyssey*, as when she discusses how placing hero and man together in the genitive case has "the grammatical effect" of combining the meaning of the two words to express a single idea. For both Homer and Joyce, in ancient Greece and in Joyce's time and in ours, there is heroism—actual, not merely potential—in the ordinary. After laying the groundwork with an analysis of the term "hero" in Homer, Ames shows how an awareness of Homer's perspective illuminates our understanding of Bloom and of Joyce's achievement in *Ulysses*.

The Incertitude of the Void: Modernist Narrative

"The Incertitude of the Void" explores a number of Joyce's narrative strategies, calling attention to the apparently infinite variety of these strategies, the exorbitance of his styles. Among the most striking of these strategies are those that seem almost prophylactic, with an enticing and courageous mode of self-censorship that forces the reader into exploring what is hidden, not said, closeted.

In "Shocking the Reader in 'A Painful Case,'" Margot Norris demonstrates how such strategies can jolt and disturb us. Norris provides cogent evidence that Joyce's story is about a "closeted" man; but she goes beyond that to argue that *the story itself* is "closeted," as she simultaneously complicates, problematizes, and clarifies Joyce's presentation of Mr. Duffy. By "retaining, initially at least, loose personifications of narrator and reader as more or less unified subjects and agents," Joyce incorporates in "A Painful Case" "egregious manipulations of the reader's emotional and ethical response." Inevitably, as Norris shows, we see the tale of Mr. Duffy and his relationship with Mrs. Sinico (and his fear of such a relationship) from our own temporal perspective, but she situates us as well "in the historical conditions that not only linked the scandals of Charles Stewart Parnell and Oscar Wilde to each other in Joyce's mind, but that extended their caution of the punishment that 'exceptionalism' visits on gifted Irishmen to himself."

Morton P. Levitt too leads us to pay attention to what Joyce does *not* say. Levitt argues in "Joyce and the Origins of Modernism: . . . What Is Not Said in 'Telemachus'" that Joyce's modernism is not a sudden spiritual manifestation arising out of nowhere in the middle of *Ulysses*, or even in *Portrait of the Artist*, but, in fact, is evident at the start of the very first story in *Dubliners*. While acknowledging a number of key "sources" in Joyce's short stories—such figures as Ibsen, Zola, and Flaubert—Levitt also recognizes the even more revolutionary additions Joyce contributed to their narrative "mix." Above all, most operative in Joyce's style is what he "does not tell us, what he does not say at all, what he knows well enough even at this early stage of his development to leave out: and thus leave to his reader. The great master of the vast, encyclopedic Modernist narrative is distinguished most by what he omits."

Levitt extends his claims for the modernism of *Dubliners* by arguing that the intense, even extreme modernism of Joyce's narrative method in *Ulysses* appears on the first page, even in the first line: "*Ulysses* is radical from its opening words, consistently radical through to its closing words. There is no break—in technique or in theme—between the first and the second parts of the novel." And Levitt amplifies this argument to assert, polemically, that "we may well need to rethink the relationship between Modernism and what follows in its wake," later in Joyce's century and into ours. He argues that to insist on a "'narrator' in *Ulysses* is a necessary post-Modernist critical invention in order to justify the existence of a post-Modernist criticism."

Examining the association of discourse with intercourse, a common subtext among writers of the early twentieth century, Thomas Rice in "Condoms, Conrad, and Joyce" argues "not only that this subtext is pervasive in modernist writing, but also that thwarted communication, both among characters in these works of literature and between their authors and their audience, comes to represent a kind of prophylaxis." The *condomization* of the text, he states, is an attempt by modernist writers "self-protectively to sheathe their texts, to shield their words from their audience, not so much from the fear that their words might be made flesh as from an anxiety that a more direct conversation with the public body might expose their works to some kind of contamination." Analyzing the symptom of textual prophylaxis in Joseph Conrad's *The Secret Agent* and Joyce's texts, particularly *Ulysses,* Rice points out that "both authors figuratively employ a mass-cultural product as a shield to protect their works from full communication with, and contamination by, mass culture itself." Andreas Huyssen, in *After the Great Divide,* claims of modernist art that "Only by fortifying its boundaries, by maintaining its purity and autonomy, and by avoiding any contamination with mass culture and with the signifying systems of everyday life can the art work maintain its adversary stance: adversary to the bourgeois culture of everyday life as well as adversary to mass culture and entertainment which are seen as the primary forms of bourgeois cultural articulation" (54). But as Rice notes, Joyce's work, unlike Conrad's, both exemplifies and critiques what Peter Bürger terms the "autonomy aesthetic" of modernism.

For Rice, "Joyce's similarly equivocal relationship to the *pas de deux* between the autonomy aesthetic of modernism and the activism of the avant-garde not only strongly distinguishes his receptiveness to the avant-gardist critique of the bourgeois institutionalization of art from Conrad's endorsement of institutional suppression in *The Secret Agent* but also acts a major, insufficiently acknowledged, governing tension in *Ulysses.*" This tension is most fully effected in the *Wake*, which Rice suggests is "the limit case of modernist textual condomization." But conversely, he points out, "in its hypercommunicativity—its superabundance of discourse, rather than thwarted intercourse—*Finnegans Wake* disseminates the seeds of the conclusion of 'Oxen of the Sun,' there held in reserve, to generate a work that stands equally as a monument of literary modernism and of the avant-garde: a socially, politically, and aesthetically revolutionary attempt to make art possible for the modern world."

In "Plausibility and Epimorphs," Fritz Senn provides new terminology for one of Joyce's most intriguing departures from traditional narrative expectations. Senn interrogates the plausibility of verisimilitude in the dialogue, interior monologue, and narrative of *Ulysses*. He questions the realism of the virtuoso verbal runs of Stephen Dedalus's speech in episodes such as "Scylla and Charybdis" and "Oxen of the Sun," or the oratory of John F. Taylor, whose unprepared speech seems quoted verbatim, despite the disclaimer by MacHugh in "Aeolus"—the episode that, as Senn notes, has after all "an editor presiding who determines what goes in." Stephen "does in fact 'act speech.'" Both speech and interior monologue are stylized by the thematic mode that drives or signs the narrative of an episode. Narrative plausibility is suspended in the second half of the novel, dissolving into narrative caprice.

Senn proposes the term "epimorph" for the "deviations away from, or superimposition on, an initial realistic mode. The ad hoc term 'epimorph' serves as a label for the particular colorings that seem to be imposed, thrust upon, as it were from above (therefore *epi*), on the chapter's shape (*morphe*)." The very language of individual episodes, including characters' speech, is fashioned by, even simulates or feigns, the thematics of those episodes, latent in the early episodes but dominant later in the novel. Thus Senn shows that the "later *Ulyssean* exorbitances (literally what leaves a conventional track) are germinally operative right from the start" of the text, forcing a retrospective arrangement of interpretation. (As Senn notes, interpretations are themselves epimorphic conversions.) And, given that "language itself is epimorphic," Joyce, through the epimorphic exorbitance of his text, reveals the processes whereby words come to mean.

All those fortunate to have heard, over the years, Zack Bowen's renditions of "The New Bloomusalem" will be glad to see, here, his determination to "lay the cornerstones of a New Critical Bowenusalem for the coming century of Joyce criticism by resolving the differences between those contemporary critics who cite Joyce in order to substantiate their favorite literary theory and others who apply literary theory merely to illuminate their favorite Joyce text." By analyzing in "Theoretical Bloom" first Stephen's and then Bloom's "theoretical" approaches to art and life, Bowen combines his characteristic wit and his expertise on the role of music in Joyce's works to illuminate the aesthetic and theoretical matters he explores: he shows that "like a chord resolving itself," Stephen and Bloom are "drawn together . . . on the only ground on which they have much in common, music," and that they may indeed "have found the source of commonality to forge the uncreated conscience of their race."

Zack Bowen has had an extraordinarily distinguished career as a scholar, critic, editor, teacher, and university administrator. His scholarship has been wide-ranging, within and beyond Irish studies. Within the present context, anyone who has worked in Joyce studies has been in Zack Bowen's debt—and knows it. Bowen's is an influence to which we are all indebted, and from which none of us can escape. So it is fitting that this volume is dedicated to him, with gratitude.

Works Cited

Connolly, Cyril. *The Unquiet Grave: A Word Cycle by Palinurus.* New York: Viking, 1945.
Derrida, Jacques. "Roundtable on Translation." In *The Ear of the Other: Otobiography, Transference, Translation,* edited by Christie McDonald and translated by Peggy Kamuf, 91–161. Lincoln: University of Nebraska Press, 1985.
Huyssen, Andreas. *After the Great Divide: Modernism, Mass Culture, Postmodernism.* Bloomington: Indiana University Press, 1986.

The Same People in the Same Place— or Different Places

Cultural Studies, History, Nationalism, and Transnationalism

"A Regular Swindle"

The Failure of Gifts in *Dubliners*

Mark Osteen

It is a striking historical coincidence that the rise of modernist literature took place concurrently with the emergence of modern anthropology and sociology. Critics were not slow to recognize certain modernists' "anthropological" approaches to comparative mythology: one recalls, for example, T. S. Eliot's explicit references to Jessie L. Weston's *From Ritual to Romance* in his notes to *The Waste Land,* and Stuart Gilbert's explication of James Joyce's use of Greek myth and epic in *Ulysses.* However, early critics had little to say about the modernists' employment of specific sociological or anthropological paradigms, perhaps because most modernist authors derived their anthropological material from literary sources—classical epic, medieval legend, Chinese poetry—rather than from social science texts. Even now, when literary scholars boast of advancing "political" or "historical" readings of Joyce and other authors, we seldom bother to acquaint ourselves with actual works of sociology, economics, or anthropology, aside from rounding up the usual suspects—Adorno, Althusser, Jameson, Foucault, or Bataille—and parading them by the observation tower. What goes largely unappreciated is the way that modernist texts, and Joyce's in particular, exemplify the discoveries of modern and contemporary social scientists. This neglect is strange, since Joyce himself sometimes described his work as a sociological document: an author who announces his intention to write a "moral history" of his country (*Letters II* 134) is adducing examples as a scientist displays specimens or tests hypotheses. That "nicely polished looking-glass" in which Joyce hoped to reflect Dubliners' foibles is also a microscope, a scientific instrument designed to advance the "course of civilisation in Ireland" (*Letters I* 64).

Hence, as a first step toward bringing Joyce criticism into the twenty-first century, we must, paradoxically, look backward, re-reading Joyce in light of the sociological and anthropological texts of his age, and thereby begin to recover the social contexts for his works. Doing so may enable us both to challenge current critical commonplaces and to establish new paradigms for the next century of Joyce studies, and indeed for an age of globalization in which the last pre-industrial economies are being converted to capitalism. Thus, in what follows I intend to scrutinize in detail the ways that Joyce uses one such socio-anthropological paradigm—that of the gift—to map his chosen terrain and to depict the collision between old and new values and practices and the effects of that collision on his fictional human beings.

One of Joyce's social science contemporaries was French anthropologist Marcel Mauss, whose brief 1925 treatise *Essai sur le don* (*The Gift*) is one of the seminal texts in comparative anthropology. Mauss compellingly argues that gifts in so-called "primitive" societies were "total social phenomena" that expressed and served religious, juridical, moral, political, and economic functions all at once (3). Mauss shows that what appear to be disinterested, gracious social rituals involve competition, obligation, and hostility as well as friendliness and generosity. By the end of his monograph, however, Mauss seems to lose sight of his own evidence and laments that the spirit of the gift has faded from modern society, much to our detriment. Those "primitives," he concludes, were "less sad, less serious, less miserly, and less personal than we are. Externally at least, they were or are more generous, more liable to give than we are" (81). He then exhorts his readers to learn from these generous "primitives," to substitute alliance and solidarity for hostility, isolation, and stagnation (82–83).

Most histories of the gift offer a similar narrative, here summarized by Jonathan Parry: "as the economy becomes increasingly disembedded from society, as economic relations become increasingly differentiated from other types of social relationship, the transactions appropriate to each become ever more polarized in terms of their symbolism and ideology" (466). According to this narrative, the domain of the gift has been gradually invaded, occupied, and finally displaced, so that it now plays only a minor role in the everyday economy, functioning almost exclusively among kin or close friends and posing no threat to the dominant ideology and practices of mercantile capitalism. Recently, however, Natalie Zemon Davis (among others) has challenged this story, arguing that gift giving and receiving have never faded entirely, and that "gift exchange persists as an essential relational mode, a repertoire of behavior, a register with its own rules, language, etiquette and gestures" (9). Even in the twentieth century (as, no doubt, it will in the new century), it takes its place beside two other "relational modes"—the "mode of sales" and the "mode of coercion" (extortion, theft, and so on [Davis 9])—as a primary means of social interaction. Davis's statement about the persistence of gift exchange applies particularly well to early twentieth-century Dublin, a city lacking a strong industrial class, whose economy had been stifled for centuries by the British presence, and whose citizens clung to a mythic vision of Ireland as a kingdom governed by ancient traditions of honor, heroism, and self-sacrifice. Joyce's Dubliners, like their real-life counterparts, and like many citizens of postcolonial nations today, reside in a transitional economy that partakes uneasily of both the premodern and the industrial. In such circumstances, gift practices become particularly powerful markers of social status and connection.

Mauss's ambivalence about the gift—his recognition that it not only expresses a purer sense of grace and generosity but also remains an instrument of power and status—also finds exceptionally strong expression in *Dubliners*. For the most part, however, Joyce's citizens seem to exemplify Mauss's sad, ungenerous moderns. Indeed, our examination will suggest that each one of the three interlocking obligations analyzed by Mauss— the obligations to give, to receive, and to reciprocate (Mauss 39)—is distorted in Joyce's Dublin. Giving fails to generate good feeling or prestige but nevertheless remains an undeniable moral imperative; receiving gifts leads to resentment or onerous debt; reciprocity is withheld, disrupted, or neglected entirely. The result is a broad and profound sense of fragmentation, frustration, and alienation. Thus, although Phillip Herring has suggested that *Dubliners* demonstrates a "persistent advocacy of the gift exchange cycles of love, trust, hospitality, and friendship together with a deep suspicion of" commerce (178), those values are conspicuous mostly by their absence. The characters' performance in gift rituals is deeply flawed, as the volume repeatedly depicts gifts mislaid, unsent, misinterpreted, or unwelcome. Handicapped by poverty, duplicity, and delusions of grandeur, the characters nonetheless seek to promote fellowship and status through gift exchanges; but the results are bribery, hostility, and despair. Efforts at displaying generosity almost inevitably metamorphose into what Little Chandler's wife, Annie, calls a "regular swindle" (*D* 71).

John Gordon has wittily demonstrated how the theme of loss and subtraction pervades the stories. The Dublin condition, he notes, is an "inordinate degree of susceptibility . . . to loss" (347). And yet, as Mauss argues, loss is natural and healthy for a society, because through economic losses citizens generate gains in other registers. The "gifts" that Mauss described in such rituals as the Kwakiutl potlatch ceremony—in which chieftains and other wealthy clansmen give extravagant reciprocal gifts and engage in orgies of property destruction in order to establish and solidify prestige—only look voluntary; in fact, he noted, they are obligatory and are practiced with the goal of crushing rivals (3, 41). In other words, what looks like generosity is actually an index of social power: citizens lose property in order to gain status. Through giving, economic capital is converted into what Pierre Bourdieu terms "symbolic capital" or "social capital"—fame, power, or rank (*Outline* 179).[1]

Mauss was, of course, far from the first to recognize this phenomenon, for the capacity to turn loss into gain through largesse has been recognized in the West as a sign of nobility at least since Aristotle's *Nicomachean Ethics*, which outlines three forms of generosity, the greatest of which is *megalopsychia* (greatness of soul), usually translated as "magnanimity." According to Aristotle, the magnanimous person confers benefits but is ashamed of receiving them, and will "repay benefits with interest, so that his original benefactor, in addition to being paid, will have become a debtor and a beneficiary" (1124b; 70).[2] Much later, Nietzsche seems to have had Aristotle in mind when in *Thus Spoke Zarathustra* he lauded the "gift-giving virtue" as "the highest" of all (186).[3] The magnanimous person exercises the gift-giving virtue by giving freely and in return receiving greater gifts, enhanced prestige, or both. The concept of magnanimity thus reveals what anthropologist Annette Weiner has identified as the essential paradox of the gift: how to "keep-while-giving" (5).[4] Magnanimity is also the ideal to which Joyce's Dubliners, particularly the males, aspire. Constrained by poverty and wedded to unproductive social habits, however, they fail to transform their losses into moral or social gains. Even when they do give, Joyce's males are oppressed rather than enriched by the giving. This phenomenon is most clearly displayed in the stories of "mature life," which disclose a spectrum of aborted largesse: Chandler, of "A Little Cloud," is humiliated by his drinking partner's gay worldliness and his wife's ingratitude; in "Counterparts," Farrington deepens his poverty of spirit and purse by leading a barroom potlatch; in the painful case of James Duffy, emotional and financial meanness signifies a rejection of all social bonds and a permanent condition of alienation.

A second key principle drawn from the anthropology of gifts also comes into play here: inalienability. Certain objects, Mauss suggests, never move outside the family, and even when handed down to the next generation are surrounded by rituals of great solemnity; these possessions are never really given at all, because they continue to bear the identity of their first owner (Mauss 43). Such objects, never fully dissociated from their original possessors even when relinquished, are said to be *inalienable*. In the enchanted world of Mauss's "primitives," "everything speaks" (44), but inalienable objects always speak in the specific voice of a person, family, clan, or tribe. Such possessions function as a "force against change" by authenticating origins and kinship histories (Weiner 9, 33); they further suggest that we can understand exchangeable objects only by juxtaposing them with objects withheld from exchange. Indeed, inalienable possessions serve as the foundation of the gift system for anthropologist Chris Gregory, who expands the distinction between alienability and inalienability into an ambitious schema in which gifts and commodities embody two vastly different social systems and visions of identity. According to Gregory, "commodity exchange is an exchange of *alienable* objects between people who are in a state of reciprocal *independence* that establishes a *quantitative* relationship between the *objects* transacted, whereas gift exchange is an exchange of *inalienable* objects between people who are in a state of reciprocal *dependence* that establishes a *qualitative* relationship between the *subjects* transacting" ("Kula" 104; emphases added).[5] Imprinted with the identities of giver and receiver, gifts promote and express connection; commodities, on the other hand, bespeak alienation. In a gift economy, objects gain personhood; in a commodity economy, people become objects (Gregory, *Gifts* 41).

The principle of inalienability arises from a fourth obligation that Mauss mentions but never develops: the requirement to give gifts to the gods (14). (This obligation has, until recently, been neglected by anthropologists as well.) From this fourth obligation, Maurice Godelier traces the hierarchical effects of gift giving: since the gods can never be fully repaid, those humans who give the most or are most closely associated with the divine are elevated to quasi-godlike status (Godelier 30). Human gifts are material remnants of the original, divine gift. At once "substitutes for sacred objects and substitutes for human beings" (Godelier 72), gifts are thus caught between the inalienability of holy things—divine relics, family heirlooms, and kinship markers inextricably linked with tribal or national identities—and the alienability of commodities freely exchanged for profit (Godelier 94). Gifts are thus double-voiced, speaking now in the timbre of ancestors or divine beings, and now in the neutral tones of mere merchandise. In sum, gift practices are the Jekyll and Hyde of social interactions, sometimes cementing social relations and encouraging friendship but at

other times promoting debt and envy. Gifts may be freighted with historical or social significance, or they may dissolve into fungible objects.

These concepts help to explain the peculiar entrapment of Joyce's Dubliners, many of whom are victimized by their adherence to a rigidly binary,
reified understanding of gifts and commodities. Characters such as the
"Araby" narrator and Chandler find themselves unable to move from an
idealized realm associated with religion, love, art, and the gift to the materialist territory of commerce and purchase. Indeed, the three stories of
male adolescence I'll treat here delineate a stark trajectory of diminishing
idealism, descending from a quasi-religious faith in the radical separation
of inalienable and alienable things, to a vision of largesse as nothing more
than an engine to generate prestige, and finally to a desperate cynicism in
which everything is alienable and presents are nothing but disguised
bribes.

"Araby" initiates the motif of the failed gift.[6] Herring suggests that the
narrator's quest for the ideal present starts with the uncle's gift of money,
but in fact it commences much earlier, when the boy recalls the generosity
of his house's former tenant, a "charitable" priest who bequeathed his
money to "institutions and the furniture of his house to his sister" (D 21).
These bequests are highly honorable, according to Aristotle's definition,
because they are "connected with the gods" (1122b; 66); more important,
the priest's death and his charity are implicitly linked to a longstanding
historical affiliation between gifts and sacrifice (see Berking 48), so that his
life gains meaning only through his sacrificial death. Although we may
doubt whether leaving one's possessions to institutions after one's death
constitutes true charity, nonetheless the boy's association of gifts and holi-
ness seems clear.[7] He therefore tries to emulate the priest, protecting his
romantic longing for Mangan's mysterious sister from the brutalities of
the marketplace by figuring his emotions as a "chalice," the very container
of Christ's sacrificial blood and the most tangible proof of a priest's power
of transubstantiation. Juxtaposed and contrasted with the raucous commercial space is the "back drawingroom in which the priest had died" (D
23) and in which the solitary boy presses his palms together in erotic
prayer. The space of gifts—of the sacred, of the inalienable—seems entirely at odds with the domain of commodities, where dwell the profane
and the alienated. On one side is the treasured chalice; on the other are
barrels of pigs' cheeks. The boy's image of the girl thus incarnates a narrative of perfect divine largesse that presages his ultimate loss. That is, because the only gift that will truly satisfy his idealized lover is the ultimate

sacrifice of the boy's life, his desire for very human erotic connection collides with his romantic narrative of Christly imitation, one that, he believes, has been enacted by the priestly steward.

The "Araby" narrator fails to grasp that the gift mode exists within and alongside the mode of sales. Indeed, to gratify his pseudo-ascetic impulses, the boy would be required to decline all rewards for his present.[8] Thus in "Araby" the gift partakes of a myth of saintly self-sacrifice that contributes a good deal to Irish social and political oppression, a myth embodied for Joyce by Parnell, and, as we'll see, for Gabriel Conroy by Michael Furey. In any case, far from being inspired by his uncle's present, the boy is delayed by the man's tardy handout and deterred from his planned expedition, so that what may have been a generous donation for the uncle "translates as a paltry sum for the recipient" (Benstock 95), one that could never be worthy of his yen for transcendence.[9] Worse, to perform his planned act of beneficence the boy must once again pass through a street "thronged with buyers" (*D* 26). When he arrives at Araby, it is bathed in a silence "like that which pervades a church after a service" (*D* 26): it has been transformed from a sacred to a profane space. One scarcely need mention the famous "fall of the coins" whose jingle aurally announces the gift's dissolution into the mercantile. Though tentatively fingering "porcelain vases and flowered teasets"—conventional symbols of femininity that seem to mock his vision of the gift as a sacred chalice—the boy is intimidated by the bazaar's crass atmosphere and fails not only to give a present but even to get one. His fervent desire to enhance his erotic capital (one that Bourdieu neglects to mention) through an extravagant gift to his loved one founders on the realities of Araby, and instead of imitating the generous priest, the boy ends up mimicking his dilatory uncle. Power borrowed from God gives way to weakness purchased at the expense of the boy's spirit; the "splendid bazaar" (*D* 23) is exposed as a cheap swindle.

This image of impotent idealism sets the tone for the rest of the volume, and the two other stories of male adolescence demonstrate how rapidly that idealism fades. In "After the Race," for example, Jimmy Doyle is depicted as little more than a tool for his father to cultivate people "worth knowing" and thereby secure for his son "qualities often unpurchaseable" (*D* 35, 37); in other words, Jimmy is nothing but human stock invested to earn social capital. Likewise, Daddy Doyle secretly approves of Jimmy's minor excesses because they reinforce his self-image as a "great-souled" man wealthy enough not to bother about small expenditures (*D* 35). Despite Jimmy's wealth, however, the other potential investors in the automobile firm act as though they are doing him a favor by including him in their card game, and eventually take him for a good chunk of that wealth. In the end, moreover, he loses his money without purchasing any of those valuable immaterial qualities. Extravagance and magnanimity thus appear here as a con-game's camouflage, and the "Araby" boy's fevered romance and spiritualized notion of the gift have yielded to a naked vulgarity unredeemed by that naïveté. Ironically, Jimmy and his father are victims not of idealism but of insufficient mercenariness. Yet in their attachment to the same bourgeois values that victimize them, they seem to epitomize the "gratefully oppressed" that populate Joyce's Dublin (D 34).

We can further explain Jimmy Doyle's victimization through reference to the work of another anthropologist, Marshall Sahlins. He has outlined a "spectrum of sociability" based on reciprocity, in which the friendlier the relations, the less specific and more extensive are the obligations. Parents, for example, do not calculate what they have given to their children and probably do not expect repayment. At the other end of the spectrum from this "solidarity" extreme lies so-called "negative reciprocity," the most impersonal sort of exchange, exemplified by haggling and theft. In these transactions, each party tries to gain advantage over the other by reciprocating with a lower value than what has been received. Between the two is what Sahlins called "balanced reciprocity," the desired goal of most exchanges in modern society, whereby each transactor receives something of roughly equal value, and in timely fashion (191–96).[10]

So far so good. But this system of relational modes depends upon what Bourdieu calls a "collective misrecognition." The delay between donation and reciprocation permits the flexible negotiation of kinship and friendship relations: time allows parties to "forget" that reciprocation is due and thus to maintain the "self-deception" that obligated repayments are really gifts and to pretend that presents are bestowed with no expectation of return (Bourdieu, "Selections" 198). Problems arise when parties disagree upon the nature of a relationship or transaction. Here, then, lies one significant source of the distortion of reciprocity in Joyce's Dublin, and, for that matter, in many transitional societies of the early twenty-first century: Bourdieu's collective amnesia has been partly cured, and the result is what I am calling *relational errors*, in which one party understands a transaction as a gift and another understands it as a contract or debt (see Herring 177). That is what occurs in "After the Race": flattered by the blandishments of his "friends," Jimmy fails to grasp that the real goal of their association is to liberate him from his money. In other words, he mistakes one set of reciprocal relations for another. Another type of relational error involves treating the inalienable as a commodity. This is the case in "Two Gallants," where Corley and Lenehan's chicanery converts love and generosity into mere coins of vantage. In this world, the ideal of magnanimity seems ludicrously archaic.

As a noted leech, Lenehan is one of the few male gift *receivers* in the collection; apparently his "vast stock" of stories and jokes lets him repay rounds of drinks with narrative currency (*D* 42). His pal Corley invokes the "Araby" boy's notion of gift giving, but only in order to mock it, boasting that he used to "pay the tram" for women, "or buy them chocolate and sweets. . . . I used to spend money on them," he confides, "And damn the thing I ever got out of it" (*D* 44). No longer chalices, women have been converted into cigars (*D* 43), boosters of phallic virility. Obviously Corley and his disciple inhabit Davis's third "relational mode" or Sahlins's domain of "negative reciprocity," where the goal is to take without paying back. Their poverty of "purse and spirit" (*D* 49) likewise drains the spirit from every transaction. Although for a moment Lenehan seems to recognize the emptiness of his life—like James Duffy, he eats alone, cast out from the social rituals associated with meals—his momentary despondency is dispelled by his fond reverie of marrying a "simpleminded girl with a little of the ready" (*D* 49): cash, that is, coin of the realm, preferably gold. The gravely revealed coin at the end of the story thus ironically reverses the fall of the coins at the conclusion of "Araby"; instead of failing to purchase a gift for a spiritualized female, these men crassly accept a "gift"—no doubt extorted—from a commodified female. Whereas the "Araby" boy weeps while gazing into the darkness, Corley smiles while opening his hand to the streetlight's blunt regard.

We might view these two as companion stories, inasmuch as they exemplify Jonathan Parry's point that the "ideology of the pure gift may . . . itself promote and entrench the ideological elaboration of the domain in which self-interest rules supreme" (469): that is, each is underwritten by a polarized notion of the gifts/commodities distinction. The "Araby" narrator's moist idealism is but the reverse face of Corley's brutal exploitation. If you can never attain the ideal, why not take what you can when you can? In each case, gift and commodity, love and exploitation, remain radically polarized. Lovers either give presents without any consideration of return or simply compete for scarce resources. But they never share anything or engage in true reciprocal exchange.

The stories of "mature life" manifest at least a vestigial belief in the possibility of magnanimous gift giving. As I noted at the outset of this essay, however, these characters' attempts to create prestige through gifts also run aground. Indeed, we can follow the trail of inept giving inaugurated in "Araby" through these tales of misshapen spending, beginning with "A Little Cloud," a story that it resembles in many respects. In this story, Little Chandler at first seems to entertain few of the "Araby" narrator's illusions, the ages having "bequeathed" him the knowledge that it is useless to struggle against fortune (D 61). Yet struggle he does, first by attempting to appropriate symbolic capital from the name of Corless's (D 61), where he has observed women with their faces powdered, lifting their dresses as they touch the earth like "alarmed Atalantas" (62). For Little Chandler as for the "Araby" boy, women embody luxury and wealth. Having failed to glean much reflected shine from these memories, however, he conjures up a review of his nonexistent poems that attributes to him the *"gift of easy and graceful verse"* (D 63).

Once at Corless's he seeks to establish his potency through a treating contest—Dublin's own version of the potlatch—with the worldly Ignatius Gallaher, a man notable for extravagant habits that belie his saintly first name (D 62). Gallaher gives the impression of the magnanimity that Joyce's males so eagerly seek.[11] After the orange-tied journalist inaugurates the potlatch, Chandler reciprocates (D 66); Gallaher buys again, and finally Chandler returns the favor. But though the drink count is balanced, Chandler still loses: he ends up feeling that he has failed to "assert his manhood" in the exchange (D 69), perhaps because Gallaher snubs Chandler's invitation to visit his home, a refusal of hospitality that suggests disdain. Also, to the recently married Chandler, Gallaher speaks of matrimony in Lenehan's mercenary terms, predicting that for him "there'll be no mooning and spooning about it. I mean to marry money. She'll have a good fat account at the bank or she won't do for me" (D 70). His metaphors express the complete commodification of his future spouse's identity: her name is equated with currency (he'll "marry money") and her body with her bankbook (she is merely a "fat account"). Gallaher's materialist metonyms interfere with Chandler's misty Atalantas.

Unintentionally contradicting his earlier defense of marriage, Chandler finds himself borrowing Gallaher's own humiliating idiom: "You'll put your head in the sack . . . like everyone else if you can find the girl," he says stoutly (D 70). Marriage has become a form of sacrifice or suicide: that besacked head, we realize, is ready to be chopped off. Once he arrives home, Chandler is reminded of his own loss of manhood. First he is reprimanded for forgetting to purchase the "parcel of coffee from Bewley's" that his wife requested, forcing her to venture out herself (*D* 71). He then recalls the "present" of a "pale blue summer blouse" he bought her, which cost him both the hefty sum of 10s 11d as well as an "agony of nervousness" (*D* 71). Chandler's generous intention was first undermined by his having to return for the "odd penny of his change," and then annihilated by his wife's reaction when she threw the "blouse on the table and said it was a regular swindle to charge ten and elevenpence for that." Scanning her picture and the room, Chandler sees his own limp largesse reflected in his wife's "mean" face—no statuesque Atalanta she—and in their "mean" furniture (*D* 72), still to be paid for. Imprisoned, the "little man" ends the story weeping, like the "Araby" narrator, over his abject failure to exercise the gift-giving virtue. Chandler has, however, sacrificed something: his ability to imagine a better future and a more generous self. Like the "Araby" boy, he is trapped by his inability to shift from one relational mode to another.

Similarly, for scrivener Farrington of "Counterparts," the gift economy only reinforces his subjection. Afraid to beg for an advance on his meager salary, he pawns his watch for six shillings, and as he walks from the pawnshop he "preconsidered the terms in which he would narrate the incident to the boys" (*D* 81). His legalistic language ("preconsidered the terms") reveals his vision of the treating contest to come as a kind of contract in which he will tender his story in return for drinks and prestige. As Carol Shloss notes, the man inarticulately believes that such gift exchanges allow him "to feel part of a larger, self-regulating system" and thinks "that each donation is an act of social faith" (193). But, as Aristotle reminds us, a poor man cannot be magnanimous and "anyone who tries is a fool" (1122a; 66). Farrington fails to heed this ancient warning.[12] Paul Delany has brilliantly illuminated the story's pattern of "homosocial consumption"—similar to the pseudo-potlatch system I have traced in the "Cyclops" episode of *Ulysses*—in which each treater feels momentarily that he is the master of revels (Delany 382; see also Osteen, *Economy,* 250–79). For a while Farrington seems able to command this economy and to bolster his social capital through the narrative currency of his sharp retort to his boss (Delany 385). It is thus no accident that the middle section of the story, where the drinking and storytelling are narrated, is the only section in which Farrington is given a name. But once again the pretense of brotherhood masks a swindle: as Delany shows in detail, Farrington spends almost all of his six shillings to pay for nineteen drinks but receives only eleven, whereas the sponger Paddy Leonard accepts nine drinks without once springing for a round.[13]

The boy in "Araby," clinking his remaining pennies together as he exits the bazaar, is, Delany reminds us, "father to the man Farrington, feeling his pennies as he waits, defeated, for his homebound tram" (386). But whereas Delany suggests that Joyce accepted such homosocial consumption as a legitimate refuge for his beleaguered males (388), "Counterparts" starkly reveals the darker side of the system on which that consumption is based. Farrington's attempts to manipulate the gift economy merely reconfirm and deepen his lack of status: in the end he spends almost all of his money and doesn't even get drunk. At home, the alleged solidarity of the pub gives way to the brutality of negative reciprocity: someone must pay for Farrington's losses, and little Tom Farrington is elected to the position. The boy tries to stave off a beating by bribing his father with a Hail Mary—a metaphorical sacrifice and ritual gift. But this Tom, like the one in the previous story, is a prisoner as well as a scapegoat. Clasping his hands in supplication, he cries "O pa," his words pathetically echoing the "Araby" boy's fervid "O love" (D 86). Alas, Tom is also his father's son, and his pitiful attempt to offer grace is arrested by the patriarch's stick.

Unlike Farrington, whose lack of magnanimity results partly from his poverty, James Duffy of "A Painful Case," with his secure middle-class position as a bank clerk, could afford to be generous, though that is not his habit. Still, during the initial stage of his relationship with Emily Sinico, Mr. Duffy loosens his usually tight grip, as shown by the verbs depicting their intimacy, all of which relate to bestowal: he "lent her books, provided her with ideas, shared his intellectual life with her." In return, she "gave out some fact" about herself (D 98). She even becomes his "confessor," as if to reinforce the "Araby" narrator's linkage of gifts and sacred ritual. But Duffy abruptly halts these tender exchanges by rejecting the obligations they have engendered: "We cannot give ourselves," his soul pronounces, "we are our own"; alas, "every bond . . . is a bond to sorrow" (D 99). Not only is Duffy guilty of emotional meanness (and Joyce's style here emulates that scrupulosity), but he is also a poor reader. That is, he should have studied more carefully his copy of *Thus Spake Zarathustra*, wherein Zarathustra urges his followers to practice the rich selfishness in which "your soul strives for treasures and gems, because your virtue is insatiable in wanting to give. You force all things to and into yourself that they may flow back out of your well as the gifts of your love" (Nietzsche 187). Zarathustra declares that the highest virtue is to become "sacrifices and gifts yourselves" (187); this is precisely what the "Araby" boy (and Michael Furey) attempt to do. In contrast, Duffy epitomizes what Nietzsche calls "sick" selfishness, which hungrily "sizes up those who have much to eat; and always it sneaks around the table of those who give" (187). The ironic result for this self-professed Nietzschean is to remain an "outcast from life's feast" (*D* 104). His inability to give cheats him of all solace.

So far we have seen how poorly male characters exercise the gift-giving virtue. As in the stories of adolescence, the stories depicting mature men trace a pattern of diminishing spirituality and shrinking gifts. Thus in Duffy the impulse to give that so tortures Chandler and Farrington has withered; whereas the latter two are frustrated by seeking and not finding it, Duffy voluntarily seeks no "communion with others" (*D* 97). But it is not only gift rituals that fail to produce solidarity in *Dubliners;* there is a paucity of meaningful rituals of any kind. Even the rituals that do exist— the elliptically narrated funeral in "The Sisters," the shotgun wedding in "The Boarding House," Duffy's solitary mealtimes, the pandering sermon in "Grace"—fail to satisfy the characters' needs for community and compassion. One might similarly argue that the males' inadequate performance in gift rituals results from an unfamiliarity with their protocols. After all, most theorists agree that the modern gift economy is generally associated with females, and several sociological studies confirm that women both give and receive gifts more frequently than do men.[14] Not in *Dubliners,* where women are no more adept at giving than their male counterparts. But whereas males in *Dubliners* attempt to generate prestige through magnanimity, women's gifts fail because the women, like Jimmy Doyle, misread their social positions and misinterpret communal norms. Their errors are relational errors.

Immediately after little Tom Farrington promises to say a Hail Mary, a virgin appears, as if invoked by that promise, in the diminutive form of Maria, who in "Clay" is initially portrayed as exactly the sort of "veritable peacemaker" needed in the Farrington home (*D* 87). She has garnered tributes in the form of gifts, such as the purse she received from Joe and Alphy Donnelly as *A Present from Belfast* (*D* 88). The two half crowns inside that purse might allow her to reciprocate for this present with gifts of her own, and indeed, she is associated with generosity throughout the early pages of the story: when she has visitors she unfailingly gives them "one or two slips from [the plants in] her conservatory" (*D* 88), and she habitually supervises the distribution of the barmbrack cakes that her fellow employees take with tea (*D* 89). She also shares the "Araby" narrator's faith in the power of the gift and, flushed with good feeling on her way to the Donnellys', buys penny cakes for the children and tops them off with an expensive slice of plumcake for the parents (cost: 2s 4d). These cakes are, of course, pale imitations of the wedding cake she desires but will never receive, as her blushing response to the brusque salesclerk's remark suggests (D 90). Although she manages to purchase her planned gifts, she fails to complete the transaction, and her humiliation again echoes that of the "Araby" boy.

Maria's fragile well-being cracks when she discovers that she has mislaid the plumcake on the tram, ruining any hope of earning gratitude from the Donnellys. Her loss of the cake serves as the story's turning point: from this moment on everything she gives or receives—her song, the clay she touches in the game, the wine that Joe forces her to accept (D 93)—is either incomplete or unwelcome. However, her loss of the plumcake really signifies an unconscious acknowledgment of hostility: the gift can't be given because the family who would receive it has been torn apart by fraternal feuding. Hence, in failing to reciprocate for their joint present she unconsciously reenacts the absence of generosity and grace in the Donnelly household. Maria's lost present, then, embodies the fractured moral economy of her hosts.

Joe claims that "Maria is my proper mother" (D 88). If so, she is as ineffectual a parent as Chandler and Farrington are. Maria's problematic motherhood also foreshadows that of "A Mother," where Mrs. Kearney's relational error again results in hostility, conflict, and exploitation. She is another character caught between "romantic ideas" she has never fully relinquished (D 124) and the mercenary reality in which a daughter is a commodity whose value one enhances with a dowry. Disguising that investment as a gift does little to change its status as a purchase price. But mixed messages end up confounding the mother. When Mr. Holohan proposes that Kathleen accompany the artistes performing for the *Eire Abu* Society, her mother enters "heart and soul" into the details of the enterprise, and finally signs a contract specifying that Kathleen will receive eight guineas for four concerts (D 125). For her mother, the contract is a business deal. Yet her behavior—"invariably friendly and advising: homely in fact" (D 125)—sends conflicting signals about the transaction that reveal her ambivalence. Indeed, it is precisely her carefully practiced hospitality during negotiations, when she insists that Mr. Holohan help himself to their biscuit barrel and beverage decanter (D 125), that complicates matters by implying that the transaction belongs within the domain of the gift, where obligations are flexible and the time for repayment elastic.

Thus when the Society decides to cancel one of the four concerts, Mrs. Kearney's insistence on obeying the letter of the contract makes her appear petty and grasping. On Saturday night, when she receives a little less than half of the money stipulated, she is outraged: "She had spared neither trouble nor expense and this was how she was repaid" (*D* 134). Mrs. Kearney's ivory indignation not only causes her to forfeit the remainder of the fee but prompts everyone to condemn her actions, and the magniloquent O'Madden Burke announces that Kathleen's musical career in Dublin is ended (*D* 133). Was the contract a market transaction or a friendly agreement? Public opinion in Dublin's clannish middle-classes proclaims the latter, decreeing that Mrs. Kearney's pinched generosity amounts to a betrayal of the "spirit" of the gift. Of course, this is a convenient charge for the sexist males of the Society, who can project their meanness onto her by implicitly invoking women's historical affiliation with gifts. She too is ensnared, like Little Chandler, albeit from the opposite direction, by an inability to negotiate a smooth transition between gift and marketplace. Caught between the vestigial kinship mores of the friendly gift and her bourgeois adherence to commercial values, she makes a relational error that leads to the loss of the social capital she has so laboriously accrued.

"The Dead" both consummates and supplements these distressing patterns.[15] At the story's opening, another male, Gabriel Conroy, attempts to impress a woman with his generosity; again he fails, this time because the coin he gives to Lily looks less like a gift or tip than what Bernard Benstock calls a "bribe to cover an embarrassing gaucherie" (105).[16] Like most tips, Gabriel's stands "at the boundary of other critically different transfers, not quite a payment, not quite a bribe, not quite charity, but not quite a gift either" (Zelizer 95). He has committed, like Mrs. Kearney, an error of relation, failing to recognize that any "gift" made to Lily at this moment can only be taken as a sign of contempt, an attempt to "get something" out of her—in this case, a sense of his own magnanimity. But Gabriel departs from the pattern established by the "Araby" boy, because his lame attempts at generosity derive not from male elders but from female ones. His aunts, the Morkan sisters, may indeed offer the volume's only examples of authentic generosity. Though far from wealthy, the aunts believe in the "best of everything" (*D* 160), both practicing largesse and condemning its absence in others, as when Aunt Kate questions the church's lack of "politeness and gratitude" to female choir members (*D* 177).

Gabriel's mother seems to have shared their graciousness, for he fondly recalls the present of a purple waistcoat that she made for him (*D* 169) and realizes that it was only "thanks to her" that he attended a university (*D* 170).

In his historical study of giving, Helmuth Berking traces the norms of gift exchange and sacrifice to the distribution of foodstuffs by primitive hunters, in which the "roast meat hierarchy corresponded to the social hierarchy" when dividing up the sacrificial meal (69). Likewise, in "The Dead," Mr. Conroy tries to solidify his role as big chief by carving and distributing the goose (see *D* 179). He also attempts to reciprocate for his aunts' generosity by praising them fulsomely in his speech as the "Three Graces of the Dublin musical world" (*D* 186), though his accolades are soured by his ungracious allusions to Molly Ivors.[17] The Three Graces invoke the spirit of the gift, that ideal which many Dubliners fail to attain, but the women pass it not to Gabriel (at least not at first) but to Gretta, who possesses an "attitude" of grace as she stands listening to Bartell D'Arcy sing "The Lass of Aughrim" (*D* 191). Gabriel's praise, of course, is meant to show what a generous soul *he* is. And even after the party he continues trying to generate social and erotic capital through giving, first overtipping the cabman (*D* 196), and then soliciting Gretta's compliment when he mentions lending a pound to Freddy Malins.

But Gabriel's most abject failure to give is disclosed only in retrospect, when Gretta romantically—if probably inaccurately—tells him that Michael Furey made the ultimate sacrifice for her, giving his life for her love. Furey's martyrdom finally fills the "Araby" narrator's chalice of desire: the perfect gift is possible after all. Once Gretta relates Michael's story, the Morkans' feast appears as a kind of Last Supper, with Michael Furey's body serving as host for Gabriel's pseudo-priestly offices. If only Gabriel could take Michael's place, or could ingest that spirit of perfect self-sacrifice and ideal largesse that Furey embodies! Gabriel seems doomed to fall short of such extravagant giving. Such a romantic gesture, sanctified in Gretta's memory and then embellished by Gabriel, would perhaps trump any human male's attempt to equal it. But should he even try? Or is Joyce pointing to the ultimate emptiness and sentimentality of the very ideal of self-sacrifice, an ideal that has contributed so much to Ireland's stultification? This question, in turn, bears on the issue of Gabriel's "generosity." Does Gabriel achieve a more authentically generous vision at the end of the story? Or does his culminating epiphany, as Vincent Pecora suggests, merely exemplify "the codified expression of the myth of self-sacrifice, of grateful oppression, lying at the heart of Joyce's Dublin" (243)? Pecora's description of the characters' self-delusion rings true, but his suggestion that Gabriel's final, impersonal vision of the unity of the living and the dead simply repeats his earlier tendency to heroicize his own self-pity fails to grant Gabriel the capacity to change.[18] Although Gabriel's previous actions were indeed designed to display a generosity that seems ultimately bogus, one could argue that one aim of the story is precisely to suggest that Gabriel, alone among Dubliners, begins to move toward a less self-absorbed appreciation of his own condition. Perhaps Gabriel's tears aren't entirely "generous" (*D* 203), but cold-hearted readings like Pecora's risk duplicating the very absence of generosity they condemn.

Behind the question of Gabriel's generosity lies the question of Joyce's. Richard Ellmann argued years ago that the Morkan sisters' graciousness may embody Joyce's regret, expressed in a letter to his brother Stanislaus, that he had not reproduced "the attraction" of Dublin, particularly its "ingenuous insularity and hospitality." According to Ellmann, "The Dead" marks his attempt to make amends for having been "unnecessarily harsh" to his native city (*JJII* 245; *Letters II* 166). After all, what is Joyce's meticulous verbal parsimony—that vaunted "scrupulous meanness" of style that he described to Stanislaus (*Letters II* 134)—but the Dublin affliction translated into the practice of composition? If so, then Joyce's admitted harshness proves nothing so much as his kinship with his characters, for his merciless dissection of his citizens' foibles—their poverty of soul, their shriveled generosity, their economic and religious paralysis—smacks of a meanness that is not only stylistic but also moral (see *Letters II* 134). In indicting their failures of generosity, Joyce mimics them, thereby proving himself even more a Dubliner. At the end of "The Dead," however, it is clear that, on the stylistic level at least, something unprecedented is occurring that may signal a shift in Joyce's attitude. The key change from scrupulous meanness to swooning melody may herald a dawning self-awareness on the part of the author, as Joyce himself shifts from the negative reciprocity of vengeance to a recognition of shared community. Although the transition remains tentative and complicated, Joyce's final story achieves, if not magnanimity, then at least tolerance.

For Pecora, there is in *Dubliners* "no distinction between princely generosity and the necessary sacrifices of poverty; the former is simply the ideological transubstantiation of the latter, the transformation of damaged experience into a mythic surplus of value" (244). But the characters' failures to act magnanimously do not necessarily invalidate the ideal. Isn't it still preferable to attempt largesse, that "princely failing" (*D* 184), than to acquiesce in the mercenary machinations of Lord John Corley or emulate the desiccated loneliness of James Duffy? Even if, as we have seen, many Dubliners are victimized by their adherence to an impracticable or archaic ideal of grace and magnanimity, the only alternative offered—a soulless bourgeois self-interest characteristic of contemporary society as well—seems even more disabling. *Dubliners* suggests, in fact, that Joyce was ambivalent about the role of the gift, understanding and exposing the paralysis that the myth of the perfect gift inflicts but also respecting its heroic quality and moral grace. *Dubliners* finally implies that only those flexible enough to negotiate the transition between the realms of gift and commodity escape self-swindling. And in the twenty-first century, a similar flexibility will be required not only of postcolonial subjects who must accommodate shifting economic and social values and habits but also of Americans or Europeans who find capitalism's drive to commodify everything, including themselves, increasingly sterile and unfulfilling. No character in Joyce's Dublin, however, except perhaps Gabriel Conroy, seems able to make this transition, because to do so requires first that they gain a clearer picture of their own world and their own natures, and then that they take active steps to change that world and that nature.

Why, then, do gifts fail in Joyce's Dublin? Certainly the pressure of Catholicism, with its powerful ethos of self-sacrifice, self-abnegation, and contempt for the world, affects both male and female characters, in some cases handicapping their economic and social agility, as we see in "Araby." Some of Joyce's Dubliners—Farrington of "Counterparts" and Maria of "Clay," for example—fail to exercise the gift-giving virtue because they lack the economic capital needed to generate social capital. For others, such as Mrs. Kearney, the transition from a precapitalist to a capitalist society has fostered conflicting, and ultimately imprisoning, norms and practices. That is, the market economy—itself distorted and crippled by the imperial British presence—coexists uneasily with a gift system left over from the country's tribal past. We may attribute both the absence of largesse and the relational errors to such forms of cognitive dissonance, to the characters' adherence to ideals that no longer fit their society. A similar rigidity in gender roles—the belief that males must give large gifts to show power, whereas females must remain flexible and receptive while also managing the domestic economy—traps certain characters in humiliating circumstances. Finally, characters such as Corley, who have bought into capitalism and scoff at any but the most self-serving motives, swindle themselves by remaining wedded to an ideology that works against their own interests.

For most of the collection, Joyce shows no propensity to forgive his city for its real and imagined slights to his genius, and his harsh scrutiny of its citizens' gracelessness dramatizes his own lack of magnanimity. In declining to tender humane compassion for their condition as victims, he may himself be perpetrating a regular swindle, blaming them for problems over which they have no control. Fortunately, Joyce's mature fiction largely abandons this Duffyesque verbal and emotional parsimony for a generosity of style, vision, and spirit. This literary largesse commences, perhaps, with "The Dead": its arguably more expansive style and ambiguously redemptive resolution exhibit signs that Joyce was learning, perhaps from his own miserable characters, the value of the gift-giving virtue. Twenty-first-century Joyce critics who hope to remain worthy of these works' enduring power to illuminate contemporary experience might well learn the same lesson.

Notes

1. Bourdieu's definitions of the various types of capital are notoriously vague and overlapping. In essence, however, he defines "symbolic capital" as "prestige and renown attached to a family and its name" (*Outline* 179); "social capital" refers to "obligations . . . and the advantages of connections or social positions, and trust"; "cultural capital" designates embodied or institutionalized knowledge or expertise. For a clarification of these terms, see Smart, who writes that symbolic capital "involves claims by the possessor that he or she be treated in particular ways by classes of others. Social capital consists of claims to reciprocation and solidarity from particular others" (396). As many critics have suggested, Bourdieu's various forms of "capital," like his description of gift practices, is flawed by economism. See, for example, Koritz and Koritz 411, and Osteen, "Questions," 23–25.

2. It's not certain how well Joyce knew the *Nicomachean Ethics*. Ellmann asserts that he had copies of the *Psychology* and the *Poetics* in his Trieste library (*Consciousness* 99). In a December 1904 letter to Stanislaus, James mentions completing a "short course in Aristotle" (*Letters II* 71). It is difficult to imagine that Joyce was not at least somewhat familiar with the *Ethics* as well.

3. For a helpful discussion of Nietzsche's debt to Aristotle in the matter of gifts and ethics, see Woodruff.

4. Richard Rowan voices a similar paradox in *Exiles* when he declares that "while you have a thing it can be taken from you. . . . But when you give it, you have given it. No robber can take it from you" (*E* 46–47): giving, in other words, is gaining,

because in giving one places one's signature upon the gift. Unfortunately for Rowan's prestige, the "thing" to which he is alluding here is his wife, Bertha.

5. Gregory's work has been widely challenged, and it is clear that the two realms interact in countless ways. For example, a single object may be at one point in its "biography" a gift and at another point a commodity. His formula also neglects one of the most significant ideas in Mauss's work: the essential duality of gifts, which are at once disinterested and interested. But despite its oversimplified picture of the complex ways that people interact with objects, Gregory's dichotomy—gifts signify inalienability, social interconnectedness, and personhood, whereas commodities stand for alienation, independence, and neutrality—underlies much anthropological, sociological, and literary scholarship on the gift. For critiques of Gregory, see Frow 127, and Mirowski 444–46. For a fuller treatment of the principle of inalienability and the gift/commodity distinction, see Osteen, "Gift or Commodity?" 233–39.

6. One might argue that the pattern really begins with the narrator's gift of snuff to Father Flynn in "The Sisters," a gift that, as Bernard Benstock notes, may be "payment" for his tutorials (93; D 6), but that would be stretching the point.

7. Vincent Pecora has remarked on the ambiguities of attribution here: does the word "charitable" issue from the naïve boy's mind, or is it the older narrator's implicitly ironic view of such a definition of "charity" (Pecora 239)? Such discourse, he aptly suggests, is already "dispossessed."

8. As Parry observes, in Christian morality, "the unreciprocated gift becomes a liberation from bondage to [the world], a denial of the profane self, an atonement for sin, and hence a means to salvation." The erection of a wall between sacred and profane domains prompts the "development of a *contemptus mundi* which culminates in the institution of renunciation, but of which the charitable gift—as a kind of lay exercise in asceticism—is also often an expression" (468).

9. Joyce never tells us precisely how much money the boy receives. As the boy strides down Buckingham Street he holds "a florin [a two-shilling coin] tightly in [his] hand" (D 25); yet when he arrives at the bazaar, he hands the gatekeeper a "shilling" (D 26), which suggests that the uncle's gift consists of a florin and a shilling, for a total of three shillings. But at the end the boy describes allowing "the two pennies" to fall against "the sixpence" in his pocket—"the" meaning "the only remaining" sixpence (D 27)—which wouldn't make sense if he had originally had three shillings. In any case, the female pictured on the florin and shilling would scarcely have contributed to his idealization of the female form, since it depicted the decidedly unromantic figure of the elderly Queen Victoria (see Seaby 158).

10. It is tempting to associate a particular economic practice with each realm (for example, generalized reciprocity = gift; balanced reciprocity = sales; negative reciprocity = theft), but in fact many transactions and relationships mix the forms.

11. By Aristotle's definition, however, Gallaher falls short, for the truly great-souled person is "like an expert, since he can see what is fitting and spend large

amounts with good taste" (1122b; 65). In contrast, even the dazed Chandler perceives Gallaher's essential vulgarity (*D* 69).

12. Farrington even fits Aristotle's example of a fool: one who feasts the members of his dining club as if they were at a wedding (1123a; 67).

13. See Delany, 383–85, for a full accounting of the drinks and costs involved.

14. The reasons for this phenomenon are complex. One is certainly the historical separation of spheres, in which men practiced business and women kept house. It is not clear, however, whether the inequality in gift giving generally exposes women's lack of genuine power, or instead becomes a method of exerting indirect authority by regulating the range and nature of kinship relations. For discussions of this issue, see Komter 124–31; Cheal 6; and Hyde 103–5. For a treatment of the connection between women and gifts in Joyce, see Osteen, "Female Property," and Osteen, *Economy*, 29–32, 423–25, 430–39.

15. I have already discussed at length the perversion of the gift system in "Grace," so I won't rehash my arguments here. Those interested may wish to read my article "Serving Two Masters," particularly 85–89.

16. Tipping became fully acceptable only around the turn of the twentieth century, and the practice incited a good deal of outrage as theory caught up with practice. In the United States there were even nationwide efforts to abolish it. For a discussion of the practice of tipping in the context of the limits on monetary gifts, see Zelizer 94–96.

17. To promote the requital of services, according to Aristotle, the Greeks gave a prominent place to the temple of the Graces, for "one ought both to perform a return service to someone who has been gracious, and another time to make the first move by being gracious oneself" (1133a; 89). Of the Three Graces, Seneca writes, "one of them bestoweth the good turne, the other receiveth it, and the third requiteth it" (quoted in Davis 12–13). This cycle of reciprocity is figured in conventional representations of the Graces, where they are often shown dancing, hands linked, in a circle. See Davis, 12, for one such representation.

18. Pecora here seems to cling to a rigidly Marxist notion of characters as mere vectors of social and economic forces. This ideological lumber weighs down any critic attempting to keep pace with Joyce's verbal and moral dexterity.

Works Cited

Aristotle. *Nicomachean Ethics*. Translated by W. D. Ross. In *The Basic Works of Aristotle*, edited by Richard McKeon. New York: Random, 1941.

Benstock, Bernard. *Narrative Con/Texts in "Dubliners."* London: Macmillan, 1994.

Berking, Helmuth. *Sociology of Giving*. Translated by Patrick Camiller. London: Sage, 1999.

Bourdieu, Pierre. *Outline of a Theory of Practice*. Translated by Richard Nice. Cambridge: Cambridge University Press, 1977.

———. "Selections from *The Logic of Practice*." In *The Logic of the Gift: Toward an Ethic of Generosity*, edited by Alan D. Schrift, 190–230. New York: Routledge, 1997.

Cheal, David. *The Gift Economy*. New York: Routledge, 1988.

Davis, Natalie Zemon. *The Gift in Sixteenth-Century France*. Madison: University of Wisconsin Press, 2000.

Delany, Paul. "'Tailors of Malt, Hot, All Round': Homosocial Consumption in *Dubliners*." *Studies in Short Fiction* 32 (1995): 381–93.

Ellmann, Richard. *The Consciousness of Joyce*. New York: Oxford University Press, 1977.

Frow, John. *Time and Commodity Culture*. Oxford: Clarendon Press, 1997.

Godelier, Maurice. *The Enigma of the Gift*. Translated by Nora Scott. Chicago: University of Chicago Press, 1999.

Gordon, John. "*Dubliners* and the Art of Losing." *Studies in Short Fiction* 32 (1995): 343–52.

Gregory, C. A. [Chris]. *Gifts and Commodities*. London and New York: Academic, 1982.

———. "Kula Gift Exchange and Capitalist Commodity Exchange: A Comparison." In *The Kula: New Perspectives on Massim Exchange*, edited by Jerry W. Leach and Edmund Leach. Cambridge: Cambridge University Press, 1983.

Herring, Phillip F. "James Joyce and Gift Exchange." In *The Languages of Joyce: Selected Papers from the 11th International James Joyce Symposium, Venice, 12–18 June 1988*, edited by R. M. Bollettieri Bosinelli, Carla Marengo Vaglio, and Christine Van Boheemen, 173–90. Philadelphia: John Benjamins, 1992.

Hyde, Lewis. *The Gift: Imagination and the Erotic Life of Property*. New York: Random House, 1983.

Joyce, James. *Dubliners*. 1914. Edited by Hans Walter Gabler with Walter Hettche. New York: Vintage, 1993.

Komter, Aafke E. "Women, Gifts and Power." In *The Gift: An Interdisciplinary Perspective*, edited by Aafke E. Komter, 119–31. Amsterdam: Amsterdam University Press, 1996.

Koritz, Amy, and Douglas Koritz. "Symbolic Economics: Adventures in the Metaphorical Marketplace." In *The New Economic Criticism: Studies at the Intersection of Literature and Economics*, edited by Martha Woodmansee and Mark Osteen, 408–19. New York: Routledge, 1999.

Mauss, Marcel. *The Gift: The Form and Reason for Exchange in Archaic Societies*. 1925. Translated by W. D. Halls. New York and London: Routledge, 1990.

Mirowski, Philip. "Refusing the Gift." In *Postmodernism, Economics, and Knowledge*, edited by Stephen Cullenberg, Jack Amariglio, and David Ruccio, 431–58. London and New York: Routledge, 2001.

Nietzsche, Friedrich. *Thus Spoke Zarathustra*. In *The Portable Nietzsche*, edited and translated by Walter Kaufmann. New York: Viking, 1954.

Osteen, Mark. *The Economy of "Ulysses": Making Both Ends Meet*. Syracuse: Syracuse University Press, 1995.

———. "Female Property: Women and Gift Exchange in *Ulysses*." In *Gender in Joyce*, edited by Jolanta W. Wawrzycka and Marlena G. Corcoran, 29–46. Gainesville: University Press of Florida, 1997.

———. "Gift or Commodity?" In *The Question of the Gift*, edited by Mark Osteen, 229–47. London and New York: Routledge, 2002.

———. "Introduction: Questions of the Gift." In *The Question of the Gift: Essays across Disciplines*, edited by Mark Osteen, 1–41. London and New York: Routledge, 2002.

———. "Serving Two Masters: Economics and Figures of Power in Joyce's 'Grace.'" *Twentieth Century Literature* 37 (1991): 76–92.

Parry, Jonathan. "*The Gift*, the Indian Gift, and the 'Indian Gift.'" *Man*, n.s., 21 (1986): 453–73.

Pecora, Vincent P. *Self and Form in Modern Narrative*. Baltimore: Johns Hopkins University Press, 1989.

Sahlins, Marshall. *Stone Age Economics*. New York: Aldine de Gruyter, 1972.

Seaby, Peter. *The Story of British Coinage*. Rev. ed. London: Seaby, 1990.

Shloss, Carol. "Money and Other Rates of Exchange: Commercial Relations and 'Counterparts.'" In *New Perspectives on Dubliners, European Joyce Studies 7*, edited by Mary Power and Ulrich Schneider, 181–94. Atlanta: Rodopi, 1997.

Smart, Alan. "Gifts, Bribes and *Guanxi*: A Reconsideration of Bourdieu's Social Capital." *Cultural Anthropology* 8 (1993): 388–408.

Weiner, Annette B. *Inalienable Possessions: The Paradox of Keeping-While-Giving*. Berkeley and Los Angeles: University of California Press, 1992.

Woodruff, Martha Kendal. "The Ethics of Generosity and Friendship: Aristotle's Gift to Nietzsche?" In *The Question of the Gift: Essays across Disciplines*, edited by Mark Osteen, 118–31. London and New York: Routledge, 2002.

Zelizer, Viviana A. *The Social Meaning of Money*. New York: Basic Books, 1994.

Joyce's Sacred Heart Attack

Exposing the Church's Imperialist Organ

Mary Lowe-Evans

> My Divine Heart . . . is so inflamed with love for men, and for thee
> in particular that, being unable any longer to contain within Itself
> the flames of Its burning charity, It must needs spread them abroad
> by thy means and manifest itself to [mankind]. . . . I have chosen thee
> as an abyss of unworthiness and ignorance for the accomplishment
> of this great design, in order that everything may be done by Me.
> **Jesus to Margaret Mary Alacoque, c. 1673 (Alacoque 67)**

I

The callow, self-effacing, seventeenth-century Visitation nun who recounts Jesus's "great design" in her *Autobiography* has been credited with
introducing to the world an icon and ritual of extraordinary transnational
influence. Margaret Mary Alacoque deployed the power of the Sacred
Heart, yet she never left the small provincial area of France where she
grew up. You have all met the Sacred Heart: the attractive bearded Jesus
with an organ exposed on his breast. That bleeding organ, which only on
close inspection reveals itself to be a heart, is encircled by a crown of thorns
and sends off copious flames. Lest you overlook this amazing out-of-body
phenomenon, Jesus points to it with his left index finger. By examining
some of the ways in which James Joyce has "mined" this seductive image
and its origins, and by locating Joyce's work in the context of late nine-
teenth- and early twentieth-century expansionist Irish Catholicism, I
hope to elucidate both the nature of Joyce's brief with Catholicism and the
potency of a specific line of discourse that continues to reverberate worldwide. The current scandals within the Catholic Church involving the
sexual abuse of young children by priests and the cover-up of that abuse by
the bishops might be interpreted as symptomatic of a system that exploits

the potential for gaining, maintaining, and extending control over the faithful by promoting the eroticization of its high priest. Joyce understood and exposed the complicated ways in which the church harnessed and manipulated the forces of human desire, and, for that reason, his works continue—in the twenty-first century—to trouble the orthodox.

The narrative of "Eveline" implies that these observations are part of Eveline's reverie, a daydream each detail of which suggests unrealized potency. The fact that Eveline has never "found out" the priest's name indicates both a reluctance to assert herself and a fear of uncovering, finding, or locating the mysterious power the priest represents. She seems both to have sought the priest's name and escaped knowledge of it. Yet the photograph is old, "yellowing," in some sense "broken" like the harmonium above which it hangs, and thus should represent no threat at all. Without a pause in the train of thought, however, the narrative moves from yellowing photograph to broken harmonium to "the coloured print of the promises made to Blessed Margaret Mary Alacoque." Only here does the sentence end. The designation "coloured print" tells us that there is, besides the list of promises, a picture included in this implied frame. Like the priest's name, the description of the image in the print is missing. In the terms Joyce sets out in "The Sisters," the opening story of *Dubliners,* such absences represent *gnomons* or gaps that elide, suppress, or censor significant information. Nonetheless the earliest readers of *Dubliners,* and indeed most Catholic readers educated before Vatican II, would have known that the "coloured print" is a picture not of Margaret Mary Alacoque as the narrative seems to hint, but of the Sacred Heart, that is, a picture of Jesus exposing his most vital organ, an icon carefully reproduced according to directions given by Margaret Mary Alacoque herself:

> The Divine Heart was shown to me placed upon a throne of fire and flames. Bright beams emanated from it on all sides; it was more brilliant than the sun and transparent as crystal. The wound which it received upon the cross was clearly to be distinguished; the Divine Heart was furthermore encircled by a crown of thorns and surmounted by a cross. (quoted in Hausherr 38)

Typically the print would also include two biblical verses: from Matthew 11:28, "Come to me all you that labor and are burdened, and I will refresh you"; and from John 14:6, "I am the way, and the truth, and the life." Eveline, however, is apparently intrigued not by the icon or the verses so much as by the twelve promises Jesus purportedly made during a series of apparitions to Alacoque. The last and "greatest" of the promises offered a kind of insurance policy: anyone who would attend mass and receive communion for nine consecutive first Fridays of the month would die in a state of grace (which in turn would ensure immediate entrance into heaven). The first Friday novena has subsequently become one of the most widely practiced devotions in the Catholic Church. In Joyce's story "A Mother," we're told that Mrs. Kearney "went to the altar every first Friday" (*D* 135). Also, as Frederick Lang observes in *"Ulysses" and the Irish God,* Joyce's own mother did so as well. In "The Trieste Notebook," Joyce recorded, under the heading "Mother," "Every first Friday she approached the altar" (quoted in Lang 96–97). Other promises made by the Sacred Heart to Margaret Mary Alacoque include establishing peace in the families of those who would promote devotion to him and providing them comfort in all their afflictions.[1]

The unacknowledged but palpable presence of the Sacred Heart, along with the complicated network of promises given and acted upon in "Eveline," constitute an argument, one of many that Joyce makes, about the church's methods of controlling its members and extending its influence. As with her failure to learn the priest's name, Eveline seems to avoid seeing the elaborate image of phallic power represented in the colored print. Rather she associates herself with the absent Alacoque—who, like herself, never left her home territory—and the security offered in the twelve promises. Donald Torchiana argues that "the identification of Eveline with the Blessed Margaret Mary is central. It highlights in Joyce's Dublin a misguided young woman who denies the sacredness of the heart, largely because of her devotion to the Order of the Sacred Heart" (70). However, Torchiana does not dwell on the sinister implications of the Sacred Heart icon in relation to its enthrallment of Eveline or on the larger issue of the church's manipulation of its seductive power.

Although Eveline apparently avoids direct confrontation with the image, she continues to muse about the nameless priest. The next sentence or segment of her reverie begins with the pronoun "He," presumably referring to the priest. Yet between the reference to the priest's photograph and the unspecified "He," the undisclosed image in the colored print intervenes. Thus a conflation of priest and Sacred Heart image seems to be invited. In the backroads of Eveline's mind, priest and icon merge, perhaps, into a powerful, unnamed, and enticing Watchman. In the next sentence, the antecedent of "He" seems clarified since "he had been a school friend of her father" could refer only to the priest. Now Eveline's father becomes implicated in this previously unnamable phenomenon. The concluding lines of Eveline's reverie reinforce the priest/Sacred Heart/father conflation and also emphasize Eveline's failure to confront the phallic gaze that this emblematic passage has been establishing. What's more, the final lines of this segment move the triumvirate and the reader away from Eveline's dusty parlor and broken harmonium into a larger arena. "Whenever he showed the photograph to a visitor her father used to pass it with a casual word:—He is in Melbourne now" (30). The repetition of masculine pronouns produces a confraternity, if you will, which seems to involve both pride of association and participation in empire building. Specifically, the priest, the Sacred Heart, and their friend (Eveline's father) are symbolically complicit in expanding the influence of Irish Catholicism beyond the confines of Ireland itself. "*He* is in Melbourne now" (emphasis added) might be taken to mean that the priest and the Sacred Heart are both there while Eveline's father, by way of his implicit approval, participates in the expansionist politics the priest's mission represents.

Eveline's part in this mission is apparently to focus on the promise emanating from the gaze of the fathers without learning the father's name or directly confronting the gaze: in effect colluding in the consolidation of that power without questioning or understanding it. Like Alacoque, deemed "an abyss of unworthiness and ignorance" by her beloved Sacred Heart, Eveline will facilitate a great design, extending and reinforcing masculinist systems in which her own father—who insists that Eveline "had no head" (31)—participates. For Raffaella Baccolini, "Eveline epitomizes the female condition in *Dubliners;* her identification with the past and her passivity foreclose any possibility of a future for her" (157). It is precisely her identification with Alacoque, however, that renders her a representative of the church's once and future imperialism.

In the remainder of the story, we learn that Eveline has "consented to go away" or "run away with a fellow." In her "new home, in a distant unknown country . . . she would be married" (30). There she would not be treated violently as her dead mother had been by her father. Eveline thinks of her rescuer, a sailor named Frank, in terms suggesting a type of Sacred Heart, a "kind, manly, open-hearted" fellow who will take her to a paradise called Buenos Ayres.[2] Thus, in spite of the fact that Eveline's father objects to her association with Frank, and notwithstanding Frank's representation as a benign rover, Frank, too, belongs to the confraternity of male potentates: "I know these sailor chaps," Eveline's father warns (32).

The most troubling of Sacred Heart advocates, however, turns out to be

Eveline's mother, who is associated with power through victimhood. In his Lacanian reading of the story, Garry Leonard sees Eveline's mother as "acting on behalf of patriarchy's need to pose as monolithic authority with no beginning and no end" (*Reading* 97). Leonard's observation works well with the argument I am making about the mother's collusion with her male victimizers. Recalling both her promise to her dying mother, to "keep the home together as long as she could" (a variation on the Sacred Heart's promise to "establish peace in their families") and her mother's final, incomprehensible words, foolishly repeated again and again, Eveline becomes terrified:

> as she mused the pitiful vision of her mother's life laid its spell on the very quick of her being—that life of commonplace sacrifices closing in final craziness. She trembled as she heard her mother's voice saying constantly with foolish insistence: Derevaun Seraun! Derevaun Seraun! She stood up in a sudden impulse of terror. Escape! She must escape! Frank would save her. He would give her life, perhaps love, too. But she wanted to live. (33)

There has been much critical debate about the words Eveline's mother utters, leading to no definitive explanation of them.[3] I will enter that debate by suggesting that they are meant to replicate the repetitive, mind-numbing, often nonsensical and contradictory words of a religious litany. Litanies to the Sacred Heart, and to Blessed Margaret Mary Alacoque, both of which conveyed at once the mysterious, seductive yet threatening tone of the phrase "Derevaun seraun," were popular in 1904 Dublin. For example, "The Litany of The Most Sacred Heart of Jesus" invokes "Heart of Jesus, desire of the everlasting hills"; "Heart of Jesus, filled with reproaches"; "Heart of Jesus, bruised for our offenses"; "Heart of Jesus, pierced with a lance" (Alacoque 138). The "Litany in Honor of Margaret Mary Alacoque" refers to her as "Victim and holocaust of the Heart of Jesus"; "Model of obedience and mortification"; and "Thou who was crucified with Christ" (Alacoque 140). While none of these invocations either sounds or looks like "Derevaun Seraun," the point I wish to make is that litanies generally are intended to infiltrate the psyches of the faithful with predetermined yet mystifying attitudes about the icon or saint being celebrated and also about the individual self who repeats the phrases. The litany thus usurps the individual's psychic space or agency, producing a kind of "craziness," as Eveline briefly understands.

Eveline's vision, unlike Margaret Mary Alacoque's, however briefly, inspires her to escape the entrapment that her mother, her father, and the whole Sacred Heart nexus represents. She hears, but does not understand, an echo of her mother's incomprehensible words in Frank's "speaking to her, saying something about the passage over and over again." However, "she answered nothing [but] out of a maze of distress, she prayed to God to direct her, to show her what was her duty" (33). Like Margaret Mary Alacoque, she relinquishes her agency. "All the seas of the world tumbled about her heart. He was drawing her into them: he would drown her" (34). Eveline's thoughts here seem to respond directly to the Sacred Heart's promise that "Sinners shall find in my heart a boundless ocean of mercy." Instead of offering comfort, however, the promise implicit in Frank's call— "Come!"—nauseates and projects Eveline into a madness not unlike her mother's wherein "she kept moving her lips in silent fervent prayer" until finally, "her eyes gave him no sign of love or farewell or recognition" (34). Frank's call echoes the verse on the colored print that hangs over the broken harmonium, "Come to me all you who labor . . ." but Eveline seems to experience a terrifying epiphany that prevents her from responding.

Eveline's sudden and unspeakable fear of Frank's imagined participation in the "maze of distress" or composite gaze of priest, Sacred Heart, father, and mother, as I read it, effectively silences and blinds her more completely than had the images on the parlor wall or the real threat of her father's violence; she thus refuses the call of this human "savior." Nonetheless, like Alacoque's, Eveline's will to live outside the bounds of the gaze is foreclosed. Notably, Alacoque observes several times in her *Autobiography* that the Sacred Heart had compromised her will: "It was my Sovereign Master, who, having taken possession of my will, did not permit me to utter any complaint"; "My Divine Master inspired me with a great fear of following my own will" (Alacoque 25, 36). Eveline presumably returns to fulfill her promise and "keep the home together" (33) for her abusive father, while Frank, unencumbered by a wife, continues on his unspecified mission.

Joyce's strategy—to make the Sacred Heart the silent and invisible puppeteer behind this brief scenario—indicates his conviction that Catholic devotional practice lends itself both to the proximate goal of developing a docile congregation and to the larger purpose of maintaining and expanding a hierarchical phallocracy. In this regard I disagree with Garry Leonard's remarks about "Eveline" in response to Thomas Richards's *The Commodity Culture of Victorian England*. Leonard insists that the print of the promises made to Alacoque hanging in Eveline's parlor "is a far cry from the jingo kitsch that Richards describes" (*Commodity* 56). Richards's point is that imperialism recognized and exploited the correlation between commodity production and kitsch on one hand, and territorial expansion on the other (Richards 133). My contention is that the imperialist church also understood that connection and thus reproduced commodities such as the Sacred Heart icon to "capitalize" on it. Joyce, in turn, reveals the complex and subtle interactions between church power and devotional practices and will return in later works to the Sacred Heart devotion both to expose and harness its power, to resist and lay bare its machinations. The question I would now like to address is: Why the Sacred Heart?

II

In his purported appearances to Alacoque, Jesus set out the "great design" mentioned in the epigraph to this essay. Though Alacoque never left her native France, she would eventually express her understanding of the great design—establishing the image and conveying the message of the Sacred Heart—in decidedly imperialist terms: "We must love His Sacred Heart with all our might and all our strength. We must love it unwaveringly and it will establish its *kingdom* and *rule* despite all that its foes may do to resist it" (quoted in Hausherr 95; emphasis added). At the behest of Jesus himself, according to the *Autobiography,* Alacoque designated her confessor, the Jesuit Father Claude de la Colombiere, the *official* facilitator of the great design: "It was to a Jesuit that the disciple of the Sacred Heart was told by Our Lord to address herself, and it was by the Jesuits that this devotion was first made public. . . . From their ranks issued the first and most zealous apostles of the devotion, as well as the founders of the greater number of confraternities, associations, and pious exercises in honor of the Divine Heart" (Hausherr 112). Speaking to Father Colombiere, who directed her to keep a journal that would subsequently be turned over to him, Alacoque insisted that "Jesus Christ made known to me in a manner that admits of no doubt that through . . . the fathers of your society He would spread this devotion everywhere" (Hausherr 116).

Having been educated by the Jesuits, James Joyce would have been immersed in Sacred Heart lore. Furthermore, in 1882, the year of Joyce's birth, a wealthy American had the twelve promises of the Sacred Heart "translated into 200 languages and printed on pictures of the Sacred Heart which he circulated by the million in all parts of the world" (Verheylezoon 236). (It is just such a commodified picture and text that hangs on Eveline's wall.) At the turn of the century, as if fulfilling the mandate Alacoque set out, Pope Leo XIII consecrated the whole human race to the Sacred Heart. There followed an immense increase in the devotion described by one Catholic commentator as an "overflowing stream, sweeping away all obstacles. . . . It [has] won nations. . . . those that consecrate themselves to the Divine Heart and submit to its royal empire are innumerable" (Verheylezoon xxii). Ireland had, in fact, been the first country to so consecrate and submit itself in 1873, a fact that Leopold Bloom recalls in the "Hades" episode of Joyce's *Ulysses* (*U* 6.955–56).

The emblematic passage from Joyce's "Eveline" that I have explicated reveals that Joyce was aware from early in his career of the power nexus emblematized by the Sacred Heart icon and the texts surrounding it. However, he probes the icon even more assiduously in his later works. By the time Joyce completed *Ulysses,* Margaret Mary Alacoque, having been designated merely "Blessed" when "Eveline" was in composition, had been officially, publicly, formally canonized by Pope Benedict XV in 1920. Both Alacoque's stock and that of the Sacred Heart had consequently increased in value while publicity about them abounded. During this period Joyce, too, would facilitate a sort of canonization by metamorphosing his early Margaret Mary—the timid virgin Eveline—into the cocksure virago Molly Bloom.

In *"Ulysses" and the Irish God,* Frederick Lang carefully and comprehensively traces references to the Sacred Heart in Joyce's oeuvre, providing historical details about the icon along the way. Among the most interesting observations Lang makes is that the "Great Apparition" of the Sacred Heart to Saint Margaret Mary Alacoque occurred on June 16, the same day as Bloomsday. Lang compares the Sacred Heart's Great Apparition, during which he exposes his flaming heart to Margaret Mary Alacoque, to Blazes Boylan's exposing his "big red brute of a thing" (*U* 18.144) to Molly Bloom on June 16, 1904. Lang compellingly argues that Joyce parodies Sacred Heart iconography, purposefully foregrounding its highly charged sexual symbolism, to reveal the church's multivalent control strategies. Joining numerous other critics who have examined Joyce's Catholicism (Robert Boyle, S.J.; William T. Noon, S.J.; Ruth Walsh; Beryl Schlossman; Darcy O'Brien; Michael O'Shea, among many others), Lang argues that Joyce transmutes Catholic doctrine, ritual, and tradition into a celebration of the divinely human over the inhumanly divine. My own reading extends Lang's and others' into a larger discourse about Joyce's contribution to our understanding of ecclesiastical empire building and identity formation. Joyce positions himself within the logic of Irish Catholicism's most cherished devotions—among which that of the Sacred Heart is prominent—to expose the spurious relationship between an otherworldly realm of eternal reward and the specific, material, real-world acts of self-abnegation and proselytizing required to reach that world. Joyce insists that we pay excessive attention to our various identities because he seems to have believed that relinquishing whatever understanding and control might be possible over them to be foolish at best and dangerous at worst.

Ironically, the widely practiced devotion to the Sacred Heart, insisting on the subservience of the faithful (more on this point later), came to prominence during the very period in Irish history when the drive for political independence was gaining the force that would result in Easter 1916. Joyce was convinced that the church's influence—imposed partly through symbols like the Sacred Heart—negatively affected the self-concepts of the Irish people especially through the women, often pressuring them to act in their own worst interests. Irish devotion to the Sacred Heart thus provided Joyce a specific, detailed emblem of the colonized psyches of the Irish people (one that effectively contributed to the myth of suffering Ireland) on one hand, and ecclesiastical ambition on the other; he seems to have used that emblem, among other religious icons, to open the way into a much larger debate involving the Irish Catholic Church, Irish independence, and sexual identity. Joyce undermined the Sacred Heart, then, for precisely the reasons that the Jesuit order promoted it. The devotion had been associated mostly with the Jesuits since Margaret Mary Alacoque commissioned Father Colombiere in 1675; then in the late nineteenth century, after years of "erudite theological discussions," having come to appreciate the power of the devotion as an empire-building tool, the papacy itself finally endorsed the Sacred Heart "in a clear and unambiguous manner" (Carroll 133). This imperialist aspect of the devotion also associates it intimately with the discourses about post-Famine Irish Catholic identity, a cultural and self-concept that expanded increasingly to include Irish Catholicism's role of missionary to the new world.

III

The mid-nineteenth century found the Irish Catholic Church in a process of redefinition involving it in two distinct but overlapping roles. While the church projected an image of itself as heroic resister of British imperialist oppression, it nevertheless, especially in the post-Famine years, increasingly fashioned itself the center of an alternative empire, with headquarters in the dioceses of Dublin and Armagh and "colonies" in the Irish Catholic sections of Canada, Australia, and North America. As the century wore on, the latter emphasis took precedence over the former, but during Joyce's early life the two currents of ecclesiastical discourse were almost equally strong. To bolster each of these positions, the church became increasingly doctrinaire about matters of faith and sexual morals, which in turn seems to have intensified a rather generalized feeling of guilt and inadequacy in the people while simultaneously providing justification for the image of the pious Irish. This double-mindedness in the Irish about their spiritual status was inevitably reinforced by discourses surrounding the Great Famine, which had represented them as both cursed and blessed—the Famine being at once a sign of God's disfavor and his recognition of their spiritual fortitude.[4] In fact, a "devotional revolution" initiated by Cardinal Paul Cullen occurred in Ireland during the last half of the nineteenth century. The transformation he instigated

> entailed for the clergy increased standards in administration, scrupulous adherence to the doctrinal positions of the papacy, and ready acceptance of the instructions of superiors, particularly the Cardinal Archbishop. Anything that smacked of irregularity or departed from the practices and procedures approved by Rome was rooted out. . . . Simultaneously, this re-invigorated clergy extended to the laity as a whole an active and all-encompassing form of religious practice. (Cairns and Richards 62)

Devotion to the Sacred Heart accommodated this new attitude of religious discipline mixed with self-abnegation especially well because it was purportedly structured for and prescribed to an adoring young female by a petulant, reproachful, but sensuous and desirable Christ. The enduring effectiveness of the Sacred Heart as disciplinarian and sensual object of desire, both of which roles fulfill the church's will to power, is strongly expressed in the words of a modern Irish devotee, the poet Eiléan Ní Chuilleanáin. In a 1995 article, Ní Chuilleanáin admitted that, "in the last decade or so, I find that it is that other icon [as opposed to the crucifix or statues of the virgin] that draws me, of the body turned inside out, the heart exposed and bleeding, the man's flesh feminised—the Sacred Heart, which was so common on the walls of Irish houses when I was a child" (577). Somewhat like the fictional Eveline and the real Margaret Mary, Ní Chuilleanáin finds herself drawn by memories of the masochistic image, "the man's flesh feminised" of the Sacred Heart, into what she believes to be an appreciation of the sacred. While Ní Chuilleanáin's experience may not seem directly relevant to ecclesiastical imperialism, the drawing away from the material and into the spiritual realm that Ní Chuilleanáin describes surely produces a kind of docility amenable to psychic colonization.

Significantly, the Sacred Heart "so common on the walls of Irish houses," as Ní Chuilleanáin recalls, was *becoming* common in Joyce's youth. In his sociological study of *The Catholic Church in Nineteenth Century Ireland,* Desmond J. Keenan notes that publication of the *Sacred Heart Messenger* dates from 1888 and that

> Popular devotion to the Sacred Heart on a wide scale probably dates from Fr. James Cullen's (no relation to the Cardinal) crusades at this period. Fr. Cullen instituted the Pioneer Total Abstinence Association, thus joining temperance with reparation to the Sacred Heart. Only women were allowed to join at first. . . . In 1873 [the year Ireland was consecrated to the Sacred Heart], the periodical *Catholic Ireland* was started, specifically to promote devotion to the Sacred Heart. (152)

Given the particular emphasis in Ireland on the Sacred Heart, it is not surprising that Mrs. Kernan, wife of the alcoholic Tom Kernan in Joyce's story "Grace," "believed steadily in the Sacred Heart as the most generally useful of all Catholic devotions" (*D* 157). The Sacred Heart contributed not only to private local devotions but also to Irish influence in the world at large. Keenan tells us that "Irish influence . . . probably reached a peak by the end of the nineteenth century when Maynooth [the Catholic seminary outside of Dublin] was the undisputed head of a world wide spiritual empire. . . . If a full study of developments in canon law were made—especially leading up to the Code by Pius X—it might well be found that the whole Church was 'hibernicised' rather than Ireland being 'Romanised'" (160). From its earliest stages in the nineteenth century, the growing power of the Irish Catholic Church had drawn on the seductions of the Sacred Heart. A confraternity of the Sacred Heart was begun in 1809 at Georges Hill convent that inaugurated a holy hour devotion, "one of the earliest examples of the holy hour practiced in Ireland" (Keenan 149). In 1812, a confraternity of the Sacred Heart was formed at Maynooth, and by 1835, "the devotion of the First Fridays [inspired by the Sacred Heart's great promise] was in full bloom in the Franciscan church in Dublin where they were celebrated with solemn high mass, litanies, benediction and indulgences" (Keenan 149).

In carrying out the dual mission of the Irish church, maintaining a docile "flock," and expanding the church's influence, the Irish Catholic priest was indispensable, just as Fr. Colombiere had been indispensable in disseminating devotion to the Sacred Heart. As Irish Catholic parishes took root in North America and Australia, it was the missionary priests more than any other single group who maintained in the people their Irish Catholic values and hence their collective identity. It is thus that the priests also came to represent a potent Irishness that spread itself outside of Ireland. Such is the priest whose name Eveline never "found out," and who is "in Melbourne now." Some historians, like W.E.H. Lecky, insisted that priests were able to expand their empire specifically because of their influence over women (144).[5] Historian Emmet Larkin points out that between 1845 and 1900, the ratio of priests to laymen in Ireland increased astonishingly, and that "the Irish Church during this period exported a very large number of priests and nuns to help staff churches in the United States and the rest of the English speaking world" (651). Paul Blanshard was prompted to argue in his 1953 polemic *The Irish and Catholic Power*:

> There are six times as many Irish Catholics outside of Ireland as there are at home, and their hold on the machinery of Catholic power has never been more impregnable. . . . The whole Catholic power system of the West is, as the *Irish World* puts it, "Ireland's spiritual empire." And, as the editor asserts, that "spiritual empire is world-wide. . . . So when fools and ignoramuses try to belittle Ireland and sneer at it and its people, we can call attention to Ireland's Empire of the soul." (5)

When Joyce's Stephen Dedalus in *A Portrait of the Artist as a Young Man* vows to assume the role of priest—albeit a priest of the eternal imagination—he fully understands the power he claims for himself among Irish Catholics. Methodically, he sets about bridging the gap between the "mystifications" (rather than the mysteries) of the faith and the apparently stunted daily lives of his class of Irish men and women. Having had "the cursed Jesuit strain . . . injected the wrong way," as Buck Mulligan insists in *Ulysses* (*U* 7.209), however, Stephen exposes how the church has manipulated the symbols of the faith so as effectively to control the minds and bodies of the faithful and extend its own empire rather than facilitate the Irish Catholic Church's redefinition of itself as defender of the colonized. In the "Circe" episode of *Ulysses* (a phantasmagoric psychodrama giving expression to the repressed fears and desires of its primary cast of characters), Stephen's mother (designated THE MOTHER, associating her both with the Virgin Mary and with all mothers) appears. She implores "O Sacred Heart of Jesus, have mercy on him! Save him from hell, O Divine Sacred Heart" (*U* 15.4232–33). When Stephen resists his mother's intercession, she persists: "(*in the agony of her deathrattle*) Have mercy on Stephen, Lord. . . . Inexpressible was my anguish when expiring with love, grief and agony on Mount Calvary" (*U* 15.4238–40). This scenario reconfigures Eveline's situation—a child in danger of entrapment by a mother's dying imprecations—and places Stephen in the endangered position. Both mothers have been compromised by association with the Sacred Heart. When THE MOTHER describes herself as "expiring with love, grief and agony on Mount Calvary," she takes on the role not only of Jesus's Mother but also of Margaret Mary Alacoque, who claims to have "taken on her shoulders that heavy cross all studded with nails" (121) and also of Christ himself. THE MOTHER's words, in fact, come from "an act of Reparation to the Sacred Heart" (Lang 231).

The most significant effect of this encounter, for me, is the way in which it assigns responsibility to THE MOTHER for passing on a particular aspect of the Sacred Heart legacy—that of the suffering victim. But Stephen rejects his mother's advances in what many critics believe to be the climax of the episode: "*He lifts his ashplant high with both hands and smashes the chandelier*" (*U* 15.4243–44). Later in the episode, however, the Sacred Heart returns, this time exposing himself not as a victimized female but as a confraternity of powerful male institutions.

Speaking to Leopold Bloom, Stephen taps himself on the brow and insists "in here it is I must kill the priest and the king" (*U* 15.4436–37). Shortly thereafter

> Edward the Seventh appears in an archway. He wears a white jersey on which an image of the Sacred Heart is stitched with the insignia of Garter and Thistle, Golden Fleece, Elephant of Denmark, Skinner's and Probyn's horse, Lincoln's Inn bencher and ancient and honourable artillery company of Massachusetts. (*U* 15.4449–53)

That the nexus of worldwide power represented here is stitched together with the Sacred Heart at its center is notable. Taken together, the two scenes—one with Stephen's mother and one with Edward the Seventh—suggest Joyce's, if not Stephen's, appreciation of the pervasive power and appeal of the church as symbolized in the Sacred Heart. Besides its sadomasochistic appeal, the church can boast of membership in a transnational military industrial complex.

Attesting to the power of this devotion, Joyce also had other lived experiences that, like my own, included daily or weekly encounters with holy cards, badges, prints, scapulars, hymns, litanies, prayers, and "ejaculations" invoking the Sacred Heart's "burning love" for those who would devote themselves to him. *The Messenger of the Sacred Heart* (a copy of which Davy Stephens attempts to sell to Bloom in the "Circe" episode of *Ulysses* [*U* 15.1122–27]) was available to Catholics at least through the 1950s. Such texts as these, as well as leaflets featuring an "Act of Consecration" to the Sacred Heart were, regularly "pressed" onto the faithful in Catholic churches and schools. Additionally, as part of Ireland's devotional revolution, enthusiastic priests frequently delivered homilies mapping the way for the faithful to achieve union with the Sacred Heart. The Enthronement of the Sacred Heart, a ritual developed during Joyce's youth, locates the icon in the home, where it is henceforth to preside "as master and King" (Carroll 328–29). It seems clear, then, that Joyce chose to expose the church's organ of empire because he recognized its designs on him and his country. One final point I would like now to consider concerns the comprehensiveness of Joyce's understanding of this powerful icon.

IV

Whether or not Joyce subjected Sacred Heart devotion to psychoanalytic scrutiny is debatable. Nonetheless, the evidence in his oeuvre leads one to conclude that Joyce recognized not only its ubiquity but also the repressed desires for which it provided spurious satisfaction. Only recently has this devotion received detailed psychoanalytic attention, and the conclusions that Michael Carroll draws in his 1989 *Catholic Cults and Devotions* lend credence to the insights exposed in Joyce's parodic transformations of the icon. As I have mentioned earlier, devotion to the Sacred Heart became the subject of much theological analysis during the second half of the nineteenth century, the primary reason for which was its growing popularity. In effect, to expand and reinforce its power base, the church sought reasons to legitimate a practice already attracting devotees in a wide range of countries. Joyce undertook a similar though inverted project in using a devotion that he knew to have both local and transnational appeal to establish his creed regarding the need for sexual honesty and "truth." He may even have intuited the psychological roots of the Sacred Heart's unprecedented popularity in the late nineteenth century.

Carroll contends that the enhanced appeal of Sacred Heart devotion may be explained by the "centrality of the reparation element" within it (137). Indeed, the entry in the 1907–12 edition of *The Catholic Encyclopedia* under "Heart of Jesus, Devotion to the" (which Joyce may have read) emphasizes its compensatory nature: "one of the essential phases of the devotion is that it considers the love of Jesus for us as a despised, ignored love [for which] He complained so bitterly to Blessed Margaret Mary" and accordingly outlined his detailed plan for making reparation (164).

Applying Melanie Klein's psychoanalytic theory to the reparation aspect of Sacred Heart devotion, Carroll hypothesizes that this desire to make amends proceeds from imagined "attacks on the father, the prototypical authority figure" (151). With no apparent knowledge of Joyce's sexually charged Sacred Heart satire, but closely aligned with Lang's observations about the phallic connotations of Joyce's Sacred Heart allusions, Carroll observes that "the primary associations evoked by the Sacred Heart seem to be that it is a body part belonging to an adult male . . . simultaneously both inside and outside that male's body . . . lacerated and punctured" (139). Lang reaches a similar conclusion:

> despite Irish Catholicism's particularly intense "contempt" for sexuality the Sacred Heart devotion seems a disguised form of genital worship. Christ's conspicuous heart does divert attention from the genitals, but, in having become visible, the organ seems external and so appears to be modeled on them. (103)

From Mulligan's irreverent epithet "Blessed Margaret Mary Anycock!" (*U* 9.646) to Bloom's reference to the Sacred Heart statue in "Hades" as "showing it" (*U* 6.954), to Molly's memory of Blazes Boylan's exposed "big red brute of a thing," which has "put some heart up into" her (*U* 18.144, 733), Joyce demonstrates throughout *Ulysses* his perception of the Sacred Heart's heart as an upwardly displaced sex organ demanding both attention and action.

Carroll justifies his reading of the Sacred Heart as "a symbolic representation of the father's penis . . . absorbed by the mother during intercourse" (141) by recounting Sacred Heart apparitions, all but one of which were experienced by women. For example, in the account of her first apparition, Margaret Mary Alacoque reveals that Christ "asked for my heart . . . placed it within his adorable Heart . . . then withdrawing it . . . like a burning flame in the shape of a heart, he replaced it . . . Saying: 'Behold my beloved, a precious pledge of my love, which is inserting into your side a tiny spark of its most fiery flames'" (quoted in Carroll 142). For Carroll, the exchange of hearts represents "the infantile memory of the father's absorbed penis [within the mother]; that is, Alacoque 'absorbed' Christ's physical heart during mystical intercourse" (142). As numerous commentators, such as Lang and Richard Brown, have noted, Joyce often converts such mystical intercourse to authentic human intercourse; this is especially so in the encounter between Molly, a profane Margaret Mary Alacoque, and her "blazing" lover, who is, significantly, an opportunist not unlike the church's own Sacred Heart.

It seems certain then that Joyce appreciated the power of the Sacred Heart devotion both in terms of its popular and its psychosexual appeal; could he also have perceived its effectiveness as an empire-building tool, as I have been arguing? Carroll examines the desires vicariously fulfilled in the Sacred Heart devotion—to make reparation to or reconcile with the wounded male authority figure—on both the individual and institutional levels. On the institutional level, he views the devotion as a means of assuaging the collective guilt of Catholics for imagined involvement in attacks on the papacy, the embodiment of patriarchal church power. Citing the nineteenth-century antipapal movements within the *Risorgimento* in Italy and similar attacks on the pope's authority during the *Kulturkampf* in Germany, Carroll contends that nineteenth-century Catholics generally, and in those countries particularly, felt the need to make reparation. Sacred Heart devotion, providing a handy means for filling that need, became popular among the laity. As a way of reinstating its power and controlling the laity, the church in turn began the process of officially sanctioning and prescribing the details of the devotional practice.

In his insightful rendering of the psycho-socio-historical implications of Sacred Heart devotion, Carroll mentions Ireland only once. But I believe his insights about the multiple causes and effects of this intriguing devotion are applicable to Ireland in ways that shed light on its prolonged colonial status. As Lang has made clear, and the early consecration of Ireland to the Sacred Heart suggests, Ireland's spirit of dedication may have surpassed that of other Catholic countries during the growth years of the devotion in the late nineteenth century. Why would this be so?

The event that cut nineteenth-century Ireland in two was, of course, the Great Famine (see note 4 below). Not only did it inaugurate the second half of the century by starving, infecting, humiliating, and driving out thou-

sands of young people, it inspired guilt and the perceived need for reparation as well as rebellion and reform. Every aspect of Irish life from economics to literature to marriage patterns was affected by the Famine. The
devotional revolution mentioned earlier was in many ways caused by the
church's role in facilitating the rise in familism after the Famine. Additionally, the Famine contributed to the growth of the Irish Catholic empire.
Paul Blanshard, an avowed critic of that empire, insists that "when half a
million people died at home and more than four million were driven out of
the country, the Irish fortuitously clinched their hold upon Catholic power
in America" (250). Emmet Larkin argues that Cardinal Cullen, who inaugurated the devotional revolution in Ireland,

> derived very great advantage from the psychological impact the fam-
> ine had on those who remained in Ireland. The growing awareness of
> a sense of sin already apparent in the 1840s was certainly deepened as
> God's wrath was made manifest in a great natural disaster that de-
> stroyed and scattered his people. Psychologically and socially, there-
> fore, the Irish people were ready for a great evangelical revival, while
> economically and organizationally the Church was now correspond-
> ingly ready after the famine to meet their religious and emotional
> needs.(639)

More specifically, the perceived need to make reparation after the Famine
may explain the astonishing popularity of the Sacred Heart devotion and
the church's willingness to sanction it so whole"heartedly." The perceived
need to make reparation would have derived from voices in the discourse
about the Famine and its causes that insisted on a certain fecklessness
among the Irish resulting from their slavish idolatry of the pope and the
priests. By some commentators this charge was particularly laid at the feet
of Irish women, whose "priest-ridden" influence was perceived to have
made the entire population so docile as to succumb to the Famine without
a fight.

If in fact the Irish generally and Irish women particularly felt the need
to compensate for these attacks on the church's authority, the Sacred Heart
devotion certainly provided them a tailor-made formula for doing so. To
the extent that he believed the church to be in some degree responsible for
the atrophied will of the Irish, Joyce seems to have accepted this version of
post-Famine discourse. He seems also to have believed that priestly enthrallment of individual women was detrimental to the collective will and
that the liberation of such women from priestly control would have to be

achieved in the place where that control was most effectively exerted, their sexual identities. Thus by transforming Margaret Mary Alacoque into Molly Bloom, a woman who is willing to experiment, break the rules, and please her own body without making reparation, Joyce carries out his own heretical priestly mission. Unlike Eveline, Molly finds out, remembers, and repeats the names of priests, disclosing the locus of their power. She shamelessly encounters, enjoys, and deflates the "big red brute of a thing" with which her Sacred Heart surrogate tries to impress her. The progression from Margaret Mary Alacoque to Eveline to Molly represents a kind of decolonization of the psyche, not only of Irish women but of the Irish and of Catholics generally.

Interestingly, in spite of Joyce's transformation and liberation of Margaret Mary, she seems to have returned in her victimized form under the name of Saint Maria Faustina Kowalska. The history of this innocent little Polish nun, who was repeatedly "visited" by Jesus during the 1930s (in the form of "The Divine Mercy" rather than the Sacred Heart) and commissioned to spread his message and image throughout the world, is remarkably parallel to Alacoque's. Her canonization on April 30, 2000, was championed by the current pope, John Paul II, whose conservatism is legend. Read in the light of Joyce's parody of Alacoque, Kowalska's story suggests that the exploitation of innocence continues to be very much a part of ecclesiastical politics.

Notes

1. The complete list of promises, oddly enough, is not given in Alacoque's *Autobiography*. However, numerous other sources, including Torchiana (72), and O'Connell (1–10), list them as follows:

I.   I will give them all the graces necessary in their state of life.
II.   I will establish peace in their families.
III.   I will console them in all their troubles.
IV.   I will be their assured refuge in life and more especially in death.
V.   I will pour out abundant benedictions on all their undertakings.
VI.   Sinners shall find in my heart a boundless ocean of mercy.
VII.   Tepid souls shall become fervent.
VIII.   Fervent souls shall advance rapidly to great perfection.
IX.   I will bless the houses in which the image of my Heart shall be exposed and honored.
X.   I will give to priests the power of touching the most hardened of hearts.

XI.   Persons who propagate this devotion shall have their names inscribed in
my Heart, and they shall never be effaced from It.

XII.   I promise that those who receive Communion on the First Friday of nine
consecutive months, shall not die under my displeasure.

2. Katherine Mullin convincingly argues that Frank may have been Joyce's version of a procurer, enticing young women to a life of prostitution in Buenos Aires.
Even this interpretation works well with the Sacred Heart associations, given that
the Sacred Heart was, in a sense, a procurer of women.

3. The note on "derevaun seraun" in the Penguin edition of *Dubliners* provides a
summary of suggested meanings for the phrase, including among others "the end of
pleasure is pain" and "the end of song is raving madness" (Gifford 52), and "worms
are the only end" (Torchiana 75–76). Brendan O'Hehir's opinion that the phrase is
"probably gibberish but phonetically like Irish" (quoted in Joyce, *D* 256) comes
closer to my own argument that, like litanies, the words preempt psychic space.

4. I have discussed the complicated responses of the Irish to the Famine in *Crimes
against Fecundity: Joyce and Population Control*. Since publication of that work in
1989, a plethora of Great Famine studies have appeared, especially in conjunction
with the sesquicentennial commemoration in 1995–97. Among the best is Cormac
Ó'Gráda's 1999 *Black '47 and Beyond: The Great Irish Famine in History, Economy,
and Memory*. As his title suggests, Ó'Gráda takes an interdisciplinary and comparative approach to the subject. He also lists and comments on many of the more recent
studies. While emigration and death statistics vary somewhat from study to study,
there seems to be no substantial disagreement with the idea that the Famine had
momentous and far-reaching consequences. In response to what Ó'Gráda calls "a
respected historian [who] described the Irish famine as no more than a detail in
European history," Ó'Gráda contends that "a little research would have shown the
opposite to have been true: a comparative perspective on the famine makes it stand
out, not only in nineteenth century European history, but in world history" (232).

5. Lecky's *History of European Morals* is especially strong on this subject.

Works Cited

Alacoque, Margaret Mary. *The Autobiography of Saint Margaret Mary Alacoque.*
Rockford Ill.: Tan Books, 1986.

Baccolini, Raffaella. "'She Had Become a Memory': Women as Memory in James
Joyce's *Dubliners.*" In *Rejoycing: New Readings of "Dubliners,"* edited by Rosa
M. Bollettieri Bosinelli and Harold F. Mosher Jr., 145–64. Lexington: University
of Kentucky Press, 1998.

Bainvel, Jean. "Heart of Jesus, Devotion to the." *The Catholic Encyclopedia.* Vol. 7.
New York: Robert Appleton, 1907–12.

Blanshard, Paul. *The Irish and Catholic Power: An American Interpretation.* Boston:
Beacon Press, 1953

Brown, Richard. *James Joyce and Sexuality*. Cambridge: Cambridge University Press, 1985.

Cairns, David, and Shaun Richards. *Writing Ireland: Colonialism, Nationalism, and Culture*. Manchester: Manchester University Press, 1988.

Carroll, Michael P. *Catholic Cults and Devotions: A Psychological Inquiry*. McGill-Queens University Press, 1989.

Childs, Matthew, "James Joyce and the Modernists: A Novelist and Novelties." *The Latin Mass* 10, no. 2 (spring 2000): 58–61.

Gifford, Don. *Joyce Annotated: Notes for "Dubliners" and "A Portrait of the Artist as a Young Man."* 2d ed. Berkeley and Los Angeles: University of California Press, 1982.

Hausherr, Rev. M., S.J. *The Glories of the Sacred Heart of Jesus*. New York: Benziger Books, 1906.

Joyce, James. *Dubliners*. Introduction and notes by Terence Brown. Penguin, 1992.

Keenan, Desmond J. *The Catholic Church in Nineteenth Century Ireland: A Sociological Study*. Totowa N.J.: Barnes and Nobles, 1983.

Lang, Frederick K. *"Ulysses" and the Irish God*. Lewisburg, Pa.: Bucknell University Press, 1993.

Larkin, Emmet. "The Devotional Revolution in Ireland, 1850–75." *The American Historical Review* 77 (June 1972): 625–52.

Lecky, W.E.H. *The History of European Morals*. Vol. 2. London: Longmans, Green, 1869.

Leonard, Garry. *Advertising and Commodity Culture in Joyce*. Gainesville: University Press of Florida, 1998.

———. *Reading "Dubliners" Again: A Lacanian Perspective*. Syracuse: Syracuse University Press, 1993.

Lowe-Evans, Mary. *Crimes against Fecundity: Joyce and Population Control*. University Press, 1989.

Mullin, Katherine, "Don't Cry for Me, Argentina: 'Eveline' and the Seductions of Emigration Propaganda." In *Semicolonial Joyce*, edited by Derek Attridge and Marjorie Howes, 172–200. Cambridge: Cambridge University Press, 2000.

Ní Chuilleanáin, Eiléan, "Acts and Monuments of an Unelected Nation: The *Cailleach* Writes about the Renaissance." *Southern Review* 31, no. 3 (July 1995): 570–80.

O'Connell, Patrick. *The Devotion to the Sacred Heart of Jesus*. Wexford: John English, 1951.

Ó'Gráda, Cormac. *Black '47 and Beyond: The Great Irish Famine in History, Economy, and Memory*. Princeton: Princeton University Press, 1999.

Richards, Thomas. *The Commodity Culture of Victorian England: Advertising and Spectacle, 1851–1914*. Stanford University Press, 1990.

Torchiana, Donald J. *Backgrounds for Joyce's "Dubliners."* Boston: Allen and Unwin, 1986.

Verheylezoon, Louis, S.J. *Devotion to the Sacred Heart: Object, Ends, Practice, Motives*. Westminster, Md.: Newman Press, 1955.

States of Memory

Reading History in "Wandering Rocks"

Anne Fogarty

Joyce's lofty declaration to Frank Budgen that in composing *Ulysses* he wanted "to give a picture of Dublin so complete that if the city one day suddenly disappeared from the earth it could be reconstructed out of my book" has become a well-worn truism in the critical afterlife enjoyed by his work (Budgen 69). The familiarity of the claim should not, however, be allowed to mask its paradoxical nature. Although Joyce suggests that fiction can wholly substitute for reality, he simultaneously maintains that his text makes fullest sense in terms of its referentiality. Dublin, it would appear as well in the double take of Joycean aesthetics, is both mirrored and eclipsed by the fictional work conceived in its likeness. The material realities of life on June 16, 1904, supply significant coordinates for our reading of *Ulysses* and yet seem also to be erased by the very processes of fictionalization and re-invention. Joyce's memorializing textuality obliterates, rearranges, and deconstructs the history and geopolitical spaces that it also pretends to safeguard and salvage.

As the material and historical realities to which *Ulysses* alludes recede further from us, one of the chief challenges facing the twenty-first-century critic is how to prevent these contexts, on the one hand, from fading, and on the other, from solidifying into falsely reductive accounts of early twentieth-century Ireland. Frequently, the time period framing the events of *Ulysses* is seen as static and unchanging and often is encapsulated in conveniently tidy chronicles of social and political stagnation or of a heroic, but downtrodden, premodernity. Criticism needs constantly to question the versions of the past that Joyce's writing mediates, or is held to enshrine, and also to remain alert to the extent to which it both interacts with and contests a very shifting and contested set of historical experiences. Rather than perceive Irish history as a determinism informing and constraining his fiction or as a fixed, immobile ground against which it can be measured, we must recognize not only the carefully textured nature of the social critique of post-Parnellite Ireland that his fiction performs but also the alternative, open-ended, and speculative histories that it constructs.

Epistemological and hermeneutic skepticism, however, is but one route by which we can revivify the reading of Joyce in a new century. Given the several decades of Joycean criticism that have elapsed, current scholars are also burdened with the weight of previous interpretations that frequently intervene between the reader and the text and superinscribe themselves in our critical engagement with it. J. Hillis Miller has noted that the de-mystified analyses promoted by late twentieth-century cultural criticism—which urge us to deconstruct texts and view them with suspicion—often seem at odds with, and to belie, the initial process of imaginative surrender to a work of literature and the uncertainties and misprisions that form part of the reading experience (113–31). The task for a further century of Joycean analysis is not just to engage in useful dialogue with a rich and voluminous inheritance of authoritative interpretations and editions but also to preserve the openness and pleasure of initial encounters with his work. Thus, current and future Joycean criticism finds itself faced with a difficult, but challenging, balancing act: it needs at once self-consciously to catalogue and take stock of the wealth of exegesis that his work has attracted; to position itself in relation to longstanding debates; inventively to formulate fresh questions and to reconnoiter new fields of inquiry; and finally to acknowledge the provisionality of all attempts to pin down the protean qualities of Joyce's fiction. The imaginative potential of Joyce's work can be made available to future generations of readers only if the scholarship it has spawned succeeds in providing us simultaneously with the necessary tools for interpreting his texts and with the means constantly to reassess and question the very grounds on which we approach and make sense of them in the first instance.

In the light of such considerations, this essay will begin by briefly examining the many persuasive and magisterial readings of "Wandering Rocks" that have been formulated. It will then look at how the intricate narrative structures of the episode utilize teasing historical allusions and techniques of spatiotemporal conjunction and displacement in order to foreground the multiple ways in which Dubliners interact with and reflect on the past. In addition, the methods in which collective memories are at once harnessed and ironized in this fragmented interlude will be considered. A further aim of my analysis will be to review the ideological underpinnings of the versions of the Irish past that inform interpretations of this chapter and to reflect on how a more densely historicist approach to Joyce's work might be deployed in order to complicate such readings. I shall argue that the web of allusions and memories that underpins this section both captures the ambivalence of the colonial subject caught between cultures and political allegiances and also gestures at a hidden narrative of dissidence and dissent that cannot be accommodated by any overarching story or single historical overview of the period. In particular, Joyce's precise rendering of the material and physical struggles of a host of minor figures, ranging from the growling truculence of the onelegged sailor to the captivating pathos of Dilly Dedalus and Master Dignam, will be shown to be not just a figuration of the miseries caused by political oppression and economic poverty but also an empathetic depiction of an abjected subjectivity that refuses to be inserted into the reigning political narratives of Gaelicization, modernization, or constructive unionism.

Additionally, attention will be given to the ideological dualisms that are often held self-evidently to provide the contours of the episode. Many assessments of "Wandering Rocks" assume that Fr. Conmee and William Humble, the Lord Lieutenant, represent the neatly counterpoised and damaging forces of church and empire that have entrapped Irish society but that can readily be dismissed by the reader equipped with the benefit of the unmasking vision of historical hindsight. This essay will demonstrate, however, that these two figures draw together many of the conflicting undercurrents in early twentieth-century Irish society and are used to delineate a carefully layered and protean view of a fluid historical scene. The divisions, decenterings, and complex allusiveness of the episode capture the tectonics of power in a colonial society but also gesture at the revolutionary changes taking place in Ireland at the turn of the twentieth century fueled by numerous conflicting movements for political autonomy and social reform. "Wandering Rocks," instead of presenting us with a picture of an enervated and dispirited community, as many critics have averred, orchestrates the multiform political possibilities of Dublin in 1904 while also subtly reworking and critiquing them. Rather than showing us a closed world in a state of animated suspension that simply courts our moral condemnation, this pivotal chapter holds all of the political, social, and cultural elements of Dublin in 1904 in fluid dissolution and invites its readers actively to immerse themselves in the unforeclosed processes and concrete materialities of a living history that it engagingly and playfully mirrors and refracts.

Paradoxically, "Wandering Rocks" sets out to break the strangulating hold of history on Irish society by pointedly concentrating on the here-and-now. The main objective of the collage of nineteen overlapping and divergent vignettes, featuring an assortment of Dublin's citizens as they move around the city at three o'clock on the afternoon of June 16, 1904, would appear to be to elude retrospection and to evade the stultifying effects of historical reminiscence. In this pivotal section, too, the text itself seems to slip its bearings by departing from its Homeric intertext. Although the Symplegades, or Clashing Rocks, are mentioned on several occasions in *The Odyssey*, the feat of passing between these twin dangers is part of the catalogue of adventures of Jason in the *Argonautica* and not of Ulysses.[1] Circe suggests the Wandering Rocks to Odysseus as an alternative route to Scylla and Charybdis. Hence, in taking up this abandoned Homeric trajectory, the episode symbolically deviates and sets out in pursuit of fictional and historical alternatives.[2] Similarly, issues of plot and characterization appear even further in abeyance here than in preceding episodes. The constraints of linearity and logic are ostensibly set aside in favor of a randomized world patterned on a potentially liberating series of present moments.

Critical reception of this central chapter, while applauding its experimentalism, has tended, by and large, to view it in two opposing ways. One group of critics sees it as an allegory and resounding indictment of the social malaise of Dublin life. A second, but smaller group, perhaps as a reaction to these negative assessments, discerns in it the lineaments of a more hopeful narrative and grapples to find a way of describing its complex dynamics and the overwhelming sense of doubleness generated in this world of clashing alternatives. The prompts Joyce supplied us in his schemata appear to endorse the readings that see this central section of *Ulysses* as describing a soulless, decentered colonial city. The terms of reference suggested in the Gilbert and Linati schemata, such as "mechanics" and "labyrinth," and the emphasis on a conflict between spiritual and secular authorities—"Cristo e Cesare" (Christ and Caesar)—in the Linati schema, as well as the description of the setting as "L'Ambiente Nemico" (the hostile milieu), have led critics to underscore the picture of urban alienation that emerges at the core of *Ulysses*.[3] The rebarbative nature of this world is held, moreover, to color and cross-infect attempts to perceive or make sense of it. In his pioneering account of the chapter, Clive Hart famously declares its fragmentation, pseudo-objectivity, false congruences, and misleading cross-references to be a series of traps for the unwary reader. The labyrinthine dead-ends and wrong turnings of Dublin are mirrored directly by the frustrating experiences of readers as they grapple with this elusive section of *Ulysses*.

However, despite this emphasis on the unreliability and intricacies of the narrative organization of "Wandering Rocks," and on the mercurial nature of the Dublin that is projected, Hart nonetheless discerns a coherent moral objective in Joyce's representation of this urban world. He argues that the falsities and incongruities of the episode allow us at once to glimpse the "city's malice" and to gain insight into the "inadequate personal relationships of the principals," that is, Stephen and Bloom (Hart 202). He also concludes that Stephen and Bloom will gain command of the city only when they learn to amend their faults and control their fantasies. Many other interpretations of "Wandering Rocks" echo and extend Hart's bleak assessment of the urban environment and the social milieu it depicts. Michael Seidel declares the episode "the black hole at the center of *Ulysses* ... [that] draws the matter of Dublin to it" (186). Richard Ellmann notes that three o'clock is, in biblical tradition, the time at which Christ's crucifixion took place and concludes that the chapter acts like a "distorting mirror-image" of *Ulysses* as a whole, in which "Dublin asserts itself as micropolis, with petty debts, petty spies, petty rebellions, petty lives and deaths" (91). In a similar summation, Trevor Williams argues that "No Man's Land" might be an appropriate subtitle for the Dublin of "Wandering Rocks" as its "citizens wander its streets freely without ever themselves becoming aware of the imprisoning structures mechanically enclosing them" (268). He further sees the section of the novel as laying bare the roots of oppression of Joyce's characters in the twin ideologies of British colonialism and Roman Catholicism.

Marilyn French arrives at an even more damning diagnosis. She contends that "Wandering Rocks" forces us to the conclusion that "Dublin is a land of the dead and dying," and she sees the failure to achieve contact with reality and the "lack of genuine encounter" as the pervasive themes of this portion of *Ulysses* (118). Moreover, she deems that the black ironies of the succession of short scenes are akin to a medieval morality drama. Hugh Kenner, by contrast, adjudges the harsh atmosphere of the chapter to be the result of Joyce's increasing reliance on amorality and depersonalization. For him, the emergence of an anonymous narrative voice that is characterized by its pursuit of relentless irony and indifference to the personal fates of the characters is at the root of the discontinuities and rhetorical games of "Wandering Rocks" (63–66). Mark Wollaeger, similarly, views the episode as imbued by an impulse to record impassively the minutiae of the urban labyrinth of Dublin. However, he connects this desire to register the lives of the inhabitants of the city while discountenancing their individualism as an ironic mirroring of the technologies of surveillance prevalent in the city at that period and as Joyce's mimicry and enactment of the subjected consciousness of the colonial subjects of this downtrodden capital (87). Len Platt, in a suggestive revisionist reading of the section, observes the extent to which it not only thematizes history but also foregrounds the activities of several amateur historians, including Fr. Conmee and the Rev. Hugh C. Love. However, he concludes that their efforts reveal the continuing Anglocentrism of Irish society and the draining inauthenticity of a colonial community.

In sum, while interpretations of the internal organization of this chapter may vary, the preponderance of critics subscribes to the consensus that views the fragmentation, confusion, and misinformation of "Wandering Rocks" as mirroring the alienation and the moral errancy of Dublin life. In particular, a generalized perception of early twentieth-century Irish society as lacking in political direction and enervated by colonial rule seems to inform the negativity of such conclusions. Inevitably, tacit assumptions about the historical era and social world portrayed by Joyce and about the political subtexts of his writing color interpretations of this central chapter of *Ulysses*.

There are, however, counterviews of "Wandering Rocks" that uncover divisions and conflicting moments within this narrative that make it less easy to see it as cohering around a single moral imperative or as answering to a unitary thesis on reigning aspects of Irish politics. Bonnie Kime Scott, in a suggestive feminist re-reading of the episode, contends that we should shift our attention to the seemingly submerged presences of female and other minoritarian figures in this urban landscape. Scott avers that the fragmented drama of this entracte of *Ulysses* aims not to instruct us in social or textual mastery but to alert us to "numerous moments of being that enact the marginal experiences of minor characters who seem to have little control over their lives."[4] Importantly, Weldon Thornton, in his narratological study of the episode, argues that "Wandering Rocks" demonstrates the limitations of the seemingly objective naturalism affected by the secondary narrator and also distances itself from the narrator's overweening irony and propensity for satire (134–42). Moreover, following on the studies of John Wenke and Vincent Sherry, he claims that the many acts of altruism portrayed in the nineteen vignettes subvert the view that this is a callous and unremittingly hostile urban world. Hence, in Thornton's estimation, the narrative is at odds with itself and provides a bifurcated and at times contradictory account of Dublin on the afternoon of June 16.

Joep Leerssen goes further still in his assessment of the positive portrait of Dublin constructed by "Wandering Rocks." He contrasts Joyce's innovative narrative techniques with the strategies used by literary and historical representations of Ireland in the nineteenth century. Borrowing a term from Bakhtin, Leerssen asserts that these latter works favored a view of Ireland as a "chronotope," that is, as a place where time passes unevenly and is frequently in a state of arrest (224–31). Furthermore, many nineteenth-century nationalist histories attempt to unify the Irish past and to replace the turbulent *Nacheinander*, or sequentiality, of events with a spectacular *Nebeneinander*, or simultaneity. Often, as a consequence, history is presented as a series of timeless tableaux transcending the causality of logic. In Leerssen's view, *Ulysses* as a whole, and the "Wandering Rocks" episode in particular, seek to undo the paralyzing freeze-frames of nineteenth-century Irish nationalist historiography by depicting Dublin as a dynamic, Newtonian universe. Joyce's representations of a vibrant modern metropolis are designedly at variance with static, romanticist mythologies about Ireland.

Whereas Leerssen's summation places a welcome emphasis on the forward-looking, modernizing impulse of this episode, Andrew Gibson's exploration of its historical dimensions suggestively opens up a possibility of attending to its dissonances and dualities. He proposes that "Wandering Rocks" allows us to discern the gaps that exist between the reigning political macronarratives of church and state, as borne out in the sections devoted to Fr. Conmee and to the viceregal procession, and the micronarratives represented by the numerous characters whose lives it stages. The interpretation put forward in this essay will build upon and extend Gibson's findings. It will examine the way in which the divergences between the framing religious and political perspectives and the lifeworlds of the individual characters are intimated, but it will also argue that it is ultimately impossible to prise these official narratives apart from the numerous personal microhistories that strew this section. Historical remembrance and ideological conflict constantly disrupt the clockwork operations of the interlocking paths of the multifarious cast of characters. Their peripatetic movements are accompanied by the divagations of communal memory and are correlated to the political discourses and debates from which they dissent but can never entirely dissever themselves.

Pierre Nora, in his multivolume study of the multiple facets of French identity, *Realms of Memory*, describes the *loci memoriae* of a culture not so much as fixed sites but as significant entities, both material and nonmaterial, that have become symbolic in the heritage of a given community.[5] In addition to physical locations, rituals, historical figures, and institutions, Nora also explores resonant spatial and temporal categories, such as the opposition between Paris and the provinces, that form French national consciousness. In the realms or sites of memory may be found sedimented all of the contradictory layers of historical knowledge and received wisdom of a society. Nora's methodology is compelling because of the way in which it probes the ambiguities of remembrance and acknowledges the role of unofficial modes of recall such as folk memory, tradition, and oral history in the creation of cultural symbolism. However, as many have pointed out, his theses about the importance of rituals of remembrance in the forging of national history and identity are also problematic because they appear to be motivated by a nostalgia for an organic past and a curious distrust of the function of history in the postmodern period.[6] Joyce, by contrast, in the coded and ambiguous historical allusions that subtend "Wandering Rocks," both harnesses the political force and radical potential of what Maurice Halbwachs terms "the social frameworks of memory" and also contests their mythologizing functions (37–40). Moreover, *Ulysses* indicates that the sites of memory in a colonial culture are always in themselves the center of conflicting significance and cannot easily be disambiguated or made to answer to the needs of the overarching narratives of nationalism, imperialism, or decolonization, or to the yearnings of individual desire.

As numerous commentators have observed, Dublin, rather than the actions of any of the characters, would appear to act as a unifying locus of the "Wandering Rocks" episode. Indeed, it quickly transpires that this is both a documentation of the city as it appears on a particular day in history and a telescoping of its eventful and multilayered forehistories. Not coincidentally, in an episode built around synchronicities and the links between receding and interconnecting temporalities, Blazes Boylan's secretary records the date on which the events of the novel as a whole occur:

Miss Dunne clicked on the keyboard:
—16 June 1904. (*U* 10.375–76)

Her newfangled typewriter, ironically, is pressed into service to create the illusion of a historic present but also to draw the readership into a temporal dimension that has already elapsed. History, moreover, permeates this episode and is inextricable from the urban scenes that it limns and catalogues with such detail.

An initial measure of the extent to which the past is a pervasive concern might be arrived at by listing the resonant street names, historic buildings, statues, and significant locations to which it alludes. In the several overlapping itineraries picked out, the text refers to Mountjoy Square (*U* 10.12), Great Charles Street (*U* 10.68), Newcomen Bridge (*U* 10.111), George's Quay (*U* 10.298), Crampton Court (*U* 10.492), Wellington Quay (*U* 10.533), William's Row (*U* 10.654), James's Street (*U* 10.674), Pembroke Quay (*U* 10.794), Bedford Row (*U* 10.830), Lord Edward Street (*U* 10.960), Parliament Street (*U* 10.981), Essex gate (*U* 10.992), Nelson Street (*U* 10.1063), Holles Street (*U* 10.1101), Clare Street (*U* 10.1114), Bloody Bridge (*U* 10.1183), Leinster Street (*U* 10.1263), and Northumberland and Lansdowne Roads (*U* 10.1277–78). The significant buildings named include Trinity College, Dublin Castle, the Viceregal Lodge, the City Hall, and St. Mary's Abbey, which is, in Ned Lambert's eyes, "the most historic spot in all Dublin" (*U* 10.409). Whereas the density of allusion might be attributed to Joycean encyclopedism and to the desire to create a sense of the dizzying facticity of urban life, it also evocatively indicates the extent to which even casual journeys in Dublin traverse a streetscape that has been molded by several centuries of colonial history. As C. T. M'Cready notes, most Dublin streets are named after English monarchical families and lord lieutenants and their consorts. Hence the workings of power and the complex legacies of a divided history are part of the very topography of the lives of Joyce's characters.

However, the chapter does not just signal the inescapability of the past; it also captures the vital changes in the political affiliations of the city that had begun to be registered in the latter half of the nineteenth century.[7] The oldest statue in Dublin is used as an ironic foil in the final section when the viceregal cavalcade passes the spot where "the foreleg of King Billy's horse pawed the air" (*U* 10.1231–32). The frantic animation of the monument transposes Denis Breen's *distrait* condition, as he is hurriedly rescued from the passing traffic by his concerned wife, and comically suggests how the colonial past is inscribed in, and also erased by, his befuddlement. For a long period this tribute to William III, which was erected in 1701 to commemorate the anniversary of the battle of the Boyne, was the only statue in the city. As Sir John Gilbert amply documents in his history of Dublin, it acted as a focal point for political demonstrations for the duration of its installation on College Green and was frequently damaged by political dissidents (26–51). "Wandering Rocks" also carefully notes recent additions to the statuary of Dublin that mark the emergence of new attempts to reconfigure the landscape of the city. Thus, the text refers to "Goldsmith's knobby poll" (*U* 10.339), to "the stern stone hand of Grattan" (*U* 10.352), and still more portentously to the "slab where Wolfe Tone's statue was not" (*U* 10.378). The statues to Goldsmith and Grattan were unveiled in 1864 and 1876 respectively, while the abortive efforts to erect a monument to Wolfe Tone had been initiated in 1898, the centenary of the 1798 Rising. Hence, the chapter captures not just the fossilization and deadening weight of colonial history but also the recent and ongoing efforts to create a new iconography that would variously express local pride, patriotic fervor, and nationalist ambition. The dual naming of the city's main bridge, however, which is designated "O'Connell bridge" (*U* 10.599) by the narrator in the tenth section but reverts to its previous alias of "Carlisle bridge" (*U* 10.747) in Ned Kernan's internal ruminations, crystallizes the conflicted loyalties of the citizens of Dublin as they severally declare allegiance to Daniel O'Connell, a nationalist hero, or to Lionel Cranfield Sackville, first duke of Dorset and Lord Lieutenant of Ireland, 1731–1737 and 1751–1755.

A listing of the historical personae invoked in this chapter might lead to a similar view of the corroding incoherence and self-divided nature of identity in a colonial city. Fr. Conmee's thoughts range across the figures of Cardinal Wolsey (*U* 10.14–16), Mary Queen of Scots (*U* 10.65), Lord Aldborough (*U* 10.83–84), Lord Talbot de Malahide (*U* 10.156–57), and Mary, first countess of Belvedere (*U* 10.165–70). This list is further extended by the allusion to Nelson in the angry snatches of "The Death of Nelson" delivered by the onelegged sailor (*U* 10.232–47), and the references to Wolfe Tone (*U* 10.378), Silken Thomas (*U* 10.408), Garret Mór, the great earl of Kildare (*U* 10.448), Robert Emmet (*U* 10.764), Sir Jonah Barrington (*U* 10.782), Lord Edward Fitzgerald (*U* 10.785), Major Sirr (*U* 10.786), the "sham squire," Francis Higgins (*U* 10.789), Charles I, "nonesuch Charles" (*U* 10.858), the Geraldines (*U* 10.930), and John Howard Parnell, Parnell's brother (*U* 10.1049). If the labyrinth is one of the reigning symbols of the episode, then this eclectic list appears, at first glance, simply to represent a random selection of hapless Irish rebels and leaders and of English victims of fortune. The cumulative effect of these scattered allusions would seem to do no more than reinforce an overwhelming sense of the adventitious nature of history. However, countervailing this view of the past as patterned around lost causes and destitute fortunes is the active desire by many of the chief participants in the episode to write histories of their own. It is striking that several of the protagonists are either aspiring historians or historians *manqués*. Fr. Conmee reflects on the Talbots of Malahide and toys with the idea of recording the history of the Jesuit foundations in Ireland; Ned Lambert narrates the story of Silken Thomas's rebellion in St. Mary's Abbey and also recounts the anecdote about the arson attack by Garret Mór, the Great Earl of Kildare, on the cathedral at Cashel; O'Madden Burke wants to write a history of St. Mary's Abbey; the Rev. Hugh C. Love is in the process of writing a chronicle about the Geraldines; while Kernan muses on the execution of Robert Emmet and the capture and betrayal of Lord Edward Fitzgerald. A preoccupation with history and a desire to appropriate and reformulate a well-worn communal legacy of historical narratives would appear to be a shared characteristic of some of the key actors in this episode. Moreover, the histories that captivate these characters hinge always on tales of loss and violence and on clashes between subordinates and authority.

Several critics have recently mooted various designs in the apparently random endeavors and contradictory internal musings of Joyce's ersatz historians. Len Platt, for instance, argues forcibly that the history that captivates all of these figures is either Anglo-Irish or British. He holds, as a result, that their aspirations are forlorn and empty, the outcome of the hijacked allegiances and intellectual dependence of a colonized people. Moreover, he argues that the episode hinges on the neatly counterpointed irony that the Catholic priest, Fr. Conmee, seems concerned with the dealings of aristocratic English settlers such as the Talbots and the Rochforts, while the Protestant minister, Rev. Hugh C. Love, is taken up with the history of an Anglo-Norman, Catholic dynasty, the Geraldines. For Platt, "Wandering Rocks," moreover, conspicuously advertises the lack of interest of its cast of characters in revivalist concerns or a native past and prominently fails to incorporate recent and current Irish history. Anglocentrism in this view has a crushing hold on the colonial imagination.

However, I would suggest that the dynamics of the episode are more complex still and that they only become apparent when we begin to consider the ways in which Joyce playfully recasts the political forces at work in Irish society in 1904 by offsetting the two seemingly clashing and neatly delimited hegemonic worldviews represented by Fr. Conmee and William Dudley. Even though these figures appear, on first reading, to stand for apparently fixed ideological domains, with Conmee advancing an insidious and authoritarian Catholic pietism and Dudley upholding a self-glorifying and obtuse imperialism, closer analysis reveals that they also act out and are carefully positioned in relation to a number of competing issues that dominated Irish political arenas in the period.

Historians are unanimous in seeing the decades that followed the death of Parnell on October 6, 1891, not just as a time of dashed hopes but also as a period of social and political change. They have sketched out the conflicting forces at work in turn-of-the-century Ireland in various ways: Joseph Lee sees as one of the key divisions of the period the opposition between the program of Douglas Hyde and the Irish-Irelanders for deanglicization and a return to traditional values and the desire of other political activists such as Patrick Pearse and James Connolly for accelerating the pace of modernization and cementing the connections between Ireland and Europe. Oonagh Walsh discerns in this era a growing polarization of constitutional and radical politics as separatist nationalists, especially in the wake of the Anglo-Boer war, began to press for political independence and to diverge from the aims of the Irish Parliamentary Party under John Redmond that still pursued a modified form of Home Rule within the Empire. Alan O'Day sees the significant shifts within the period as resulting from the designs of successive Conservative governments effectively to quell Irish demands for Home Rule by introducing a series of significant reforms in the country, especially in the areas of economic development, land ownership, and local administration. The so-called policy of "killing Home Rule by kindness" was designed as a sop to Irish nationalism, as well as a means of pandering to the desire of Northern Unionists to retain connections with Westminster.

Joyce's depiction of the clashing rocks of church and state in the central episode of *Ulysses* carefully constructs multilayered figures that act, on one level, as ciphers of the false ideologies with which they are associated and, on another level, as expressive vehicles for a range of political choices and possibilities. In portraying Fr. Conmee and William Humble, the earl of Dudley, Joyce is, of course, in both instances producing fictionalizations and ironic refractions of real historical figures. Moroever, although their respective journeys—Conmee's walk and tram trip northward to Artane, and the Lord Lieutenant's cavalcade southward to Ballsbridge—seem to suggest that they are pulling in diametrically opposed directions, they also have many intersecting features. Albeit both men act as embodiments of the oppressive power relations in Irish society, they are both engaged in charitable missions: Fr. Conmee attempts to come to the aid of the Dignam family by finding a place in an orphanage for Master Dignam, while the Lord Lieutenant is on his way to the Mirus Bazaar, which is raising funds for Mercer's Hospital. Even though they are representatives of an exploitative authority, both appear to be advocates and supporters of local self-help movements and of philanthropic institutions. The curious moment in which Fr. Conmee boards an outward-bound tram on Newcomen Bridge is mirrored by a ghostly and unidentified Nicholas Dudley C.C. (*U* 10.107–12) stepping off an inward-bound tram; this mirroring playfully intimates the collusion between church and state and also hints at the shared characteristics of these two figures.

From the opening lines, Conmee seems to be typified by his smug sense of superiority and his devotion to order and regulated containment: "The superior, the very reverend John Conmee S.J. reset his smooth watch in his interior pocket as he came down the presbytery steps" (*U* 10.1–2). In addition, his obsequiousness to those of high social standing, "the wife of Mr David Sheehy M.P." (*U* 10.17) and Lady Maxwell, for example, and his grating condescension to those he sees as his inferiors, such as the "three little schoolboys" (*U* 10.40), would appear to reinforce this impression of servility and conservatism. However, as Ruth Frehner points out, movement and a constantly altering perspectivism define the narrative dynamics in operation throughout this episode.[8] Hence these insistent ironies that cast Conmee's behavior in one particular light compete with, and are qualified by, other recognitions. Indeed, each of the individuals depicted in this section of *Ulysses* may be seen as caught between rival political possibilities and opposing social forces. While Fr. Conmee's constant invocation of aristocratic figures, such as Lord Talbot de Malahide, or Mary, first countess of Belvedere, and his recurrent recourse to British history in his inner communings, might seem to indicate his Anglocentrism, it also styles him as a modernist who refuses to accept the ideal of a self-sufficient Irish-Ireland. However, another angle cast by the narrative intimates a further set of contradictions. The historical Conmee authored in real life a short pamphlet titled *Old Times in the Barony*. This text was first published in part in *New Ireland Review* in 1895 and subsequently issued by the Catholic Truth Society in three imprints in 1900, 1902, and 1907. His study is an idiosyncratic but heartfelt meditation on a traditional rural world in the vicinity of "Luainford," the author's designation for Athlone. Conmee depicts this forgotten locality in idyllic terms as a self-sufficient feudal economy, an epitome of Celtic civilization, and an organic community undisturbed by class divisions and populated by local figures, survivors from a bygone age, such as Barney, the rentless proprietor of a small cottage and the spalpeen, who are held in high esteem.[9] Joyce insinuates phrases from this essay and mocking riffs upon its quaintly archaizing discourse into his character's stream of consciousness: "Those were old worldish days, loyal times in joyous townlands, old times in the barony" (*U* 10.159–60). Thus, while the text may seem to set Conmee up as the opposite of the Gaelic League priest who argues for a return to native, Gaelic values, the historicism with which he is associated is not wholly out of sympathy with such a mind frame. In section one of "Wandering Rocks," his thoughts consistently gravitate outward to the rural outskirts of Dublin, whether to Malahide, the shore of Lough Ennel, or Rathcoffey, a village in the vicinity of Clongowes Wood College. His disruptive memory of himself walking "by the stubble of Clongowes field" (*U* 10.185–86)—which intrudes as an interpolation in later sections—insistently underlines his interest in documenting lost rural worlds that are threatened by the forces of modernity and in recuperating historical periods and figures that have been forgotten or sidelined. The prismatic optics of the text at once cast Conmee as determinedly advancing Catholic hegemony, as serving as nativist spokesperson for the forgotten zones of an authentic Ireland, and as appropriating and kowtowing to English imperial values in the interest of self-advancement.

His ready citation of fragments from British history and his fascination with the fortunes of Anglo-Irish families also reveal themselves under close scrutiny to extend beyond a reflex Anglocentrism. As David W. Miller and D. George Boyce have argued, the nineteenth century is marked by Catholic resurgence and by the church's increasing consolidation of its power base in political and educational affairs. Conmee's conversations with the wife of David Sheehy, an M.P. in the Irish Parliamentary Party, and his determination to fix up the future of young Master Dignam might be seen as symptomatic of such an alignment between religious, social, and political institutions. The nature of these alliances is shown, however, to be uneasy and still uncertain. His praise of the "wonderful man" (*U* 10.25), Father Bernard Vaughan, and thus his seeming approbation of the high Tory, evangelical Catholicism advanced by his English counterpart, is undermined by his less than flattering recollection of his "droll eyes and cockney voice" (*U* 10.34). The masculinist zealotry associated with Bernard Vaughan's missionary renewal of the Catholic Church is at once welcomed and xenophobically dismissed because of its tainted Englishness.

Moroever, his ambivalence about Vaughan may be read not just as professional or national rivalry but as an outcome of the growing disaffection with the unionist sympathies of this preacher that led to the decline of his popularity in Ireland.[10]

Indeed, even though Fr. Conmee's imagination seems to be peopled by members of the English or Anglo-Irish ruling class, the stories that he mentally unearths either revolve around motifs of Catholic rebellion against Protestant autocracy or pick out tales that highlight the contradictory power relations within Irish colonial families. Cardinal Wolsey and Mary Queen of Scots belong, of course, in a catalogue of Catholic martyrs. The Talbots of Malahide, however, represent a more complex history of religious and political allegiance. They were an Anglo-Norman, Catholic family who were granted land in Malahide by Henry II in the late twelfth century. The continuity of the Talbot tenure at their estates, which extended to the late twentieth century, was made possible by the strategic alliances of the family and by their loyalty to the Crown. Though dispossessed by Cromwell, they were one of the few Catholic families to be reinstated and to retain their entitlements in the Restoration period. The family only converted to Protestantism in 1779.[11] Conmee's seemingly inconsequential toying with their history thus, while it might seem a romantic tangent, implicitly tracks the fortunes of an Anglo-Norman, colonial dynasty in Ireland and acts as a reminder of the way in which power was consolidated and maintained throughout a lengthy history: "The joybells were ringing in gay Malahide. Lord Talbot de Malahide, immediate hereditary lord admiral of Malahide and the seas adjoining. Then came the call to arms and she was maid, wife and widow in one day" (U 10.156–59). Moreover, the logical leaps in his associative memories expose the difficulty of giving coherence to a history that must incorporate the story of settlers who have become natives and yet at the same time acknowledge the constant loss and dispossession suffered by the indigenous Irish. The bereft Anglo-Irish bride seems a discreet but inadequate synecdoche for this aspect of history that Conmee omits.

Kevin Collins has recently argued that the clergy who played a prominent role in the revivalism fostered by the Gaelic League saw themselves as "the guardians of Ireland's historic identity" (172). Joyce's Conmee seems to arrogate just such a role to himself. The narratives he sets in train are suffused with the antimodernist romanticism typical of much of revivalist historicism, but they also lay claim to an enlarged perspective on Irish history that includes the chronicles of colonial settlers. However, the plots he uncovers seem unable to settle into a reliable shape. Instead, they disclose the divisions embedded in colonial history and are also colored by the uneasy political compromises of early twentieth-century Ireland. In reading this first section of "Wandering Rocks," we are initiated moreover into the complicated narrative structures of the episode and familiarized thereby with the peculiar practices of reading history in a colonial community. As with Conmee's multiple lines of identification with Cardinal Wolsey, Mary Queen of Scots, and Mary Rochfort, daughter of Lord Molesworth, the narrative performs spatial and temporal leaps and alternates between anticipations of upcoming plot elements and retroversions to previously narrated motifs. While critics have tried to order the unruly mobility of Joyce's internal links and prompts through identifying and listing the multiple interpolations and occasional false leads, it proves ultimately impossible to establish reliable causal sequences or fully coherent semantic patterns. Thus, the allusion to "Mr Denis J Maginni, professor of dancing &c" (U 10.55) may be explained as an interpolation that anticipates the description of this character's genteel advance across O'Connell Bridge in section ten. However, there are many other temporal dislocations that do not follow this pattern and seem like involuntary memories or unmotivated narrative flashbacks. Thus, Fr. Conmee is suddenly transported to the vicinity of Clongowes: "Father Conmee, reading his office, watched a flock of muttoning clouds over Rathcoffey" (U 10.184–85). Earlier his empathetic musings on Mary Rochfort issue in a vivid reminiscence of her imprisonment by her husband: "A listless lady, no more young, walked alone the shore of lough Ennel, Mary, first countess of Belvedere, listlessly waking in the evening, not startled when an otter plunged" (U 10.164–67). In each case the privatized memories suppressed by history appear to cut across our field of vision and break the continuity of the visual and temporal fields of the narrative in the present. Despite the sense of disconnection, the effect is to create what Fritz Senn has called a repertoire of "interlocations" (163–71) in which the dividing lines between past and present are blurred. In "Wandering Rocks," the past is presented as hospitable to contemporary imaginings but also dangerously susceptible to appropriation and misrepresentation. Conmee's conjuring up of the stalwart Cardinal Wolsey and of the powerful Lord Talbot de Malahide, on the one hand, and of the tragic Mary Queen of Scots and Mary Rochfort, on the other, suggests that the histories on which he dwells, divided as they are between stories of heroism and of romantic oppression, pander to his bifurcated view of the world and to the torn and often compromised loyalties of a colonial subjectivity. While his historical sympathies span a broad compass and may in part be associated with the attempts by revivalist writers to restore ownership of the past to the local community, they are also indicative of how ideological positions might harden and of the ever-strengthening ascendancy and authoritarianism of the Catholic Church.

William Humble Ward, the viceroy whose shadowy but portentous presence forms the second symbolic axis of the chapter, has received surprisingly little critical attention. The deftly orchestrated satire of the vice-regal cavalcade that concludes this episode, in which imperial power is at once enacted on the streets of Dublin and eclipsed by the distracted attention and subversive obliviousness of its citizenry, seems to obviate any further investigation. However, as in the case of Conmee, the depiction of the Lord Lieutenant does not confine itself solely to parody but also achieves a rich counterpoint of historical moments. In the first instance, his symbolic urban journey is in itself a fictionalized history. In actuality, Dudley opened the Mirus Bazaar on Tuesday, May 31, and arrived there, as the *Irish Times* of June 1, 1904, reports, at "full speed" from Cork.[12] Joyce thus deliberately delays and slows down the progress of the viceroy. The anachronism of imperialism is borne out even by the fictional license that rearranges the documentary details of Dudley's visit to the bazaar. His comic invisibility in the nineteenth section of "Wandering Rocks," in which most passersby either fail to see him or misrecognize him, is further compounded by the fact that this seeming presence is in itself a fictional phantom.

William Humble Ward, second earl of Dudley, was appointed Lord Lieutenant in August 1902 and held the office until 1905.[13] Although the entry on him in the *Dictionary of National Biography* deems his tenure in Ireland a "great social success" (890), it was also marked by conflict because of his support of the devolution policy of his friend, the Chief Secretary, George Wyndham, which alienated Northern Unionists. Dudley's speeches during his brief appointment in Ireland reveal him to be an assiduous and well-meaning imperial official who, however, subscribed to the views that land ownership should be transferred to Irish tenants and wholeheartedly supported schemes for the modernization and economic improvement of the country. He was an ardent advocate of Horace Plunkett's cooperative movement and frequently grappled in his speeches with a problem with which he was particularly exercised, the task of developing and enhancing rail transport in the country. His interest in transport also was expressed by his passion for motoring. He prided himself on his frequent trips to far-flung corners of the country that extended his knowledge of Irish affairs. Dudley, thus, was a supporter of the local self-help movements, which were such a feature of the radicalized politics of early twentieth-century Ireland, but he married these sympathies with a belief that the resolution of the land question and the fostering of local entrepreneurship would both further the cause of colonial capitalism and engender a spirit of prosperity that would cancel out all political disaffection. The addresses that he gave just prior to the date of Joyce's fiction provide evidence of the multiple ironies that frame this section of the text. In a speech on the occasion of the opening of the Crosshaven extension to the Cork and Passage Railway on May 30, 1904, he proclaimed that "rapidity and regularity, safety and cheapness of transit are factors in determining the commercial condition of any country," whereas he berated a Northern gathering on June 3, 1904, and instructed them that the common goal of "increased fertility" should unite the country and render it indifferent "whether our shirts are made of orange or green" (Dudley 74, 80).

Joyce's confinement of this forward-looking viceroy, who hailed the advent of modern transport systems, to the slow-motion procession of horse-drawn carriages hence nicely punctures a well-intentioned progressivism that is nonetheless the by-product of the desire for imperial domination. However, the mixture of apathy and misdirected obsequiousness with which the cavalcade is greeted might also be read as a commentary on the ultimate inefficacy of the conservative policy of appeasement by granting concessions in the area of landownership and the reform of local government. The streamlined, mechanized modernity that Dudley saw as a solution to Irish ills is here portrayed as a chaotic reality peopled by divergent needs and desires. The coda to "Wandering Rocks" is thus a parodic rendering of both the emptiness and the insidiousness of the processes of power, a reflection on Irish complicity with colonial rule, and an anticipation of the imminent self-eclipsing and ousting of imperial control in the country. Ironically, the faceless and invisible Dudley, with his militaristic entourage of outriders that threaten to trample unsuspecting onlookers, acts as an insignia both of political oppression, on the one hand, and of its possible dissolution, on the other. The final phrase, "the salute of Almidano Artifoni's sturdy trousers swallowed by a closing door" (U 10.1281–82), at once gestures at the stifled conditions of this society and at the means by which it might achieve liberation.[14]

This doubling effect is also evident in the other key historical figures invoked in the chapter. Ned Lambert declares the council chamber of Saint Mary's Abbey to be "the most historic spot" (*U* 10.409) in Dublin because it is the location where Silken Thomas proclaimed himself a rebel. In a chapter that represents the contradictory trappings of a contemporary Lord Lieutenant, it seems no accident that the Rev. Hugh C. Love is engaged in writing the history of the Geraldines, the Anglo-Norman dynasty to which Silken Thomas belonged. The Geraldines were the most powerful rulers in the Renaissance Pale, and several members acted as lord deputies throughout the sixteenth century. Silken Thomas's rebellion in 1533, although often painted as a misdirected uprising, was, as Laurence McCorristine has illustrated, a calculated move by a powerful Irish nobleman to inject dimensions of the Europe-wide, Catholic crusade against Henry VIII into a local feud in order to topple the king's power in Ireland. In addition to quelling the revolt, the English government took measures to ensure that Old English ruling families would never again acquire such preeminence. The Rev. Hugh C. Love is, in a subsequent section, revealed to be a landlord who has distrained for rent on Father Cowley. He thus seems to belong to the later echelons of post-Reformation, Protestant property owners who displaced the earlier generations of English settlers in Ireland. His obsession with the Geraldines is hence depicted as an ironic cross-identification and as the product of the confused fealties in a colonial community. The history that he is writing erupts, moreover, into the very topography of Dublin and asserts a spectral but uncanny reality in the present: "The reverend Hugh C. Love walked from the old chapterhouse of saint Mary's abbey past James and Charles Kennedy's, rectifiers, attended by Geraldines tall and personable, towards the Tholsel beyond the ford of hurdles" (*U* 10.928–31).

This facility for converting history into the memorial acts as one of the unifying and dynamizing energies of Dublin society in the episode. Tom Kernan, who seems much more concerned with matters of business and with his appearance, also lapses into reflections on the history that is at once cryptically inscribed, but also palpably present, in the urban scenes that he is passing through: "Down there Emmet was hanged, drawn and quartered. Greasy black rope. Dogs licking the blood off the street when the lord lieutenant's wife drove by in her noddy" (*U* 10.764–66). Later he thinks about the betrayal of Lord Edward Fitzgerald by "that sham squire" (*U* 10.789) and cross-links this recollection with a confused intermingling of two recently composed ballads commemorating the 1798 rebellion:

They rose in dark and evil days. Fine poem that is: Ingram. They were
gentlemen. Ben Dollard does sing that ballad touchingly. Masterly
rendition.
    At the siege of Ross did my father fall. (U 10.790–93)

The scattered references to historical events and figures in "Wandering
Rocks" appear to have a double impetus: they alert us to the inchoate and
splintered nature of history in the divided collectivity of a colonial society,
but they also resurrect potent memories of a buried, yet continuous, Irish
counterinsurgency.

In a manner that anticipates Pierre Nora's investigation of the multifarious aspects of French national identity, Joyce's fictional probing of the
various sites of memory that form the competing axes of Irish political
history aims not simply at invalidating or parodying them but also at disclosing the multiple pathways by which collective memory is constructed
and put to service in national communities. The historical allusions strew-
ing the course of this narrative to Parnell's forgotten chess-playing
brother, the failed rebellions of Silken Thomas, 1798, and Robert Emmet
may be, in part, the product of the self-annulling aspirations of romantic
nationalism, with its predilection for stories of tragic self-sacrifice and
tales of doom-laden uprisings, but they also issue from the subversive
mobilization of national memory in late nineteenth- and early twentieth-
century Ireland that acted as a force for modernization and change.[15] History in "Wandering Rocks" is both a hodgepodge of disconnected fragments and a potent archive on which all of the inhabitants of Dublin,
despite their divisions and muddled assumptions, draw.

Above all, it is the simultaneous spectrality and living immediacy of
this history that this central episode with its parallelisms, cross-cuts, and
displacements draws to the fore. The broken chronicle centering on the
multiple cast of characters traversing the city streets must, however, also
be seen as part of this dual narrative in which history is exposed as an
ideological construct and a fluid, unfinished continuity. The conflicts of
power conjured up by the pointed historical allusions in the successive
sections of the chapter are implicitly at tension, but interconnected, with
the more material struggles of many of the subaltern figures who also
occupy our visual field. Just as history seems to be a tapestry of presences
and absences, so too an alternating pattern of startling images of embodiment and disembodiment illustrates the jagged connectivities between

history, politics, and the abject condition of many of the characters featured here. The recurrent allusions to the onelegged sailor begging for money and to the disembodied "generous white arm" (*U* 10.222) of Molly Bloom donating a coin to him capture the destitute economic conditions of the city. As elsewhere in *Ulysses,* the narrative insistently focuses on the physicality and material dimensions of concrete existence. The over-determined attention given to movement, gestures, and bodily posture in the chapter highlights the human misery created by political systems. Father Conmee notes the awkward man "sitting on the edge of the seat" (*U* 10.129–30) and also recalls his difficulty in giving Communion to "the awkward old man who had the shaky head" (*U* 10.132). The violent gait and "vigorous jerks" (*U* 10.246) of the onelegged sailor are underlined, as are the "darkbacked" shape of Bloom (*U* 10.315), the "grave deportment" (*U* 10.599) of Denis J. Maginni, the "Phlegmy coughs" of the shopman (*U* 10.632), the "high shoulders" of Dilly Dedalus (*U* 10.855), Ben Dollard's ambling gait (*U* 10.903), the "ghostbright" eyes of John Howard Parnell (*U* 10.1052), the "butty and short" (*U* 10.1169) physique of Paddy Dignam, and his son's "mourning" posture reflected in the sidemirrors of the milliner's shop window (*U* 10.1130–33). James Connolly contended in an essay, published in *The Workers' Republic* in 1899, that "the subjection of Ireland which is represented to-day as a mere political question is instead an economic, a social question" (33). "Wandering Rocks" seems imbued by a similar realization. Jimmy Henry's dismissal of debates in the city council about "their damned Irish language" (*U* 10.1007) may be seen not so much as a rejection of revivalism as an indication of the increasing tensions between nationalist and socialist platforms and of the gap between political ideologies and economic struggles in the era. The accentuation of the abject plights of Dilly Dedalus and Master Dignam, among many others in the chapter, seems to underline the widening gulf between cultural politics and economic struggle, but it also insists on the interconnections between the two spheres. Stephen's searing recognition that his sister "is drowning" (*U* 10.875) is brought home not only by her poverty and hunger but also by her purchase of Chardenal's French primer. Master Dignam's trip to purchase pork steaks is similarly accompanied by his need for cultural sustenance as he muses on a boxing match that he has just missed. The abjection of these figures emphasizes their oppression and distance from narratives of power but also signals their ongoing struggles and pertinence to the political debates animating their community.

In Nora's outline of *lieux de mémoire,* or states of memory, the most resonant sites of communal history are formed through perpetual sedimentations of new meanings. They are hence constantly subject to flux even though they may be deployed as a way of maintaining tradition and combating change. The investigations of historians intent on tracing the operations of cultural memory underscore the fact that objects of veneration from the past or events of note remain alive only to the extent that they are rethought and remade. Joyce's *Ulysses*, under the accumulated weight of almost a century of glosses, commentaries, and interpretations, has itself become a redolent site of memory that is frequently used in order to anchor reassuringly simple views of Irish history and politics. This essay has considered how a historical interpretation of "Wandering Rocks" might allow us to interrogate and reconsider the histories that we draw upon in exegeses of his work and to preserve its openness and pluridimensionality. It has argued that the historiography we extrapolate from, or impose on, Joyce's writings needs constantly to be reviewed. The memorializing symbolism of Joyce's narrative is elusive and multilayered and does not easily allow itself to be reduced to one-sided political allegories. Criticism of "Wandering Rocks" has too readily assumed that it can be seen as a reliable moral and political indicator of Dublin in 1904. However, Joyce's subtle historicization and playful fictionalization of the material realities of the afternoon of June 16, 1904, refuse to yield up any fixed political diagnostic. Although the satiric thrust of much of the narrative performs a critique of reigning ideologies and depicts the seeming stagnation of Dublin life as a symptomology of the colonial condition, the fluid, unsettled narrative also presents us with a portrait of the multiple political currents and countercurrents shaping Irish society in this period and develops an unfurling history that can be captured with a masterly precision but that remains always unforeclosed.

Notes

1. See Leslie F. Smith for a discussion as to whether Joyce associates the Plangktai rocks mentioned in *The Odyssey*, which seem to be situated in the vicinity of Scylla and Charybdis, with the Wandering Rocks on the Bosporus Straits, which feature in the Argonaut legend of Jason's adventures. Michael Seidel, however, argues that Joyce, influenced by Victor Bérard, translates the Wandering Rocks to a Mediterranean location (182–85). The account of Athena's intervention to aid Jason and his crew to pass safely between the Clashing Rocks may be found in Apollonius of Rhodes (50).

2. See Fritz Senn for an interpretation of the way in which Joyce playfully inter-polates a non-Homeric sequence into *Ulysses*.

3. For details of these interpretive grids established by Joyce, see "Appendix A: The Gilbert and Linati Schemata," (Joyce, *Ulysses*, edited with an introduction by Jeri Johnson, 734–39).

4. Scott 136. Kathleen McCormick, by contrast, argues that the pleasure of read-ing this chapter depends on alternating between the desire to master and the desire to submit to its indeterminacies (45–46).

5. Nora, "From *Lieux de mémoire* to *Realms of Memory*," In *Conflicts and Divi-sions*, vol. 1, *Realms of Memory*, xv-xxiv.

6. For a critique of Nora and of postmodern reifications of memory, see Noa Gedi and Yogal Elam, and Kerwin Lee Klein.   ·

7. See Joseph Brady for a history of early twentieth-century Dublin that portrays it not as a decayed capital but as a site of change and expansion.

8. Frehner discusses the way in which the puzzling spatial and semantic relations and interconnectivities of this episode resemble the disruption of perspective in cub-ist painting, in which elements are not set off against each other by use of form or color or by the differentiation between foreground and background (179).

9. Len Platt, however, views Conmee's pamphlet in a different light and dismisses it as a "Catholic elegy to Protestant landlordism" (151).

10. See Martindale (146–49) for an account of Vaughan's visits to Ireland and of his family connections with Mayo, where his father owned an estate.

11. For the history of the family, see Noel Flanagan, and Joseph Byrne.

12. See "Mirus Bazaar: Opening Ceremony." Joyce also alters the fact that Lady Dudley was absent that day due to illness.

13. Details of Dudley's life are outlined by Charles O'Mahony (313–25), and K. C. Wheare (890).

14. See Enda Duffy for a discussion of the absences, gaps, and other spaces in the text.

15. For a discussion of the various ways in which memory was politicized in nineteenth-century Ireland, see Lawrence McBride, Anne Fogarty, and Luke Gib-bons.

Works Cited

Apollonius of Rhodes. *Jason and the Golden Fleece*. Translated by Richard Hunter. Oxford: Oxford University Press, 1993.

Boyce, D. George. *Nineteenth-Century Ireland: The Search for Stability*. Vol. 5, *New Gill History of Ireland*. Dublin: Gill and Macmillan, 1990.

Brady, Joseph. "Dublin at the Turn of the Century." In *Dublin through Space and Time*, edited by Joseph Brady and Anngret Simms, 221–81. Dublin: Four Courts, 2001.

Budgen, Frank. *James Joyce and the Making of "Ulysses" and Other Writings*. 1934. Oxford: Oxford University Press, 1972.

Byrne, Joseph. *War and Peace: The Survival of the Talbots of Malahide 1641–1671*. Dublin: Irish Academic Press, 1997.

Collins, Kevin. *Catholic Churchmen and the Celtic Revival in Ireland 1848–1916*. Dublin: Four Courts Press, 2002.

Conmee, John S., S.J. *Old Times in the Barony*. 1900. Blackrock, Co. Dublin: Carraig Books, 1976.

Connolly, James. "The Re-Conquest of Ireland." 1899. In *The Lost Writings of James Connolly*, edited by Aindrias Ó Cathasaigh, 32–35. London: Pluto, 1997.

Dudley, William Humble Ward, Earl of. *Milestones on an Irish Journey: Some Speeches Delivered by His Excellency the Earl of Dudley During His Vice-Royalty in Ireland*. Dublin: A. Thom and Co., 1905.

Duffy, Enda. "Disappearing Dublin: *Ulysses*, Postcoloniality, and the Politics of Space." In *Semicolonial Joyce*, edited by Derek Attridge and Marjorie Howes, 37–57. Cambridge: Cambridge University Press, 2000.

Ellmann, Richard. *Ulysses on the Liffey*. London: Faber and Faber, 1972.

Flanagan, Noel. *Malahide Past and Present*. Dublin: Noel Flanagan, 1984.

Fogarty, Anne. "'Where Wolfe Tone's Statue Was Not': Joyce, 1798, and the Politics of Memory." *Études Irlandaises* 24, no. 2 (1999): 19–32.

Frehner, Ruth. "Warum ein Pater dünnbesockt durch eine fremde Küche läuft: Gleichzeitigkeit in den 'Irrfelsen.'" [Why a Thin-socked Clergyman Walks through Other People's Kitchen: Simultaneity in "Wandering Rocks."]. In *James Joyce: "Gedacht durch meine Augen" ["Thought through My Eyes"]*, edited by Ursula Zeller, Ruth Frehner, and Hannes Vogel, 157–87. Basel: Schwabe, 2000.

French, Marilyn. *The Book as World: James Joyce's Ulysses*. 1976. London: Abacus, 1982.

Gedi, Noa, and Yogal Elam. "Collective Memory: What Is It?" *History and Memory* 8 (1996): 30–50.

Gibbons, Luke. "'Where Wolfe Tone's Statue Was Not': Joyce, Monuments and Memory." In *History and Memory in Modern Ireland*, edited by Ian McBride, 139–59. Cambridge: Cambridge University Press, 2001.

Gibson, Andrew, "Macropolitics and Micropolitics in 'Wandering Rocks.'" In *Joyce's "Wandering Rocks,"* edited by Andrew Gibson and Steven Morrison, 27–56. Amersterdam: Rodopi, 2002.

Gibson, Andrew, and Steven Morrison, eds. *Joyce's "Wandering Rocks." European Joyce Studies* 12. Amsterdam: Rodopi, 2002.

Gilbert, Sir John T. *A History of Dublin*. Wellington Quay, Dublin: Joseph Dollard, 1903.

Halbwachs, Maurice. *On Collective Memory*. Edited and translated by Lewis A. Coser. Chicago: University of Chicago Press, 1992.

Hart, Clive. "Wandering Rocks." In *James Joyce's "Ulysses": Critical Essays*, edited by Clive Hart and David Hayman, 181–216. Berkeley and Los Angeles: University of California Press, 1974.

Joyce, James. *Ulysses.* Edited by Jeri Johnson. 1922. Oxford: Oxford University Press, 1993.

Kenner, Hugh. *Ulysses.* Rev. ed. Baltimore: Johns Hopkins University Press, 1987.

Klein, Kerwin Lee. "On the Emergence of *Memory* in Historical Discourse." *Representations* 69 (winter 2000): 127–50.

Lee, Joseph. *The Modernisation of Irish Society 1848–1918.* Dublin: Gill and Macmillan, 1973.

Leerssen, Joep. *Remembrance and Imagination: Patterns in the Historical and Literary Representation of Ireland in the Nineteenth Century.* Cork: Cork University Press, 1996.

Martindale, C. C., S.J. *Bernard Vaughan, S.J.* London: Longmans, Green and Co., 1923.

McBride, Lawrence W., ed. *Images, Icons, and the Irish Nationalist Imagination.* Dublin: Four Courts, 1999.

McCormick, Kathleen. *"Ulysses," "Wandering Rocks," and the Reader: Multiple Pleasures in Reading.* New York: Edwin Mellen, 1991.

McCorristine, Laurence. *The Revolt of Silken Thomas.* Dublin: Wolfhound, 1987.

M'Cready, C. T. *Dublin Street Names Dated and Explained.* 1892. Blackrock, Dublin: Carraig Books, 1975.

Miller, J. Hillis. *On Literature.* London: Routledge, 2002.

Miller, David W. *Church, State, and Nation in Ireland 1898–1921.* Dublin: Gill and Macmillan, 1973.

"Mirus Bazaar: Opening Ceremony (Address of the Lord Lieutenant)." *Irish Times,* June 1, 1904.

Nora, Pierre. *Realms of Memory: The Construction of the French Past.* 3 vols. Translated by Arthur Goldhammer. 1992. New York: Columbia University Press, 1996–98.

O'Day, Alan. *Irish Home Rule 1867–1921.* Manchester: Manchester University Press, 1998.

O'Mahony, Charles. *The Viceroys of Ireland.* London: John Long, 1912.

Platt, Len. "Moving in Times of Yore: Historiographies in 'Wandering Rocks.'" In *Joyce's "Wandering Rocks,"* edited by Andrew Gibson and Stephen Morrison, 141–54. Amsterdam: Rodopi, 2002.

Scott, Bonnie Kime. "Diversions from Mastery in 'Wandering Rocks.'" In *"Ulysses"—En-Gendered Perspectives: Eighteen New Essays on the Episodes,* edited by Kimberly J. Devlin and Marilyn Reizbaum, 136–49. Columbia: University of South Carolina Press, 1999.

Seidel, Michael. *Epic Geography: James Joyce's "Ulysses."* Princeton: Princeton University Press, 1976.

Senn, Fritz. "Charting Elsewhereness: Erratic Interlocations." In *Joyce's "Wander-*

ing Rocks," edited by Andrew Gibson and Steven Morrison, 155–85. Amsterdam: Rodopi, 2002.

Sherry, Vincent. "Distant Music: 'Wandering Rocks' and the Art of Gratuity." *James Joyce Quarterly* 31, no. 2 (Winter 1994): 31–40.

Smith, Leslie F. "Homer and Apollonius on the Wandering Rocks." *James Joyce Quarterly* 9, no. 4 (Summer 1972): 479–81.

Thornton, Weldon. *Voices and Values in Joyce's "Ulysses."* Gainesville: University Press of Florida, 2000.

Walsh, Oonagh. *Ireland's Independence, 1880–1923.* London: Routledge, 2002.

Wenke, John. "Charity: The Measure of Morality in 'Wandering Rocks.'" *Eire-Ireland: A Journal of Irish Studies* 15, no. 1 (1980): 100–113.

Wheare, K. C. "Ward, William Humble." *Dictionary of National Biography 1931–1940.* London: Cumberlege, 1949.

Williams, Trevor. "'Conmeeism' and the Universe of Discourse in 'Wandering Rocks.'" *James Joyce Quarterly* 29, no. 2 (winter 1992): 267–79.

Wollaeger, Mark A. "Reading *Ulysses:* Agency, Ideology, and the Novel." In *Joyce and the Subject of History,* edited by Mark A. Wollaeger, Victor Luftig, and Robert Spoo, 83–104. Ann Arbor: University of Michigan Press, 1996.

Cyclopean Anglophobia and Transnational Community

Re-reading the Boxing Matches in Joyce's *Ulysses*

Richard Brown

A new millennial retrospect on some of the potential ideological implications of the boxing matches represented in *Ulysses*, I want to argue, might lead us toward the position that Joyce's presentation of Stephen's contretemps with the soldiers in the "Circe" episode, in which echoes of the sport of boxing are heard and transformed, can usefully be understood as an attempted renegotiation of the binary model of national conflict. This model of conflict is also, perhaps, typical of sport, and especially of the popular cultural spectacle of sport, in terms of which the activity of boxing has earlier been presented in *Ulysses*, especially in the "Wandering Rocks" and "Cyclops" episodes. This thread of sporting reference might then serve in *Ulysses* as more than popular-cultural documentary, demonstrating how Joyce's texts can draw attention to the ways in which cultures tend to make strategic monstrosities out of their "others." We may also find analogies both for Stephen's utopian but emergent model of the transnational kind of community that might be imagined as a goal of his aspiring literary production and for Bloom's sometimes transcendently pragmatic politics of the everyday.

My title foregrounds the Anglophobia that is one particularly evident aspect of the binarizing discourses of political nationalism characteristic of the "Cyclops" episode, where the report of the "Keogh-Bennett" boxing match is given. It also gestures toward the notion of a "transnational" community that has been voiced in social and cultural theory of the movements of peoples across national borders. This notion of a community formed out of transnational migrancy may seem to suggest a parallel with, for instance, the formulation of a "transcultural" idea of Joyce in Karen Lawrence's volume of that title, which works to link the phenomenon of cultural displacement with that of translation.[1]

Ulysses, of course, is an encyclopedia of the everyday life of the modern urban world; its reserves of popular cultural reference have increasingly been explored by popular-culturalist and post-Bakhtinian critics such as Cheryl Herr, R. Brandon Kershner, M. Keith Booker, Garry Leonard, and others.[2] Within this work, the discussion of sports and games has occasionally emerged, with references to horse racing, cycling, motor racing, running, tennis, and Eugen Sandow's body-building exercises being among the relevant items that turn up in the text and in criticism of it. The boxing matches themselves have not escaped notice, with, for instance, an essay by J. Lawrence Mitchell filling in several useful background details and contexts and even providing a contemporary print of the Heenan-Sayers fight prominently mentioned in the text.

Mitchell invokes a brief allusion made by David Hayman to the fight reported in "Cyclops," but he cautiously steers away from Hayman's brief description of it as "a paradigm for the English-Irish conflict."[3] Of course it is good to be lighthearted about much of this material when we can, but several serious issues of cultural legitimation, of social class, of gender (especially, I think, of masculinity), of ideology, of cultural identity and community are played out within the representation of sports and games in our cultures and, of course, also in *Ulysses. Ulysses* is never only ideology. It is definitively counterintuitive and almost always offers a distinctive and usefully playful twist in response to whatever topic we might bring to it. Significantly, in this case, it offers the chance to make a rapprochement between this glimpse of popular cultural history and the classic theorizing of the popular cultural discourses of *Ulysses,* which, according to Herr for instance, can be characterized as "complex subversions" of the binary oppositions upon which contemporary ideologies were constructed (16).

In *Ulysses,* the boxing match that gets the most prominent treatment is that between Myler Keogh and Sergeant-Major Bennett, glimpsed in "Lestrygonians" (*U* 8.800–803), considered by young Paddy Dignam in the penultimate subsection of "Wandering Rocks" (*U* 10.1121–52), discussed and offered in parodic report in "Cyclops" (*U* 12.939–87), and then more surrealistically recast in the action of "Circe" (*U* 15.4370–800). The fight as it appears in the text is significantly adapted by Joyce from the actual bout that took place in April 1904, the details of which were first recorded by Robert Martin Adams; it is not my intention to reveal more of the background of the original (Adams 70, 170, 240).

In "Wandering Rocks," Stephen observes a print of a different, older match, that between Heenan and Sayers that took place in the 1860s. But the Keogh-Bennett fight is perhaps all the more interesting in its adaptation by Joyce from fact, in the mediation of its appearance in the text through the mourning consciousness of young Dignam, and in its later development through the gigantizing discourses of journalistic report in which it appears in "Cyclops." These transformations into and through the text work to provide the analogies for aspects of Stephen's literary aspirations and what they may have in common with Bloom's politics of the everyday.

Aside perhaps from the grotesque "butting match"—a report of which is read by Alfie Bergan in "Cyclops" when he is looking for sensational "spicy bits" in the newspaper (U 12.1322, 1321)—boxing is one of the most violent of sporting spectacles, and, arguably, a sport in which the agonistic contention of the two participants is most clearly evident. Boxing is therefore ideally placed to serve in *Ulysses* as a symbol or paradigm for the dangers of binary oppositions themselves in the cultural as in the political sphere. It is a sport where the line between raw lawless violence and the imposition of a fair and elegant set of rules seems especially interesting to draw and one where the tendency of commercially driven journalistic discourses to produce exaggerated constructions of alterity is evident. (For today's generation of television viewers, the commercial spectacle of professional wrestling as offered by the American World Wrestling Federation and the World Championship Wrestling bodies shows this tendency even more forcefully.) I argue that these are some of the issues raised in "Wandering Rocks," highlighted by exaggeration in "Cyclops," and which the apparent chaos of "Circe" attempts to deconstruct.

Writers, especially American writers from Ernest Hemingway to Norman Mailer and Bob Dylan (not to mention scriptwriters for the Hollywood cinema), have, of course, frequently exploited the potential of the sport of boxing, usually as a medium for the expression of rude masculine emotions and sensibilities that are often tragically muted, inarticulate, or self-censored in our modern urban communities.[4] Joyce anticipates them all in the potent little scene in "Wandering Rocks," where the episode's protocol of divergent narrative perspectives allows us a unique glimpse into the personal mourning of the young Paddy Dignam for his lost father, articulated indirectly through his thoughts about this boxing match.

It was Joyce's forte (as we know from the early stories of *Dubliners* and the early chapters of *A Portrait*) to present the perspective and psychology of children (and especially the impact of politics from this perspective), so it is no surprise to find this textual moment such a clever and interesting

vignette in these terms. Master Dignam speaks his own Edwardian idio-
lect, much of which can be almost opaque to the modern reader. He calls
the boxers "puckers" and their fists "props," and, when he sees in the window what is presumably a reflection of one of the posters of the music hall
singer Marie Kendall that are dotted around the episode, he thinks to himself that she is "One of them mots that do be in the packets of fags Stoer
smokes that his old fellow welted hell out of him for one time he found
out" (*U* 10.1142–44). Master Dignam is out and about in the streets because the mourning atmosphere of his house is one that he says he finds
"too blooming dull" (*U* 10.1124–25); but it would be wrong to read him
as being superficial or callous. The repetition of his favorite adjective,
"blooming," may work as one of a number of parallels to Bloom that are
suggested, just as other aspects of the scene (including Stephen's thoughts
on the Heenan-Sayers print earlier in the episode) link him to Stephen.
The scene is all the more powerful for its understated terms. Dignam
dreams of going to the boxing match, but this wish adds another element
of pathos, since he quickly realizes that he is looking at a two-week-old
advert for a fight that has already taken place. Indeed, from the start,
Stuart Gilbert presented him as one of several of the characters in the episode who are subject to false illusions of various kinds (208).

Like Bloom and Stephen, who are to be reflected in the mirror in
"Circe," Dignam sees a reflection of himself in the figures of the "two
puckers stripped to their pelts and putting up their props." He sees that
"From the sidemirrors two mourning Masters Dignam gaped silently" (*U*
10.1131–33), and this doubling of his mourning self seems to be echoed in
the personae of the two boxers who are clearly marked as representatives
of Dublin and London respectively. The opposition of the two symbolically
masculine figures of the boxers may be seen as in some ways reflecting a
psychic split in Dignam's emergent masculinity, connected to the sudden
death of his father. Equally, by a further doubling in the process of reflection, we may see Dignam's mourning as itself symbolic, presenting him as
the psychological victim of a traumatic contention between the two boxers or, indeed, the two sibling cities for which they stand. That the boy
glimpses the "red flower in a toff's mouth" (*U* 10.1150)—that is, Blazes
Boylan's—in this context raises the uglier side of Boylan (who we know
has had a role in promoting and/or has bet on the fight) and sets up an
inevitable contrast between the self-admiring cheat and the impression-
able childish sensibilities that his profiteering is calculated to exploit.
These connections further invoke reflection on the way the contestation

between sportsmen such as boxers can be exaggerated for the self-interest of those manipulating the spectacle; the scene also provides one of the moments in which Boylan shows up in a less than heroic light.

Symbolic regional or national rivalry or contestation is, of course, a vital aspect of sports and games and especially of their construction as popular spectacle in the modern media. Often quite pointed local and regional rivalries between otherwise relatively well-attuned and mutually respecting communities can emerge in relation to such sporting competitions. In most cases, the sporting spirit of sporting rivalries (bound by the rules intrinsic to the game) is strong enough to contain and override any amount of partisanship, thereby preventing actual violence between participants or supporters of rival groups. We might invoke the extremely successful cultural contributions both to emerging national identities and to international welfare and cooperation made during the twentieth century by such bodies as the international Olympic movement established during the 1890s under the guidance of the Frenchman Baron de Coubertin. However, the contentious potential of otherwise peaceful sporting rivalries is not always easily contained, and such modern phenomena as football hooliganism may remind us that sporting rivalries and criminally or politically violent contestations can sometimes overlap or become confused.

It is this latter kind of phenomenon, the very intense spirit of contestation and partisanship and its commercial and journalistic exploitation, that is invoked in the "Cyclops" episode, where the full parodic account of the Keogh-Bennett boxing match appears. "Cyclops," with its increasingly drink-fueled bar-room talk and its parade of thirty or so interpolated parodic passages or asides (partly of the medieval English and Irish romance literature of heroes and giants but importantly also of the giant- or monster-making modern discourses of journalistic and mediated report), is one of the episodes of *Ulysses* where the largest quantity and the widest diversity of popular or quasi-cultural phenomena can be found. It is also the episode where distorted or partisan perspectives seem everywhere to drown out the possibility of consensus, let alone a shared sense of truth. Binary political constructions and contentions are found in their most exaggerated form here, as is certainly the case in the reporting of the boxing match where the local hero Myler Keogh is puffed and cosseted by the reporting discourse as "Dublin's pet lamb," whereas the English soldier Percy Bennett is cast as the more villainous-sounding "Portobello bruiser," whom even the referee intervenes to oppose—and whose punishment and eventual defeat the strongly partisan crowd delights to cheer (*U* 10.1133–34).

Joyce, we know, modeled his character of the Citizen on the historical figure Michael Cusack, whose campaign for the revival of Gaelic sports and games provided Joyce with a microcosm for an implied critique of the cultural separatism, provincialism, or even xenophobia he found in aspects of the contemporary nationalist agenda. So here we find the discussion and parodic report of the boxing match taking place immediately after the parodic account of a meeting discussing the promotion of Gaelic sports, a meeting whose not-so-hidden political agenda is suggested by the list of those present, in which the clergy comically outnumber the laity by twenty-five to two. The politics of the partisanship of both crowd and report is not difficult to discern, and whereas we might expect such partisanship in a discussion of sports in a bar, it is made more disturbing here, where the political and historical debate of the episode and also the taunting and exclusion of Bloom are carried on in this same discursive mode.

Bristling with perspectival distortions and discursive binaries, the characteristic mode of the "Cyclops" episode is, as Christy Burns has pointed out, both paranoid and one that may have the dangerous tendency to stimulate further reflective or reduplicated paranoid responses (121–30). The readerly position that Joyce himself apparently envisaged for the chapter is stated clearly enough in his explanatory letter to Budgen, where he refers to what he calls the "colossal vituperativeness" of the Citizen, who, as Joyce says, "unburdens his soul about the Saxo-Angles in the best Fenian style."[5] The cave of Polyphemus perhaps has, then, something in common with that of Plato's *Republic* (inasmuch as it is a place where the truth cannot be seen except through shadowy mediations); and the "gigantism" that is the style of the episode may invoke not only the giants who speak but also the monstrosities that their discourses produce. Significantly, it is in that other monster-making episode, "Oxen of the Sun," that Joyce shows us the process by which Mulligan creates a comically monstrous and exaggerated villain out of the apologetic Englishman Haines, by narrating the incident at Moore's in the style of gothic fiction.

Bloom's encounter with the Citizen, by this kind of reading, is clearly an echo of Joyce himself in Stephenesque mode, attempting to evade the paranoid tendency of overenthusiastic nationalisms to silence his art by ideological appropriation. Interestingly, the same letter includes a "private" section referring to an awkward brush between Joyce and Martha Fleischmann's jealous patron and lover Rudolf Hiltpold, which casts Hiltpold as an angry Polyphemus to Joyce's Odysseus as he escapes Zürich at the end of the First World War (*SL* 239).

The possible personal-political analogies that may seem to be invoked in the episode are not all on the one side, however, since, for instance, several of the details used in the partisan history of Anglo-Irish relations that are exaggerated by the Citizen's "colossal vituperativeness" overlap with the sketched history Joyce himself wrote in his lecture on "Ireland, Island of Saints and Sages" and his Trieste articles for *Il Piccolo della Sera* on the passage of the Home Rule Bill. In addition, renaming the actual English boxer Garry of the 6th Dragoons after the English consular official Bennett (with whom Joyce had been in dispute over his trousers) and introducing the name of the Norwegian consular official, Wettstein, to the parodic report suggest that Joyce was also paying off his preposterously exaggerated score against amateur theatrical British officialdom as well as nationalistic bombast here.

Much of the function of the episode seems to be to exaggerate polarities to an extreme, placing Bloom as much in a situation of having to steer a course between mutually exclusive and opposed alternatives as is Stephen in "Scylla and Charybdis." Yet Bloom is, willingly or unwillingly, a contender as well as an observer here. And, lest any attempt be made to recuperate too easily the figure of the Citizen as an opponent whose position is somehow equally legitimate to Bloom's, Joyce provides us with the additional twist of the prejudice of the nameless narrator of the episode: a corrupt debt collector who voices a range of dodgy attitudes and who, right from the start, proves himself unqualified to judge or even reliably to record by his tacitly approving racist account of the duping of the Jewish tea merchant Moses Herzog by the thief Geraghty.

A conspicuous problem with some contemporary attempts to reclaim the political discourses of the Citizen and the nameless narrator as, in some ways, justifiable critiques of imperialism (or even, more subtly, as reflective modes of imperialistic discourse to which colonized peoples may be subject) is that they are so deeply compromised by Joyce's placement of the Citizen's Anglophobia alongside and among so many other xenophobic modes of discourse, beginning with the narrator's account of the Herzog incident.

The anti-Semitism of this narrator goes menacingly hand in hand with the xenophobia of the Citizen, of which his Anglophobia serves as a convenient example, since he does indeed memorably vituperate against the Saxo-Angles he calls the "foe of mankind" (*U* 12.1249), and who are char-

acterized according to the monstrous paradigm of Rumbold the Liverpud-
lian barber (who has apparently written an illiterate letter offering his
services as hangman to the High Sheriff). Such a picture of a monstrous
militarized Britain sadistically intent on vicious disciplinary practices of
corporal and capital punishment hardly serves as legitimate political critique, not least since it is so obviously anachronistic to the modernizing
liberalizing Britain of the 1904 to 1922 period of the book.[6] The best the
Citizen can say of British civilization is to repeat some of the familiar
Joycean jokes that were exchanged in the "Aeolus" episode about water
closets, here the "thrones of alabaster" (U 12.1213), and to refer to the
English people as "bloody thicklugged sons of whores' gets! No music and
no art and no literature worthy of the name. Any civilisation they have
they stole from us. Tonguetied sons of bastards' ghosts" (U 12.1198–
1201).

   English reticence is, of course, an internationally admired quality (all
the more admirable in the context of the dangerous verbal exaggerations
of this episode). The capacity of the early twentieth-century London literary metropolis not only to absorb but fully to foreground the Irish literary
achievement of the later nineteenth and earlier twentieth centuries—of
which the character Haines may, in a way, serve as one kind of example—
may also surely be construed as in itself admirable. But that is not quite the
point, in an episode in which supposed characteristic traits of a variety of
national groups are paraded not as celebrations of difference but as forms
of abuse. The French appear as a "Set of dancing masters! . . . They were
never worth a roasted fart to Ireland" (U 12.1385–86); the Germans are
represented as "sausageeating bastards" (U 12.1391); the Alaki of Abeo-
kuta (who could, presumably, have told the Citizen a thing or two about his
favorite subjects of famine, economic underdevelopment, and South African wars) is held up to patronizing ridicule. And when Alfie sees in the
paper a horrific picture of a racist lynching in America, the narrator describes it by culturally stereotyping the perpetrators (in a predictable play
on the dime-novel character) as "A lot of Deadwood Dicks" (U 12.1325).

   The function of voicing these verbal assaults in the episode (which are
of the kind now usually silenced by political correctness) is partly to do
politics and history in the manner of extreme or deliberate partisanship
usually reserved for the commercial exploitation of spectator sports and to
draw attention to the ways in which binary polarities and partisan discourse go hand in hand. Few would propose that all readers approach
Ulysses in the mode of the Denis Breen of the "Cyclops" episode, ever

more absurdly running around Dublin trying to find the lawyers who are all too willing to litigate on his behalf against the imagined or actual slight of the postcard he has received. There is, as Christy Burns suggests, no doubt some danger of the reactive paranoid replication in such voicings of that which we might rather leave unvoiced. On the contrary (given a reasonably self-critical reader or group of readers), the language works to gather sympathy for precisely the things the Citizen wishes to attack, so that here, for instance, Bloom is moved to come to the defense of British culture. It is only in the case of the terrible disaster of the Irish famine that Bloom, under all this local pressure to conform, concedes any justice at all to the Citizen's rant and, even then, there is an obvious irony in his agreeing that what the Citizen says is "Perfectly true" (U 12.1376).

According to Benedict Anderson's much-discussed terms of reference, the nation remains the most powerful political construction in modern life, the political entity that has the power to legislate and even to take or to require the sacrifice of human life: "nation-ness," he writes, "is the most universally legitimate value in the political life of our time" (3). Yet the nation is not as much an organically lived or mechanically connected society as it is an ideological or, as Anderson says, "imagined community" in which most of the members need not see or know each other in a direct way. Consequently the "origins of national consciousness" are coterminous with and directly dependent upon the rise of what he calls "print culture" as the medium through which this imagined community can be conceived, defined, adapted, and communicated to its members (37–46). In this context we might perhaps pause to consider the implications of the voicing of the Citizen's partisan national discourse in the context of the print cultures of Dublin's popular journalism, with its insistently regionalizing agenda and the consistently distancing play with the circumstances, personalities, and discourses of popular and nationalistic journalism that Ulysses repeatedly performs.

The Marxist critic of nationalism Tom Nairn, whose book The Break-Up of Britain is much discussed by Anderson, goes so far as to quote the Citizen's Anglophobic outburst as evidence of the divisive contentions within Britain that he sees as threatening its social progress and coherence. Yet to go one stage further and overliteralistically to identify the imaginary imagined community of Barney Kiernan's with the actual imagined community of an independent Ireland would be a dangerous oversimplification and as much an anachronistic misconstruction of any currently existing democratic political state as is the Citizen's picture of a hanging and flogging Britain.

The Citizen's discourse is locked within the kind of binary mode that postcolonial critics describe as a problematic reduplication within emerging nationalist discourses of the imperialistic authority they wish to resist, or else, as Joseph Valente puts it, the special double bind of colonial hypermasculinity that may be said to react to a sense of political oppression with violence.[7] However, one more positive intention of the discourse (if we accept Joyce's letter to Budgen as indicating his primary intention), and hopefully even its primary effect, may be to create precisely the sense of transnational cosmopolitan community that is the inverse or opposite side of the one-eyed discourse that the Citizen and the narrator of "Cyclops" produce.

It might perhaps be argued that we are all now working in a virtual twenty-first-century Joycean hyperspace, in an imagined community linked by the print media of our specialist journals and by the newer media of air travel, e-mail, and the Internet, and that this fact might be held to provide some evidence that such utopian effects of works like those of Joyce can, at least occasionally, actually be observed. For many of us, at any rate, certainly one strong justification for our continuing to read, research, and teach Joyce's texts is that they repeatedly confront us with the ideals, the necessities, and the practicalities of producing bi-, multi-, or even post-partisan kinds of cultural community.

We can play this argument out further in terms of the theoretical arguments of Anderson, Said, and Bhabha but also perhaps more immediately in terms of our *Ulyssean* sporting thread. Bloom, of course, in the "Cyclops" episode opposes his pragmatic definition of nation against the exclusivist and essentialist ones that surround him. His passionately understated declaration on behalf of love against the "Force, hatred, history" (*U* 12.1481) of the discourses of partisan contention voiced by the others in the bar represents one of his strongest moments of ethical vindication in the text. In our sporting terms, he opposes the extreme partisanship of the Gaelic Athletic Association (which extends to the lengths of setting up its own independent kind of game and set of rules) and the stark agonism of a boxing match to his ideal of playing the "shoneen" game of tennis (*U* 12.889), a game that, anticipating the health-club culture of the turn of our twenty-first-century millennium, he recommends for "agility," "training the eye," and for the "circulation of the blood" (*U* 12.945–46, 952–53), rather than in terms of competition or conflict (which are also of course possible in tournament play at tennis).

As I indicated at the start of this essay, we can see the scene of Stephen's contestation with the soldiers in "Circe" as a further continuation and transformation of these themes along the same lines as Bloom's advocacy of pragmatic definitions of nation, of universal love, and even of this symbolic kind of tennis. In "Wandering Rocks," Stephen has, we recall, also seen a picture of a boxing match in a shop window—a print of the epic bare-knuckle bout between Heenan and Sayers in the 1860s, the violence of which was a factor in leading toward the establishment of the Marquis of Queensberry rules in 1867 to regulate the sport and attempt to protect the participants against excessive life-threatening injury. In the farcical fight with the soldiers that transpires on Stephen's exit from Bella Cohen's in "Circe," several disjointed seriocomic references to what Stephen calls the "Noble art of selfpretence" occur (U 15.4413). A phantasm of Edward VII enters like a boxing referee to try to ensure a "clean straight fight" (U 15.4461). But, although Stephen recognizes him as one of the "philirenists" (U 12.4435)—a lover of peace—the issue is irresolvably complicated in his mind by the paradox that he wishes imaginatively to subvert the "priest and the king" (U 12.4437) whose authority may be the only guarantee of any such "clean straight fight" taking place.

Complex issues of legitimacy and legitimation arise during the fracas, including the laws or conventional codes of chivalry, hospitality, and legitimate boxing. Compton's prompt to Carr ("Eh, Harry, give him a kick in the knackers" [U 15.4484]) incites a transgression of one of the most distinctive and deeply held rules of Queensberry for boxing: that contestants can score credit by directing blows at their opponent's head or upper torso but are strictly denied any blow "below the belt." (This idiomatic phrase, incidentally, occurs in "Cyclops" in a different context, where the sexual spying of censorious priestly "sky pilots" is described as being "below the belt" [U 12.695–96].) Issues of politics, nation, and empire are inextricably threaded through the ever more complex maze here, but the attempt to construe the incident in the terms of a binary Anglo/Irish, colonial/anticolonial battle is further undercut not least by Joyce's construction of the scene upon what was to him a definitively English paradigm of the story of William Blake's tussle with the soldiers in his garden in the Sussex town of Felpham.

The Blakean analogy encourages the reader to construe the scene primarily as a kind of battle between the potentially transgressive expansions of poetry itself (or what Stephen calls "The intellectual imagination" [*U* 15.4227]) on the one hand and the reductive binaries of political force on the other. As with Bloom in "Cyclops," rather than a boxing match like the Keogh-Bennett bout that can be seen as a battle between two opposing nations, what seems to be at stake in this, as it were, "not-quite" fight is a deconstructive contestation with the imaginary notion of nation itself and its capacity to act on the one hand as a guarantor of peaceful order, legality, and legitimacy, and on the other as the potential legitimator of life-threatening conflict: "You die for your country," as Stephen says to the soldier. "Not that I wish it for you. But I say: Let my country die for me. Up to the present it has done so. I didn't want it to die. Damn death. Long live life!" (*U* 15.4471–74).

One way of reading the references to boxing here and earlier in the text, then, is to argue that they work to construct an opposition that can be understood in terms of two different notions of gaming and "play," a difference that was, arguably, implied by Bloom's advocacy of tennis as opposed to boxing in "Cyclops." It seems an especially lucky coincidence that Stephen's godfather, Mr. Fulham, in the idyllic Mullingar fragment appended to *Stephen Hero*, arranges "tennis tournaments" for Stephen as part of the program of happy summer entertainment there (*SH* 212). One point is that in tennis the contenders hit the ball rather than, as in boxing, hitting each other; but behind that point there seem to be subtler distinctions at work.

On the one hand, we have the notion of play as contestation between two or more opponents, according to a set of rules that orders and inhibits the wilder aspects and makes for "fair play" between the contenders but that may also perhaps be said to legitimate the very terms of their contestation. On the other hand, we have what would appear to be Stephen's notion of play here, which seems more imaginatively open and deconstructive and which may be seen to consist in an attempt to decompose the binary terms in which such opposition can take place. One side might be thought to be playing the game in the conventional sense; the other may be said to approximate more closely an activity that is sometimes called "shifting the goalposts."

We might further gloss these two notions in terms of two contrasting philosophical senses of the word "game." The first may be seen in the world picture of Wittgenstein's language philosophy, in which all that can be said is to be understood within the determinate rule-bound confines of certain language games. The second may be found in the more open, libidinal, and deconstructive postmodern notions of gaming or play elaborated by Jean-François Lyotard and Jean-Loup Thébaud in *Just Gaming* (*Au juste*), and especially in "Structure, Sign, and Play in the Discourse of the Human Sciences" by Jacques Derrida, with its notion of the "center" as that which both enables play and yet resists itself becoming the subject of play. That both of these arguments explore the idea of play in relation to the potentially playful and characteristically self-re-legitimating hermeneutic practices of interpreting cultural texts makes them especially interesting to us, of course, in the cultural sphere. It may go without saying or it may be going too far to say that to tie these arguments back to Anderson might even lead us to see the goal (or at any rate one possible effect) of young Dignam's plight and of both Bloom's and Stephen's complex struggles to consist in the creation of the kind of ideal bi-, multi-, or even post-partisan international community based on the play of interpretation of suitable literary texts that we could, for the sake of argument, call an ideal kind of international James Joyce foundation.

However, we may, as ever, need to guard against an uncritically euphoric Joycean deconstructivism. At this moment in "Circe" (which, as I have argued, can be seen to provide a parallel with and development from Bloom's paradoxically triumphant encounter with the Citizen in "Cyclops"), Stephen may win the symbolic and intellectual side of the argument with the soldiers hands down. But he still gets knocked over in the more literal and representative sense, as if to imply that his imagined postmodern future of nations that lie down in order to allow their subjects to be poets are (or in 1904 or 1922 were) still paradoxical chimerae of an unimaginably utopian future. Violent contestations on behalf of more-or-less "imagined" nations may not be so easy to transcend, and, as Benedict Anderson's work serves to remind us, the legitimacy of "nation-ness" remains dominantly strong.

Reading *Ulysses* from a twenty-first-century perspective may remind us how far we have come in our cultural consciousness since the book was written and how far it has helped to construct the stages of that progress away from reductive binaries and toward something else in our present and future states. But it may also remind us of how far we still have to go.

Notes

1. For definitions and discussion of the term "transnationalism," see Vertovec, "Conceiving and Researching Transnationalism"; for "transcultural," see Lawrence, ed., *Transcultural Joyce*.

2. See also Donald Torchiana on "After the Race"; James Atherton and, more recently, David Pierce on cricket, for instance in the *James Joyce Broadsheet*.

3. See Hayman's chapter on "Cyclops" in *James Joyce's "Ulysses": Critical Essays*, ed. Clive Hart and David Hayman (267).

4. Hemingway's story "The Undefeated" in *Men without Women* may be the genre-defining work. See also Mailer's *The Fight* and Dylan's "Hurricane" on the album *Desire* (1975). Among relevant English writers, Mitchell usefully lists Byron, Hazlitt, and Arthur Conan Doyle as the author of the 1896 novel *Rodney Stone*.

5. *SL* 239; and see also his reference to the "erection allusion" and its excision for the November 1919 printing, in his letter of January 3, 1920 (*SL* 246).

6. Public hanging was abolished in Britain as a criminal punishment in 1865, and the anachronism of its placement here might be seen in juxtaposition with the case of Thomas Hardy, who (having witnessed the public hanging of Martha Brown in 1856, when he was a child in Dorchester) made hanging a campaigning theme of *Tess of the D'Urbervilles* (1891). The issue is further complicated in *Ulysses* by the connection between this scene and multiple references to the historically distant hanging of Robert Emmet in 1803 for treason, regularly documented in standard annotations to *Ulysses*.

7. See, for instance, the review by Neil Levi, in the *James Joyce Literary Supplement*, of *James Joyce and the Tradition of Anti-Colonial Revolution*, by Roxanne Dunbar-Ortiz. And see Joseph Valente, "'Neither Fish nor Flesh.'"

Works Cited

Adams, Robert Martin. *Surface and Symbol: The Consistency of James Joyce's "Ulysses."* Oxford: Oxford University Press, 1967.

Anderson, Benedict. *Imagined Communities: Reflections on the Origin and Spread of Nationalism.* Rev. ed. London: Verso, 1991.

Atherton, James S. *The Books at the Wake: A Study of Literary Allusions in James Joyce's "Finnegans Wake."* New York: Viking, 1960.

Attridge, Derek, and Marjorie Howes, eds. *Semicolonial Joyce.* Cambridge: Cambridge University Press, 2000.

Booker, M. Keith. *Joyce, Bakhtin, and the Literary Tradition: Toward a Comparative Cultural Poetics.* Ann Arbor: University of Michigan Press, 1997.

Burns, Christy L. *Gestural Politics: Stereotype and Parody in Joyce.* Albany: State University of New York Press, 2000.

Derrida, Jacques. "Structure, Sign, and Play in the Discourse of the Human Sciences." In *Writing and Difference,* translated by Alan Bass, 278–93. London:
Routledge and Kegan Paul; Chicago: University of Chicago Press, 1978.

Dunbar-Ortiz, Roxanne. *James Joyce and the Tradition of Anti-Colonial Revolution.*
Working Papers Series of Comparative American Cultures Department. Wash-
ington State University, 1999.

Gilbert, Stuart. *James Joyce's "Ulysses."* Harmondsworth: Penguin, 1963.

Hart, Clive, and David Hayman, eds. *James Joyce's "Ulysses": Critical Essays.* Berkeley and Los Angeles: University of California Press, 1974.

Hemingway, Ernest. *Men without Women.* New York: Scribner, 1970.

Herr, Cheryl. *Joyce's Anatomy of Culture.* Chicago: University of Illinois Press,
1986.

Kershner, R. Brandon, ed. *Joyce and Popular Culture.* Gainesville: University Press
of Florida, 1996.

Lawrence, Karen, ed. *Transcultural Joyce.* Cambridge: Cambridge University Press,
1998.

Leonard, Garry. *Advertising and Commodity Culture in Joyce.* Gainesville: University Press of Florida, 1998.

Levi, Neil. Review of Dunbar-Ortiz in *James Joyce Literary Supplement* (fall 2000):
14.

Lyotard, Jean-François, and Jean-Loup Thébaud. *Just Gaming (Au juste).* Translated
by Wlad Godzich. Manchester: Manchester University Press, 1985.

Mailer, Norman. *The Fight.* London: Hart-Davies, McGibbon, 1976.

Mitchell, J. Lawrence. "Joyce and Boxing: Famous Fighters in 'Ulysses.'" *James Joyce
Quarterly* 31, no. 2 (winter 1994): 21–30.

Nairn, Tom. *The Break-Up of Britain.* London: New Left Books, 1977.

Pierce, David. "Arthur Shrewsbury" and "Frank Budgen." *James Joyce Broadsheet*
(February 2000): 1, 4.

Torchiana, Donald T. *Backgrounds for Joyce's "Dubliners."* Boston: Allen and
Unwin, 1986.

Valente, Joseph. "'Neither Fish nor Flesh'; or How 'Cyclops' Stages the Double-Bind
of Irish Manhood." In *Semicolonial Joyce,* edited by Derek Attridge and Marjorie
Howes, 96–127. Cambridge: Cambridge University Press, 2000.

Vertovec, Steven. "Conceiving and Researching Transnationalism," *Ethnic and Ra-
cial Studies* 22, no. 2 (March 1999): 447–62.

The True Story of Jumbo the Elephant

Sebastian D. G. Knowles

Love loves to love love. Nurse loves the new chemist. Constable 14A
loves Mary Kelly. Gerty MacDowell loves the boy that has the bicycle. M. B. loves a fair gentleman. Li Chi Han lovey up kissy Cha Pu
Chow. Jumbo, the elephant, loves Alice, the elephant. (*U* 12.1493–96)

But did he? These lines are always deeply satisfying, showing the narrator
at his scathing best, piling on the pieties of Bloom ("I mean the opposite of
hatred" [*U* 12.1485]) and the antipathies of the Citizen ("He's a nice pattern of a Romeo and Juliet" [*U* 12.1492]) with equal abandon, throwing
them both into the mincer.[1] The mock peroration to love has even, I was
surprised to learn, found its way into the Yahoo personals, where a desperate Joycean (can there be any other kind?) uses these very lines as an unlikely come-on, under the advertising heading "Tired of the bar scene?"[2]
This citation not only gives the lie to Judge Woolsey, who famously
claimed in 1933 that nowhere in the text does the effect of the book "tend
to be an aphrodisiac" (*U* xii). It also proves once and for all that the Internet and its users are oblivious to irony.

But to return to Jumbo. Jumbo the elephant was born in the African
jungle, acquired by a Herr Schmidt for the Paris Zoo, and traded to the
London Zoo in 1865 for a rhinoceros and a pachyderm to be named later.
At his peak, he weighed seven tons, stood twelve feet high, and had a fond-
ness for whiskey. In the 1870s, Jumbo was a favorite of Queen Victoria, her
son the Prince of Wales, and the young Winston Churchill. In March 1882,
P. T. Barnum bought the elephant for £2,000 for his circus in America, an
event that caused widespread panic. Children flocked to see the departing
elephant (see fig. 5.1). The *Times* of March 9, 1882, reported a gargantuan
increase of 2,061 percent in daily attendance: "The total number of visitors
for the day was 4,626, as against 214 for the corresponding Wednesday last
year." "The eagerness of children and young girls to ride on its back," said
the *Illustrated London News* of March 18, "is beyond all precedent. There
were 43,653 admissions last week." The *Times* of March 9 also reported, to

Fig. 5.1. Cover of the *Illustrated London News*, Sunday, March 18, 1882.
Copyright The Zoological Society of London. Reprinted by permission.

the presumed horror of its readers, that the superintendent of the *Assyrian Monarch*, the steamship on which Jumbo was to sail, had requested to be "provided with the means of killing the animal should such a necessity arise," displaying the kind of scare tactics for which the paper has always been justly famous.

The elephant's sale was seen as a loss for all England and for its empire (fig. 5.2). Retired colonels came out of the woodwork, as they always do on such occasions, writing to the *Times* to reject the theory that Jumbo had "must," the disease that leads elephants to charge madly into crowds and kill people in zoos, for which A. D. Bartlett, the head of Regent's Park Zoo, had sensibly wanted to get rid of it. Though Major General Agnew of Belsize Park Gardens, drawing on his thirty-four years of experience with elephants in Assam, could applaud the Council of the Zoological Society for taking "the wise step of getting rid of a very dangerous animal" (*Times,* March 18, 1882), George Bowyer claimed to the contrary that "any mahout or qualified keeper could control him" (*Times,* March 16, 1882). Bowyer further compared the action of the council to a sale by the trustees of the British Museum of the Codex Alexandrinus.

The country went Jumbo-mad: there were Jumbo cigars, Jumbo collars, Jumbo fans, and a Jumbo polka. "Why Part with Jumbo" (words by G. H. MacDermott, music by E. J. Symons) was one of many popular songs writ-

Fig. 5.2. "Jumbo, England's Loss and America's Gain." Cartoon c. early 1882. Copyright Bridgeport, Conn., Public Library Historical Collections. Reprinted by permission.

Fig. 5.3. "Why Part with Jumbo, The Pet of the Zoo." Song by G. H. Macdermott and E. J. Symons. Copyright The Zoological Society of London. Reprinted by permission.

ten for the occasion (fig. 5.3). Jumbo was imagined at the opera, at the bar, and even as an aesthete, after the fashion of Bunthorne in Gilbert and Sullivan's wildly popular operetta *Patience*, which was still running at the time (fig. 5.4). The Moore and Burgess minstrels advertised, on the day of Jumbo's departure, that their own "original Jumbo, who will never perform out of London, whom wild horses cannot tear from St. James' Hall,

Fig. 5.4. "Jumbo Aesthetic." Trade card, c. April 1882. Private collection. Published in A. H. Saxon, *P. T. Barnum: The Legend and the Man* (New York: Columbia University Press, 1989). Reprinted by permission.

will make his entrée together with his keeper, Elephant William" (*Times,* March 18, 1882). The London *Daily Telegraph* cabled Barnum on February 22 as follows: "EDITOR'S COMPLIMENTS. ALL BRITISH CHILDREN DISTRESSED AT ELEPHANT'S DEPARTURE. HUNDREDS OF CORRESPONDENTS BEG US TO IN- QUIRE ON WHAT TERMS YOU WILL KINDLY RETURN JUMBO" (Bryan 159), to which Barnum replied that £100,000 would be no inducement to cancel purchase. Dante Gabriel Rossetti and Henry Wadsworth Longfellow died, and a lunatic attempted to assassinate the queen, but no one paid very much attention to anything else.

The departure of Jumbo for America, as recorded by the *Times*'s society page of Monday, March 27, 1882, has a strangely familiar ring:

By the 12 5 train from Fenchurch-street travelled Lady Burdett-Coutts to bid the great animal farewell. In her ladyship's saloon carriage were also Lord Tenterden, Lady Tenterden, Admiral Sir E. Commerell, Mr. Ashmead Bartlett, M.P., and Mrs. Ashmead Bartlett, Mr. Henry Wagner, Mrs. Scott, and Mr. Rendell. Mr. Vickers, a partner in the managing owners' firm (John Patton, junior) and Mr. Hosack travelled by the same train, and at Gravesend General Sir John and Lady Douglas and other visitors came on board, where the emigrants who had not joined on the previous day embarked, and Captain Wilson, the chief executive officer for the port, provisionally passed the vessel, leaving Captain Scone to make the final examination. The Baroness, who received a bouquet of sweet-scented violets from Mr. Vickers, went with her party to visit the elephant on the forward part of the 'tween decks, gave him his last bun, and wished him "Goodbye," expressing her opinion that he would find as warm friends in America as he had in England, and that he would be safe in the hands of Newman, with whom, as well as Scott, her ladyship shook hands. Lady Burdett-Coutts afterwards inspected the emigrants' quarters, and spoke to the poor people themselves, their Russian interpreter translating her remarks. When she passed them to go away the Jews pressed forward to kiss the hem of her garment, and they cheered her as she left. The Baroness left money to be employed in purchasing sweets and other trifling luxuries for the women and children. The Assyrian Monarch was gaily dressed out with bunting. (*Times*, March 27, 1882)

"Blimey it makes me kind of bleeding cry, straight, it does" (*U* 12.676–77): this is written with the same pathos and eye for social detail as the send-off for the Croppy Boy in "Cyclops." Parnell was not there to see Jumbo off, because he was in jail for the first and only time in his life: in the same edition of the newspaper a small entry reads: "Mr. Parnell has declined to write, unless under very exceptional circumstances, letters from Kilmainham" (*Times*, March 27, 1882). While Jumbo was caged on a steamer, "able by the wonderful flexibility of his trunk to explore very fully by the touch the places immediately outside his prison" (*Times*, March 28, 1882), Parnell was in prison for protesting against the 1881 Land Act. During the time of Parnell's incarceration, the Moonlighters—Parnell's term for the agrarian secret societies of Ireland—had taken over; murders in Dublin were up 371 percent in the first quarter of 1882 (Lyons 177). Parnell was released from Kilmainham on the day after Jumbo arrived in New York, twenty-six days before the assassination of Burke and Cavendish in Phoenix Park on May 6.

Jumbo, then, was both a reprieve from and a representation of the problems of empire. The call for the voiding of the contract with Barnum, seriously pursued by the press, was brought up in Parliament on March 11 and "received with cheers and laughter" (*Times*, March 11, 1882); but it was sandwiched between two far more serious discussions of an atrocity committed in the Boer War and a request for additional protection from members of the Irish Land League.[3] As the *Times* said in its leader on the topic of March 9, 1882:

> For our own part, while we are sorry to part with a favourite, we cannot say that our zeal in Jumbo's behalf has kept pace with that of the many correspondents who have been roused by his wrongs. People who have no suspicion that the friendly relations between Russia and Germany have been endangered by Skubeleff's speeches, who have a vague idea of the Irish as a tiresome people, who are far from comprehending the issues raised by the appointment of the Lords' Committee, and who confess that they have not followed the discussion upon Parliamentary procedure, have taken a keen interest in Jumbo's destiny. Others have let fall the thread of public events while they gaped open-mouthed at Jumbo reconnoitring [*sic*] his trolley. It is well enough that children should crowd in thousands to the Zoological Gardens, and, as a parting act of kindness, or cruelty, stuff the hero of the hour with buns innumerable. But it speaks volumes for the fundamental levity of adult nature that men have, for the last fortnight, given the first and foremost place in those of their thoughts which did not regard themselves, not to kingdoms and their destinies, but to Jumbo.

This, for the *Times* of 1882, or for the *Times* of any year, is quite wonderful. The newspaper agrees with Zack Bowen, and with Bakhtin, that the carnival spirit is a positive, regenerating force.[4] The comedy, played on a hyperbolic stage, is a distraction, as it is in "Cyclops," and a distraction from the same subject: the loss of a gigantic imperial dream.

But Jumbo was not just carnivalesque; he was in a carnival, and on his arrival in America his circus career took off. In six weeks he earned Barnum a third of a million dollars. Barnum advertised him as "The Colossus of the Old and New World," "The Universal Synonym for All Stupendous Things" (Bryan 162). And he did become the universal synonym for all stupendous things: it's because of this elephant that we have jumbo-sized fries, jumbo shrimp, and the jumbo jet. Even his excrement was jumbo-size, as seen in fig. 5.5 by the size of the Jumbo-the-elephant sticker that a Puritanical librarian placed on the photograph underneath the elephant's tail. Jumbo's arrival into small towns in America was compared to the coming of Christ: "The shouting at Jerusalem," according to his keeper, Matthew Scott, "for the 'Son of Man' when he rode triumphantly on an ass, could not have exceeded the shout that has gone up from the children of the United States as they have watched and waited by hours to get a sight of Jumbo" (quoted in Saxon 297). The deity *is* a nickel dime bum-show. Bloom is Ben Bloom Elijah, and Jumbo is Jesus: both stories operate according to the principle of gigantism and parody, overkill and under-cutting, Jumbo and the Jumbo sticker.

The end of Jumbo the elephant is tragic and affecting in the extreme

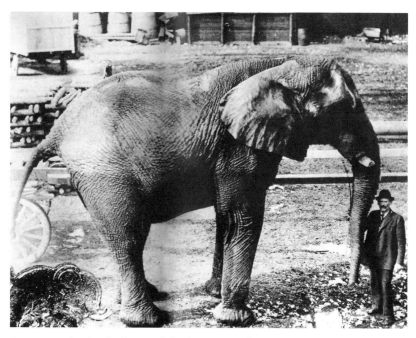

Fig. 5.5. Jumbo the elephant with his keeper, Matthew Scott. Copyright Bridgeport, Conn., Public Library Historical Collections. Reprinted by permission.

Fig. 5.6. Jumbo the elephant lying dead after his collision with a goods train in September 1885. Private collection. Published in A. H. Saxon, *P. T. Barnum: The Legend and the Man* (New York: Columbia University Press, 1989). Reprinted by permission.

(fig. 5.6). Here I must let *The True Story of Jumbo the Elephant*, a children's book from 1963, pick up the tale:

> One evening, in September 1885, Barnum's circus had been visiting the town of St Thomas, Ontario, in Canada. As usual, the show had been packed and Jumbo had been the great success of the evening. The men were busy taking down the circus, getting ready to move on to the next stopping place. Most of the animals had already been loaded into their vans on the special train. Thirty-one lesser elephants who appeared with Jumbo were already safely aboard. Last of all, it was Jumbo's turn. He was led out, with his inseparable companion Tom Thumb [a smaller elephant], by his old friend Matthew Scott towards the grand "Palace Car."
>
> To get to the car, they had to cross an old, unused piece of railway track; at least it had not been used for a long time. It disappeared round a large bend several hundred yards away from them, to join on to the Grand Trunk Railway. As Jumbo was making his stately way towards his car, without any warning, Matthew Scott heard the

sound of an approaching train. He stood quite still for a moment, not knowing what to do, holding firmly on to Jumbo's chain. Jumbo pawed the ground nervously at the sudden noise. Suddenly, Scott was horrified to see an unexpected goods train appear round the bend of the supposedly unused branch railway line. He tugged frantically at Jumbo's chain and shouted for him to move. But Jumbo, by now quite terrified, braced his huge legs and would not move. The engine, moving very quickly, rushed down on them.

At the very last moment, Matthew Scott jumped aside. The engine hit little Tom Thumb on the back leg, throwing him down on the ground. Jumbo, standing right across the track, was hit by the full weight of the oncoming engine. His great bulk was hurled down with a terrifying crash. The engine itself was derailed.

At once there was noise and steam and confusion. People rushed to the scene. The dazed and frightened keeper picked himself up and went straight across to his old friend, lying there on his side. But one glance was sufficient for Matthew Scott to see the truth. Jumbo was dead. Blood was oozing from his great mouth. He had been killed at once, before he could possibly know what had happened.

The old keeper went down on his knees beside the dead elephant. His eyes filled with tears and, although knowing it was useless, he spoke to Jumbo. He put his arms around the animal's great trunk and he remembered the frightened, skinny little creature who had arrived at London Zoo all those years before. (Mathieson 37–39)

Shades of the death of Mrs. Sinico. Imagine reading that as a child.[5] The town of St. Thomas, Ontario, built a statue in 1985 to mark the centenary of this occasion: it weighs 138 tons. More immediate attempts to capitalize on the elephant's death were made predictably by Barnum himself, who exhibited both hide and skeleton of the elephant together, in a singularly disgusting attempt to recoup some of his losses, which were estimated at 50 percent of the total show's worth (fig. 5.7). In "Double Jumbo," as this ghoulish exhibit was affectionately known, you have a perfect match for the "Cyclops" theme of life in death and death in life: Barnum, like Bloom, is trying to downface you that dying is living. As Dignam's boots are preserved and resoled in the Blavatsky parody in "Cyclops" (U 12.338–76), so Jumbo is reexhumed, both flesh and bone, sole and soul, a metempsychosis devoutly to be avoided.

To add insult to injury, Alice was brought over from London, the same Alice who had pined so much for Jumbo that people said, "Alice will be

Fig. 5.7. "Double Jumbo." Copyright Circus World Museum, Baraboo, Wisconsin. Reprinted by permission.

broken-hearted if Jumbo goes" (Mathieson 23). Alice was exhibited in a widow's cap that was an exact replica of Queen Victoria's (Saxon 299). The elephant was tethered beside the remains of Jumbo, and billed, in a crowning example of the romantic grotesque, as Jumbo's "widow." "His Majesty the King loves Her Majesty the Queen" (*U* 12.1498–99): everyone associated Jumbo with the queen, not just because the queen visited him with her son, but because they were both larger than life, both symbols of empire. The *New York Times* playfully reported in happier days, at the height of Jumbo-mania, that "the Queen would romp with him, rolling with him in innocent delight upon the turf. Later in life when the danger that her Majesty might by accident roll upon Jumbo and seriously injure him became too obvious to be disregarded, the Queen ceased" (Saxon 295).

To a shocked world the news of the death of Jumbo the elephant was as incomprehensible as the death of JFK or Princess Diana: as in the two latter-day cases, conspiracy theories sprang up as to the manner of his death. People said that Barnum had planned the elephant's death as a publicity stunt, an accusation that led Barnum to slap a libel suit on the newspaper that carried the story. Some said that the elephant was a drunkard or was suffering from a chronic disease and needed to be disposed of. But the most startling, and most Joycean, theory was that he was killed for excessive

flatulence. (Here the size of the Jumbo sticker in fig. 5.5 should be re-
called.) "The huge animal," says Barnum's principal biographer, "so stank
up the circus that Barnum and his partners out of sheer embarrassment
decided they had no choice but to do away with him" (Saxon 301).

Tram kran kran kran. Good oppor. Coming. Krandlkrankran. I'm sure
it's the burgund. Yes. One, two. *Let my epitaph be.* Kraaaaaa. *Written.*
I have.
Pprrpffrrppffff.
Done. (*U* 11.1290–94)

As Bloom waits for a passing tram, so Barnum, also an advertising man,
waits for a passing train on the Grand Trunk Railway.[6] Larry Quigle, the
putative Barnum assassin in this theory, was meant to have been ordered
to "shoot Jumbo through the eye" (Saxon 301), ending Jumbo's Odyssean
journey with a truly Cyclopean gesture.

Jumbo's hide is preserved at Tufts College in Medford, Massachusetts,
or was, until the museum burned down in 1975, taking Jumbo's hide with
it (fig. 5.8). Tufts still calls its football team the Jumbos. The skeleton, the
other half of "Double Jumbo," is found in the American Museum of Natural History in New York. And Alice? Did Jumbo the elephant love Alice the
elephant? Sadly, the answer is no. Jumbo showed no love at all to Alice,
often instead menacing her angrily and violently (Saxon 293). The pining
that Alice was meant to have displayed at Jumbo's imminent departure
was more likely the result of the excessive crowds outside her cage.

In "Circe," the beatitudes mumble:

THE BEATITUDES
(incoherently) Beer beef battledog buybull businum barnum bug-
gerum bishop. (*U* 15.2241–43)

Though there is no evidence that P. T. Barnum ever buggered a bishop, he
did practically everything else. He was a "businum," or businessman, and
he did buy a bull, or bull elephant, and though "buybull" is a reference to
the Bible, it also refers to buying the products of John Bull, or buying
English. In buying Jumbo—the giant and mythological figure who be-
strides two continents and one *Ulysses* episode like a colossus—Barnum
bought English all right. Barnum's acquisition of Jumbo the elephant from
the Regent's Park Zoo in 1882 sent up a wail of lamentation through British society, a cry that was also, as the *Times* acutely observed, a celebration

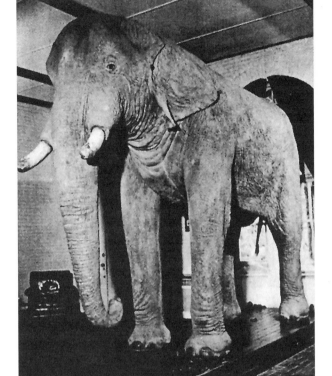

Fig. 5.8. Jumbo's hide, displayed at Tufts College in Medford, Massachusetts, until destroyed by a museum fire in 1975. Copyright Duette Photographers, Boston.

of the fundamental levity of adult nature. It was not Alice who loved Jumbo, in all the ways that "Love loves to love love." It was England.

H. G. Wells famously likened the syntactical contortions of the late Henry James to a hippopotamus intent on picking up a pea at all costs; if this essay has the same ponderous quality it is because *Ulysses* requires an extraordinary and faintly ridiculous level of concentration. *Ulysses* is an elephant in the zoological gardens of modern literature, and we are its keepers. Sometimes, like Matthew Scott, we stand proudly and proprietorially at its head; sometimes, like the puritanical librarian, we diligently place our sticker on its fundamentals; at other times, like P. T. Barnum, we are reduced to displaying its carcass. To know the whole of *Ulysses,* as we move into the twenty-first century, is impossible. Instead, we must focus on a line here—"Jumbo, the elephant, loves Alice, the elephant"—or there—"yes I said yes I will Yes"—and by carefully following that single line of inquiry, a tiny piece of the whole, a fold and a wrinkle of its flesh, will be illuminated. The book's final line has now been revealed, by Michael Groden in a report (on new acquisitions by the National Library of Ireland of Joyce materials) at the Trieste International James Joyce Symposium in 2002, to have originally read "yes I would Yes," a reading, had it been retained, that would have sent the novel cascading into the subjunctive and forced the rescreening of the T-shirts of thousands of college women everywhere. The preceding examination of a pea-sized unit of Joycean meaning is the method of the electronically annotated editions: each entry may not seem to amount to much, but the details build and matter.

So Jumbo the elephant didn't love Alice the elephant: maybe God doesn't love everybody after all, and perhaps Gerty is more interested in Cissy Caffrey than in the boy that has the bicycle. Jumbo was sold under the eyes of a nation in March 1882: that same nation was beginning to lose control of colonies in Africa and Asia and was about to hear, in May, of an event that would galvanize the issue of Home Rule for Ireland, with the assassination of two of its government employees in a park in Dublin. Jumbo lived on after death, a ghostly carnival afterimage of himself: so does Paddy Dignam, and the beautiful May Goulding, but more than that, so does Queen Victoria. Jumbo the elephant, like Victoria, was a defining figure of the age, inhabiting a long-dead world of buns and violets on the *Assyrian Monarch*, of six-year-olds piling into the howdah for the *Illustrated London News*, a world that has been lost by 1904, along with the Fauntleroy suit that little Rudy would have worn and the songs that are no longer sung around the Dedalus piano. And all that is still to be seen and heard in Dublin in 1904 has been lost by 1922, for Joyce, and for his postwar readers. It is up to the twenty-first-century reader to make these excavations. Sometimes, if one is in a carnival mood, the temptation comes to trumpet one's findings, making a meal of them, advertising them like a side-show barker. For only then can Jumbo lumber through the undergrowth of "Cyclops," squash the narrative mockery that surrounds him, stand tall at seven tons against Bloom's eleven stone four pounds, and be recognized.

Notes

1. Satisfying except for the dropped "l" from "gentleman" in the 1961 edition, a classic boner in the "Steelyrining" tradition of that edition (corrected to "Steelyringing" [U 11.1]). Bloom is nettled by a similar, but authorized, "l"-drop from the Telegraph's funeral report (U 16.1260).

2. For someone who has spent the better part of the last ten years of his life studying "Sirens," this line strikes a particular chord.

3. Perhaps not incidentally, a question immediately followed on the reports of foot-and-mouth disease in a county in Cornwall, further linking the Barnum episode to the historical background of Ulysses.

4. See Bowen, "Ulysses" as a Comic Novel 18–19, and Bakhtin, The Dialogic Imagination 58.

5. Jumbo's death cannot, unfortunately, be the inspiration for the death of Anna Karenina, because Tolstoy's heroine threw herself under a train eight years earlier, in 1877. Austin Briggs reminds me that Carker is killed by a train in Dombey and Son, and in Mrs. Gaskell's Cranford a character is killed as he crosses the tracks, too absorbed in reading Pickwick to notice the oncoming train. The St. Thomas train wreck of 1885 then joins a long literary line of tragic railway accidents, from Dombey to Duffy.

6. The name of the Grand Trunk Railway Line is nearly as good a joke as Lenehan's, though it can only be a cosmic accident. Barnum indulges in a similar pun in a letter to an unidentified correspondent of March 7, 1882: "All my thoughts & cares at present are locked up in two trunks—one of which belongs to Jumbo" (Saxon, Selected Letters 223).

Works Cited

Bowen, Zack. "Ulysses" as a Comic Novel. Syracuse: Syracuse University Press, 1989.

Bakhtin, M. M. The Dialogic Imagination: Four Essays. Edited by Michael Holquist. Translated by Caryl Emerson and Michael Holquist. Austin: University of Texas Press, 1981.

Bryan, J., III. The World's Greatest Showman: The Life of P. T. Barnum. New York: Random House, 1956.

Lyons, F.S.L. Charles Stewart Parnell. London: Collins, 1977.

Mathieson, Eric. The True Story of Jumbo the Elephant. New York: Hamish Hamilton, 1963.

Saxon, A. H. P. T. Barnum: The Legend and the Man. New York: Columbia University Press, 1989.

———, ed. Selected Letters of P. T. Barnum. New York: Columbia University Press, 1983.

Time Travel on Wings of Excess

"Ithaca" and a Message in a Bottle

John Rocco

> In the words of the Cyclops narrator the curse of my deaf and
> dumb arse light sideways on Bloom and all his blooms and blos-
> soms. I'll break the back of *Ithaca* tomorrow so 'elp me fucking
> Chroist.
>
> **James Joyce to Frank Budgen (SL 281)**

Ulysses, that wily novel of stratagems, is excessive in its tricks, traps, and
trips through history. Its excesses grow with its narrative. Its penultimate
chapter, "Ithaca," seems to be the safe rock the reader finally reaches after
the exploding carnival of "Circe" and the cliché minefield of "Eumaeus." It
is also the most Joycean-obsessive chapter in the book and, as Frank
Budgen tells us, Joyce called it his favorite of all the episodes of *Ulysses*
(264). Modeled on a catechism, "Ithaca" gives the reader questions, answers, lists, catalogues, property appraisals, Bloom's budget for June 16,
1904 (*U* 17.1455–78), the description of products like The Wonderworker
("It heals and soothes while you sleep, in case of trouble in breaking wind,
assists nature in the most formidable way, insuring instant relief in dis-
charge of gases, keeping parts clean" [*U* 17.1826–28]), and, in what is the
most cited passage of the chapter, the movement of something as vital as
water into the Bloom household (*U* 17.163–70). As Joyce told Budgen, all
these details are given so that "the reader [will] know everything and
know it in the baldest coldest way" (*SL* 278). This is the end point of mimesis: everything is given to the reader as reality becomes not something we
are supposed to feel and see, but something we are supposed to understand
at *every* level of operation and production. As Erich Auerbach notes, Joyce
is representative of the modernists who break with the established Western reliance on mimesis to "find a method which dissolves reality into
multiple and multivalent reflections of consciousness" (487). "Ithaca," to
put it bluntly, "dissolves reality" into facts, figures, itemizations, lists. The

penultimate chapter of *Ulysses* seems to dissolve "reality" or, at least, nov-elistic diegesis to report what one diligent TV detective defined as "just the facts." And the "facts" are given to an excessive degree. The chapter is one of *excess*: excessive details, excessive descriptions, excessive facts, excessive questions, and excessive answers.[1] The "Ithaca" chapter is an excess of rep-resentation: the Road of Excess leads to the Facts of "Ithaca." But, as we shall see, this excess of facts is complicated by history. The nature and ef-fect of this narrative excess can be judged only by experiencing it, and we begin with the facts as nonobjective, as not "just the facts" but rather as something personal and historical and excessive.

"Ithaca" is pronounced "impersonal" in the schema reproduced in Stuart Gilbert's *James Joyce's "Ulysses,"* and Hugh Kenner describes the chapter as resembling "the final chapter of a Victorian novel" because it "abounds in detailed revelations that refocus what we had thought we knew and substantiate what we only guessed" (141). However, "Ithaca" moves beyond the modernist will-to-interiorize and the Victorian obses-sion with categories and explanations; we are given a different cosmos of mimesis wherein someone like Esther Summerson would be completely lost despite the fact that Dickens tells us that in *Bleak House* he "purposely dwelt upon the romantic side of familiar things" (ix). In "Ithaca," Joyce does not dwell on the "romantic side" of anything: he just gives us the *thing* itself. There may not be any spontaneous combustion in *Ulysses,* but there is a blowing up of the "humanist" novel. Human "voice" and "thoughts" seem to be the only things missing from the vast collection of objects and ideas assembled in "Ithaca." Karen Lawrence succinctly states the problem of the chapter: "Joyce does everything possible in 'Ithaca' to destroy our sense of a narrating, human voice" (183–84). And yet, surpris-ingly, what we discover among the objects and facts is something exces-sively human. "Ithaca" is the literary equivalent of the vast storehouse of objects at the end of *Citizen Kane*: there is a puzzle and a labyrinth of things, but in the overlooked fire is the burning heart of the man everyone is seeking. Turning to the vast storehouse of facts and objects of "Ithaca" entails examining an old reaction to Joyce's "excessive" challenge to repre-sentation.

The Soviet director Sergei Eisenstein was an ardent admirer of Joyce even when to be so became politically dangerous.[2] Throughout his career Eisenstein publicly championed Joyce's work, and the two met in Paris in the early thirties. In his autobiography, Eisenstein describes their meeting by first evoking the impact the Irish novelist had upon his films: "The year that gave birth to the idea of intellectual cinema was the year I became acquainted with Joyce's *Ulysses*" (213). Intellectual cinema, according to Eisenstein, is film constructed around ideas instead of purely emotional scenes. His conception of intellectual cinema was made up of the "effective montage of *intellectual attractions*" to "develop a film language capable of making an abstract idea blossom in an emotional way" (207–8). The great project Eisenstein had in mind for the culmination of intellectual cinema was a film version of Marx's *Capital*. A movie based on *Capital* sounds as possible, and as entertaining, as a movie called *Phenomenology of Spirit*. There is an obvious problem with such an undertaking: how do you film complex ideas and theories that have no correlation with common film images or cinematic techniques? However, as James Goodwin describes it in his study of Eisenstein's use of history, the director took *Ulysses* as a kind of guide for his thinking about filming the unfilmable:

In order to give *Capital* "the form of a discursive film," Eisenstein contemplated a "de-anecdotalization principle" that would diminish storyline to a level of *historettes*, or petty events. Seeking an adequate triviality for the 'spinal' "theme," he identifies an example within literary modernism: "In Joyce's ULYSSES there is a remarkable chapter of this kind, written in the manner of scholastic catechism. Questions are asked and answers given. The subject of the question is how to light a Bunsen burner. The answers, however, are metaphysical." The chapter in question is the seventeenth, identified by Joyce critics as the "Ithaca" section. As in *Ulysses*, in the *Capital* project the methods of representation—rather than the persons or events represented—are foregrounded, textual dominants. (122)

Through the example of "Ithaca," history is made manageable; the processes behind the machine of history—industrialization, imperialism, colonialism, class conflict—are depicted on a level that can be grasped as a "petty" event. The alienating and impersonal movement of history is made human through the structure of the storytelling. This is exactly the effect Fredric Jameson describes as "de-reification" throughout the pages of the novel; through this kind of intervention, history and politics are made manageable in the minds of the Dublin citizen and the reader. The alienation of modern society, according to Jameson, is disrupted, and "everything seemingly material and solid in Dublin itself can be dissolved back into the underlying reality of human relations and human praxis" (136). The key word here is "everything": through narrative excess the world of modernity is made a world where people can live. This movement toward the personal, the human, is the aspect of Joyce's work that influenced Eisenstein and helped shape his thinking about the future of film. But how can we read this "human" aspect in "Ithaca," the chapter described as "impersonal" and stuffed with inanimate objects ("Describe the alterations effected in the disposition of the articles of furniture" [U 17.1279–80)? The answer lies in the fact that, as critics from A. Walton Litz to Patrick McGee have pointed out, "Ithaca" is a not a completely "objective" chapter.[3] The consciousness of Bloom pervades many of the questions and answers and, in a certain sense, "Ithaca" represents the ultimate frontier of the interior monologue. This is the point where we can begin to understand Eisenstein's interest in "Ithaca." "Ithaca" may be seen as the chapter where interior monologue meets history, or where history itself is cracked open to reveal its inner rumblings. The "objective" facts of the chapter—facts representing the lived experience of the characters and the very movement of the heavens—are shot through with Bloom's consciousness, and "objectivity" is brought into question. This kind of questioning leads to a human response and a human participation in history. It leads to the reader opening Bloom's drawer to examine its contents. But before opening one of Bloom's drawers to look at what is inside, we must become unstuck in time like Vonnegut's Billy Pilgrim and fall into No Man's Land right before the attack on the Somme during the First World War.

Paul Fussell tells us that the Somme affair came to be known among the troops as "the Great Fuck-Up." It was a British offensive that began on the first of July and ended five months later. The operation was designed to take pressure off the French at Verdun. On the first day of the attack, the British lost over sixty thousand men.[4] Fussell quotes a description from the beginning of the battle that sums up the early thinking about the war and how modern thinking itself changed: "As the gun-fire died away I saw an infantryman climb onto the parapet into No Man's Land, beckoning others to follow. . . . As he did so he kicked off a football. A good kick. The ball rose and traveled well towards the German line. That seemed to be the signal to advance" (27). This is the most famous instance of the British display of bravado in the face of the enemy (the man who reportedly organized the kicking of four footballs before the offensive, Captain W. P. Nevill, was killed instantaneously).

This is an archetypal incident that Fussell points to as possible in the early stages of the war. Something like this was conceivable before the war and during its early stages, but it would appear deluded and insane during the later stages of the conflict. After the war, this kind of thinking, this kind of romantic bravado and innocent outlook, was lost to the world, and Fussell points to a new kind of consciousness arising from the battlefields: "there seems to be one dominating form of modern understanding [and] it is essentially ironic" (35). As Fussell describes it, the war marked a break in modern thinking about reality and truth. Stephen Kern points to the war as a crucial point during the modern questioning between time as "atomistic or a flux" (20–29). And for Gertrude Stein the war was a cubist composition. This bloody "composition" provided for the new way of experiencing modernity that Fussell points to and the questioning about time that Kern describes. For Stein, the war is cubist because it cannot be looked at in any *one* way. The war is cubist because it has no one view, no one perspective, no one controlling idea or motion. The war reflects the state of being that people found themselves in during the second decade of the new century. This assault on meaning and the world at war was what Nietzsche had pointed to and prophesied throughout his writing. In a famous passage from *The Will to Power*, Nietzsche described the prevailing belief in the "ego" and its concomitant influence over truth: "facts is precisely what there is not, only interpretations." This was what Nietzsche believed people should understand, and the Great War gave them a push in this direction by showing them that

if the word "knowledge" has any meaning, the word is knowable; but it is *interpretable* otherwise, it has no meaning behind it, but countless meanings—"Perspectivism."

It is our needs that interpret the world; our drives and their For and Against. Every drive is a kind of lust to rule; each one has its perspective that would like to compel all the other drives to accept as a norm. (267)

In 1914, "drives" broke out all over the world. And facts became different; facts became something to be interpreted, not relied upon as solid instances of "truth."

From the relative safety of exile in Trieste and Zürich, Joyce witnessed and read about these "drives." Some of this reading came from Nietzsche, a reading that lasted Joyce's entire life and, in the words of Joseph Valente, formed an "alliance . . . of spiritual revolution" (88). According to Valente, Joyce's relationship to Nietzsche centered on their concern with perspectivism, a concern that "traces the monologism of Western metaphysics to a misplaced belief in the ego, rather than an illusory sense of objective existence" (89). I would point out here that this interest revolves around their attack upon ocularcentrism[5]—Nietzsche began his attack upon Western metaphysics in *The Birth of Tragedy* when he described the Dionysian quest to "transcend all seeing" (140)—and that Joyce took this attack into a different direction by creating an oeuvre of work embodying this critique of perspectivism. But Joyce also had a personal interest in reading the "drives" that were tearing the Europe of "entrenched and marshalled races" apart.

In 1916, two of Joyce's friends from his school days were killed—one in the uniform of a British officer and the other at the hands of a British officer. Francis Sheehy-Skeffington, the model for MacCann in *A Portrait* and one of the organizers of the protest against Yeats's *The Countess Cathleen,* was killed during the Easter Rising when he attempted to stop his fellow Dubliners from looting. A British officer caught the pacifist Skeffington in the streets and had him shot without a trial for rioting.[6] Tom Kettle, the model for Robert Hand in *Exiles,* died an even more ironic death, and he knew it when he sat in the trenches after the terrible beauty was born: "These men will go down in history as heroes and martyrs and I will go down—if I go down at all—as a bloody British officer" (Cross 41). Kettle was an Irish nationalist who disapproved of *Dubliners* because he thought its paralyzed view of his fellow citizens would be harmful to Ireland. He joined the British army at the beginning of the war because he believed that England would reward Irish participation with Home Rule (this false hope was held by other Irish poets such as Francis Ledwidge, and the overall colonial situation is illustrated by the "onelegged sailor" in "Wandering Rocks": "—For England. . . . " [*U* 10.232]). Kettle was killed in September during the Somme offensive. The contrast and ironic similarities between these two deaths were highlighted by the fact that Kettle and Skeffington were brothers-in-law. Joyce wrote a letter to Kettle's widow and invoked Skeffington's death in his last sentence: "I am grieved to hear that so many misfortunes have fallen on your family in these evil days" (*SL* 222).

Joyce wrote "Nestor" during those evil days from November to December 1917. He began writing the chapter almost exactly one year to the day that the Somme offensive was called off. As James Fairhall describes it, 1917 was "an especially demoralizing year dominated by the idea that attrition would decide the war" (165).[7] (Is it significant that the chapter I will be pointing to as the most influenced by the war's shattering of conven-

tional perspective—"Ithaca"—is the *seventeenth* of the novel?) The reason I bring up the second chapter of *Ulysses* in this discussion of "Ithaca"
is that if we are to see "Ithaca" as the chapter where history itself is given
an interior monologue, then "Nestor" must be examined as the chapter
where history first talks. The "art" of "Nestor," we are told in the Gilbert
schema, is "history" (30). E. L. Epstein suggests that because of this concentration on history "many later passages in *Ulysses* depend for their
interpretation upon their understanding of 'Nestor'" (17). And part of the
significance of this chapter is Stephen's teaching of history and his awareness of the weight of the past. The relationship of "Nestor" to "Ithaca" is
particularly important here: "Nestor" is the "Telemachiad" parallel to the
"Nostos" positioning of "Ithaca." The chapters have mirrored positions
within the text—middle chapters in triads at the beginning and ending of
the novel. And, as the Gilbert schema tells us, the two chapters are directly
related in their forms: the technique of "Nestor" is described as "Catechism (personal)," whereas "Ithaca" is described as "Catechism (impersonal)" (30). Stephen begins "Nestor" by asking a question: "—You, Coch-
rane, what city sent for him?" (*U* 2.1); and the chapter ends with the
anti-Semitic Mr. Deasy asking Stephen a question: "Ireland, they say, has
the honour of being the only country which never persecuted the jews. Do
you know that? No. And do you know why?" (*U* 2.437–39). These questions and answers will go on to form the structure of "Nestor's" twin,
"Ithaca."

"Nestor" begins with a question to a child, but the quiet and fidgety
classroom quickly dissolves into the destruction of war: "Fabled by the
daughters of memory. And yet it was in some way if not as memory fabled
it. A phrase then, of impatience, thud of Blake's wings of excess. I hear the
ruin of all space, shattered glass and toppling masonry, and time one livid
final flame" (*U* 2.7–10). This "excessive" Blakean meditation on the force,
production, and communication of history—what Fritz Senn points to as
the chapter's highlighting of history as something "unfathomable" that
for "some reason . . . escaped oblivion" (767)—leads to an image of destruction. As E. L. Epstein points out, the "resemblance of this vision to a
scene of the First World War, a building hit by artillery," is due to the
events occurring in Europe as Joyce wrote the chapter (22). In fact, it is
hard to imagine that any reader of the novel in 1922, or a page turner
throughout the twenties and thirties, could read this vision from Stephen's
mind without conjuring up visions of the Great War.

Time and space itself were casualties of the war. This blowing up of time and space occurs again after Stephen's one great burst of action: the smash-ing of the chandelier in Bella Cohen's: "*He lifts his ashplant high with both hands and smashes the chandelier. Time's livid final flame leaps and, in the following darkness, ruin of all space, shattered glass and toppling masonry*" (*U* 15.4243–45). At this point in the novel, Stephen has finally thrown off the agenbite of inwit associated with his guilt over his mother's death and shrugged off another effort of the "fathers" (church and state) to control him. But this is also a mock heroic—and drunken—gesture, and we are reminded of the beginning of Marx's *The Eighteenth Brumaire of Louis Bonaparte*: "Hegel remarks somewhere that all facts and personages of great importance in world history occur, as it were, twice. He forgot to add: the first time as tragedy, the second time as farce" (594). If the events in "Circe" border on farce, they also have their tragic side. Right after Stephen "destroys" time and space, he is confronted by the arm of the British military in the form of Privates Carr and Compton. And during this confrontation, the city that gave birth to Stephen becomes involved in the fight: "*Brimstone fires spring up. Dense clouds roll past. Heavy Gat-ling guns boom. Pandemonium. Troops deploy. Gallop of hoofs. Artillery. Hoarse commands. Bells clang. Backers shout. Drunkards bawl. Whores screech. Foghorns hoot. Cries of valour. Shrieks of dying. Pikes clash on cuirasses. Thieves rob the slain*" (*U* 15.4661–65). Dublin burns. The imag-ery invokes the war and 1916, when British warships sailed up the Liffey and turned their guns on the city. As Declan Kiberd argues in *Inventing Ireland*, the myths surrounding 1916 and the war were "almost identical" (247). And, in the light of the deaths of Kettle and Skeffington, they be-came conflated in *Ulysses*.

The First World War changed language because it changed how we see the world. For the soldier in the trenches, the world looks different; as Fussell argues, things that were taken for granted before the war become "new" to the "new" eyes of the experienced soldier: "It was the sight of the sky, almost alone, that had the power to persuade a man that he was not already lost in a common grave" (51). In a reaction to a chapter from *Mod-ern Painters*, Max Plowman summed up the experience of the new vision of the soldier: "Was it Ruskin who said that the upper and more glorious half of Nature's pageant goes unseen by the majority of people? . . . Well, the trenches have changed all that. Shutting off the landscape, they compel us to observe the sky" (quoted in Fussell 54). This upheaval took place all over the Western world, and it revolutionized how the world is talked about and how consciousness is perceived.

The Great War also provided artists and thinkers with a new way of "seeing" reality. And this brings me to my point about "Ithaca" and the war: of all the chapters in *Ulysses,* the style of "Ithaca" is the most representative of the "upheaval" of historical events surrounding Joyce as he composed the text. World War I is what Jameson would call the "subtext" of the chapter; even though "Nestor" is filled with imagery from the war, "Ithaca," partly because it is the mirror of "Nestor," is more reflective of the war in its very form. In "Nestor," we are given blood-soaked battlefields and buildings blown apart; in "Ithaca," we are given the conventional novel being blown apart. Granted, Joyce pushed the novel to its limits throughout the text, but the position of "Ithaca" in the novel highlights its power in dismantling the traditional form of the novel at the same time that it highlights Joyce's challenge to representation. The language of the novel is changed in "Ithaca" because the Great War changed thinking about words and identity. Fussell describes language and consciousness as being one of the great casualties of the war. In *A Farewell to Arms,* Hemingway gives a description that Fussell says would have been incomprehensible before the war; Frederic Henry tells us, "Abstract words such as glory, honor, courage, or hallow were obscene beside the concrete names of villages, the numbers of roads, the names of rivers, the numbers of regiments and the dates" (191). This is an important formulation because "concrete names," "numbers," "the names of rivers," and "dates" are the exact things "Ithaca" is constructed upon. The end of *Ulysses*—"Penelope" being beyond the end in its timelessness and its eight sentences turned toward infinity—dispenses with traditional form and language because "abstract words" no longer apply. "Ithaca" is the end point of novelistic "truth" and representation, as depicted in the loss of "innocent" language; and the strange large dot at the end of the chapter may be taken as the period after the last sentence of the "last" novel. The reader will know "everything" after "Ithaca," but this new, "excessive" knowledge is colored by the postwar reevaluation of everything. And to see this we must (finally) open Bloom's drawer.

Before Bloom opens the unlocked "first drawer," we are given a catalog of the items contained in it in one of the longest descriptions in the chapter. Bloom opens it to deposit the most recent of Martha Clifford's letters, and the drawer is opened to us as we become literary archeologists picking through the objects making up Bloom's life. The "2nd drawer" contains important documents such as his birth certificate, his endowment assurance policy, his bank passbook, and the official notice of Rudolph Virag changing his name to Bloom (*U* 17.1855–72). But the first drawer contains detritus that is more telling of Bloom's existence and his desires. The first drawer is packed with stuff, and the catalogue of the items is long and detailed:

> A Vere Foster's handwriting copybook, property of Milly (Millicent) Bloom, certain pages of which bore diagram drawings, marked *Papli*, which showed a large globular head with 5 hairs erect, 2 eyes in profile, the trunk full front with 3 large buttons, 1 triangular foot: 2 fading photographs of queen Alexandra of England and of Maud Branscombe, actress and professional beauty: a Yuletide card, bearing on it a pictorial representation of a parasitic plant, the legend *Mizpah*, the date Xmas 1892, the name of the senders: from Mr + Mrs M. Comerford, the versicle: *May this Yuletide bring to thee, Joy and peace and welcome glee*: a butt of red partly liquefied sealing wax, obtained from the stores department of Messrs Hely's, Ltd., 89, 90, and 91 Dame street . . . (*U* 17.1775–85)

The list goes on to mention other objects such as the letters from Martha Clifford; "a press cutting from an English weekly periodical *Modern Society*, subject corporal chastisement in girls' schools" (*U* 17.1801–3); condoms; a chart describing Bloom's measurements "compiled before, during and after 2 months' consecutive use of Sandow-Whiteley's pulley exerciser" (*U* 17.1815–17); and a tool that is symbolic of our sift through the drawer and the overall reading of the chapter of "facts": "a lowpower magnifying glass" (*U* 17.1808–9). In all, there are twenty-nine different items in the drawer. Ezra Pound once called *Ulysses* "a summary of pre-war Europe" in which is depicted "the blackness and mess and muddle of a 'civilization.' Bloom very much *is* the mess" (251). Bloom is the prewar mess under the microscope of the new language given to the world by the Great War. And the drawer is a mess, an excess of novelistic description. There are no empty words describing the contents of the drawer that Frederic Henry would object to: there are only lists, dates, addresses, concrete descriptions, "objective" appraisals. The list of articles is reminiscent of the comic exaggerations of Rabelais, Cervantes, and Sterne, but it has a modern sense and a modern impact. This may be better assessed by bringing up the writer who gave Stephen his artistic model and "Circe" its basis in psychodrama. It may also be said that it was Gustave Flaubert who gave "Ithaca" its examination of bourgeois history.

In the words of Michel Foucault, Flaubert's work emerged from his "discovery of a new imaginative space in the nineteenth century" that removed itself from the "sleep of reason" and entered the cosmos of human "fact": "The imaginary now resides between the book and the lamp. The fantastic is no longer a property of the heart, nor is it found among the incongruities of nature; it evolves from the accuracy of knowledge, and its treasures lie dormant in documents" (90). Flaubert's great subject was the world of the bourgeoisie, and he spent his career attacking its hypocrisy, callousness, and stupidity. This modern subject required a modern literature. For Foucault, this "modern" shift in Flaubert was epitomized in *The Temptation of St Antony*, a work Flaubert spent his entire career rewriting. Through its invocation of spiritual ecstasy and nightmare vision, Flaubert created a highly experimental novel combined with an impossible play. *The Temptation of St Antony* is rooted in Flaubert's personal psychic disturbances (now believed to have been epilepsy); his fascination with religion; his interest in the "everyday"; and what Foucault calls his resistance to deny "reality" in an effort to amass "minute facts, monuments reduced to infinitesimal fragments, and the reproductions of reproductions" (91). In other words, Flaubert was interested in the contents of Bloom's drawer. It is this concentration on bourgeois "knowledge" and experience that Foucault points to as the "modern" element in Flaubert, and it triggers something in literature itself: "In writing *The Temptation*, Flaubert produced the first literary work whose exclusive domain is that of books: following Flaubert, Mallarmé is able to write *Le Livre* and modern literature is activated—Joyce, Roussel, Kafka, Pound, Borges. The library is on fire" (92). This flaming library is behind modernism, *Ulysses,* and, in Hélène Cixous' words, that "opera-out-of-gear" called "Circe" (387).

If we take Flaubert's *The Temptation* as the spark behind Nighttown, then it is Flaubert's last unfinished novel that gives "Ithaca" its bonfire of facts. Edmund Wilson was one of the first critics to describe the similar "modern" theme in Flaubert and Joyce: "*Ulysses* is, I suppose, the most completely 'written' novel since Flaubert. The example of the great prose poet of Naturalism has profoundly influenced Joyce—in his attitude toward the modern bourgeois world and in the contrast implied by the Homeric parallel of *Ulysses*" (203). And *Bouvard and Pécuchet* was Flaubert's last foray into the "modern bourgeois world"; the story of two law-copyists who come into money, Flaubert's unfinished novel examines their search for knowledge and the "facts" of the world. It is a story of two Bartlebys who search for the "facts" of the brick walls outside their windows. Bouvard and Pécuchet retire and move to Chavignolles, a small village in Normandy. In this seclusion they study every subject they can think of. Their studies include chemistry, politics, love, medicine, geology, psychology, and a host of other topics. Flaubert is rumored to have read 1,500 books in preparation for this exhaustive examination of bourgeois knowledge. However, as in "Ithaca," "facts" in *Bouvard and Pécuchet* are not something to rely on, something to believe in, something belonging to "truth." (Flaubert planned on having a *sottisier*, or dictionary of moronic "common ideas," as an appendix.) This is repeatedly shown to our bourgeois researchers, until they reach a point in their education that removes them from their earlier conceptions of life and knowledge. Flaubert describes in one sentence what may be taken as his own reading of the "facts" of his own world: "Then a lamentable faculty developed in their minds, that of noticing stupidity and finding it intolerable" (217). As the great bourgeois epic, *Ulysses* follows in this search for the "facts" of modern life.[8] And yet, as the example of "Ithaca" indicates, something changed in modern existence. This change occurred with the guns of August.

Late in *Bouvard and Pécuchet*, after the two copyists notice "stupidity" and find it "intolerable," they become teachers of two of the town's orphans. And like Stephen, they come upon the subject called history: "Pécuchet explained Europe to him with an atlas, but bewildered by so many lines and colours he could not find the names. Basins and mountains did not fit in with kingdoms, the political order became confused with the physical. Perhaps that would all be cleared up by studying history" (263). History will provide the "facts" that will clear up the confusing "lines and colours" of the map; but their search for history provides for a pedagogical Catch-22. They realize there is only one way to know history: "Conclusion: history can only be learned through much reading. This they would do" (263). The "facts" of history, what Pécuchet calls "a real maze," can only be learned through books, or the repository of "facts." "Truth" is a circle without a beginning or an ending. (Nietzsche: knowledge is "*interpretable*" and "it has no meaning behind it, but countless meanings— 'Perspectivisim.'") Flaubert drew the circle; Joyce broke it.

The form of "Ithaca" is symbolic of the modern break with the reliance on "fact" and the stability of "truth." Henry James once described the novels of Walter Scott as "triumphs of fact," but the novel of "facts" was changed by the war, excessively defeated at the Somme, at Verdun, at Passchendaele. In many ways, modernism itself was changed by the war, or, as Michael Levenson describes it, the modernists changed their focus because of the great interruption of worldwide battle: "Before the war, the modernists had assumed the role of violence-inciting artistic *provocateurs* whose aim was to startle the culture out of lethargy. But after August 1914, lethargy was no longer the dreaded ill. The problem for the moderns became what posture to adopt in the face of general social disarray" (140). The explosion of war drowned out Wyndham Lewis's *Blast*. The war killed many of those at the heart of European modernism, including Guillaume Apollinaire, Henri Gaudier-Brzeska, and T. E. Hulme. It wounded a young Hemingway who went to Europe looking for romance and ended up filled with shrapnel from an Austrian mortar. After the war, Hemingway went in search of "one true sentence," the "true" being an adjective for something that had not existed before the war; not "truth" but a "true" sentence like that at the beginning of "In Another Country": "In the fall the war was always there, but we did not go to it anymore" (206). And Joyce wrote *Ulysses* surrounded by the chaos of war and the destruction of that bourgeois artifact Flaubert crafted called the novel. "Ithaca" follows Flaubert's fascination with and critique of the bourgeois "fact"; but at the same time, the penultimate chapter of *Ulysses* excessively announces the end of history, the end of bourgeois mimesis, and the end of the novel.

The excessive ending of *Ulysses* from "Oxen of the Sun" until Molly's final word stretches the "facts" of the novel and provides for the death of the genre. These narrative experiments bothered Edmund Wilson. A great admirer of the book as a whole, Wilson nevertheless felt that the latter part of the text was "artistically absolutely indefensible" (216). Although he praised the artistic virtuosity behind "Circe" and "Penelope," Wilson felt the narrative experiments near the end of the text "bogged" down the important meeting between Bloom and Stephen. He described "Ithaca" as "the scientific question-and-answer chapter which undertakes to communicate to us through the most opaque and uninviting medium possible Dedalus's conversation with Bloom" (216). This is the kind of reading Kiberd comes away with after examining the "anti-climax" of Bloom bringing Stephen home for cocoa, but he discerns a different impact: "Joyce concludes that there can be no freedom for his characters within that society: they exist in their interior monologues with a kind of spacious amplitude which proves impossible in the community itself. So his refusal to provide a 'satisfactory' climax in their final meeting is his rejection of the obligation felt by realists to present a coherent, stable, socialized self" (354). This reading seems to be in direct contrast to Jameson's conclusion that the people of Dublin transcend reification in the novel through lived speech and achieve a kind of human world in the face of global contingency. I think both are correct in their thinking because they both approach "Ithaca" as the chapter where this kind of reading is possible; reading "Ithaca" enables Kiberd to conclude that *Ulysses* "is a prolonged farewell to written literature and a rejection of its attempts to colonize speech and thought" (355); reading "Ithaca" enables Jameson to ask: "Why do we need narrative anyway? What are stories and what is our existential relation to them? Is a non-narrative relationship to the world and to Being possible?" (140). And the reason these two critics can come to such different conclusions is that the excesses of the chapter—the lists, the descriptions, the questions, the answers—provide for an opening into the interior monologue of history itself. The last object I want to point out in Bloom's drawer brings together these two interpretations as meditations upon history and also points to the overall influence on the form of the chapter.

The objects we have seen in Bloom's drawer tell us things about the lived history of Bloom, his family, and his country. This is the force behind the entire chapter: the "voices" and "thoughts" of Bloom *and* history itself color the narrative, soak it in a manner akin to what Kenner describes as the Uncle Charles Principle; the excess of "Ithaca" is a narration seeped in the consciousness of Bloom and modern history. In this light, the last object we pull from the drawer gives us Bloom himself telling us about history; we open Bloom's drawer and find "a sealed prophecy (never unsealed) written by Leopold Bloom in 1886 concerning the consequences of the passing into law of William Ewart Gladstone's Home Rule bill of 1886 (never passed into law)" (*U* 17.1787–90). This tiny time capsule is not opened for us: we do not know what Bloom's "prophecy" describes, but we do know that Bloom was for Home Rule and that the prophecy probably reflects this position. The Home Rule bill of 1886 was the first bill to be introduced by Gladstone but was defeated, as Don Gifford tells us, on June 8, 1886 (596).

Ulysses almost takes place—it misses it by eight days—on the eighteenth anniversary of the first defeat of a Home Rule bill. This dating, to my mind, is heavily symbolic and, in the context of "Ithaca," it takes on an interesting light. *Ulysses* has eighteen chapters, eighteen installments of modernity and bourgeois culture and history since the defeat of Home Rule. As I have mentioned, the promise of Home Rule was one of the reasons many Irishmen served in the British army during the First World

War. Tom Kettle and others like him fought and died for this postwar reward that never came. In his popular history of the war, Martin Gilbert
takes time out of a detailed description of troop movements during the
Somme offensive to mention Kettle and the Irish company he led into the
captured village of Ginchy: "Before the attack the officers were given
pieces of green cloth to be stitched on the back of their uniforms, a symbol
of Irish patriotism. Touching his patch, Tom Kettle told his soldier servant:
'Boy, I am proud to die for it!' Leading his men into the village that day,
Kettle was killed. His soldier servant, in a letter of condolence to Kettle's
wife, wrote: 'He carried his pack for Ireland and Europe. Now pack-carry-
ing is over. He has held the line'" (283–84). As I have pointed out, Joyce
also wrote a letter to Kettle's widow. In a certain sense, Bloom's sealed
prophecy is a message in a bottle Joyce attempted to send to Kettle before
he put on that British uniform and before he added a patch of green to it.
The unsealed prophecy is never unsealed because of the failure of the British Parliament to pass Home Rule into law. After the fall of Parnell, Home
Rule became an even more elusive goal, and Bloom's prophecy lay in his
drawer untouched for eighteen years and eight days. Kettle went to defend
Catholic Belgium because he saw it as a defense for all small nations. But
the war was good-bye to all that. It is as if "Ithaca" is a time machine and
Joyce was attempting to send a message in a bottle back to Kettle: Home
Rule will remain a broken dream. And he sends this message back through
the symbolic history of one Dubliner who has been out too late on one
June night. It is a message sent back to Kettle and Skeffington and Joyce's
father and all Parnellites. It is a shout through history to the rebels of 1916.
The message is never received, the prophecy is never opened, but its meaning spreads throughout the entire chapter to follow Frederic Henry's in-
junction, "Abstract words such as glory, honor, courage, or hallow were
obscene besides the concrete names of villages, the numbers of roads, the
names of rivers, the numbers of regiments and the dates." History does not
speak in abstractions; it speaks through excess, through war, through
people.

Joyce gives us a new "meaning" in "Ithaca." The chapter's excess is
similar to Bataille's "expenditure": it consumes, wastes, exaggerates, destroys in order to arrive at something "new," something *revolutionary*.[9]
"Ithaca's" reflection of the Great War and the Easter Rising, its montage of
objects and "facts," and its place within the novel called *Ulysses* pushes
"meaning" elsewhere, pushes *Ulysses* into what Barthes describes as the
excess of "The Third Meaning," or "obtuse meaning": "An obtuse angle is

greater than a right angle: *an obtuse angle of 100*, says the dictionary; the third meaning also seems to me greater than the pure, upright, secant, legal perpendicular of the narrative, it seems to open the field of meaning totally, that is infinitely" (55).[10] This new "obtuse" meaning of the novel leads to the infinity of "Penelope," but before "Ithaca" can end its excess it must ask one last simple question: "Where?" (*U* 17.2331). But the last answer is not so simple after the Somme offensive, the Great War, the shelling of Dublin, and the chapter called "Ithaca." Barthes: "The obtuse meaning is a signifier without a signified, hence the difficulty in naming it. . . . If the obtuse meaning cannot be described, that is because, in contrast to the obvious meaning, it does not copy anything—how do you describe something that does not represent anything?" (61). There is no last answer, no last fact, no last description. There is only a large dot and the end of excess.

Postscript

On the morning of September 11, 2001, a line from *Ulysses* took on prophetic fire: "I hear the ruin of all space, shattered glass and toppling masonry, and time one livid final flame." This essay was written before the World Trade Center went down in New York City. Since then that line and the essay have taken on other meanings: "[I]t is hard to imagine that any reader of the novel in 1922, or a page turner throughout the twenties and thirties, could read this vision from Stephen's mind without conjuring up visions of the Great War." It is hard to imagine a reader today not thinking of that day in New York.

If "Ithaca" is a "time machine" teaching us that history speaks "through excess, through war, through people," then what does Joyce tell us about our past, and what will we say about his work in the twenty-first century? I think the answer lies not in the critical/historical/cultural tools used on Joyce but in the work itself. The "excess of meaning" in "Ithaca" is indicative of the play with meaning throughout Joyce's work. This "excess" of Joyce will always provoke new readings, new meanings, new influences, new Joyces. This "excess" will always raise new questions and new answers.

Define Joyce's "excessive" place within world culture. Big question, little answer. Let's ask Alain Robbe-Grillet, the novelist and filmmaker (*L'Immortelle* [1963], *Eden and After* [1971], *La Belle Captive* [1983]):

I admire Joyce's *Ulysses*. But I am persuaded that I do not see more than about a tenth of what Joyce put into the novel. He had a Shakespearean culture, a Catholic culture, an Irish culture, and I see these intersecting at only a few points while he himself was permeated by these three cultures. I fully know that I will never see the wealth of allusions that will, in a single word, draw together Shakespeare, Ireland, and the Catholic religion. But there will always be someone who will see one aspect or other. When a work will have enough readers or spectators, this totality—what Riffaterre has called the arch-reader (or arch-spectator for cinema)—will have, in essence, recovered something close to the totality of the meaning. (Fragola 45)

The twenty-first century will see a further accumulation of Joyce readers moving toward Riffaterre's "arch-reader." But these readers are not confined to the profession of critic; often these readers are artists themselves. Robbe-Grillet's fiction and films are influenced by Joyce's play with narrative; Eisenstein was also a "reader." Alfred Hitchcock saw something else in Joyce; as Donald Spoto has described it, Hitchcock used Joyce as a kind of shocking Rorschach test:

On the desk was a copy of Joyce's *Ulysses*, which Hitchcock casually picked up and opened to a marked page. And then, calmly as if he were reading a news story, he read the notorious toilet scene to his embarrassed secretary, who could not . . . repress her discomfort nor determine why Hitchcock was subjecting her to this odd initiation into the unconventional "new literature." (163)

Bloom's visit to the outhouse provided the background for the first shot of a flushing toilet in mainstream American cinema. Marion Crane performs the deed in *Psycho* (1960) directly before taking her final shower.

Define Joyce's impact on American culture. Joyce rocks. Joyce is an influential figure in American popular culture from the films of Richard Linklater—his first film, *Slacker* (1991), is structured upon the movement of a city in "Wandering Rocks," and his *Waking Life* (2001) is a play within an American dreamworld—to *The Simpsons* (Joyce himself appeared during a St. Patrick's Day parade in Springfield). You can feel Joyce rocking throughout the legacy of Beat literature. The poet Ron Whitehead moves toward Joyce in a poem called "Dublin":

Space. Time. Rhythm. Static. Kinetic. Truth. What is truth? Silence.
Do you know? Movement. Rhythmic movement. What is the shortest distance between two points? Creative distance. How do we move
forward? Imagination? Mysticism? Lies? We move forward by the
aid of symbols and we change those symbols as we move forward.
Who said that? Who is in this dark room with me? Who is standing
by my side? Whispering in my ear? Breathing on my neck? Gig-
gling? Who is laughing? (162)

The traveling voice in the poem opens a window and listens to the Dublin
night: "In the distance I hear the two songs I hear so often: Jimi Hendrix
playing Bob Dylan's 'All Along the Watchtower' and Bob Dylan playing
Bob Dylan's 'All Along the Watchtower.' Where is Jimi Hendrix? Where is
Bob Dylan?" (164). This is the culture of rock playing back upon itself in
the Hibernian Metropolis. This playback begins with Kerouac, who went
in search of his family's roots in *Satori in Paris*:

Of course they all smelled the liquor on me and thought I was a nut
but on seeing I knew what and how to ask for certain books they all
went in back to huge dusty files and shelves as high as the roof and
must've drawn up ladders high enough to make Finnegan fall again
with an even bigger noise than the one in Finnegans Wake, this one
being the noise of the name, the actual name the Indian Buddhists
gave to the Tathagata or passer-through of the Aeon Priyadavsana
more than Incalculable Aeons ago:—Here we go, Finn:—
GALADHARAGARGITAGHOSHASUSVARANAKSHATRA
RAGASANKUSUMITABHIGNA. (33)

Kerouac mixed spirituality with excess and an artistic method drawn from
Joyce ("Telling the true story of the world in interior monolog" ["Belief"
72]). As Kerouac pointed out, Beat writing and Beat culture are the backgrounds for the birth of rock: "Beatles is spelled Beatles and not Beetles"
(*Selected Letters* 404).

Describe any personal connections with this connection between Joyce and
rock. When I was editing *The Doors Companion*, I had the good fortune of
meeting Patricia Kennealy Morrison, the wife of Jim Morrison of the
Doors. She told me that Morrison had been an admirer of Joyce and often
read aloud from his poetry. She also told me that her own reading of Joyce
began in college when she was inspired by a young instructor who set

Joyce's words on fire for her. The college instructor's name was Zack Bowen.

Notes

1. As Phillip Herring describes them in *Joyce's "Ulysses" Notesheets in the British Museum*, the very preparations that Joyce took to write the chapter employed an excess of information and specialized terminology:

His approach . . . required a considerable amount of cribbing from handbooks on mathematics, astronomy, and physical geography. In the "Ithaca" notesheets one finds algebraic equations, calculations for interest on loans, geometric doodling, curious statistics, ciphers, and above all lists of impressive scientific words. Although almost none of these are above the high-school level, many of them are calculated to amuse and confound. As with the notes on embryology, Joyce's mind is continually drawn to the curious and exotic; and where distortion is not inherent in the material, he exaggerates for comic effect. When Joyce exaggerates here, it is usually in one of two ways: either he produces ludicrous results by a *reductio ad absurdum* of scientific method or he parodies scientific prose by the exaggerated use of jargon. The result in both cases is monstrous, but absurdly humorous. (59)

2. For an examination of a lecture Eisenstein gave during this period to his film students about the importance of Joyce, see Tall.

3. See Litz and McGee for discussions of the "subjective" nature of the chapter from two different critical perspectives.

4. In *The Great War: 1914–1918*, Captain Cyril Falls, formally the official British historian of the First World War, breaks through his solid history to write about the Somme: "On nearly half the Allied front and three-quarters of the British there was at most temporary progress. The rest of the story is complete and bloody defeat. Heroic deeds were performed all along the battlefield, but heroism was not enough" (200). And in his classic work on warfare, *The Face of Battle: A Study of Agincourt, Waterloo, and the Somme*, John Keegan calls the offensive a "human tragedy" and goes on to assess its impact on our thinking about the war and his writing of it:

Accounts of the Somme produce in readers and audiences much the same range of emotions as do descriptions of the running of Auschwitz—guilty fascination, incredulity, horror, disgust, pity and anger—and not only from the pacific and tender-hearted; not only from the military historian, on whom, as he recounts the extinction of this brave effort or that, falls an awful lethargy, his typewriter keys tapping leadenly on the paper to drive the lines of print, like the waves of a Kitchener battalion failing to take its objective, more and more slowly towards the foot of the page; but also from professional soldiers. Anger is the response which the story of the Somme most commonly evokes among professionals. Why did the commanders not do something about it? Why did they let the attack go on? Why did they not stop one battalion following in the wake of another to join it in death? (255–56)

5. Ocularcentrism is structured around a powerful metaphor: seeing is truth, seeing is believing, believing is seeing. As the force behind Western metaphysics, ocularcentrism emerges from Plato's cave and colors philosophy, art, and the sciences. For discussions of the hegemony of sight, see Jay and Levin.

6. For details about the Rising and a description of Skeffington's arrest and execution, see Caulfield. As Caulfield notes, there was a private in the Citizen Army named James Joyce. A bottle washer by trade, this rebel Joyce had the distinct pleasure of "liberating" the pub he worked in (63–65).

7. Fairhall's reading of Joyce's interaction with history is an important study of the relationship, and I am indebted to his chapter on Joyce and the Great War (161–213). For an invaluable look at the impact of the Great War on the novel and what he calls "the historical textures of *Ulysses*," see Spoo 120–35.

8. In *Time and Western Man*, Wyndham Lewis negatively associates Joyce's work with the world of the bourgeoisie: "Joyce is the poet of the shabby-genteel, impoverished intellectualism of Dublin. His world is the small middle-class one, decorated with a little futile 'culture,' of the supper and dance-party in 'The Dead'" (75). For a persuasive reading of the importance of bourgeois culture in *Ulysses*, see Benstock.

9. See Bataille 116–29.

10. The subtitle to Barthes's "The Third Meaning" is "Research Notes on Some Eisenstein Stills," and the essay deals specifically with a "new" or "different" kind of meaning provoked by Eisenstein's film text, which "exceeds the copy of the referential motif" (53). This "excess" of meaning is the product of "intellectual cinema," a form Eisenstein said he learned from reading Joyce.

Works Cited

Auerbach, Erich. *Mimesis: The Representation of Reality in Western Literature.* Translated by Willard R. Trask. Princeton: Princeton University Press, 1953.

Barthes, Roland. "The Third Meaning." In *Image-Music-Text,* edited and translated by Stephen Heath, 52–68. New York: Noonday Press, 1977.

Bataille, Georges. "The Notion of Expenditure." In *Visions of Excess: Selected Writings, 1927– 1939,* edited by Allan Stoekl and translated by Allan Stoekl, Carl R. Lovitt, and Donald M. Leslie Jr., 116–20. Minneapolis: University of Minnesota Press, 1985.

Benstock, Bernard. "Middle-Class Values in *Ulysses*—and the Value of the Middle Class." *James Joyce Quarterly* 31 (summer 1994): 439–54.

Budgen, Frank. *James Joyce and the Making of "Ulysses."* Bloomington: Indiana University Press, 1960.

Caulfield, Max. *The Easter Rebellion.* Dublin: Gill and Macmillan, 1995.

Cixous, Hélène. "At Circe's, or the Self-Opener." *boundary* 2, no. 3 (winter 1975): 387–97.

Cross, Tim, ed. *The Lost Voices of World War I.* Iowa City: University of Iowa Press, 1988.

Dickens, Charles. *Bleak House.* New York: Signet, 1964.

Eisenstein, Sergei. *Immoral Memories,* translated by Herbert Marshall. Boston: Houghton Mifflin, 1983.

Epstein, E. L. "Nestor." In *James Joyce's "Ulysses,"* edited by Clive Hart and David Hayman. Berkeley and London: University of California Press, 1974.

Fairhall, James. *James Joyce and the Question of History.* Cambridge and New York: Cambridge University Press, 1993.

Falls, Cyril. *The Great War: 1914–1918.* New York: Perigee Books, 1959.

Flaubert, Gustave. *Bouvard and Pécuchet.* Translated by A. J. Krailsheimer. New York and London: Penguin, 1976.

Foucault, Michel. "Fantasia of the Library." In *Language, Counter-Memory, Practice: Selected Essays and Interviews,* edited by Donald F. Bouchard and translated by Donald F. Bouchard and Sherry Simon. Ithaca: Cornell University Press, 1977.

Fragola, Anthony N., and Roch C. Smith. *The Erotic Dream Machine: Interviews with Alain Robbe-Grillet on His Films.* Carbondale and Edwardsville: Southern Illinois University Press, 1992.

Fussell, Paul. *The Great War and Modern Memory.* London and Oxford: Oxford University Press, 1975.

Gifford, Don, with Robert J. Seidman. *"Ulysses" Annotated: Notes for James Joyce's "Ulysses."* Berkeley and Los Angeles: University of California Press, 1988.

Gilbert, Martin. *The First World War: A Complete History.* New York: Henry Holt and Company, 1994.

Gilbert, Stuart. *James Joyce's "Ulysses."* New York: Vintage, 1955.

Goodwin, James. *Eisenstein, Cinema, and History.* Urbana and Chicago: University of Illinois Press, 1993.

Hemingway, Ernest. *A Farewell to Arms.* London and New York: Penguin, 1970.

———. "In Another Country." In *The Complete Short Stories of Ernest Hemingway.* New York: Charles Scribner's Sons, 1987.

Herring, Phillip. *Joyce's "Ulysses" Notesheets in the British Museum.* Charlottesville: University Press of Virginia, 1972.

Jameson, Fredric. "*Ulysses* in History." In *James Joyce and Modern Literature,* edited by W. J. McCormack and Alistair Stead, 136–48. London: Routledge and Kegan Paul, 1982.

Jay, Martin. *Downcast Eyes: The Denigration of Vision in Twentieth-Century French Thought.* Berkeley and London: University of California Press, 1993.

Keegan, John. *The Face of Battle: A Study of Agincourt, Waterloo, and the Somme.* New York: Vintage, 1977.

Kenner, Hugh. *Ulysses*. Rev. ed. Baltimore and London: Johns Hopkins University Press, 1987.

Kern, Stephen. *The Culture of Time and Space: 1880–1918*. Cambridge: Harvard University Press, 1983.

Kerouac, Jack. "Belief & Technique for Modern Prose." In *Good Blonde and Others*. San Francisco: Grey Fox Press, 1996.

———. *Satori in Paris & Pic*. New York: Grove Press, 1985.

———. *Selected Letters: 1957–1969*. Edited by Ann Charters. New York: Viking, 1999.

Kiberd, Declan. *Inventing Ireland: The Literature of the Modern Nation*. Cambridge: Harvard University Press, 1995.

Lawrence, Karen. *The Odyssey of Style in "Ulysses."* Princeton: Princeton University Press, 1981.

Levin, David Michael, ed. *Modernity and the Hegemony of Vision*. Berkeley and Los Angeles: University of California Press, 1993.

Levenson, Michael H. *A Genealogy of Modernism: A Study of English Literary Doctrine 1908–1922*. Cambridge and New York: Cambridge University Press, 1984.

Lewis, Wyndham. *Time and Western Man*. Edited by Paul Edwards. Santa Rosa: Black Sparrow Press, 1993.

Litz, A. Walton. "Ithaca." In *James Joyce's "Ulysses": Critical Essays*, edited by Clive Hart and David Hayman, 385–405. Berkeley and London: University of California Press, 1974.

Marx, Karl. *The Eighteenth Brumaire of Louis Bonaparte*. In *The Marx-Engels Reader*, edited by Robert C. Tucker. New York: Norton, 1978.

McGee, Patrick. *Paperspace: Style as Ideology in Joyce's Ulysses*. Lincoln and London: University of Nebraska Press, 1988.

Nietzsche, Friedrich. *The Birth of Tragedy and the Case of Wagner*. Translated by Walter Kaufmann. New York: Vintage, 1967.

———. *The Will to Power*. Edited by Walter Kaufmann. Translated by Walter Kaufmann and R. Hollingdale. New York: Vintage, 1968.

Pound, Ezra. "Past History." In *Pound/Joyce*, edited by Forrest Read. New York: New Directions, 1967.

Senn, Fritz. "History as Text in Reverse." *James Joyce Quarterly* 28 (summer 1991): 767–78.

Spoo, Robert. "'Nestor' and the Nightmare: The Presence of the Great War in *Ulysses*." In *Joyce and the Subject of History*, edited by Mark A. Wollaeger, Victor Luftig, and Robert Spoo, 120–35. Ann Arbor: University of Michigan Press, 1996.

Spoto, Donald. *The Dark Side of Genius: The Life of Alfred Hitchcock*. New York: Ballantine, 1983.

Tall, Emily. "Eisenstein on Joyce: Sergei Eisenstein's Lecture on James Joyce at the

State Institute of Cinematography, November 1, 1934." *James Joyce Quarterly* 24 (winter 1987): 132–42.

Valente, Joseph. "Beyond Truth and Freedom: The New Faith of Joyce and Nietzsche." *James Joyce Quarterly* 25 (fall 1987): 87–103.

Wilson, Edmund. *Axel's Castle.* New York: Charles Scribner's Sons, 1931.

Whitehead, Ron. *Beaver Dam Rocking Chair Marathon.* Louisville, Ky.: Wasteland Press, 2002.

Wollaeger, Mark A., Victor Luftig, and Robert Spoo, eds. *Joyce and the Subject of History.* Ann Arbor: University of Michigan Press, 1996.

Dagger Definitions

Translation and Language

Joyce *en slave* / Joyce Enclave

The Joyce of Maciej Słomczyński—A Tribute

Jolanta W. Wawrzycka

Once upon a time, and a communist time it was, there was a Polish translator who worked on *Ulysses*, and that translator made the nicest historical contribution to Poland's literary culture.[1] Why would readers of Joyce in general care to read an essay about a translator? Non-native English language readers of Joyce may find this essay—yet another tiny facet on the disco-ball of the international Joyce industry they help to perpetuate—akin to their own interests. On the other hand, readers of Joyce born into the English (any English) language, reflecting on the floor-to-ceiling apparatus of dictionaries, lexicons, annotations, and encyclopedias that aid their "translation"-riddled activity of reading Joyce, may stay with this essay to catch a glimpse of the workshop of an outsider, a reader-as-translator, a reader-translator. Translation, the ultimate act of close reading and interpretation, partakes in a variety of late twentieth-century postmodern and postimperial phenomena by having engendered theoretical stances that opened venues for re-reading received sociocultural milieus. A trite dictum that all "reading" is, ultimately, translation merits revisiting at the brink of the twenty-first century. This essay, by taking stock of the centrality of translators' efforts—and by paying tribute to one translator's labors—seeks to bring into focus the mechanism that determines the survival and/or demise of translated literary works, while touching as well on the difference between translating what a text *says* and translating what a text *means*.

Contexts: This Translation Theory and the Other Translation Theory

When Sylvia Beach and Sergei Eisenstein agreed to exchange contemporary books in English for the newest Russian writings, she felt disappointed with what she had received: "Judging by what he sent me, nothing particularly important seemed to be appearing in Russia at the time; or perhaps it was *the translations that were lacking"* (Beach 110; emphasis added). This casual pronouncement speaks to Beach's recognition of the profound importance of translators as mediators between cultures, as forgers of writers' reputations, as co-creators (or spoilers) of literary greatness, or, to take it one step further, as "writers"—or "re-writers"—of works of literature in a target language. A crucial factor in the reception of a translated work in the target culture—and Beach's reflection speaks to that too—is the translator's linguistic intuition, which can range from mere skill, to talent, to genius. Were the translators of those Russian books native speakers of Russian who had acquired English, or were they native English speakers with acquired Russian? Would that make a difference? As Fritz Senn reflects, "we do not know what can be reasonably expected of a translation. What are its prime requirements? If principles like correctness, accuracy, internal consistency, preservation of motifs, correspondences, overtones, symbolic superstructures, tone, music, and many others are at variance, as they undoubtedly are, what are the preferences?" (*Dislocutions* 20).

Some or all of these criteria must have triggered Beach's reaction to the books she received, and she surely did not read them in Russian first. There is a rich record of postulates, definitions, and prescriptions published by practicing translators and philosophers of language; of particular benefit to this discussion is a contribution by Roman Ingarden. By defining at least four layers of literary works of art, Ingarden described with considerable precision the possibilities and limits of translation. Briefly, the four strata are: word sounds and phonetic formations; semantic units; represented objects; and schematized aspects. The fact that they coexist in a polyphonic harmony highly limits the degree of fidelity to be achieved in translation, for the process of translation necessarily affects this harmony.[2] For some thinkers, what passes for translation is "a convention of approximate analogies, a rough-cast similitude" (Steiner 77), and for others translation is a "labor of approximation" (Valéry 119). Still, there seems to be a great need for "approximate analogies," for new translations of old classics continue to make headlines in the literary world, and translation studies continue to flourish, all of which points to the fact that, after all, translation is, in Senn's words, "the art of the possible" (20).

Mikhail Bakhtin's claim that "a language is revealed in all its distinctiveness only when it is brought into relationship with other languages," although originally contextualized by his discussion of novelistic hetero-

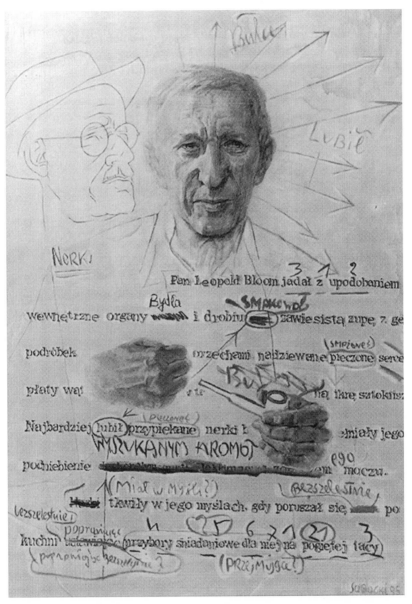

Fig. 7.1. Image of Słomczyński and his translation of the opening of "Calypso."
Painted by Leszek Sobocki. Photographed by Kuba Śliwa. Reproduced with permission of the Słomczyński family.

glossia (411), describes the effects of translators' immersion in the translating process. For translators face the split not only along the "original-
target language" axis but also along the internal axes within them: a variety of original "languages" contained in a translated work and the variety
of the "languages" to be rendered in the target language (one thinks of all
the Englishes in "Cyclops," or "Nausicaa," or "Oxen"). It follows then that
works purged of what Bakhtin calls the "brute heteroglossia" (410) for the
sake of "single-imaged, 'ennobled' language" would present fewer problems in translation—say, works of art produced to advance an ideology, to
conform to demands of censorship, or to excite a variety of feelings (Joyce's
"kinetic art"). In works where "the dialogic nature of heteroglossia is revealed and actualized," says Bakhtin, "languages become implicated in
each other and mutually animate each other" (410): how should translators proceed in rendering that in a target language? What is their task?

After Walter Benjamin tackled these questions in the 1920s, few philosophers of translation dared to dispute his ideas. But, from the practical—translator's—point of view, the high level of abstraction of Benjamin's description of the translator's task appears to be, well,
philosophical. In "The Task of the Translator," Benjamin states that "the
translator's task consists in finding that intended effect which produces in
it the echo of the original" so as to "to release in his own language that
pure language which is under the spell of another, to *liberate the language
imprisoned in a work in his re-creation of that work*" (77; 80–81; emphasis
added). It goes without saying that all translators of literature, and certainly of *Ulysses*, have labored to re-create a translated work in a target
language—though the bellicose metaphors of "imprisonment" and "liberation" can strike one as quite categorical in their presumption of equiva-
lence: they say that there *is* language that *is* imprisoned (encoded?) and *is
therefore* capable of being liberated (decoded?). The Chinese translator of
Joyce, Jin Di, prefers to follow "the principle of closest possible approximation to the overall effect of the original" (Szczerbowski 126), a clever
phrasing that grants translators of "Oxen of the Sun" the right to choose
their own equivalents of "The Wanderer" or designate their own Swifts in
their respective literatures, as they should. Also, for Benjamin, the artist
and the translator are differently motivated in their work: where the
artist's intention is "spontaneous, primary, graphic," the intention of the
translator is "derivative, ultimate, ideational." It is all too easy for Joyce
scholars to dispute this dichotomy, considering that volumes have been
written on Joyce's artistic intentions and workshop: little about Joyce's art

is spontaneous, primary, or graphic (if "graphic" refers to γραφικός, *of* or *for writing*), and everything is derivative, ultimate, and ideational (Joyce was, after all, translator par excellance, working, like Stephen, with an acquired speech). Benjamin differentiates between the aims of translation and of literary work: translation is directed "at language as totality" rather than at "specific linguistic and contextual aspects" (77), another dichotomy that all of Joyce's oeuvre only too obviously obliterates. Finally, Benjamin sees works of literature as being "in the center of the language forest" and translation "on the outside facing the wooded ridge" (77). This evocative metaphor rings true for all Joyce translators who, indeed, more often than not, feel not only outside the wooded ridge but also outside the eye-level fence around that ridge, on the tips of their toes; however, it gives them no tool to cut into that forest. One can proliferate metaphors like that endlessly—Benjamin's essay prompted many such re-readings, including one by Jacques Derrida. Derrida savors those moments in Benjamin's text that address the task of the translator who has to respond to the

> *demand for survival* which is the very structure of the original text. (Notice Benjamin does not say the task of the translation but rather of the translator, that is, of a subject who finds him/herself immediately indebted by the existence of the original, who must submit to its law and who is duty-bound to do something for the original.) To do this, says Benjamin, the translator must neither reproduce, represent, nor copy the original, nor even, essentially, care about *communicating* the meaning of the original. *Translation has nothing to do with reception or communication or information. . . .* Translation augments and modifies the original . . . even as it also modifies the translating language. This process—transforming the original as well as the translation—is the *translation contract between the original and the translating text. . . .* [T]he contract is destined to assure a survival, not only of a corpus or a text or an author but of languages. (122; emphasis added).

Unlike Benjamin's "liberation" metaphor, Derrida's metaphor of "survival," by shifting focus from translator to the process of translating, speaks precisely to the dynamics of linguistic immersion in the process of what I would call *languaging* the original in the target language. Such a process, indeed, "has nothing to do with . . . communication," and if at first this assertion seems baffling, it helps to remember Beach's reaction to Russian translations that apparently communicated nothing to her—

something was at variance in those books. In the process of becoming, those translations failed to modify the target language sufficiently: a well-turned translation "succeeds in promising success" (Derrida 123), by fulfilling the *contract* Derrida speaks of, whereby it is read by target readers as if it were written in their language, with Ingardenian strata or Bakhtinian heteroglossia largely preserved. Derrida's "survival" of translation then, like the original, is predicated on readership—it assures not only the circulation of a translated work but also the survival of literature(s) and language(s).

Among Joyceans, critics such as Rosa Maria Bosinelli have used translation studies effectively as "a critical approach that can contribute to the understanding of a literary work" (quoted in Frehner and Zeller 457).[3] But, more relevantly, Fritz Senn—who has forged his Joyce scholarship on the issues of translation and reading-as-translation—has commented in all of his works on what survives from "Joyce(an)" when it migrates to other languages and on what survives of "Homer(ic)" when it migrates to "Joyce." Concerned that "we rarely trouble to distinguish between reading the original and reading a translation," Senn pointed out as early as 1967 ("The Issue Is Translation" 163) what he reiterated in 1984: that thousands of "readers who do not know English have 'read' *Ulysses* when in fact they have not been exposed to a single word as Joyce wrote it" (*Dislocutions* 4). They rely on the renditions by the translators, who ultimately hold "an awful power" over their captive target audience. For that audience gets only "a complete running commentary of the original," as Senn describes translation (*Dislocutions* 2). And if most translators work, as I suspect they do, under the tacit assumption that translation has everything to do with communication or information (and deal deathly blows to the original by interpreting/determining), how does that assumption change the outcome of their labor? Later in this essay, I discuss some aspects of the Polish "Joyce voice," mindful that translation is a process of "almosting" a translated text by capturing in the target language those language curve balls that Joyce threw to scholars and professors.

The Joyce of Słomczyński

The existence of Joyce in Poland began in the 1920s. The critical interest in Joyce and his works brought sporadic attempts to translate his works into Polish in the 1930s, but they did not fully materialize until the 1950s and

1960s: *A Portrait of the Artist as a Young man* (*Portret artysty z czasów młodości*), translated by Zygmunt Allan, first appeared in Polish in 1937 and was republished in 1957, to be joined in 1958 by *Dubliners* (*Dublińczycy*), translated by Kalina Wojciechowska. A decade later, in 1969, the Polish *Ulisses* was published amid much publicity and critical acclaim for the translator, Maciej Słomczyński, who in 1970, 1972, and 1973 also published translations of *Giacomo Joyce*, Joyce's poetry, and "Anna Livia Plurabelle."[4] In the early 1970s, a "Joyce enclave" of sorts emerged in Poland, a two-faceted cultural phenomenon. On the one hand, there was a "Joyce" in a popular sense, a readily recognizable name of the literary icon of the West and almost a cult figure, for just to own a copy of Słomczyński's 1969 translation of *Ulysses* amounted to a status symbol.[5] On the other hand, "the Joyce of the stage" became a prominent feature of cultural life in Poland, the land of theatergoers, thanks to numerous stage adaptations based on Słomczyński's texts, starting with the 1970 production *Ulisses*, "written by Słomczyński, after Joyce."[6] The impact of theatrical productions could be appreciated by wider audiences owing to coverage in the daily press, in cultural television programs, and in literary magazines. Joyceans in the West were kept appraised of these and other Polish Joyce events through the English-language essays, reports, and reviews in the *James Joyce Quarterly*.[7]

Thus "the Polish Joyce" emerged as the Joyce of/by Maciej Słomczyński, in many respects a genius-translator and in every respect a giant figure in Poland's reception of Anglo-Saxon and American literature, whose death closed a very important chapter of literary history in Poland.[8] Some Joyceans who had met Słomczyński at early Joyce Symposia remember him as a highly energetic and inventive Joyce scholar and translator, but it is important to stress that Słomczyński had also translated a vast array of works ranging from Chaucer to Faulkner to Nabokov.[9] Słomczyński's associates are at work compiling a full bibliography of his works and translations; it will be of interest to other translators, especially because so many Polish sources mention his uniquely phenomenal achievement of translating all of Shakespeare. Słomczyński's landmark translation, however, is *Ulisses*, a monumental achievement that has fixed "Joyce" permanently in the center of the Polish cultural and theatrical avant-garde of the time and for the years to come, given that the stage productions continue to be popular with Polish literary audiences.

But it is important to remember that both *A Portrait* and *Dubliners* have been available in Polish since the late 1950s, and, to date, these are the only full translations of these works available to Polish readers. However, Wojciechowska's *Dublińczycy* and Allan's *Portret* have enjoyed none of the acclaim of Słomczyński's *Ulisses* (which is also partly true of the originals). But before one echoes Sylvia Beach that maybe "it was the translations that were lacking" and speculates whether their reception would have been different had Słomczyński been the translator, one has to consider the political situation of the early communist years in Poland, when a brief cultural thaw of the late 1950s allowed for a momentary relaxation of rules of censorship and for a slew of translations of foreign literature to flood the Polish literary market. It was then that Słomczyński began his work on his Polish *Ulysses*, publishing "Telemachus" in Polish in *Twórczość* (Creativity) magazine in 1958, just as Allan's and Wojciechowska's translations of Joyce's earlier, arguably "simpler" texts appeared on the market (to limited critical attention, one might add). In the 1990s, Słomczyński came full circle and began translating *Dubliners* and *A Portrait*, making a few passages available to Zenkasi Theatre stage productions of Joyce's texts. They were printed for the first time in the 1999 Polish-language collection *Wokół James'a Joyce'a*. Analyzed side by side with translations by Allan and Wojciechowska in the section titled "Contents: This Translation and the Other Translation," they help to determine some aspects of Słomczyński's craft.

The Workshop of the Translator

Słomczyński as a translator published little about his "philosophy of translation." The foreword to his translations of "Circe" published in the Polish literary monthly magazine *Dialog* in 1964 offers an overview of *Ulysses* for the benefit of the Polish reader, but only one paragraph refers to its complexity: "But let us go back to the book itself. In spite of appearances, Ulysses is not an enigmatic book, nor is it multivalent or—difficult. Surely, at times the sense of individual sentences is shrouded by an unusual writing technique, but if one reads Joyce with great concentration (for there is no other way of reading him) one will easily avoid the traps of style and plot which at one time so amused Joyce."[10] Three years later he reiterated his position in a brief statement printed in the 1967 issue of the *James Joyce Quarterly* on translation: "I'm sorry to say that I never found *Ulysses* to be a difficult book. 'Oxen of the Sun' and 'Sirens' gave me some headache but the Polish language is very rich and has great elasticity. Once you get used to *Ulysses* there is nothing mysterious or enigmatic about it" ("Point of View" 236).

Słomczyński's focus on avoiding the "traps of style and plot" and his dismissal of difficulties with *Ulysses* prompt a conclusion that for him translation was roughly a process of transposition of one linguistic surface to the other. The Polish language is, indeed, "very rich and has great elasticity," but that is true of many other languages, differently. In addition, as ćwiąkała reports ("O polskim *Ulisessie*" 178; 182), Słomczyński recorded instances when he worked on *Ulysses* with dizzying speed, translating ten to fifteen pages a day. When he finished his *Ulisses*, he wrote: "The whole translation took 150 days spread over 9 years!"[11] Incidentally, Joyce himself thought that a "translation would take nearer 10 years than 1 year" (*Letters* III 59). Speed might have compromised some of Słomczyński's solutions, for scrutiny reveals a number of mechanical transpositions of lexical units from one language to another that produced, among other results, numerous calques. Some of the most qualified early critics to comment on Słomczyński's translation praised his work, though they also pointed out a number of errors that, indirectly, confirm Słomczyński's method of mechanical transposition.[12] On the whole, however, merits outweigh the errors, and most of the solutions offered by Słomczyński are truly formidable in their ingenious renditions of Joyce's verbal pyrotechnics—one emerges feeling victorious after having successfully hunted down errors in Słomczyński's *Ulisses*.

In 1973, Słomczyński revealed some aspects of his "workshop" when he published an essay, "Klucze odchłani" (The Keys to the Abyss), in the May issue of the Polish literary monthly *Literatura na Świecie* (Literature in the World). The essay, never published in English, wittily dramatizes Słomczyński's numerous attempts to "read" the *Wake* and his search for fragments to "translate" into Polish—he was working on the bilingual volume *Utwory Poetyckie—Poetical Works*—as well as his discovery of the keys to *Finnegans Wake*. As he states in "Klucze odchłani," his decision to translate a fragment of the *Wake* was prompted by

> a simple pride or megalomania, often so eagerly labeled as confidence. For, yes, Joyce is Joyce, but I too can do with my own native language whatever I wish and, after all, one man's masterpiece has to be within the reach of another man. Of course, in the case of *Finnegans Wake* that other man would have to be someone extraordinarily.... Well, extraordinarily what? I didn't even know what superlative [skills] would be necessary and appropriate to do the job.[13]

He continues by evoking his doppelganger, Joe Alex, his "breadwinner" (chlebodawca; 23) and "a friend" (przyjaciel; 27), as he pretends to "imitate" Joe Alex's deductive reasoning in his own search for the keys to the abyss of the *Wake*'s text (27). The essay seems to confirm that for Słomczyński translation (not only of Joyce but also of Milton and Carroll) was a matter of resolving formal issues of language "in the sense of workshop" (w sensie rzemieślniczym; "Klucze" 12): transposing stylistic, semantic, and lexical layers. But, significantly, Słomczyński also constructs an interesting metaphor for translation when he states: "Whereas translated work should resemble a living organism . . . very few people can take note whether the heartbeat of that organism is even or uneven. After all, [a translator's] efforts to find the best language and style [should] actually vanish from the text if the job is well done and therefore [those efforts] will be later almost invisible."[14] Słomczyński's belief that the translator can recreate a text that "lives" in the target language the same way it does in the original (with the translator's effort invisible to the readers) seems to coincide with the purpose behind Chinese translator Jin Di's "principle of the closest possible approximation to the overall effect of the original." Ingarden, however, would be skeptical about the translatability of all four strata of a work of art into another language, for the transfer of "word sounds from one language to another only too often leads to changes in higher order linguistic sound formations. As a result, new disturbances occur in the structure of the work's strata, as well as in their polyphonic harmony" (Ingarden 153). Ingardenian at heart, I would speculate that Sylvia Beach's concern about the translations of Russian writers might have been prompted by some of these disturbances. Or perhaps, in terms of Słomczyński's metaphor of a work's heartbeat, it was the heartbeat she was missing. As to the Polish *Ulisses*, few Polish readers would find it lacking: Joyce's heartbeat is there, although, as I illustrate below, here and there it skips a beat.

Contents: This Translation and the Other Translation

Comments by Polish critics on the merits and defects of *Ulisses* tend to be selective in what they discuss. Most recently, the Polish scholar and critic Tadeusz Szczerbowski, in his *Gry językowe w przekładach Ulissesa*, has presented a more systematic analysis of one particular aspect, the language games in translation.[15] To see how Joyce's voices fare in Polish, I offer below a brief discussion of a few idioms and colloquialisms from "Cyclops" (and from a fragment of "The Sisters") that illustrates how surface reading of Joyce's lexical layer in *Ulysses* can be a trap for translators because it neglects Bakhtinian heteroglossia, upsets Ingardenian polyphonic harmony of the work's strata, and causes arrhythmia in the heartbeat of the Polish *Ulisses*.

The "Cyclops" episode presented Słomczyński with a set of stylistic obstacles that he seems to have underestimated. If the parodistic asides of the chapter are rendered well and if Bloom's Polish voice sounds, well, Bloomian indeed, it is the narrator's distinctly lower-class Dublin jargon that here and there suffers in translation, as well as the voices of all the drinkers in Kiernan's pub. The truism that idiomatic expressions do not travel well across languages is, on the whole, very well defied by Słomczyński: he is frequently highly successful in rendering Irish/English colloquialisms by finding parallel idiomatic expressions in Polish ("the principle of closest possible approximation to the overall effect of the original"). But when Słomczyński nods off, at least two kinds of inaccuracies enter his translation: inventions/erasures/substitutions that—even if carried out in the spirit of Joyce's writing—falsify the original by rewriting it; and calques, which syntactically, stylistically, and idiomatically have no meaning in Polish and falsify Joyce's text with unwarranted inscrutabilities.

Idioms are an obstacle from the start: "I was just passing the time of day with old Troy" (*U* 292) is translated as: "Byłem właśnie o tej porze ze starym Troyem" (*PU* 227). Back-translated, the opening reads as: "I was just at this time with the old Troy," where ordinary Polish obliterates the narrator's idiomatic voice and introduces a calque, "stary," for "old" (which in this case, refers to Troy's age in Polish). Also, the phrase "and be damned but the bloody sweep" ("kiedy nagle, a niech to, jakiś przeklęty kominiarz") back-translates as "when, suddenly, darn it, some cursed sweep." "Damned" is rendered as "a niech to" (an innocent ellipsis meaning something like "darn it," or "oops," "ouch," "heck") and, paired up with "bloody" as "przeklęty" (Polish for "cursed"), does little to introduce the narrator's rather lowly brogue. "Bloody" becomes "cholerny" in the phrase "the most notorious bloody robber" ("najcholerniejszy, najtwardszy łotr," which back-translates as "the bloodiest, the toughest scoundrel"). However, as soon as the bloody mongrel Garryowen appears, "bloody" is translated as "pieprzony," a vulgarism that corresponds roughly to "frigging" when one wants to avoid its stronger counterpart. And if accumulation of "bloody" has a comical effect and betrays the narrator's fear of dogs (for example, *U* 295, 299, 305), the accumulation of "pieprzony" in those same contexts does not really amuse, and it connotes a generalized malevolence. Incidentally, Garryowen's growling, which "would give you the creeps" (*U* 295), "put the fear of God in you" (*U* 299), or "give you the bloody pip" (*U* 305), is rendered in Polish as "że ciarki by cię przeszły" in the first and second (*PU* 229, 232) case, back-translating as "creeps," and in the third case as "mógł człowieka od tego szlag trafić" (*PU* 237), idiomatic in Polish for the kind of fury that makes one lose control or gives one a stroke. Neither "bloody" nor "the fear of God" enters the translation.

"God" is, however, evoked in the Polish text every time the narrator says "gob" and "begob," either as "na Boga" (by God) or as "dobry Boże" (good God). This particular substitution gives the narrator's voice in Polish an altogether different tone than he has in the original. The example below illustrates this shift in tone but also shows the effect of random invention in the face of obscurity in the original: when the narrator hears Bloom defending Boylan[16] as an excellent organizer of Molly's summer tour, he thinks: "Hoho begob, says I to myself, says I. That explains the milk in the cocoanut and absence of hair on the animal's chest" (*U* 319). Because that really explains nothing (Joyce's annotators are silent on the potential allusions here), the translator copes the best he can by rewriting it as follows: "Ho, ho, good God, I am saying to myself internally, oy, I am saying. This explains how he gets the coconuts and why the goat jumps."[17] Now, "cocoanuts" appears in idiomatic Polish in the phrase "robić kokosy" (to get or become rich), but "why the goat jumps" is not an idiom, and the phrase is as enigmatic to the Polish reader as it is funny in back-translation to the English reader.

Another example of rewriting can be observed in the passage where Jack Mooney reportedly threatened Bob Doran for his drinking, and the narrator says, "Gob, Jack made him toe the line. Told him if he didn't patch up the pot, Jesus, he'd kick the shite out of him" (*U* 314), which in Polish reads "God, how Jack made him straight [straightened him out]! He told him that if he doesn't get his act together, he swears by Jesus that he'll tear his legs out of his arse,"[18] the last phrase being idiomatic Polish for beating somebody up. The introduction of Polish "dupa," "arse," gives the Polish phrasing even more vulgar overtones than "kicking the shite" has in the original. In addition, the business of "swearing by Jesus" strikes the Polish reader as odd; when Poles swear by God they use a colloquialism—"jak

Boga kocham" (meaning more or less "as much as I love God")—that, of course, carries no more religious overtones than Joyce's "Jesus" does.

Generally, Joyce's "Jesus" does not fare too well in Polish, mainly because it is not used idiomatically in the same manner. Each time the narrator exclaims "Jesus," Słomczyński translates it as an archaic "na Jezusa," which is not how colloquial Polish would handle that exclamation. Joyce uses "Jesus" roughly in the same manner as Poles would use "Jezu," with the semantic range of the American "gee." When Poles say "Jezu, ale piękne" (gee, how beautiful), they do not mean "na Jezusa, ale piękne" (by Jesus, how beautiful). But Słomczyński opts for that strange-sounding "na Jezusa" (*PU* 266) even when Joyce uses "for Christ's sake" (*U* 342) right before the pub fight breaks out—an unexplainable choice especially since the Polish language has a good equivalent in "na litość boską." One of the few instances when "Jesus" is rendered well in Polish is when the narrator says, "Jesus, full up I was" (*U* 335), "Jezu ależ byłem pełny" (*PU* 261), as he urinates. But many instances of the pub-specific Irish parlance had to be rewritten in Polish: the idiomatic "Could you make a hole in another pint?" (*U* 312) manages to preserve the metonymy but is otherwise rendered as ordinary Polish: "Could you have [could you down] another mugful?" (*PU* 243). The punning answer "Could a swim duck?" (*U* 313) had to be translated simply as "Can a duck swim?"[19] and, alas, makes no sense in Polish. Other instances of slips include such calques as "*Nie bardziej umarł niż ty!*" (*PU* 234) for "He is no more dead than you are" (*U* 301); "*na Boga* powiadam *do siebie*" (*PU* 261) for "*gob* says I *to myself*" (*U* 335); or "*Matka trzymała* burdel" (*PU* 235) for "Mother *kept* a kip (*U* 303), and so on. The last example is problematic because "burdel" (brothel) is stronger than "kip," and because "trzymała" in Polish refers to holding something in your hand, where "prowadziła," if we want to refer to brothel, would benefit the translation here. In effect, one reads Polish words forced into syntactically foreign arrangements that injure the semantic stratum and thus give the Polish text an aura of strangeness nonexistent—at least in those cases—in the original.

Until the late 1990s, Słomczyński's translations could not be studied in the context of other translations of the same texts, with the exception of the "Calypso" episode that was published side by side with a pre–World War II translation of the same episode by Józef Czechowicz.[20] However, the publication of his recent translations of a few passages from *A Portrait* and from *Dubliners* gives an alternative sound to the Polish Joyce. In the case of *A Portrait*, the only fragments available in the volume *Wokół James'a Joyce'a* are the passages from the retreat ("kazanie," or "sermon"), and they are as superb in Słomczyński's translation as they are in the original. There is a puzzling avoidance on the part of the Polish Father Arnall to address the boys as "boys"—Słomczyński has "moi drodzy," as well as "moi mili" (my dear ones) (Bazarnik and Fordham 269) where Joyce writes "my dear boys" (*P* 110) twice—but since the text was translated for the stage and directs an actor to point to the audience, the address, one supposes, had to be generalized. However, when the boys are asked to banish their "worldly thoughts," the Polish reader is misled by the "*światowe* myśli" (that is, thoughts pertinent to the *world*), where in fact "*świeckie* myśli," that is, *lay* thoughts, are to be relinquished. Allan's translation avoids these errors and is equally powerful in forging in Polish the images evoked by the retreat's sermon.

From *Dubliners*, Słomczyński translated a fragment from "The Sisters" with the Polish title "Czuwanie," meaning "Vigil," which presents a conversation between "Aunt Nannie" and "Aunt Eliza" as they hold a vigil by Father Flynn's coffin. What strikes the Polish reader about the conversation is the language that the two women use: their Polish is a mix of good, flowing language and of strangely forced unnatural syntactical constructs very different from those devised by Joyce to betray Eliza's social status and lack of education. Departures from standard Polish in Słomczyński's translation consist of transpositions of English idiomatic colloquialisms directly into Polish—those calques again—which give one the impression of reading a working draft, with the original roughed out in the target language but never really polished up.

Calques can result in mistranslations and affect meaning. For instance, Eliza says: "Only for Father O'Rourke I don't know what we'd have done at all" (*D* 16). Wojciechowska preserves the semantic range by rendering this faithfully as "Gdyby nie ojciec O'Rourke, nie wiem jak dałybyśmy sobie radę" (*PD* 11). Słomczyński introduces a slight change ("Żeby nie ojciec O'Rourke, sama nie wiem *czy byśmy w ogóle coś zrobiły*" [Bazarnik and Fordham 272]), and we hear Eliza say, "Only for Father O'Rourke, I don't know myself *if we would have done anything at all.*" Senn reminds us that "translators' errors too may serve as useful portals of discovery" (*Dislocutions* 6), for anagnostically, one wants to look back at the sisters and their reliance on Father O'Rourke more closely. One also wants to consider again the meaning of the following remark by Eliza: "Ah, there's no friends like the old friends, she said, when all is said and done, no friends that a body can trust" (*D* 16), because the Polish translators render this fragment differently. To begin with, there is a perfect Polish idiom about old friends (nie ma to jak starzy przyjaciele), which, though it operates on different syntactical wave, as most idioms do, makes a translator's job here easy; Słomczyński opts for a literal transposition of the English idiom, however, which makes my back-translation read quite well: "Ah, there are no friends such as the old friends, *to tell all the truth*. There are no other friends that one can trust."[21] In addition, the translator's interpretive choice influences the meaning of the second part of Eliza's remark, because the idiomatic "when all is said and done" has vanished from his Polish version to be replaced by a calque, "żeby już powiedzieć całą prawdę," from "all truth be told." Thus, in Słomczyński's translation, Eliza comments on the old friends as *the only* friends one can trust. In Wojciechowska, the semantic range of the second phrase changes: "Ah, there is no friends like the old friends, she said. But when all is finished, even they cannot help."[22] The two translations rendered opposing meanings in Polish—and the original suddenly does not help either. To resolve the ambiguity of Eliza's statement, one has to decide whether only old friends count when all is said and done, or whether, when all is said and done, there are no friends to trust. This rhetorical ambiguity is ontologically redundant. As for Joyce, he offers no parachute; he is busy paring his fingernails.

As the examples above indicate, some valuable lessons can emerge from studying translators' choices and translation-as-close-reading by the native English speakers. Benjamin considered translation to be a *mode*, and the original, a *source* containing "the law of translation: its translatability," which connects the original with the translation (Benjamin 72). "Duty-bound to do something for the original," as Derrida says, the translators of Joyce submit to that law as they navigate through textual pitfalls, in pursuit of the Sennian "art of the possible," and minding the minefields of heteroglossia inherent in language. It could never be doubted that the Polish translator of *Ulysses* felt for the heartbeat of Joyce's masterpiece to render it in Polish as he soared and erred in the process of negotiating the perilous traps of idiom and style. As a result, the Polish translation of *Ulysses*, though a bit arrhythmic, goes a long way to preserve Joyce's heartbeat. Sylvia Beach could never find it wanting.

Notes

1. This study is dedicated to the memory of the Polish translator of *Ulysses,* Maciej Słomczyński, who died on March 21, 1998. I'd like to express my gratitude to Fritz Senn of the Zürich James Joyce Foundation for materials on Słomczyński. I'm equally grateful to Polish scholars Katarzyna Bazarnik, Zdzisław Kudelski, and Tadeusz Szczerbowski for sending me their publications and numerous other Polish sources, and to Wojciech Słomczyński who, through Katarzyna Bazarnik, made Słomczyński's bibliography available to me.

2. In "On Translation," Roman Ingarden offers a thorough theoretical analysis of translation as he delineates differences in translating works of literature and scholarly/philosophical works. Whereas the latter would emphasize lexical and semantic precision and aim at cognition, translation of the former requires, in addition, a thorough attention to aesthetically relevant dimensions as it aims at preserving the polyphonic interstratum harmony (see Ingarden, esp. 313–52, 177–84)

3. For similar preoccupations, see also Wawrzycka, "Text at the Crossroads," in Bosinelli and Mosher.

4. *Giacomo Joyce* first appeared in Polish in *Twórczość* magazine in 1970; it was reprinted in 1972 in a bilingual volume of *Utwory poetyckie—Poetical Works,* which also includes *Chamber Music, Pomes Penyeach,* "Ecce puer," *Epiphanies,* as well as three fragments from *Ulysses* and two from *Finnegans Wake.* A thorough review of the volume by Jadwiga Ćwiąkała-Piątkowska, Słomczyński's secretary and aid from 1963 to 1966, was published in 1973 in *Literatura na Świecie,* and the same issue also carried the first Polish publication of "Anna Livia Plurabelle." In addition, in 1971 Słomczyński published his translation of Stanislaus Joyce's *My Brother's Keeper* as *Stróż brata mego.*

5. For an overview of Poland's literary scene and initial reception of the Polish *Ulisses,* see Ćwiąkała in the *James Joyce Quarterly.*

6. In 1971, the readers of the *James Joyce Quarterly* were treated to Zbigniew Lewicki's and Daniel Gerould's detailed account of "*Ulysses* in Gdansk," a tour de force theatrical undertaking based on Słomczyński's dramatization of Joyce's novel. As the authors put it, "This extraordinary success for a work that seems impossible for the stage is due in large part to Słomczyński's genius in turning Joyce's novel into a highly original stage play in its own right, even for those totally unacquainted with the novel, while at the same time remaining remarkably faithful to Joyce. Although all the episodes and almost all the dialogue (with the exception of a few simple explanatory remarks identifying characters) are Joyce's, Słomczyński's *Ulysses* is not an adaptation of the novel but rather is a new work built out of Joyce's words. The program states that the play is 'written by Słomczyński, after Joyce,' and in fact, the whole theatrical conception and new arrangement of material are the work of Słomczyński" (Lewicki and Gerould 100). See also Lewicki in *Literatura na Świecie.*

7. Besides Lewicki and Gerould, see also Rocco-Bergera and Sullivan. For other mentions of Słomczyński's thought, see Leo Knuth. Słomczyński's presence in

Joycean publications includes the 1967 reprint of his translation of the opening of "Proteus" in the *James Joyce Quarterly* 4 (1967): 238–39. Also, the premiere issue of the *James Joyce Literary Supplement* carried at the back the replica page of Słomczyński's rendition of the fragment of *ALP*, and a note titled "Plurabelle in Polish." See the last page of *JJLS* (May 1987).

8. Joyce scholars in the West knew him for his translations, but few Joyceans knew that he began as a poet and writer of children's literature, or that, as "Joe Alex," he was a best-selling author of quite sophisticated detective novels (which, under communism, generated income to cover the costs of his brief sorties to the West), or, finally, that he authored film scripts, radio plays, and television programs. When I still lived in Poland, I remember seeing a witty television program featuring Maciej Słomczyński and "Joe Alex" (with one of them—it must have been Joe Alex—in the shadow) as the "two authors" talked about art and literature.

9. Upon Słomczyński's death, a note by Katarzyna Bazarnik of Kraków's Jagiellonian University appeared in the *James Joyce Broadsheet*, titled "In Memoriam Maciej Słomczyński." Bazarnik states: "Apart from Joyce, [Słomczyński] translated all of Shakespeare (apparently the only man in the world to do so), Chaucer, Milton, Lewis Carroll, Barrie's *Peter Pan* books, Nabokov, and some of Blake's poems" (Bazarnik 4). Słomczyński's daughter, Małgorzata Słomczyński-Pierzchalska, has just published a biography of her father, *Nie mogłem być inny. Zagadka Macieja Słomczyńskiego* (I Couldn't Have Been Any Different: The Mystery of Maciej Słomczyński). Kraków: Wydawnictwo Literackie, 2003.

10. "Ale wróćmy do samego utworu. Wbrew pozorom, *Ulisses* nie jest książką ani enigmatyczną, ani wieloznaczną ani—trudną. Oczywiście, chwilami sens poszczególnych zdań bywa zawoalowany przez dość niezwykłą technikę pisarską, ale ktokolwiek zechce czytać Joyce'a ze skupioną uwagą (a inaczej w ogóle nie da się go czytać), ominie z łatwością zasadzki stylu i pułapki konstrukcyjne, które niegdyś tak bawiły autora" (*Dialog* 21).

11. "Cały przekład zajął mi 150 dni rozrzuconych przez 9 lat!" Ćwiąkała (Bazarnik and Fordham 182)

12. For instance, Polish professors of English and linguistics Grzegorz Sinko and Elżbieta Muskat-Tabakowska and professor of comparative literature Jerzy Paszek have written about Słomczyński's translation errors: Sinko listed about two dozen instances of "Anglicisms" and borrowings that sound particularly foreign, artificial, or plain wrong in Polish (59–60); Muskat-Tabakowska pointed out the mistranslation of the "french letter" that Molly knows Bloom to carry in his pocketbook, which Słomczyński rendered literally as a "letter in French" (that error has been corrected in the 1992 edition of *Ulisses*) (147), and Paszek pointed out that "Madam I'm Adam" is perfectly reproducible in Polish as "Madam a jam Adam" and not as "Kobyła ma mały bok," which means "A mare has a small side" (129).

13. "A pchała mnie zwykła pycha czy megalomania, tak chętnie nazywana wiarą we własne siły. Że niby Joyce Joycem, a przecież ja też potrafię zrobić z własnym ojczystym językiem, co zechcę i w końcu dzieło jendego człowieka musi przecież leżeć

w zasięgu innego człowieka. Oczywicie, w wypadku *Finnegans Wake* ten inny człowiek musiałby być kim niezwykle. . . . Właśnie, niezwykle jakim? Nie wiedziałem nawet, jake superlatywy byłyby konieczne i stosowne do wykonania tej pracy" ("Klucze" 13–14).

14. "Ale chociaż tłumaczenie powinno przypominać organizm . . . bardzo niewielu ludzi potrafi zauważyć, czy serce tego organizmu bije równo czy nierówno. Zresztą wszystkie próby znalezienia najwłaściwszej struktury języka i stylu nikną i roztapiają się w tekście, jeżeli praca jest przeprowadzona jak należy, i w związku z tym są później niemal niedostrzegalne" ("Klucze" 12–13).

15. This polyglot study analyzes aspects of translations of *Ulysses* into sixteen(!) languages. A much-needed English-language review of this book is in the works.

16. His name in Polish is translated as "Bujny," a masculine adjective whose meaning ranges from "exuberant, rich, abundant, bushy, fertile, lush" to "gross, rampant, wanton."

17. "Ho, ho, dobry Boże, powiadam ja sobie w duchu, oj, powiadam. To wyjaśnia na czym robi takie kokosy i czemu kózka skacze" (*PU* 248).

18. "Boże, jak Jack go wyprostował! Powiedział mu że jak się nie poprawi, to klnie się na Jezusa, że mu nogi z dupy powyrywa" (*PU* 244).

19. "Czy mógłbyś łyknąć jeszcze kufelek? Czy kaczka umie pływać?" (*PU* 243).

20. *Literatura na Świecie* 5 (1973): 242–67.

21. "Ach nie ma takich przyjaciół jak dawni przyjaciele, *żeby już powiedzieć całą prawdę*. Nie ma innych przyjaciół, którym człowiek może zaufać" (Bazarnik and Fordham 272).

22. "Ach, nie ma to jak starzy przyjaciele, powiedziała. Ale kiedy już wszystko się skończy, wtedy i oni nie mogą nic pómoc" (*PD* 11).

Works Cited

Bakhtin, Mikhail. *The Dialogic Imagination.* Translated by Caryl Emerson and Michael Holquist. Austin: University of Texas Press, 1981.

Bazarnik, Katarzyna. "In Memoriam Maciej Słomczyński." *James Joyce Broadsheet* 50 (June 1998): 4.

Bazarnik, Katarzyna, and Finn Fordham. *Wokół James'a Joyce'a.* Kraków: Universitas, 1999.

Beach, Sylvia. *Shakespeare and Company.* New York: Harcourt, Brace, 1959.

Benjamin, Walter. "The Task of the Translator." In *Theories of Translation,* edited by Rainer Schulte and John Biguenet, 71–82. Chicago: University of Chicago Press, 1992.

Bosinelli Bollettieri, Rosa Maria. "'Who is she when she is not at home?': Molly's Journey through the Italian Language and Culture." In *A Collideorscape of Joyce. Festschrift for Fritz Senn,* edited by Ruth Frehner and Ursula Zeller, 444–60. Dublin: Lilliput Press, 1998.

Bosinelli Bollettieri, Rosa Maria, and Harold F. Mosher Jr. *ReJoycing: New Readings of "Dubliners."* Lexington: University Press of Kentucky, 1998.

Ćwiąkała-Piątkowska, Jadwiga. "Joyce in Poland." *James Joyce Quarterly* 9 (fall 1971): 93–98.

———. "Poezja Joyce'a." *Literatura na Świecie* 5 (1973): 269–78.

———. "O polskim Ulissesie." In *Wokół James'a Joyce'a*, edited by Katarzyna Bazarnik and Finn Fordham, 175–84. Kraków: Universitas, 1999.

Derrida, Jacques. *The Ear of the Other: Otobiography, Transference, Translation.* Lincoln: University of Nebraska Press, 1988

Frehner, Ruth, and Ursula Zeller, eds. *A Collideorscape of Joyce. Festschrift for Fritz Senn.* Dublin: Lilliput Press, 1998.

Ingarden, Roman. "On Translations." Translated by Jolanta W. Wawrzycka. *Analecta Husserliana* 33 (1991): 131–92.

Joyce, James. "Anna Livia Plurabelle." Translated by Maciej Słomczyński. *Literatura na Świecie* 5 (1973): 43–53.

———. *Anna Livia Plurabelle.* Translated by Maciej Słomczyński. Kraków: Wydawnictwo Literackie, 1985.

———. "Czuwanie" [fragment of "The Sisters"]. In *Wokół James'a Joyce'a,* edited by Katarzyna Bazarnik and Finn Fordham, 272–74. Kraków: Universitas, 1999.

———. *Dubliners. Text, Criticism, and Notes.* Edited by Robert Scholes and A. Walton Litz. London: Penguin, 1976.

———. *Dublińczycy.* Translated by Kalina Wojciechowska. Warsaw: Oskar, 1991. This translation of *Dubliners* is identified in text citations by the abbreviation *PD*.

———. *Giacomo Joyce.* Translated by Maciej Słomczyński. *Twórczość* 7/8 (1970): 103–11.

———. "Kazanie" [fragment of *A Portrait*]. In *Wokół James'a Joyce'a,* edited by Katarzyna Bazarnik and Finn Fordham, 269–70, 283–85. Kraków: Universitas, 1999.

———. "Polish: The Opening of the Proteus." Translated by Maciej Słomczyński. *James Joyce Quarterly* 4 (spring 1967): 238–39.

———. *Portret artysty z czasów młodości.* Translated by Zygmunt Allan. Bydgoszcz: Pomorze, 1992.

———. *Ulisses.* Translated by Maciej Słomczyński. Revised and corrected by the translator. Bygdoszcz: Pomorze, 1992. This translation of *Ulysses* is identified in text citations by the abbreviation *PU*.

———. "*Ulisses:* Epizod piętnasty, Circe." Translated by Maciej Słomczyński. *Dialog* 12 (1964): 20–90.

———. "*Ulisses:* Rozdział pierwszy [Telemachus]." Translated by Maciej Słomczyński. *Twórczość* 3 (1958): 40–56.

———. *Ulysses.* New York: Vintage, 1961.

———. *Utwory poetyckie—Poetical Works.* Bilingual edition. Translated by Maciej Słomczyński. Kraków: Wydawnictwo Literackie, 1972.

156 Jolanta W. Wawrzycka

———. "*Ulisses* (fragment [Calypso])." Translated by Maciej Słomczyński. *Literatura na Świecie* 5 (1973): 242–66.

———. "*Ulisses* (fragment [Calypso])." Translated by Józef Czechowicz. *Literatura na Świecie* 5 (1973): 242–67.

Joyce, Stanislaus. *Stróż brata mego.* Translated by Maciej Słomczyński. Warsaw: Państwowy Instytut Wydawniczy, 1971.

Knuth, Leo. "The *Finnegans Wake* Translation Panel at Trieste." *James Joyce Quarterly* 9 (winter 1971): 266–69.

Lewicki, Zbigniew, and Daniel Gerould. "*Ulysses* in Gdańsk." *James Joyce Quarterly* 9 (1971): 99–116.

Lewicki, Zbigniew. "Sceniczny *Ulisses* Słomczyńskiego." *Literatura na Świecie* 5 (1973): 219–40.

Muskat-Tabakowska, Elżbieta. "The Polish Translation of James Joyce's *Ulysses* and Some Underlying Problems." ZNUJ (Zeszyty Naukowe Uniwersytetu Jagiellońskiego). *Prace Historycznoliterackie* 24 (1972): 141–56.

Paszek, Jerzy. *Sztuka aluzji literackiej: Żeromski, Berent, Joyce.* Katowice: Uniwersytet Śląski, 1984.

Rocco-Bergera, Niny. "*Ulysses* by Joyce in a Modern Performance at Palazzo Grassi in Venice." *James Joyce Quarterly* 3 (spring 1972): 397–99.

Schulte, Rainer, and John Biguenet. *Theories of Translation.* Chicago: University of Chicago Press, 1992.

Senn, Fritz. *Dislocutions: Essays on Reading as Translation.* Edited by John Paul Riquelme. Baltimore: Johns Hopkins University Press, 1984.

———. "The Issue Is Translation." *James Joyce Quarterly* 4 (spring 1967): 163.

Sinko, Grzegorz. "*Ulisses* jakim go mamy." *Miesięcznik Literacki* 7 (1970): 53–61.

Słomczyński, Maciej. "Klucze odchłani." *Literatura na Świecie* 5 (1973): 4–41.

———. "Od tłumacza" [foreword to translation of "*Circe*"]. *Dialog* 12 (1964): 20–24.

———. "Point of View." *James Joyce Quarterly* 4 (spring 1967): 236.

Steiner, George. *After Babel. Aspects of Language and Translation.* New York: Oxford University Press, 1992.

Sullivan, Philip B. "Anna Livia in West Berlin." *James Joyce Quarterly* 15 (winter 1978): 184–85.

Szczerbowski, Tadeusz. *Gry językowe w przekładach 'Ulissesa' James'a Joyce'a.* Kraków: Instytut Języka Polskiego PAN, 1998.

Valéry, Paul. "Variations on the Eclogues." In *Theories of Translation,* edited by Rainer Schulte and John Biguenet, 113–26. Chicago: University of Chicago Press, 1992.

Wawrzycka, Jolanta W. "Text at the Crossroads: Multilingual Transformations of James Joyce's *Dubliners.*" In *ReJoycing: New Readings of "Dubliners,"* edited by Rosa Maria Bosinelli Bollettieri and Harold F. Mosher Jr., 68–84. Lexington: University Press of Kentucky, 1998.

The Rebirth of Heroism
from Homer's *Odyssey* to Joyce's *Ulysses*

Keri Elizabeth Ames

Safe!

(*U* 8.1193)

There she found Odysseus among the bodies of the murdered, splattered with blood and gore like a lion who comes from devouring an ox from a farm; and his whole chest and his cheeks on both sides are covered with blood, and he is dreadful to look upon, just so had Odysseus been splattered, his feet and his hands above.

(*Od.* 22.401–6)

So Leopold Bloom in Joyce's *Ulysses* is delighted to escape confronting his wife's lover, Blazes Boylan, by turning into the National Library, whereas in Homer's *Odyssey* the nurse Eurykleia discovers Odysseus after he slaughters Penelope's suitors standing fearsome and awesome (δεινός), drenched in blood like a lion who has just finished eating.[1] Odysseus has already killed so many suitors that "the whole floor flowed with blood" (*Od.* 22.309), and his house must be washed and purged with sulfur before he can reunite with Penelope (*Od.* 22.437–94). In contrast, Bloom chooses to return silently to a marriage bed befouled by his wife Molly's sexual encounter with Blazes Boylan:

What did his limbs, when gradually extended, encounter?

New clean bedlinen, additional odours, the presence of a human form, female, hers, the imprint of a human form, male, not his, some crumbs, some flakes of potted meat, recooked, which he removed. (*U* 17.2122–25)

Such a pitiful cuckold seems like the antithesis of Homeric heroism and Joyce's proof of its demise. So, at first glance, Joyce's depiction of heroism appears to supersede Homer's entirely: the extraordinary victor has become an ordinary victim.

Yet perhaps this position only allows us to dismiss the significance of Joyce's title too precipitously, for in his notes to his only play, *Exiles,* Joyce observes, "Since the publication of the lost pages of *Madame Bovary* the centre of sympathy appears to have been esthetically shifted from the lover or fancyman to the husband or cuckold" (*E* 150). With the choice of his title *Ulysses,* Joyce focuses upon precisely this problem. Just as Molly has become the adulteress Penelope is not, so Bloom has become the cuckold Odysseus could never be. Yet if we consider the possibility that such contradictions between the Blooms and their Homeric counterparts do not simply serve to present a parody of the Homeric intertext invoked by Joyce's title, a remarkable convergence between Joyce's and Homer's conceptions of love and heroism emerges.[2] The obvious contradiction between Penelope's chastity and Molly's adultery can be reconciled to a certain degree with the acknowledgment that both marriages are fraught with ambivalence and infidelity.[3] In the same vein, how might the heroism of the cuckold in *Ulysses* and the heroism of the avenging husband in the *Odyssey* depend upon the same heroic virtues? One answer may be found in the way in which Homer's and Joyce's uses of the word "hero" (ἥρως) function to create and confirm a remarkably similar meaning of heroism, thus endowing Joyce's title with great resonance.[4] Let us then explore the idea that certain instances in which Homer and Joyce use the word "hero" (ἥρως) serve to define one particular kind of heroism that Odysseus and both attain.[5]

We first encounter the word "hero" (ἥρως) in the *Odyssey* in the context of divine aid and wrath, a context that reveals what constitutes this sort of heroism. Athena has just sprung into action on behalf of Odysseus, after receiving Zeus' permission to help him return home: "So she spoke, and beneath her feet she bound beautiful sandals, immortal, golden, which bore her over both the deep waters and the boundless land with the breath of the wind. And she seized her strong spear, tipped with sharp bronze, heavy, huge, and stout, with which *she overpowers the ranks of hero-men* (ἀνδρῶν ἡρώων) whoever are the kind that tend to anger her, that daughter of an oh-so-powerful father" (*Od.* 1.96–101; emphasis added).[6] Being a hero, the audience learns here, is the task of a man. Previously, the word "hero" is quite noticeably absent from the proem (*Od.* 1.1–10), where Homer initially refers to Odysseus only as a man without even mentioning his name, accentuating his humanity and his masculinity rather than his heroic status: "Tell for me the man, muse" (*Od.* 1.1). We next find the words "man" (ἀνήρ) and "hero" together in the genitive case, with the grammatical effect of denoting "a connection or dependence between two words.... The substantives may be so closely connected as to be equivalent to a single compound idea" (Smyth 314). I justify my hyphenation of "hero-men" based upon the interdependence Homer's grammar accentuates, emulating how Smyth hyphenates his examples. By inextricably binding up his first use of "hero" with "man" in the grammatical sense, Homer announces that his heroes are definitively not gods, but ordinary mortal men who quiver and suffer beneath the gods' wrath.

Hero-men must cope with force, symbolized by Athena's spear. For Athena does not only come to the aid of hero-men like Odysseus; she frequently subdues them (δάμνημι) with her spear when they anger her. Homer's use of an aorist subjunctive (κοτέσσεται [*Od.* 1.101]) implies that her anger is customary (Stanford, *Homer* 218). By introducing his hero-men as those who suffer from habitual divine wrath, Homer implies that they cannot avoid being mastered by the gods. The hero-men beneath the spear exemplify the complexity of the heroic task: Homer's heroes face the double task of knowing when to suffer patiently the forces beyond their control and when to use the force at their disposal for their own benefit. Heroic endurance depends upon negotiating a very delicate balance between accepting what cannot be changed and fighting to alter what can be changed. Joyce gestures toward this idea in the "Scylla and Charybdis" section with an incredible economy of words: "Act. Be acted on" (*U* 9.979). This duality encapsulates the heroic task in the *Odyssey* and *Ulysses*. Just as Athena controls hero-men with the force of her spear, so hero-men must control their own forces, the desires of the heart (θυμός), in order to endure.[7] Hero-men must resist being entirely overcome by external forces while overcoming the forces that emanate from within. As hero-men, their challenge, and the test of their endurance, is taming themselves.

By presenting this image of Athena in conjunction with his first use of the word "hero," Homer portrays a kind of heroism to which every human being can aspire, and in which every human being alive can and must participate. Everyone faces the task of controlling desire (θυμός) while suffering forces beyond one's control. Because suffering itself, regardless of its source, provides the opportunity for human distinction, even the most ordinary person has the same chance of becoming heroic as an epic warrior does. R. Havard comments upon the chances of attaining such heroism: "Pain provides an opportunity for heroism; the opportunity is seized with surprising frequency" (Lewis 157). Extraordinary endurance within ordinary human life lends this heroism its special quality. Since rising to the challenges of suffering is its only imperative, one can qualify for this sort of heroism just as easily in Dublin in 1904 as in ancient Ithaca, or in the United States in the twenty-first century. Still, such heroism is ordinary only because it is possible for ordinary people in any time and place. It requires a strength that is quite extraordinary.

The first person upon whom Homer bestows the title "hero" epitomizes the demands and requirements of such an ordinary brand of heroism. Athena names him while speaking to Telemachus, after arriving at the home of Odysseus, disguised as Mentor: "Our fathers were guest-friends from long ago, which you would learn if you just go and question *old-man-hero-Laertes*, who, so they say, no longer comes to the city, but far away in the fields suffers pains, together with an old woman servant, who puts out food and drink for him, once exhaustion has seized his limbs as he struggles to move up the hill of his vineyard" (*Od.* 1.188–93; emphasis added). Surprisingly, Laertes is much like Bloom, suffering pitifully without any obvious resistance to his plight. Later, Penelope begs for the suitors' patience until she can finish "a funeral shroud for Laertes-hero" (*Od.* 2.99), while the goat-herd Melanthius holds "an old, stout shield, speckled with rust, the one belonging to Laertes-hero, which he would always carry during his youth" (*Od.* 22.184–85). Young Laertes used to fight in battle. Now, like his rusty shield, he is old and worn, leading Thomas Falkner to suggest, "Like the dusty shield . . . Laertes' heroic abilities are hidden from sight. . . . in spite of his age, Laertes retains his heroic ability" (45, 46). By endowing Laertes with the title "hero" on these occasions, Homer emphasizes that heroes can be old, decrepit, and unquestionably vulnerable to suffering and death, but no less heroic for that condition. He portrays how hero-men bravely extend their mortal existence with every effort.

Other old fellows are worthy of the appellation "hero" as well. Aegyptius is also infirm: "Among them then Aegyptius-hero was the first to speak, who was bent with old age and whose wisdom was past measure" (*Od.* 2.15–16). Like Laertes, he is bent (κυφός) by old age, but not broken. Homer manages to include the reason why Halitherses is a hero at the same time as he overtly names him as such: "Then among them spoke old-man-hero-Halitherses, son of Mastor, for he alone excelled all of his contemporaries in knowledge of bird omens and in speaking according to fate" (*Od.* 2.157–59). Far beyond anyone else, Halitherses knows the pain the future holds. As the last hero explicitly titled in the poem, Halitherses cautions the families of the suitors about the consequences of the suitors' recklessness, imploring them to shun violence (*Od.* 24.454–62). Halitherses is named a hero while counseling restraint, not vengeance, stressing how crucial self-control is for this kind of heroism. Such temperance, along with great perseverance, earns hero-men a considerable degree of respect.

Hence Homer's actual use of the word "hero" refutes the idea that heroism is connected to the transient vitality of youth usually presumed to be one of its immutable requirements.[8] Homer's extension of the idea of heroism to include elders raises endurance to the same status and prestige as more traditionally heroic actions like battle. The youthful, martial heroism of the *Iliad* has thus been transcended and replaced with a new brand of heroism in the *Odyssey*, as Falkner observes: "Where the *Odyssey* differs from the *Iliad*, with regard to old age as with so much else, is in reformulating and even redefining the nature of heroism and heroic values" (35).[9] In the *Odyssey*, Homer's use of the word "hero" betrays how endurance itself has become a worthy form of heroism.

Homer's language further expresses how Laertes' extraordinary endurance distinguishes him as a hero. When Odysseus goes to the orchard to greet his father upon his return home, he finds Laertes gardening, digging dirt around a plant while "πένθος ἀέξων" ("fostering his pain") (*Od.* 24.231). This verb "ἀέξω" literally means to increase, but it can also mean to foster, nourish, exalt, glorify, grow, or help to flourish or blossom (Liddell and Scott; Cunliffe). The verb describes crops thriving with rain (*Od.* 9.111, 9.358), waves rising (*Od.* 10.93), Telemachus growing (*Od.* 13.360, 22.426), and the day waxing toward noon (*Od.* 9.56). Eumaeus uses it to characterize how the gods reward labor and make his efforts prosperous (*Od.* 14.65, 66; 15.372). It seems like a very odd verb to apply to one's pain until we recognize what it connotes: the heroic embrace of the pain that fate and the gods inflict upon us. Laertes makes his pain bloom, just as a gardener tries to make a plant bloom. For Laertes relishes his suffering just as he relishes life. He cherishes his pain not because he is a masochist and enjoys suffering, but because he has no other options if he wants to survive. Since he has not yet found any remedy for the triple wound of losing his only son and his wife and being besieged by the suitors, he must persevere. For Homer, Laertes is heroic because he keeps struggling to live just as he struggles to inch through his orchard. He values life no matter how agonizing living has become. By naming him as the first hero in the poem, such endurance is presented as a kind of heroism.

Remarkably, Homer and Joyce each name Odysseus and Bloom directly as their heroes in the context that best illustrates what this heroism of endurance comprises: the context of earning homecoming. Bloom receives the title "our hero" in the "Eumaeus" section, when he finally decides to return home with Stephen: "I propose, *our hero* eventually suggested after mature reflection while prudently pocketing her photo, as it's rather stuffy here you just come home with me and talk things over. My diggings are quite close in the vicinity" (*U* 16.1643–45; emphasis added). Bloom is proposing that he and Stephen seek homecoming (νόστος), while our narrator is proposing that Bloom deserves to be accepted as our hero. We may be inclined to interpret this naming ironically or sarcastically, but Bloom is truly "our hero" when he is rescuing Stephen at the same time as he is rescuing himself. "After mature reflection," he tries to withstand the pain of Molly's adultery, pocketing her old picture and his memories along with any rancor. Bloom, like Laertes and Odysseus, refuses to give up on life and on love, resolved in his belief that "talking things over" at home is the best possible course of action.

With striking similarities, only once in the *Odyssey* is Odysseus named a hero directly. While he is telling the story of his endurance to the Phaeacians, Odysseus describes how Kirke told him to travel to the rock in Hades where the two rivers meet, the very edge of death itself. Then he quotes her next instructions: "There and then, *hero*, draw near, just as I order you and dig a pit of a cubit on each side, and around it pour a libation to all of the dead. . . . and then right away the prophet [Teiresias], leader of the people, will approach you, and he will tell you your way and the extent of your journey and your return [νόστος]" (*Od.* 10.516–18, 538–40; emphasis added). Kirke addresses Odysseus as a hero when he is attempting to return home by gaining and following this advice from Teiresias: "Still, despite everything, you may yet return, even though suffering many evils, if you resolve to restrain your desires and those of your companions [αἴ κ᾽ ἐθέλῃς σὸν θυμὸν ἐρυκακέειν καὶ ἑταίρων], as soon as you shall bring your well-benched ship to the isle of Thrinacia, fleeing the violet sea, and grazing there find the cattle and good flocks of Helios" (*Od.* 11.104–9). Teiresias warns Odysseus that only through self-restraint will he accomplish his homecoming to Ithaca. As Kalypso confined Odysseus in her caves (ἐρύκω) (*Od.* 1.14), so Odysseus must curb his own desire (θυμός) so as not to devour the oxen of the sun. Again the utter duality of Odysseus' task cannot be ignored: as he was being restrained, he must also restrain himself. He must resist enough to restore his agency but must still resist any reckless impulses. Thus Kirke names Odysseus a hero while sending him to Hades to learn the importance of the self-restraint, patience, and determination that Bloom displays when he pockets Molly's photo and invites Stephen home.

Odysseus previously erred in this effort, for he is not the perfect hero in perfect control of himself. He sometimes fails to master his own desires and passions (θυμός), and the context in which Kirke names him a hero also calls attention to his inconsistency in this regard. Barely a hundred lines earlier, Eurylochus has accused him of having lost his men to the Cyclops through his own recklessness (*Od.* 10.431–37), recalling how Odysseus' comrades were reputed to have destroyed themselves in the same way by eating the oxen of the sun and how Halitherses condemns the suitors' folly (ἀτασθαλίη) (*Od.* 1.7, 10.437, 24.458). Odysseus stifles the urge to kill him (*Od.* 10.438–45), and Kirke invites the men to stay, claiming that they need to seize desire (θυμός) in their chests again, because so much suffering has made them withered (ἀσκελής) and without desire (ἄθυμος) (*Od.* 10.456–65). Desire has dried up and shriveled, like a plant without water, and now requires cultivation. So they remain with Kirke, feasting and drinking wine, until Odysseus' men caution him to remember his home (*Od.* 10.466–74). Up to this point, Odysseus forgets his own return for an entire year, so busy and content is he cultivating and satisfying his heart (θυμός)! Even though he then takes full credit for his decision to leave, never alluding to his comrades' intervention when he announces to Kirke: "My heart (θυμός) is now eager to go, as are those of my comrades" (*Od.* 10.484–85), we the audience witness how his ability to control himself wavers.

Only in this context, the context of the crisis of controlling desire (θυμός), does Kirke call Odysseus a hero. The location of his heroic naming stresses the quality that fuels Odysseus' endurance and characterizes his heroism: the willingness and the self-control to endure pain. Joyce names Bloom "our hero" at the same kind of critical juncture. For Bloom too has hesitated about returning home, thinking, "Go home. Too late for *Leah. Lily of Killarney*. No. Might be still up" (*U* 13.1212–13). Bloom delays his own return on purpose until Molly will be asleep, while Odysseus forgets his return while luxuriating with Kirke. Both then proceed to accomplish homecoming by following the advice that Odysseus gives to Aias in Hades, precisely the sort of advice that Odysseus himself previously received from Teiresias: "Subdue your passion [μένος] and your daring spirit [θυμός] δάμασον δὲ μένος καὶ ἀγήνορα θυμόν]" (*Od.* 11.562). Notably,

Odysseus uses the verb "δαμάζω," meaning to tame, master, control, which correlates very closely with the verb "δάμνημι," which conveys how Athena overpowers hero-men with her spear (*Od.* 1.100; see Liddell and Scott; Cunliffe). Heroes must treat desire (θυμός) in the way Athena treats men with her spear, once again highlighting the duality of the heroic task in trying to subdue one's internal forces while being threatened by external ones. Only the proper balance between initiative and submission makes homecoming possible.

Odysseus further clarifies the nature of this task to Telemachus when they are plotting revenge against the suitors, counseling him to resist his urge to intercede too soon: "Even if they insult me within the house, still let the dear heart [κῆρ] endure in your breast while I am suffering evilly" (*Od.* 16.274–75). Father and son agree upon the nature of their task of endurance, so Telemachus responds, "Father, most certainly, I think in time to come you will know my heart [θυμός], for no weakness at all has a hold on me" (*Od.* 16.309–10). Earlier, Telemachus described how passionate wrath rose within him while desiring revenge against the suitors ("ἀέξεται ἔνδοθι θυμός") (*Od.* 2.315). But as the suitors insult his disguised father, he increases his own pain rather than yielding to his desire, enabling him to abstain from immediate action and plot revenge in silence as his father requested ("μέγα πένθος ἄεξε") (*Od.* 17.489ff.). During the bow contest, Homer is careful to inform us that Telemachus frustrates his desires by restraining himself: "Three times he made it [Odysseus' bow] quiver with his strength [βίη], hoping in his heart [θυμός] to string the bow and shoot an arrow through the iron. And now, finally, trying to pull it on the fourth try, he would have strung it with his strength [βίη], but Odysseus shook his head and held him back, even as eager as he was" (*Od.* 21.126–29). At his father's silent command, he sacrifices his own success, relying upon his strength to conceal itself rather than exhibiting it. Valuing patience over bold and brazen initiative, he masters himself accordingly through the fierce control he exercises over his force (βίη) and his passions (θυμός). Telemachus shares with his grandfather and father the ability to foster his pain and control his desires, rather than engaging in self-destructive behavior.

Joyce is admittedly somewhat ironic in his depiction of this kind of Homeric heroism, but not in such a way that relegates heroism to meaninglessness. His narration of how Bloom acts "heroically" mocks Homer's conception of ordinary heroism in the *Odyssey* at the same time as he justifies its worth. His parody of heroism functions to confirm its persistence in a new form, not to render it null and void. Consider this example from the "Eumaeus" section, after Bloom fails to hail a ride, the only time in *Ulysses* in which the word "heroically" appears:

> This was a quandary but, bringing common sense to bear on it, evidently there was nothing for it but put a good face on the matter and foot it which they accordingly did. So, bevelling around by Mullett's and the Signal House which they shortly reached, they proceeded perforce in the direction of Amiens street railway terminus, Mr Bloom being handicapped by the circumstance that one of the back buttons of his trousers had, to vary the timehonoured adage, gone the way of all buttons though, entering thoroughly into the spirit of the thing, he *heroically* made light of the mischance. (*U* 16.31–39; emphasis added)

Here is nurturing pain ("πένθος ἀέξων") in more absurdity than we could have imagined. Bloom remains undaunted by a lost button, while Odysseus and Laertes remain undaunted by nineteen years of misery! Yet despite Joyce's switch from the epic to the comic, Bloom does bear up bravely and patiently, exactly like his Homeric predecessors, despite the contrast in their circumstances. The heroic thing for Bloom to do is to endure—not to whine or complain, nor to try to find a safety pin with which to effect a repair. Bloom is heroic because he refuses to be discouraged. By subscribing wholeheartedly "into the spirit of the thing," he resigns himself to his bad luck that his button has "gone the way of all buttons." Like Laertes, he accepts the necessity of his own suffering. Like Odysseus, he returns home handicapped by mischance, but with great determination, refusing to be deterred by anything.

Of course, the most significant pain that Bloom suffers on Bloomsday is Molly's sexual betrayal. That the button has gone the way of all buttons means only a little embarrassment. But Bloom does not want his wife to go the way of all wives, so to speak, and leave him. The pain that he cherishes is the pain of cuckoldry. Bloom accepts the pain that loving Molly inflicts upon him rather than trying to escape from it by getting divorced. Joyce captures the various ramifications of this decision when Bloom kisses his wife's rump in bed, thinking, "Divorce, not now" (*U* 17.2202). Bloom is impressively forgiving and desperately pathetic as he tries to save his home and his marriage. Yet the patience that sustains Bloom and fuels his efforts to save his home mirrors the same patience with which Odysseus salvages his home. Despite the violence with which Odysseus finally punishes the suitors, that triumph operates through the self-restraint that preceded it. Only by waiting patiently and preparing shrewdly for the right moment will he be victorious, as Athena impressed upon him beneath the olive tree: "So endure even by necessity, and tell no one of them all, neither man nor woman, that you have come back after your wanderings, but in silence suffer many pains, submitting to the force [βίη] of men" (*Od.* 13.307–10). Bloom has exercised exactly that sort of restraint by deciding to return home with Stephen in tow. "Prudently" pocketing his wife's photo (*U* 16.1644), he reins in his emotions, what Homer would name desire (θυμός), for the sake of his homecoming. Still preserving his self-control, he later brushes out of his bed without a word the potted meat that Molly and Boylan shared (*U* 17.2125) in an impressive display of "equanimity" (*U* 17.2155, 2177, 2195). Joyce names Bloom "our hero" (*U* 16.1643) when he is exhibiting the virtues of restraint and patience that Odysseus learned in Hades and from Athena beneath the olive tree. Bloom is described as acting "heroically" (*U* 16.38) when he is relying upon the silence and forbearance Odysseus also exercises in order to restore his home, ignoring the wounds to his dignity.

Given this congruence, Homer's *Odyssey* and Joyce's *Ulysses* both depict a very ordinary kind of heroism at the same time as they portray an extraordinary way to triumph. In avowing that "Joyce wrote *Ulysses* about a new kind of hero, an ordinary hero. In a way, so did Homer. . . . Like Odysseus, if Bloom is to be a hero, he must find a new kind of heroism" (Nelson 63, 79), Stephanie Nelson is observing how the *Odyssey* reformulates the heroism of the *Iliad*. Consequently, the ordinary kind of heroism that Joyce's *Ulysses* represents is not an invention by Joyce at all, but an embrace of the kind of heroism depicted in the *Odyssey* and an implicit rejection of the heroism depicted in the *Iliad*. Odysseus and Bloom are the same kind of ordinary human hero who triumphs through extraordinary endurance. Odysseus, an extraordinary hero in an extraordinary situation, endures by very ordinary means, controlling his impulses. Bloom is in an ordinary situation, yet he endures in an extraordinary way by the same ordinary means. Despite Joyce's objection that "A writer . . . should never write about the extraordinary. That is for the journalist" (*JJ I* 470), his focus upon the ordinary unveils how the extraordinary is not only hidden within the ordinary but emerges from it.[10] Any ordinary mortal can aspire to the heroism of endurance, but only extraordinary ones can achieve it. The endurance of heroism between the *Odyssey* and *Ulysses* is demonstrated by the heroism of endurance, exemplified by Laertes, Odysseus, Telemachus, and Bloom.

So, in a complex intertextual echo, Joyce portrays how Bloom remains an unconquered hero like Odysseus despite his humiliations. To this end, Lenehan makes this pronouncement about Blazes Boylan: "See the conquering hero comes" (*U* 11.340). Blazes is the conqueror who ravishes Molly and makes the Blooms' connubial bed jingle on Bloomsday. But that is only part of the story, for, "Between the car and window, warily walking, went Bloom, unconquered hero. See me he might" (*U* 11.341–42). Again Bloom prefers to avoid any encounter with Boylan, as he has already done earlier at the National Library. Bloom's tactics of evasion while "warily walking" may seem disgraceful when compared to ancient standards, yet in the modern context, they reflect the degree to which his patience, perseverance, and self-restraint enable him to preserve his home. Joyce exploits his contrasting uses of the word "hero" to prove how extraordinary and impressive Bloom actually is even when coping with such a degrading situation.[11]

Bloom's choice to avoid confrontation with his wife or with her suitor on Bloomsday and thus to acquiesce impassively to being cuckolded may seem antiheroic, but the choice to avoid struggle is often Odysseus' best strategy as well.[12] As Pietro Pucci remarks, the "choice—to do nothing— seems *implicitly* the best thing to do. . . . the posture of endurance emerges repeatedly as the solution Odysseus embraces, it being the more advantageous for his survival and protection" (74–75). In both cases, our hero-men seem less than admirable, mostly because, as Pucci concedes, "'enduring' necessarily implies survival, and so a questionable form of heroism" (49).[13] This skepticism about the merit of such heroism may be countered by the acknowledgment that the qualities promoting such endurance are commendable. For the manner of Bloom's reentry into bed names those qualities and establishes why he is much more like Odysseus than we first imagined possible.

How?

With circumspection, as invariably when entering an abode (his own or not his own): with solicitude, the snakespiral springs of the mattress being old, the brass quoits and pendent viper radii loose and tremulous under stress and strain: prudently, as entering a lair or ambush of lust or adders: lightly, the less to disturb: reverently, the bed of conception and of birth, of consummation of marriage and of breach of marriage, of sleep and of death. (*U* 17.2114–21)

Bloom returns to his bed with the same degree of self-discipline and caution with which Odysseus returns home: "with circumspection . . . solicitude . . . prudently . . . lightly . . . reverently," Odysseus' return in disguise, his testing of Penelope, and his decision to unveil himself to his son and recruit his help in killing the suitors all occur in a similar manner and by a similar method as Bloom's return to bed. But Odysseus' rage at the suitors has become so suppressed in Bloom that he manifests it only with the flick of the wrist with which he cleans off his sheets and with his private condemnation, "Is there anything more in him that they she sees? Fascination. Worst man in Dublin" (*U* 6.201–2). As Bloom counsels himself over his tormenting thoughts about Molly's affair—

> Touch. Fingers. Asking. Answer. Yes.
> Stop. Stop. If it was it was. Must. (*U* 8.591–92)

—he resigns himself to the pain of her infidelity as necessity because he "must," much as Odysseus accepts his hunger on Thrinacia and his humiliation by the suitors while in disguise.

Bloom, however, refrains from inflicting pain on others as punishment or revenge, as Odysseus and Telemachus relish during the slaughter (*Od.* 22.171–93, 462–77). Violence for Bloom is not an option: "Duel by combat, no" (*U* 17.2201–02). Herein lies one instance of a "revelation of the irreducible differences" that Wolfgang Iser finds an inevitable result of Joyce's Homeric intertext (Iser 200). Still, both Odysseus and Bloom prevail due to their extraordinary patience and capacities for self-restraint. Joyce employs the word "hero" in *Ulysses* to endorse this sort of heroism portrayed in the *Odyssey*, even as he purposely transforms how such heroism is expressed in a new place and time. *What* Bloom endures in *Ulysses* is very different from *what* Odysseus endures in the *Odyssey*, but *how* they endure is the same. As with Odysseus, Bloom's patience and self-control generate his endurance, an endurance that constitutes a particular kind of heroic excellence and that makes homecoming possible. So, while the expressions of enduring heroism have changed between the *Odyssey* and *Ulysses* due to the modern context, the meaning of this kind of heroism has not. For this reason, Joyce's conception of heroism simultaneously revolutionizes Homer's conception and reinforces it.

This insistence upon enduring and remaining unconquered despite enormous sufferings unites the Homeric and Joycean conceptions of hero-ism. Homer's inclusion of the title "hero" at the point when Odysseus is about to visit Hades while still alive draws attention to his choice to remain mortal and heroic, joining his father in embracing suffering. Kalypso of-fered Odysseus immunity from suffering, aging, and death: "I told him I would make him without death and old age for all his days" (*Od.* 5.135–36), she confides to Hermes. But in spite of Kalypso's admonition that if he knew the extent of his future suffering, he would stay with her (*Od.* 5.206–10), Odysseus aspires to become an old-man-hero who dies at home, gently, out of the sea, as Teiresias predicts (*Od.* 11.134–37), accept-ing suffering, old age, and death as the necessary prerequisite of his heroic glory. Odysseus' absolute refusal to yield in this regard causes him to en-dure like a hero instead of living like a god, because accepting the invulner-ability of immortality would mean the death of his humanity and of his heroism. Life, suffering, and death are the horizons of heroism for Homer; to try to escape them is to lose any eligibility for heroism. For this reason, Jean-Pierre Vernant insists that accepting Kalypso's offer is the equivalent of rejecting heroism: "Sharing divine immortality in the nymph's arms would constitute for Odysseus a renunciation of his career as an epic hero" (188). Homer's gods enjoy a transcendence of time that heroes cannot share. As Jasper Griffin confirms, "If the hero were really godlike, if he were exempt, as the gods are, from age and death, then he would not be a hero at all" (92–93). Kalypso's offer therefore presents Odysseus with a choice of deaths: the death-in-life of immortality, or a heroic death in Ha-des. His choice lends veracity to Dean Miller's conclusion that "Death therefore *is* the limit—the *only* limit—the hero accepts without demur" (383–84).

Heroic endurance thus requires an extraordinary will to live and the tenacity to welcome suffering until a fully inevitable death arrives. Joyce's fascination with the hero's need to endure life's pain until a fully fated and inevitable death arrives is borne out by his notes. Two passages of the *Od-yssey* cited in Joyce's notes, "Od. XI.118.130–XXIII.250.275" (Herring 28), betray Joyce's attention to Odysseus' decision to endure pain until his fated death. Joyce notes Teiresias' prediction to Odysseus: "You will make them [the suitors] pay the penalty for their violence [βίη] when you come home" (*Od.* 11.118); and Odysseus' pronouncement to Penelope: "Hereaf-ter there are still countless toils, many and difficult, which I must complete in full" (*Od.* 23.249–50). The rest of both citations detail Odysseus' next journey, wandering until he finds the man who calls his oar a winnowing fan, at which point he must plant it in the ground and make offerings to Poseidon. Only then can he return home for good. Joyce's notations comprise his recognition that Odysseus must punish the suitors and then leave home again to finish the full measure of his suffering. Joyce's notice of the lines in the *Odyssey* establishing why Odysseus' homecoming is only temporary alerts us to a curious and crucial connection between Bloom and Odysseus. They share the same need to endure suffering as they try to return home, knowing they must only leave again. After all, every new day in Dublin is a new journey, regardless of who prepares breakfast. Despite the banality of that daily departure, love always seems to require another return in both texts. Homecoming is not a single, discrete task, but a constant and continual effort.

In that endeavor, why do Odysseus and Bloom sustain the will to live? They may very well have learned from the examples of their parents' failure to do so. That Bloom's father Virag is a suicide is no surprise, but Odysseus' mother, Antikleia, is not typically categorized as one. She is normally described as dying of a broken heart. Why is she too a suicide, and in whose opinion? In Hades, Odysseus asks her what fate of sad death overwhelmed her (δαμάζω) (*Od.* 11.171ff.). She attributes her death to her longing for the extraordinary kindness of heart of her son, his unmatched ἀγανοφροσύνη (*Od.* 11.203, a full *hapax legomenon*): "Nor did the sharp-sighted archer attack me in my halls with gentle arrows and kill me, nor did any sickness come to me, such as the wretched wasting away that removes the spirit [θυμός) from the limbs. No, it was longing for you and for your advice, shining Odysseus, and for your kindheartedness [ἀγανοφροσύνη] that stole my honey-sweet will to live [θυμός]" (*Od.* 11.198–203). Death conquers Antikleia because she cannot master her own desires. She later enumerates how death ensues once desire (θυμός) has left the bones: "For the sinews no longer keep the bones and flesh together, and the strong force of the blazing fire destroys them, as soon as the spirit [θυμός] leaves the white bones behind, and the soul [ψυχή] like a dream, floats away, to hover and drift" (*Od.* 11.219–22). In death, Antikleia details the cause of her own death. She explains that the pain of her yearning for her son was so strong that it erased her will to live, forcing Odysseus to confront the fact that death is often the consequence of failing to control desire (θυμός).

Moreover, Antikleia recognizes that Laertes is managing to endure what she could not, telling Odysseus, "[your father, Laertes] lies grieving in the orchard and nurtures great pain [πένθος ἀέξει] in his heart, longing for your return" (*Od*. 11.195–96). Unlike her husband, who is able to endure his agonies, her longing for her son kills her, leading to Joyce's judgment in his notes that her death is tantamount to suicide: "Antikleia dies of grief (suicide)/ Laertes goes to country" (Herring 15). Joyce also wrote "Suicide 15.356" and beneath it, "Sisyphos—Anticleia" (Herring 30). Antikleia failed to endure her pain, whereas Laertes and Sisyphos submitted to its necessity. In the passage Joyce cites, Eumaeus tells the disguised Odysseus, "Laertes still lives, but he is always praying to Zeus that his spirit [θυμός] may pass away from his limbs in his halls. For relentlessly he grieves for his absent son, and for his lawful and respected wife, whose death agonized him most of all and brought him to old age before his time" (*Od*. 15.353–57). Joyce specifically marks *Od*. 15.356, the line in which Laertes grieves most of all for Antikleia, the only place in the *Odyssey* where the depth of his grief for his double loss of wife and son is emphasized. He is so devastated by losing his beloved wife that he wishes for death, but he nonetheless renounces suicide and tolerates his agony. Joyce's consideration of Eumaeus' description of the extent of Laertes' grief justifies the suspicion that Joyce intended to emulate Homer's focus upon the need to endure grief from the loss of loved ones. *Ulysses* demonstrates how Joyce learned the same lessons that Odysseus did from Teiresias and Antikleia in Hades, and that he appreciated their implications for the meaning of heroism.

　　Odysseus, like his father, succeeds where his mother failed. Bloom too succeeds, but where his father failed.[14] Virag and Antikleia died for the same reason: grieving for a lost beloved. Bloom remembers finding his father after his suicide and ponders what death incites: "No more pain. Wake no more" (*U* 6.365). Virag's suicide note states that life has ceased to hold any attraction for him in his grief: "it is no use Leopold to be . . . with your dear mother . . . that is not more to stand . . . to her . . . all for me is out" (*U* 17.1883–85). Choosing to commit suicide is the ultimate failure of this kind of ordinary heroism that extends and values human life above all else. Virag seems to have made that choice by poisoning himself: "Verdict: overdose. Death by misadventure" (*U* 6.363–64, see also 6.529). His note indicates that he sought his own death for the sake of joining his wife, while Antikleia just pined away until she died.

　　Love, then, has the power to kill in *Ulysses* and in the *Odyssey*. As Bloom muses, "Poor papa too. The love that kills" (*U* 6.997). The pain that belongs to love killed Virag and Antikleia. Neither one can recover from grief, and so the loss of love kills them. Stephen has not yet experienced the pain of love: "Pain, that was not yet the pain of love, fretted his heart" (*U* 1.102). But the pain that has not yet become the pain of love for Stephen is fully in bloom for Bloom, Virag, Odysseus, Antikleia, and Laertes. Recalling Stephen's declaration that "*Amor matris*, subjective and objective genitive, may be the only true thing in life" (*U* 9.842–43), we wonder how to interpret the pain of love. No one has any love for pain in the objective genitive sense. But Bloom and Odysseus do feel the pain that belongs to love, in the subjective genitive sense. They know that to survive love's pain, they must follow Laertes' example. Only by cultivating pain ("πένθος ἀέξων") can they resist succumbing to death. Treasuring pain has become another part of treasuring life. The insistence of Laertes, Odysseus, and Bloom upon the value of living and loving is the hallmark of their heroism.

By the standards of the heroism of endurance, Virag is no hero. Heroes are supposed to save lives, not end their own. Ironically, given the title of Joyce's *Stephen Hero*, Joyce relies upon Stephen to protest that he is not a hero at all for this very reason, telling Buck Mulligan, "Out here in the dark with a man I don't know raving and moaning to himself about shooting a black panther. You saved men from drowning. *I'm not a hero, however.* If he stays on here I am off" (*U* 1.60–63; emphasis added). Because the only life Stephen is trying to save is his own, he maintains that he is no hero. But by this measure, Odysseus is not a hero either, because as the only hero to come home, in the end he saves only himself. After all, Odysseus is the hero who does not even try to save drowning men! Instead, when Zeus strikes their ship with a thunderbolt after his men have eaten the oxen of the sun, he paces their sinking ship and watches his men drown: "Like sea crows they were tossed upon the waves around the dark ship, and the god stole from them their homecoming" (*Od.* 12.418–19). No examples of altruistic, heroic rescue like those to which Stephen avers are enacted by Odysseus in the *Odyssey*. In the *Odyssey* and *Ulysses*, heroism first requires saving one's own life, not sacrificing it for the sake of others.

Exposing such complexities in the notion of heroism, while insinuating that heroism may actually be much more ordinary, and even more pitiful or contemptible than one normally presumes it to be, was likely one of Joyce's aims in selecting his novel's title. Joyce's words to his brother Stanislaus reveal that heroism was not a universal ideal he sought to embrace and glorify, but an illusion he sought to dispel: "Do you not think the search for heroics damn vulgar—and yet how are we to describe Ibsen? . . . I am sure however that the whole structure of heroism is, and always was, a damned lie and that there cannot be any substitute for the individual passion as the motive power of everything—art and philosophy included" (*Letters II* 80–81). Setting aside the problem of Ibsen here, Joyce's notion of heroism as a lie veiling the potency of a single individual's capacities is borne out by Homer's *Odyssey*. The prominence Homer gives to the power of desire (θυμός), and the hero's need to master it and yield to it at the right moments, constitute exactly the individual motive power to which Joyce alludes. For in some sense, Odysseus, the victor of the Trojan War who devised the stratagem of the Trojan horse, gives up on the "damn vulgar" search for heroics in the *Odyssey* for the sake of simply surviving and returning home. Odysseus is both victor and victim as he seeks homecoming. Thus, by creating a conception of heroism fraught with ironies, tensions, and contradictions, the *Odyssey* demands the reconsideration and revision of its own premises.[15] Both Homeric poems critique the very notions that they depict, simultaneously accomplishing the presentation and the revision of those notions. Joyce's *Ulysses* engages in the same struggle with traditional heroic values, assuming the same posture of self-reflexivity, self-critique, and self-contradiction, exposing why "the whole structure of heroism is, and always was, a damned lie." Heroism deconstructs itself in the *Odyssey* and in *Ulysses* by discrediting the lie that only the extraordinary is heroic. In both texts, heroism is ordinary and extraordinary at the same time, without becoming entirely ineffable or incommensurable.

The preceding inquiry thus confirms Hugh Kenner's suspicion that Odyssean and Ulyssean heroism might somehow intersect in the realm of meaning in spite of the undeniable contrasts in its forms: "Was Odysseus perhaps a Bloom perceived through Ionic hexameters? . . . is this 1904 Ulysses perhaps the same man, reclad in circumstance as also in headgear and idiom? In Homer he seems different, very; may we say, though, thanks only to parallax?" (Kenner, *Ulysses* 106). Of course, Bloom shares Kenner's preoccupation with parallax, wondering, "what's parallax?" (*U* 8.578). Joyce provokes his readers to ask the same question about heroism, having imposed parallax on heroism itself by transplanting the story of homecoming into a new cultural and historical context. In so doing, Joyce has not subverted Homer's heroism but given it a new birth in a new guise. His readers must resort to the patience and perspicacity of Bloom and Odysseus if they are to appreciate the rebirth of heroism in Dublin. Yet from the stance of patience and endurance, there is no heroic parallax whatsoever between the *Odyssey* and *Ulysses*. Bloom is Ulysses is

Odysseus, who "would somehow reappear reborn above delta . . . and after incalculable eons of peregrination return" (*U* 17.2019–20).

Notes

1. I thank Morris Beja, Wendy Doniger, Paul Friedrich, John Gordon, David Grene, Ellen Carol Jones, Patrick McCarthy, Stephanie Nelson, Fritz Senn, and Anthony C. Yu for their comments on earlier versions of this essay. All quotations are from the Greek text of Homer's *Odyssey*, edited by T. W. Allen. All translations are mine. Citations refer to book and line number.

2. Ezra Pound first called Joyce's Homeric correspondences simply "a scaffold, a means of construction" (406). Most recently, Morton Levitt argues that *Ulysses* "makes use of Homer only as an aspect of its parody and social satire, in order to demonstrate the inversion of mythic values in modern times" (32, 53), joining the general consensus proclaimed by Richard Madtes that "little is to be gained from a study of Homeric references" (30; see Ames, "Convergence" 1–11, for a review of the literature). Like Constance Tagopoulos, who disputes how "Joyce scholarship has termed the Homeric parallels in *Ulysses* incomplete, idiosyncratic, and noninstrumental to the work" (184) in her study of return, disguise, and recognition in the two texts, I seek to affirm the value of intertextual reading of the *Odyssey* and *Ulysses* by establishing how their glaring divergences conceal the same brand of heroism, thus beginning to nullify Kenner's old but still valid complaint: "That the fundamental correspondence is not between incident and incident but between situation and situation, has never gotten into the critical tradition" (*Dublin's Joyce* 181).

3. Therefore, despite the gender switch of the adulterous partner, *Ulysses* can be understood to affirm Homer's depiction of "real love . . . between married folk" (*U* 16.1385–86) in a new time and place. For my full argument concerning why Molly and Penelope should both be viewed as faithful wives in loving marriages, see Ames, "Oxymoron."

4. While Homer's use of epithets and formulae may have depended more upon metrical expedience than any intentional pattern, it is intriguing to contemplate how certain words complement the contexts in the poem in which they occur. Alice Radin makes a compelling case for why Homer's repetition of a single, apparently inconsequential word can connote enormous meaning through its context: "Homer limits the temporal conjunction ἦμος . . . to link a proverbial, time-reckoning event to an event that is actually happening within the narrative . . . the clause derives its meaningfulness from a view of time as cyclical. In Homer, ἦμος always connects a recurring point in cyclical time to a specific moment in the linear narrative" (293). I submit that Homer uses the word "hero" (ἥρως) to great effect as well, inserting it at moments that express the special kind of heroism he is depicting in the *Odyssey*.

5. Homer uses "hero" (ἥρως) forty times in the *Odyssey*, while Joyce uses "hero," "heroine," and its adverbial and adjectival forms twenty-seven times in

Ulysses. An exhaustive analysis of all such uses lies beyond the scope of the present inquiry but can be found in "Convergence."

6. Only here in the *Odyssey* does Athena ever wield her own spear. A. P. David noted to me that shortly thereafter Telemachus puts her spear in a rack, where it rests with Odysseus' abandoned spears for the entire poem, never to be mentioned again (*Od.* 1.120–29; personal conversation, the Committee on Social Thought at the University of Chicago, June 5, 1998). Athena's spear watches over the action of the household, just as it hovers over the actions of men, unacknowledged but everpresent.

7. Caroline P. Caswell superbly explores how the semantic range of θυμός creates "approximations in meaning which range from 'soul' to 'anger,' but it is clear that these words do not adequately express what was intended by the Greek" (1). I offer various translations in this essay for the sake of conveying its depth of meaning, in concurrence with Caswell's claim that "the uses of θυμός are so varied, covering almost every important aspect of human experience, that it seems possible only to translate each occurrence as is fitting to that passage without attempting consistency" (1).

8. Falkner discusses how the *Odyssey* depicts another kind of heroism that does not depend upon victory in battle nor upon youth: "While the word ἥρως in Homer may not be age-specific, heroism clearly means youthful heroism. . . . there is within the heroic line of Laertes a rich agricultural tradition, one characterized specifically as an alternative to heroic warfare" (30, 43). Homer's valuation of heroes beyond the bloom of youth perhaps contributed to the evolution in the meaning of heroism in ancient Greece discussed by Douglas Adams: "The Greek words [hero (ἥρως) and Hera ('Ηρα)] can now be seen as the regular outgrowth of an important Indo-European cultural emphasis on youthful vitality. This cultural perspective had lost some of its power in the classical Greek polis but had still been very much alive in the heroic age" (177). Further, see Adams and Mallory 362ff., and Frisk 644ff.

9. For more on classical attitudes toward old age, see Falkner and deLuce, eds.

10. David Hayman comments that Joyce "has managed to show the extraordinary as a quality of the ordinary" (17), while Richard Ellmann speaks of Joyce's "need to seek the remarkable in the commonplace" (*JJII* 156). For Ellmann, "Joyce's discovery, so humanistic that he would have been embarrassed to disclose it out of context, was that the ordinary is the extraordinary" (*JJII* 5).

11. Heroism thus depends upon one's reaction to circumstances, regardless of the nature of those circumstances, as Francis Mackey implies of Bloom: "Heroic, undaunted, he has refused to bow to the sad fate that seems to await him, that coincidence and chance seem to assure" (62). John Henry Raleigh agrees that Bloom is "indomitable and thus heroic. . . . The really splendid originality of Joyce's conception was to place his hero in the most unheroic of circumstances" (595).

12. Odysseus' lineage raises doubts regarding his heroic status. Of his grandfather Autolycus, S. G. Farron states, "It would be difficult to imagine a more unheroic or unaristocratic ancestor" (64). W. B. Stanford contends that Joyce echoes this am-

biguity: "Though Odysseus in Homer is (by mere convention) an aristocrat, much of his conduct and many of his associates are far from aristocratic, especially in the *Odyssey*. . . . Homer was no snob. When Joyce is criticized for unheroic elements in Bloom, he is all the more clearly in the traditional succession" ("Ulyssean Qualities" 126).

13. This equivocal sort of excellence accounts for why Morris Beja praises Bloom for his lack of histrionics, albeit cautiously: "Bloom's attitude toward Molly's infidelity may in part—not entirely, to be sure: I am trying not to exaggerate but to set up what I perceive as a proper perspective—be correct, arguably heroic, even wise" (119–20). Lauding Bloom's forbearance seems especially justified in light of how Odysseus too prevails by preferring equanimity to violence at certain points in time.

14. Both men resist any temptation to suicide. Odysseus considers whether to drown himself or continue to endure in silence after his comrades release the winds of Aeolus (*Od.* 10.49–54). He also loses his will to live momentarily when Kirke commands him to visit Hades (*Od.* 10.496–502). Bloom views neither murder nor suicide as a satisfactory remedy, fearing the abandonment of reason:

What did he fear?

The committal of homicide or suicide during sleep by an aberration of the light of reason. (*U* 17.1765–67)

He does consider hurting himself to be one kind of "retribution" (*U* 17.2200) he might seek: "Suit for damages by legal influence or simulation of assault with evidence of injuries sustained (selfinflicted), not impossibly" (*U* 17.2203–5).

15. Seth Schein makes a similar claim about the *Iliad*: "Its style, mythological content, and heroic themes and values are traditional, but it generates its distinctive meanings as an ironic meditation on these traditional themes and values. Through parallels, contrasts, and juxtapositions of characters and actions, a dramatic structure is created that forces us to consider critically the traditional heroic world and the contradictions inherent in this kind of heroism" (1).

Works Cited

Adams, Douglas. "῞Ηρως and ῞Ηρα: Of Men and Heroes in Greek and Indo-European." *Glotta* 65 (1987): 171–78.

———, and J. P. Mallory, eds. *Encyclopedia of Indo-European Culture*. London: Fitzroy Dearborn, 1997.

Ames, Keri Elizabeth. "The Convergence of Homer's *Odyssey* and Joyce's *Ulysses*." PhD diss. University of Chicago, Committee on Social Thought, June 2003.

———. "The Oxymoron of Fidelity in Homer's *Odyssey* and Joyce's *Ulysses*." *Joyce Studies Annual* 14 (Summer 2003): 132–74.

Beja, Morris. "The Joyce of Sex: Sexual Relationships in *Ulysses*." In *Light Rays: James Joyce and Modernism*, edited by Heyward Ehrlich, 112–25. New York: New Horizon, 1984.

Caswell, Caroline P. *A Study of Θυμος in Early Greek Epic.* Leiden: Brill, 1990.

Cunliffe, Richard John. *A Lexicon of the Homeric Dialect.* Norman: University of Oklahoma Press, 1963.

Falkner, Thomas M. *The Poetics of Old Age in Greek Epic, Lyric, and Tragedy.* Norman: University of Oklahoma Press, 1995.

Falkner, Thomas M., and Judith deLuce, eds. *Old Age in Greek and Latin Literature.* Albany: State University of New York Press, 1989.

Farron, S. G. "The *Odyssey* as an Anti-Aristocratic Statement." *Studies in Antiquity* 1 (1979–80): 59–101.

Frisk, Hjalmar. *Griechisches Etymologisches Wörterbuch.* Heidelberg: Carl Winter, 1960.

Griffin, Jasper. *Homer on Life and Death.* Oxford: Oxford University Press, 1983.

Hayman, David. *"Ulysses": The Mechanics of Meaning.* Englewood Cliffs, N.J.: Prentice-Hall, 1970.

Herring, Philip. *Joyce's Notes and Early Drafts for "Ulysses": Selections from the Buffalo Collection.* Charlottesville: University Press of Virginia, 1977.

Homer's *Iliad.* Edited by David B. Monro and T. W. Allen. In *Homeri Opera.* New York: Oxford University Press, 1902–20.

Homer's *Odyssey.* Edited by T. W. Allen. In *Homeri Opera.* Oxford: Oxford University Press, 1917–19.

Iser, Wolfgang. *The Implied Reader: Patterns of Communication in Prose Fiction from Bunyan to Beckett.* Baltimore: Johns Hopkins University Press, 1974.

Kenner, Hugh. *Dublin's Joyce.* New York: Columbia University Press, 1987.

———. *Ulysses.* Rev. ed. Baltimore: Johns Hopkins University Press, 1987.

Levitt, Morton R. *James Joyce and Modernism: Beyond Dublin.* Lewiston, N.Y.: Edwin Mellen, 1999.

Lewis, C. S. *The Problem of Pain.* New York: Collier, 1962.

Liddell, Henry George, and Robert Scott. *Greek-English Lexicon.* Oxford: Clarendon, 1968.

Mackey, Peter Francis. "Chaos Theory and the Heroism of Leopold Bloom." In *Joyce through the Ages: A Nonlinear View,* edited by Michael Patrick Gillespie, 46–65. Gainesville: University Press of Florida, 1999.

Madtes, Richard. *The "Ithaca" Chapter of Joyce's "Ulysses."* Ann Arbor: UMI Research Press, 1983.

Miller, Dean A. *The Epic Hero.* Baltimore: Johns Hopkins University Press, 2000.

Nelson, Stephanie. "Calypso's Choice: Immortality and Heroic Striving in the *Odyssey* and *Ulysses.*" In *Literary Imagination, Ancient and Modern: Essays in Honor of David Grene,* edited by Todd Breyfogle, 63–89. Chicago: University of Chicago Press, 1999.

Pound, Ezra. *Literary Essays of Ezra Pound.* Edited by T. S. Eliot. London: Faber and Faber, 1954.

Pucci, Pietro. *Odysseus Polutropos: Intertextual Readings in the "Odyssey" and the "Iliad."* Ithaca: Cornell University Press, 1987.

Radin, Alice P. "Sunrise, Sunset: ἦμος in Homeric Epic." *American Journey of Philology* 109 (1988): 293–307.

Raleigh, John Henry. "Bloom as a Modern Epic Hero." *Critical Inquiry* (1977): 583–98.

Schein, Seth L. *The Mortal Hero: An Introduction to Homer's "Iliad."* Berkeley and Los Angeles: University of California Press, 1984.

Smyth, Herbert Weir. *Greek Grammar.* Cambridge: Harvard University Press, 1984.

Stanford, W. B. *Homer, "Odyssey" XIII-XXIV.* London: Bristol Classical Press, 1996.

———. "Ulyssean Qualities in Leopold Bloom." *Comparative Literature* 5 (1953): 125–36.

Tagopoulos, Constance. "Joyce and Homer: Return, Disguise, and Recognition in 'Ithaca.'" In *Joyce in Context,* edited by Vincent Cheng and Timothy Martin, 184–200. Cambridge: Cambridge University Press, 1992.

Vernant, Jean-Pierre. "The Refusal of Odysseus." In *Reading the "Odyssey,"* edited by Seth Schein, 185–89. Princeton: Princeton University Press, 1996.

The Incertitude of the Void

Modernist Narrative

Shocking the Reader in "A Painful Case"

Margot Norris

James Joyce's story "A Painful Case" is about a *story* that is painful for a reader: a newspaper article of the same title that gives Mr. Duffy a disturbing shock when he reads of Mrs. Sinico's death. This shocked reading produces a moment of classical *anagnorisis* when the man recognizes his implication in the woman's fate. But is Joyce's *story* "A Painful Case" painful for the reader as well? I hope to concur with critics who have thought so,[1] and argue that even though the reader is not implicated in Mrs. Sinico's pain, the narration obliges "us" to experience vicariously the shocks to her heart, the last of which kills her. "Death, in his opinion, had been probably due to shock and sudden failure of the heart's action" (*D* 114), the surgeon reports to the *Dublin Evening Mail.* The thematic presentation of James Duffy's painful shock upon reading "A Painful Case" is encased in a performative reenactment of reader shock—potentially *twice.* I will argue that the narrator treats us precisely as Mr. Duffy treats Mrs. Sinico, and suggest on less hermeneutical evidence that it also treats Mr. Duffy as Mrs. Sinico treats him—thereby producing a second aftershock. In the process, the reader is given an opportunity to feel what the woman feels[2]—and, in a more surprising way, to realize that the man's subjectivity might have been as occluded as the woman's, and can be retrieved only at the price of painful readerly implication. There is a method to Joyce's careful contrivance of reader shock and discomfort. I will suggest it is to engage the reader not only in an ethical re-thinking, but an ethical re-feeling of the two great Irish sex scandals of the late nineteenth century: the case of Charles Stewart Parnell, and the case of Oscar Wilde.

Before embarking on this exploration of readerly shock, I must consider the status and function of the narrative voice and the narration. Taking as their cue the narrative description of Mr. Duffy's "odd autobiographical habit" that leads him "to compose in his mind from time to time a short sentence about himself containing a subject in the third person and a predicate in the past tense" (*D* 108), many critics of the story have held that the narrative voice is closely reflective of Duffy's own, and may be

identified with him. "Indeed, Joyce foregrounds Duffy's dialogic participation in several places, suggesting that Duffy may be his own narrator,"
R. B. Kershner writes (111). This identification does not preclude unreliability or irony, and the debates surrounding the sincerity and significance
of Duffy's epiphany at the story's end suggest that registers of hypocrisy
and fatuity may coexist with despair not only in the character's soul but in
the narrational rhetoric as well. However, I hope to demonstrate much
more problematic complicities between the narrative voice and Duffy with
much more egregious manipulations of the reader's emotional and ethical
response. Heuristically this demonstration is best served by retaining, initially at least, loose personifications of narrator and reader as more or less
unified subjects and agents that are rendered increasingly fragmented and
cognitively disrupted as the reading process offers conflicting interpretive
possibilities that cannot be resolved.[3] This demonstration is heuristically
abetted also by framing the imagined reading of this story temporally as a
first reading—a virgin reading, as it were—followed by immediately
troubled re-readings that are set historically in the intellectual milieu of
Joyce and his brother Stanislaus. The young Joyce brothers were two turn-
of-the-century readers excited both by the great nineteenth-century Continental fiction they encountered in school and disturbed by the sex scandals that had shaken the Irish political and literary landscape during their
youth and adolescence. I will therefore proceed by reading "A Painful
Case" twice. My aim the first time is to pay special attention to the parallels between Mr. Duffy's treatment of Mrs. Sinico and the narrator's treatment of the reader. But the second time I will draw attention to a kind of
black hole in the narration that effectively decenters the story and leaves
not only Duffy's moral nature in pieces but also our own.

I begin, then, with a first reading of the woman's story, and with the
moment when both Mrs. Sinico and the reader receive a simultaneous
shock. In the passage describing the growing attachment between Duffy
and the woman, the prose betrays "every sign of unusual excitement" (D
111)—to cite its own description of Mrs. Sinico—and applies the brakes of
Duffy's own techniques of aphorism and "disembodiment," to use R. B.
Kershner's term (112):

> The dark discreet room, their isolation, the music that still vibrated in
> their ears united them. This union exalted him, wore away the rough
> edges of his character, emotionalised his mental life. Sometimes he
> caught himself listening to the sound of his own voice. He thought
> that in her eyes he would ascend to an angelical stature; and, as he

attached the fervent nature of his companion more and more closely
to him, he heard the strange impersonal voice which he recognised as
his own, insisting on the soul's incurable loneliness. We cannot give
ourselves, it said: we are our own. The end of these discourses was
that one night during which she had shown every sign of unusual
excitement, Mrs. Sinico caught up his hand passionately and pressed
it to her cheek.

Mr Duffy was very much surprised. Her interpretation of his
words disillusioned him. He did not visit her for a week. (*D* 111)

The prose here leads us to believe (like Mrs. Sinico herself) that we are
caught up in a love story that is racing toward consummation. Like Mrs.
Sinico, we are set up to overreach our romantic expectations and suffer a
verbal version of a rude coitus interruptus. "Mrs Sinico caught up his hand
passionately and pressed it to her cheek. // Mr Duffy was very much surprised" (*D* 111). Indeed, it is we as readers who are very much surprised by
Mr. Duffy's surprise. Why on earth would he be surprised by her gesture?
This man and woman are reported to have shared the vibrations of exalt-
ing music, entangled their thoughts in an emotionalized discourse, and
shared an intimacy that had given expression to the woman's fervent nature—"he attached the fervent nature of his companion more and more
closely to him" (*D* 111). Duffy's cold surprise must have felt to Mrs. Sinico
like a figurative slap in the face for having presumed an amorous expectation—an expectation that Duffy treats as a woman might treat a threatened date rape. Is Duffy offended by the sexual overture or scandalized by
the adulterous advance? In either case, why? We are never told.

I will return to this complex moment of romantic and ethical misprision
and its strange gender reversals again, after generically contextualizing
the reader's parallel shock. The entire narrative leading up to this moment
has conditioned the reader to expect an *adultery story*. Both the social
scene that is set, and the emotional climate that is rhetorically created,
point in this direction. For a story that will be about the refusal of intimacy,
the opening narrative of "A Painful Case" begins by offering a curious
excess of intimate information about James Duffy, so much so that its sharing with the reader becomes itself an invitation or seduction to intimacy. In
a carefully arranged sequence of opening revelations, the narrative descriptions penetrate this impenetrable man's environs, his room, his book-
shelf, his desk, his private journal, his temperament, his mental habits, his
daily routine, his tastes. We are allowed to scrutinize his face as an intelligent and sympathetic woman might scrutinize it, attempting to read his

character from his physiognomy. "His cheekbones also gave his face a harsh character; but there was no harshness in the eyes which, looking at the world from under their tawny eyebrows, gave the impression of a man ever alert to greet a redeeming instinct in others but often disappointed" (D 108). Even before Emily Sinico has appeared on the scene, the reader has been made the solitary and privileged witness, or voyeur, to a self-styled, post-Nietzschean Romantic hero—"sublime, contemptuous, ironic" —as René Girard might describe his *askesis*.[4]

Nothing in this opening description prepares us for the surprising turn the narrative takes when this man who "had neither companions nor friends, church nor creed," and who "lived his spiritual life without any communion with others" (D 109), meets a woman at a concert who begins a conversation with him. The narrative makes a curious maneuver at this moment—ignoring the conversation, which is not reported—to register Duffy's surprisingly alert curiosity and attention to the woman's character, face, and body. Engaged in the most casual of conversations, he tries to memorize her face: "he tried to fix her permanently in his memory" (D 109). He goes on to interpret the emotional meaning of her eyes: "Their gaze began with a defiant note but was confused by what seemed a deliberate swoon of the pupil into the iris, revealing for an instant a temperament of great sensibility" (D 109). The narration that earlier looked into Duffy's eyes for signs of his character now shows Duffy looking into Mrs. Sinico's eyes for signs of hers. The reader feels drawn into the cross-hairs of a love story that almost literally begins "at first sight." Although Duffy meets *two* women, he remarks the daughter only as a gauge to the mother's age. The narration further promises a level of frank maturity when it traces Duffy's gaze from the woman's eyes to her breast—"and her astrakhan jacket, moulding a bosom of a certain fulness, struck the note of defiance more definitely" (D 110).

When Duffy meets the woman again a few weeks later at a concert at Earlsfort Terrace, he takes surprising initiative in awaiting a moment when her daughter is diverted "to become intimate" (D 110). The context gives "intimate" no sexual connotations. But Duffy's arrangements to speak to the woman privately, learn her name and that of her husband, and make dates to meet her alone, function as gestures that signal to Emily Sinico, and to the reader, that he prepares to court her as a lover. The expectation of adultery is further reinforced by certain semiotic prompts. These include the woman's name, which reminds Mary Lowe-Evans of Emma

Bovary (Lowe-Evans 397); the story's locale of Chapelizod, the putative chapel of Tristan and Iseult;[5] and the gloss—in the professional title of Captain Sinico—of the unsympathetic husband in the Parnell affair, Captain O'Shea.[6] Once this last gloss is registered, other tacit similarities to the adulterous romance between Charles Stewart Parnell and Katherine O'Shea come into view. These are mature relationships: Emily Sinico is thirty-nine when she meets the forty-year-old Duffy; Katherine O'Shea was thirty-five when she met the thirty-three-year-old Parnell. Duffy, like Parnell, gains access to the Sinico home as a family friend; and Captain Sinico, like Captain O'Shea, is frequently absent from home and judged by Duffy to be indifferent to his wife. "In Parnell's view the lady in question had been deserted by her husband for several years," biographer Paul Bew wrote of O'Shea (42). And Margery Brady contends that Katherine O'Shea wished to contest her husband's divorce suit on the ground of his infidelities (90)—infidelities insinuated too in reference to Captain Sinico's "gallery of pleasures" (D 110).

The narration of the couple's romantic adventure—"Neither he nor she had had any such adventure before" (D 110)—contextualizes itself as an adultery story, and as the relationship blossoms into greater intimacy, the narration becomes lyrical with metaphorical intimations of impending sexuality. "Little by little, as their thoughts entangled, they spoke of subjects less remote" (D 111). We are not told what these "less remote" subjects are, but the trope of entanglement, with its botanical imagery of enfolding vines and branches, points toward the sexual imagery of enfolding human limbs.[7] The botanical imagery is further infused with allusions to temperature, nurturance, and gestation—"Her companionship was like a warm soil about an exotic" (D 111). On the narrative level, the image of Mrs. Sinico's unlit lamps darkening the room, the lingering vibrations of distant music, and the chords of transcendence in the prose describing Duffy's feelings: all set a discursive stage for consummation when Mrs. Sinico passionately catches his hand and presses it to her cheek. "Mr. Duffy was very much surprised. Her interpretation of his words disillusioned him" (D 111). This moment produces a highly imbricated crisis of interpretation that involves not only the man and the woman but also the narrative voice and the reader. The narration had clearly interpreted Duffy's words, gestures, and feelings in precisely the same way Emily Sinico interpreted them, and the narrative voice, deeply embedded in Duffy's feelings during this culminating discourse, suggests that Mrs. Sinico had misinterpreted nothing. Duffy's cold and instantaneous withdrawal is therefore as shocking to the reader as to her—following upon the provocative arousal stimulated by both the narrative voice and Duffy.

Duffy's abrupt withdrawal has turned the impending adultery narrative into a frigidity narrative, a mode of storytelling that orchestrates a reader deprivation and frustration that recapitulate Emily Sinico's deprivation and frustration. Or, to put the matter more extremely, the story has turned into an emotionally sadistic narrative. It has ventured on a mode of storytelling that incites in the reader a desire for romance, a wish for a story about the fulfillment of love even if illicit, only abruptly to punish that desire with a brutal refusal and rebuff. And for the reader, as for Emily Sinico, insult is added to injury when not only is passion withdrawn and withheld, but its withdrawal is justified with a tacit, self-righteous indictment of the woman as guilty of vulgar lechery. Not only have the narrative redactions of the trysts deprived the reader of the expected love scenes, but also the narrative withdrawal embarrasses the reader as Duffy's withdrawal embarrasses Mrs. Sinico. We expect the narrative voice to come to Emily Sinico's defense, but it does not. Instead, it colludes with Duffy's course of aggressive withdrawal—telling us nothing of what she feels, nothing of what she says during the painful three-hour-long argument as they walk in the Park in the cold. The narrative reports only the outcome of what must have been a painful and emotionally charged break-up, and its justification, in Duffy's terms: "They agreed to break off their intercourse: every bond, he said, is a bond to sorrow" (D 112). Only Emily Sinico's body is given mute expression in this scene: "she began to tremble so violently that, fearing another collapse on her part, he bade her good-bye quickly and left her" (D 112).

Four years later, when the *Dublin Evening Mail* reports her death by a slow-moving train, we again learn nothing of what Emily Sinico has felt or suffered in the intervening four years, and nothing of what she felt or suffered as the slow-moving train bore down on her. "The evidence showed that the deceased lady, while attempting to cross the line, was knocked down by the engine of the ten o'clock slow train from Kingstown, thereby sustaining injuries of the head and right side which led to her death" (D 113). This report nonetheless produces a stunning moment of literary déjà vu as we are transported back to nineteenth-century Moscow, to another railroad track on which another woman in despair confronts an oncoming train, a woman whose polysyllabic name echoes that of Emily Sinico: Anna Karenina. Tolstoy gives us what Joyce withholds—the exquisitely painful body language of the woman supplemented by the riot of the woman's thoughts and feelings:

> A feeling such as she had known when about to take the first plunge in bathing came upon her, and she crossed herself. That familiar gesture brought back into her soul a whole series of girlish and childish memories, and suddenly the darkness that had covered everything for her was torn apart, and life rose up before her for an instant with all its bright past joys. But she did not take her eyes from the wheels of the second carriage. And exactly at the moment when the space between the wheels came opposite her, she dropped the red bag, and drawing her head back into her shoulders, fell on her hands under the carriage, and lightly, as though she would rise again at once, dropped on to her knees. And at the same instant she was terror-stricken at what she was doing. "Where am I? What am I doing? What for?" She tried to get up, to drop backwards; but something huge and merciless struck her on the head and rolled her on her back. (Tolstoy 894)

There is strong evidence that Joyce had Tolstoy's *Anna Karenina* in mind as he was writing "A Painful Case." On September 24, 1905, Joyce wrote to Stanislaus to ask him to verify certain details in the story. "Are the police at Sydney Parade of the *D* division? Would the city ambulance be called out to Sydney Parade for an accident? Would an accident at Sydney Parade be treated at Vincent's Hospital?" (*SL* 75). Six days before he wrote this letter, Joyce had written another in which he gratefully responded to Stanislaus for detecting Russian influences in his stories. However, "As for Tolstoy I disagree with you altogether," Joyce wrote. "Tolstoy is a magnificent writer. He is never dull, never stupid, never tired, never pedantic, never theatrical! He is head and shoulders over the others" (*SL* 73). A little later in the letter, Joyce excoriates the English liberal press for its political criticism of Tolstoy. "Did you ever hear such impudence? Do they think the author of *Resurrection* and *Anna Karénin* a fool?" (*SL* 73).

Bringing Emily Sinico and Anna Karenina into dialogue with each other dramatizes Joyce's inversion and perversion of the adultery narrative. The nineteenth-century Continental adultery novel was ideologically ambivalent about adultery: creating sympathy for the woman who pursues it, yet devising her self-punishment in a maneuver designed to be ethically uncomfortable for the reader. Access to the adulterous woman's motives and feelings gave readers insight into the pain and sublimity of the *Liebestod* that is her fate. Why would Joyce write "A Painful Case" as a story in which there is *no* adultery; in which it is the *failure of adultery*—not its commission—that putatively drives the woman to suicide; and in which her *Liebestod*, if that's what it is,[8] is brutally stripped of all romance and transcendence? At least one plausible possibility may be that fifteen years after the scandalous adultery, divorce, censure, and death of Charles Stewart Parnell, the topic of adultery and its punishments remained an unresolved ethical wound in the Irish conscience. Joyce, who would revisit the scandal a decade later in the famous Christmas dinner scene in *A Portrait of the Artist as a Young Man*, may in 1905 have created a satirical parable about the self-righteous prescriptions of Parnell's censors. "A Painful Case" could be read as an imaginary scenario of a hideously ironic outcome had Parnell resisted the temptations of adultery and behaved as the priests, and Joyce's Dante Riordan, demanded.

In the censorious version of the Parnell scandal, Kitty O'Shea was thought to have acted the whore—as the story of "a very famous spit" that John Casey retells at the Dedalus family Christmas dinner in *Portrait* makes plain. Casey tells of a crowd in Arklow protesting against Parnell shortly before his death, when an enraged old woman "called that lady a name that I won't sully this Christmas board nor your ears, ma'am, nor my own lips by repeating" (*P* 36). Clearly Joyce did not share this view of the woman Parnell addressed in his letters as "My own wifie" and "My own darling Queenie" (Bew 43), who bore him three illegitimate children in her late thirties, and who held him as he died, eleven years after they had met. Margery Brady reports that Parnell's last words were, "Kiss me, sweet Wifie, and I will try to sleep a little" (126). In his 1912 Triestine article on "The Shade of Parnell," Joyce characterized Parnell's fall "like lightning from a clear sky":

> He fell hopelessly in love with a married woman, and when her husband, Captain O'Shea, asked for a divorce, the ministers Gladstone and Morley openly refused to legislate in favour of Ireland if the sinner remained as head of the Nationalist Party.
> . . . The high and low clergy entered the lists to finish him off. The Irish press emptied on him and the woman he loved the vials of their envy. (*CW* 227)

Reading "A Painful Case" as a satirical rendition of a man doing the right thing by the public Irish mores negatively pays unique tribute to Parnell's uxorious adultery as one of the defining features of his greatness. Joyce endowed Duffy with what he called Parnell's "sovereign bearing, mild and proud, silent and disconsolate" (*CW* 226). But he made James Duffy—a man who flirts with politics, literature, philosophy, and woman with no willingness to give, commit, or risk—the absolute antithesis of Charles Stewart Parnell, who wholeheartedly gave, committed, and risked everything for both a country and a woman.[9] Parnell refutes in advance Duffy's retroactive social exoneration: "He asked himself what else could he have done. He could not have carried on a comedy of deception with her; he could not have lived with her openly" (*D* 116). Why not? Given his complete social indifference, what had Duffy to lose except his adventureless job as a bank cashier? As a popular, powerful, and highly visible politician, Parnell had everything to lose and he risked and lost it all. In 1936, Winston Churchill wrote of Parnell:

> He dedicated himself to a single goal, the goal of Ireland as a nation, and he pursued it unswervingly until a rose thrown across his path opened a new world, the world of love. And, as he had previously sacrificed all for Ireland, so, when the moment of choice came, he sacrificed all, even Ireland, for love. A lesser man might have given more sparingly and kept more. (quoted in Brady 133)

If it is the business of the adultery novel to explain to us why there is adultery, "A Painful Case" refuses to explain to us *why there is no adultery* when all the presumptive conditions for its commission are clearly in place. Given Duffy's atheism, indifference to society, and amorality, what possible inner or outer constraints could have prevented him from yielding to Emily Sinico's overture? His reaction to this warm and giving woman made no sense at the time of his rejection of her, and it continues to make no sense after he reads of her death. Duffy's anguished self-examination gives only oblique and suspect explanations for why he rejected the woman. His moral excoriations of her are histrionic and exaggerated: "He saw the squalid tract of her vice, miserable and malodorous. . . . Just God, what an end! Evidently she had been unfit to live, without any strength of purpose, an easy prey to habits, one of the wrecks on which civilisation has been reared. But that she could have sunk so low!" (*D* 115). And as he generalizes her alcoholism to a wider, and retroactive, degeneracy, the troublesome excess of recoil at her gesture is reiterated again: "He remembered her outburst of that night and interpreted it in a harsher sense than he had ever done. He had no difficulty now in approving of the course he had taken" (*D* 115–16). If Duffy's behavior was inexplicable then, his self-justifications after her death are even more so. There is something simply wrong with this whole story whose central question—"Why had he with-held life from her?" (*D* 117)—is never answered by either Duffy or the narrator.

And yet we are given a clue to this mystery—a solution in plain sight, like Poe's purloined letter, a solution totally obvious and yet functionally so shocking that critics and readers have overwhelmingly failed or refused to see it.[10] This clue has surprising authority, for it is provided not by the narration but by James Duffy himself, when we are given a glimpse into a journal entry he wrote two months after his break-up with Mrs. Sinico: "One of his sentences, written two months after his last interview with Mrs Sinico, read: Love between man and man is impossible because there must not be sexual intercourse and friendship between man and woman is impossible because there must be sexual intercourse" (*D* 112). The narration has pried into the most private recesses of Duffy's papers in his desk, given us his most secret comment on his break-up with the woman, and yet makes nothing of this aphorism, and gives us no encouragement to ponder its significance for explaining Duffy's action. As a result we are distracted by its clever style that R. B. Kershner elegantly summarizes as "enumeration and inventory, classical balance and antithesis, analysis, neat causal connection, passive-voice construction" (111). But what if this utterly private thought, intended to be shared with no other human being, is taken at face value: as a revelation that James Duffy cannot give himself to this woman because if he could love, he would love a man? The narration has not authorized this interpretation, and it has told us nothing ex-plicitly that would support it.[11] Consequently, to speculate in explicit ways about James Duffy's sexuality obliges the reader to come to terms with what Joseph Valente has called "the compulsory heterosexuality that has encumbered even the most critically astute, theoretically sophisticated, and politically progressive Joyce scholarship" (1). By opening the gap into a queer interpretation of the story, the reader's shock or surprise becomes an ethical boomerang, exposing the strength of the heterosexual assump-tions and their control of the generic conventions of romantic fiction that we have reflexively brought to the story. In treating Duffy as a promising heterosexual lover, the reader had treated him with Emily Sinico's own expectations.

The indeterminacy of the failure of adultery in the story has previously obliged the reader to adjudicate whether its cause was Duffy's morality, prudery, asceticism, asexuality, frigidity, or the simpler possibility that Duffy, while heterosexual and attracted by the woman's personality, was simply not attracted to Mrs. Sinico sexually. Once the possibility of homosexuality is considered, the reader must take ethical responsibility for now imagining the thoughts, feelings, and anxieties of the possibly homosexual man. If we remember that Duffy lives in a social world that punishes homosexuality even more harshly than it punishes adultery, Duffy's isolation, asceticism, aloofness, and misanthropy take on a wholly different character. His abstemiousness could now imply an avoidance of temptation: for example, by dining in the dull eatery in George's Street "where he felt himself safe from the society of Dublin's gilded youth" (*D* 109). The narrative assurance that opera and concerts "were the only dissipations of his life" (*D* 109) now takes on a hint of defensiveness. We can now understand differently why he cannot write his thought, why his most intimate emotional expressions take impersonal and general form, and why a woman's romantic overture could have caused him surprised distress. Duffy's dismissive scorn of "the criticisms of an obtuse middle class which entrusted its morality to policemen and its fine arts to impresarios" (*D* 111) reminds us that the trial of Oscar Wilde would have been recent history at the time of this conversation.[12] If the concealment of Duffy's sexuality may be imagined not only in a social closet but further internalized in latency, then his autobiographical resort to a "disembodied" voice no longer seems particularly "odd" (*D* 108). We now also have a better explanation of why Duffy never registers the looks or charms of Sinico's daughter, and why Duffy might have misconstrued Emily Sinico's open nature and generous feelings.[13]

In this light, Joyce's narrative description of the growing intimacy between James Duffy and Emily Sinico becomes a rhetorical tour de force that enacts the fluidities of emotional need, personal response, and spiritual longing dammed by an erotic threshold:

> He thought that in her eyes he would ascend to an angelical stature; and, as he attached the fervent nature of his companion more and more closely to him, he heard the strange impersonal voice which he recognised as his own, insisting on the soul's incurable loneliness. We cannot give ourselves, it said: we are our own. (*D* 111)

The rhetorical gestures in this passage strain toward intimacy even as they snap away from confession in a torque of impersonal obliquity and generalized prohibition. We can now better understand Duffy's subsequent transformation of painful personal meaning into a style of equivocal epigrammatic pronouncement. The epigrammatic structure of "Love between man and man is impossible because there must not be sexual intercourse and friendship between man and woman is impossible because there must be sexual intercourse" (D 112) now resonates with much greater clarity to the encrypting signature of Oscar Wilde. Garry Leonard's astute observation—"Duffy very much wants to be his own third person so that other people might become entirely extraneous to what would then be the closed circuit of his identity" (215)—also takes on special poignancy if we imagine a homosexual Duffy. As a closeted or latent homosexual, Duffy would be consigned to a life without interlocution or dialogic possibility, with no one to whom he could safely disclose himself and communicate his true thoughts or feelings.

Duffy's rhetorical torsion away from confession infects the narrative voice as well to replace emotional representation with the facticity of externalized reportage. Once we interpret Duffy's rebuff of the woman's romantic overture as homosexual recoil,[14] the reader must revisit with a queer perspective the redacted scenes in the story. We remember that we learned nothing of what transpired during the week of silence: "He did not visit her for a week; then he wrote to her asking her to meet him" (D 111–12). And we learn virtually nothing of the transactions of the break-up: "It was cold autumn weather but in spite of the cold they wandered up and down the roads of the Park for nearly three hours" (D 112). In order speculatively to retrieve these narratively censored scenes that conceal from us the drama at the heart of this story, the heterosexual reader experiences a thickening of identity and a doubling of vision as different questions pose themselves in an effort to enter a gay subjectivity. What sensation of panic and responsibility might Duffy have felt upon recognizing that this woman had fallen in love with him? How did his own feelings of recoil present themselves to him? What choices was he able or obliged to ponder?[15] Would he tell her or not tell her his predicament? What psychological vulnerabilities and social risks would the disclosure of such a secret pose to him? What, if anything, did James Duffy tell Emily Sinico of his dilemma during that three-hour break-up in the Park? Perhaps he explained why he could not love her. Perhaps he told her nothing. If he told her nothing of his dilemma, what forms of discursive deception and indirection would have been required to justify the break-up of their relationship? Was her fit of trembling caused by disappointment and embarrassment only, or did Emily Sinico glimpse the larger and more tragic meaning in Duffy's pronouncement that "every bond . . . is a bond to sorrow" (D 112)?

The narration tells us nothing of this and thereby puts us in a risky interpretive quandary. Why doesn't the narrative voice tell us more and let us hear the break-up dialogue so that we might infer with more security what went on between this couple? If "A Painful Case" is indeed a story about a man in the closet, then it is also a closeted story.[16] Why would Joyce have written it like this? A plausible answer may lie in the historical conditions that not only linked the scandals of Charles Stewart Parnell and Oscar Wilde to each other in Joyce's mind, but that extended their caution of the punishment that "exceptionalism" visits on gifted Irishmen to himself.[17] Joyce tropes the fates of Wilde and Parnell in similar figures of hunted animals in the essays he published in 1909 and 1912 respectively in the Trieste paper *Il Piccolo della Sera*. Joyce writes of the persecuted Wilde: "He was hunted from house to house as dogs hunt a rabbit" (*CW* 203). He described Parnell: "He went from county to county, from city to city, 'like a hunted deer,' a spectral figure with the signs of death on his forehead" (*CW* 227–28). Given the unrelenting and serious censorship problems Joyce faced in his protracted nine-year struggle to get Maunsel & Company to publish *Dubliners*, could he have hoped to write openly about either adultery or homosexuality? In 1906, Grant Richards objected to mere allusions to "a man with two establishments to keep up" (*SL* 82). As late as 1912, Joyce's solicitor, George Lidwell, urged Joyce not to run afoul of Dublin's Vigilance Committee. Its object, Lidwell explained, "is to seek out and suppress all writings of immoral tendencies," and he cautioned Joyce that "if the attention of the Authorities be drawn to these paragraphs it is likely they would yield to the pressure of this body and prosecute" (quoted in *JJII* 330). One may gauge the extent to which this climate of censorship was internalized in the circumspection of the oblique allusions with which Joyce and his brother Stanislaus discuss the unnamed homosexual theme of Oscar Wilde's *Dorian Gray* in their private correspondence.[18] Writing a homosexual story in the climate of 1905 and 1906 would have been unthinkable, particularly if we remember the scandal produced as late as 1928 by the obscenity trial and banning of Radclyffe Hall's chaste lesbian novel, *The Well of Loneliness*.

My speculative reconstruction of "A Painful Case" remains indeterminate and unverifiable—itself a somewhat scandalous shadow or double of the adultery narrative with which it is entangled in ambiguity and equivocation. But this inability to "prove" the reading can itself be read as a performative effect. The narration enacts the "love that dare not speak its name" by refusing to speak it and refusing to let Duffy speak it except as a prohibition: "Love between man and man is impossible because there must not be sexual intercourse" (D 112). These narrational effects make the reader the enforcer of a regime of unknowing that requires the speculative crossing of a cognitive line to turn the narrative closet to glass, as Eve Sedgwick might put it. Sedgwick writes of *The Picture of Dorian Gray:*

> Published four years before Wilde's "exposure" as a sodomite, it is in a sense a perfect rhetorical distillation of the open secret, the glass closet. . . . Reading *Dorian Gray* from our twentieth-century vantage point where the name Oscar Wilde virtually *means* "homosexual," it is worth reemphasizing how thoroughly the elements of even this novel can be read doubly or equivocally, can be read either as having a thematically empty "modernist" meaning or as having a thematically full "homosexual" meaning. (165–66)

Since Joyce did not read *Dorian Gray* until he revised "A Painful Case" in 1906, James Duffy may be assumed not to have read it—although the narrator's failure to mention Wilde among Duffy's authors does not prove that Duffy had no Wilde on his shelves. Further, since the history of English usage does not translate "gay" into "homosexual" until the 1930s or later (*The New Fowler's Modern English Usage* 324), one cannot read a coded meaning into Duffy's acquisition of Nietzsche's *The Gay Science* after his break-up with Mrs. Sinico. Yet Eve Sedgwick reads Nietzsche through a Wildean optic.[19] She thereby finds his writings "full and over-full of what were just in the process of becoming, for people like Wilde, for their enemies, and for the institutions that regulated and defined them, the most pointed and contested signifiers of precisely a minoritized, taxonomic male homosexual identity" (133). From the retrospective intertextualization of both Wilde and Nietzsche into the homosocial jousting of "Telemachus" in *Ulysses*, Joyce may have planted *The Gay Science* in Duffy's library as an overdetermined referent.

"A Painful Case" therefore remains, more than *Dorian Gray*—of which Joyce wrote, "It is not very difficult to read between the lines" (*SL* 96)—an opaque closet at best. But nonetheless, once a queer reading is considered, the reader must contend with ethical incrimination in "the epistemology of the closet." As Sedgwick explains: "'Closetedness' itself is a performance initiated as such by the speech act of a silence—not a particular silence, but a silence that accrues particularity by fits and starts, in relation to the discourse that surrounds and differentially constitutes it" (3). In "A Painful Case," the discourse that constitutes "the closet" is the one that resolutely interprets Duffy's refusal of heterosexual love as volitional in specific registers of ethical culpability coded as egotism, narcissism, solipsism, and coldness. An ethical leap is required to imagine that Duffy's "hunger-strike against desire" (as Earl Ingersoll suggestively calls it [126]) could be prompted by a criminalized, prosecutable, and therefore frustrated and perhaps repressed desire for a same-sex object. This possibility does not readily *occur* to either the narrator or the reader, and it is this *not-occurring* that is precisely the epistemologically closeting gesture. Once the queer interpretation does occur to the reader, it produces the Tiresian optics that abash the reader in ethically productive ways. At story's end, Duffy's regret and remorse may enfold not one but two closeted lives: that of the abandoned wife ("how lonely her life must have been, sitting night after night alone in that room" [D 116])[20] and that of his own monological existence. If Emily Sinico may be imagined as the only person on earth who might have known his secret ("it revolted him to think that he had ever spoken to her of what he held sacred" [D 115]), then her loss represents the loss of his only witness, his only validation. This insight restores an achieved fullness of pain to the loss of the woman's friendship expressed in the other half of Duffy's private aphorism, "and friendship between man and woman is impossible because there must be sexual intercourse" (D 112).[21] These reflections bend our attention to the exceptional possibility of absolute closeting that Sedgwick ascribes only to the homosexual. Can Duffy's life be construed as consignment to a life undisclosed to anyone and thereby reduced to a Derridean trace, unregistered on any consciousness? "His life would be lonely too until he, too, died, ceased to exist, became a memory—if anyone remembered him" (D 116). Duffy's mourning for the dead woman is accompanied by his mourning for himself, as though he were already ontologically dead. Perhaps nowhere in Joyce's work is paralysis invoked more poignantly than in this subject's inability—on literal peril of death, if we recall that Parnell and Wilde were both dead within a few years of their scandals—to be anything other than static, still, and silent.

Notes

An earlier version of this essay appeared in the *James Joyce Quarterly* 37, no. 1–2.

1. Tanja Vesala-Varttala's fine discussion of "A Painful Case" argues that "The painful case is contagious in several senses" and that "the idea of a painful case radiates even beyond James Duffy, pointing unrelentingly at the reader" (108). She

makes the argument for readerly implication ("the reader's 'moral nature' becomes problematic and problematized in the process of re-reading Joyce's story") by keeping her focus on "the textual entanglement [that] never allows the reader to break all bonds to Duffy" (80, 109).

2. Wolfgang Wicht writes: "Female subjectivity is occluded from the narrative. But since its absence from the male-dominated and conventional newspaper report and from Duffy's dismissive perspective is made conspicuously present by the text, the reader is urged to criticize these reactions" (136–37). I concur but go further to argue that the female feelings occluded on the representational level are retrieved on a performative level—in the act of reading.

3. Tanja Vesala-Varttala invokes Ross Chambers's notion of the oppositional character of the narrative function and the textual function of fictional writing (*Room for Maneuver: Reading (the) Oppositional (in) Narrative* [1991]) in her examination of the problems of ethical reading in *Dubliners* (6–12). Wolfgang Wicht also registers this oppositionality in "A Painful Case": "Rather, the 'story' represents a person who constructs himself as subject of his ego, whereas the 'text' deconstructs this self-reflexive construct of the 'I.' This was a paradigmatic innovation in fiction. By 1906, Joyce was far from being a traditional short story writer" (131).

4. Girard 266; see also his discussion of "The Hero's *Askesis*" (153–75). Barbara Sloan, in a 1971 essay on the narrator in "A Painful Case," finds in Gabriele D'Annunzio, among others, Joyce's model for the isolated figure of the artist as superman. "D'Annunzio belonged to the group of great nineteenth century egotists of whom Wagner (another of Joyce's favorites) was also one," she writes (29). Joseph Voelker in 1980 revisits the intertextual analogues for Duffy's isolation by adding Yeats's "The Tables of the Law" to the works of Nietzsche and Hauptmann as sources of the *Übermensch* type that Duffy represents.

5. Don Gifford writes, "some Irish versions of the Tristan and Iseult story say that it was here that they consummated their ill-fated love" (81). Donald Torchiana gives the topographical significance of the Tristan and Isolde legend for the landscape of James Duffy's and Emily Sinico's relationship a full and interesting explication in *Backgrounds for Joyce's "Dubliners"* (165–75).

6. Wolfgang Wicht notes that "Joyce criticism has perhaps not noticed that the triangle involving Mrs. Sinico, Mr Duffy and Captain Sinico parallels the situation of Kitty O'Shea, Parnell, and Captain O'Shea." Wicht draws this point from the allusion: "Unlike Parnell, who went ahead and married at the cost of his career, Mr Duffy is a coward, an egocentric neurotic, a nothing" (137). I will take this parallel much further in the direction of exploring Joyce's generic play with the adultery narrative, only then to complicate it by layering it with another scandal narrative.

7. Garry Leonard writes of this scene, "Their conversations, held in a 'dark discreet room' are described as though the act of rhetorical intercourse was equivalent to the act of sexual intercourse" (221).

8. See Mary Lowe-Evans's "Who Killed Mrs Sinico?" for a comprehensive discussion of scholarly dissent with Duffy's judgment, that he had "sentenced her to

death" (*D* 117). Lowe- Evans makes the fascinating argument that it is Mary Sinico, Emily Sinico's daughter, who is "the proximate cause of her mother's demise" (398).

9. Significantly, one of the few conversations between James Duffy and Emily Sinico we are given to hear concerns Duffy's disenchantment with the Irish Socialist Party—"The workmen's discussions, he said, were too timorous. . . . they resented an exactitude which was the product of a leisure not within their reach" (*D* 111). After the abolition of the Land League, Parnell too seems to have shared his disenchantments with Kitty O'Shea—"It is certainly true that he was tired of a mass movement which—in a moment of exasperation—he described to Mrs O'Shea as hollow and wanting in solidarity" (Bew 60). Parnell, however, overcame his discouragement and went on to become leader of the Irish National League, whereas Duffy abandoned the ISP.

10. Discussions of Duffy's possible homosexuality have resurfaced after my first presentations and drafts of this argument. Prior to the appearance of both her and my essays on homosexuality in "A Painful Case" in the fall 1999/winter 2000 issue of the *James Joyce Quarterly,* Roberta Jackson reports, "Just two articles note that Joyce's story is about homosexuality—a 1963 psychoanalytic study by Stephen Reid and David Norris's 1994 survey, 'The "unhappy mania" and Mr. Bloom's Cigar: Homosexuality in the Works of James Joyce'" (87). Her footnotes indicate that Reid's article, "'The Beast in the Jungle' and 'A Painful Case': Two Different Sufferings," appeared in *American Imago* 20 (1963): 221–39. David Norris's essay appeared in the spring 1994 issue of the *James Joyce Quarterly* and notes that James Duffy's journal reference to love between men is "the most positive, if again passing, reference to homosexual activity in *Dubliners*" (365). I have since noted that Thomas Connolly, in the Clive Hart collection of essays on *Dubliners,* mentions Reid's argument and notes that "With his homosexual and heterosexual fears, James Duffy appears to be an adult version of the young boy of the first three stories, especially the boy as he is depicted in 'An Encounter,' who is so fearful in the presence of the old paederast" (114). At the time Jackson's essay was in press, Colleen Lamos's superb theoretical analysis, "Duffy's Subjectivation: The Psychic Life of 'A Painful Case,'" appeared in *Masculinities in Joyce/Postcolonial Constructions, European Joyce Studies 10.* Lamos uses Judith Butler's theory of the construction of the subject to argue that "Duffy's is a case of foreclosure that, as Butler explains, entails a 'double disavowal, a never having loved, and a never having lost'" (63). The consequence of this double disavowal for Duffy is that "the foreclosure of same-sex love coincides with the foreclosure of other-sex love; he disavows *both* homosexuality and heterosexuality" (66). This foreclosure consequently ensures that "Duffy's position is off the hetero/homo binary grid that Butler's theory maps for subjectivation" (66). This reading is an extremely significant supplement to the critical tradition of diagnosing Duffy's failing as one of narcissism, because it engages in a psychoanalytically sophisticated discourse the roles of the foreclosure of both homosexual and heterosexual desire in the story.

11. Indeed, knowledge that Joyce "stole" Duffy's aphorism from his brother

Stanislaus's diary militates against our reading it as a veiled expression of homosexual desire, or attributing anything other than a stylistic significance to it. Warren Beck writes, "As for the other sentence, Joyce's cribbing it suggests the deplorable fact that people sometimes steal things they don't really need" (223)—as though this epigram baldly announcing society's homosexual taboo were an excrescence in "A Painful Case."

12. David Wright's interesting discussion of the dates in the story concludes: "In any case, Emily Sinico's death obviously occurs late in 1903. Since the story covers a four-year period, its action therefore must, according to the data in *Ulysses*, begin in late 1899, which might or might not be significant" (111). Yet I would argue that an important possible significance for setting the story in 1899 is its temporal proximity to the imprisonment of Oscar Wilde in 1895, and his release from prison to an unforgiving public in 1897. Joyce's description of Wilde's plight upon his release from prison elaborates its pathos: "One after another drove him from the door, refusing him food and shelter, and at nightfall he finally ended up under the windows of his brother, weeping and babbling like a child" (*CW* 203).

13. Suzette Henke draws our attention to the combined maternal and platonic attraction of Emily Sinico for Duffy: "Because the narcissistic Duffy wants a matriarchal muse rather than a flesh-and-blood lover, he strategically represses the amorous dimensions of their simmering liaison" (35). Henke's indictment of Duffy for narcissism and solipsism is widespread in the critical responses to the story and is perfectly legitimate, given the narrative prompts that point the reader toward just this conclusion. I argue only that, on one level at least, these prompts might also function as an ethical trap for the reader.

14. In her analysis of Joyce's draft revisions of "A Painful Case," Jana Giles notes that "Joyce rewrites, '. . . Mrs. Sinico threw her arms around forward into his lap and seemed to faint' to read '. . . Mrs. Sinico caught up his hand passionately and pressed it to her cheek'" (202–3). Although I agree with Giles that the final version is "less melodramatic, less sexual, and more poignant" (203), I find that it concurrently makes Duffy's response *more* melodramatic, sexual, tinged with hysteria. By changing Emily Sinico's movement from one that thrusts her arms into Duffy's lap (in what could justifiably be misconstrued as a vulgar gesture) to one of extreme emotional tenderness, the focus on sexual expression is shifted from the woman to the man.

15. Although an earlier draft copy (*JJA* 4: 129) gives Duffy's retroactive contemplation of his choices an amplitude more in tune with thoughts of an adulterous elopement, I would argue that even this passage remains ambiguous and equivocal:

The fact discomposed him because his own statement of it to himself seemed something of an accusation. He asked himself what else could he have done—carried a furtive comedy which must have ended in mutual disgust or gone away with her out of Ireland. Either course would have been impossible the one of an undignified intrigue the other a ridiculous elopement. He had acted for the best: (*JJA* 4, 129; quoted in Giles, 208).

These contemplated choices rule out neither an uncomprehending latency of homosexual feeling nor Duffy's entertaining the kind of personally complex domestic arrangement (like Wilde's own marriage and household) that were not uncommon among British homosexuals, lesbians, and bisexuals in Duffy's day.

16. Roberta Jackson's excellent essay discusses the historical context of homosexual censorship and repression, including particularly the gloss on the "medicalization of male same-sex desire" in the story's title (89), along with the delayed advent of queer critical readings of the story.

17. In *Quare Joyce,* Joseph Valente writes: "the fact that Joyce apprehended social persecution as the price of such exceptionalism cannot only be traced, as it most often is, to the childhood trauma wrought by the ruin of his political hero, Charles Stewart Parnell, but also to the commotion created by Wilde's three trials" (8).

18. On August 12, 1906, Joyce wrote to Stanislaus: "I am thinking of rewriting *A Painful Case* so you might send me the MS along with the book of notes I had in Paris and the Latin quotations from the prophecies of the Abbot Joachim of Flora" (*SL* 94). Four days later, on August 16, 1906, he tells Stanislaus: "I am reading *The Picture of Dorian Grey* [sic] in Italian" (*SL* 95). Three days later, on August 19, 1906, Joyce writes Stannie that he has finished *Dorian Gray*:

I can imagine the capital which Wilde's prosecuting counsel made out of certain parts of it. It is not very difficult to read between the lines. Wilde seems to have had some good intentions in writing it—some wish to put himself before the world—but the book is rather crowded with lies and epigrams. If he had had the courage to develop the allusions in the book it might have been better. I suspect he has done this in some privately-printed books. (*SL* 96)

There is no evidence that the Wilde novella conditioned Joyce's desire to revise "A Painful Case," but a link is not impossible.

19. Sedgwick offers an important antidote to the kind of constructions of Nietzsche that allowed John William Corrington to read Duffy's acquisition of Nietzsche as suggesting an intensification of his fascist predispositions. He writes, "The total effect cannot but put us in mind of the similarities between Duffy and certain minor Nazi functionaries whose whole study was to reduce the animate world to a collection of things, to bring the 'order' of death and silence from the 'chaos' of brawling undirected humanity" (134).

20. Captain Sinico's testimony at the inquest allows us to reconstruct his absence on the day of his wife's death. Although "he had arrived only that morning from Rotterdam," he "was not in Dublin at the time of the accident" (*D* 114). Emily Sinico

died at ten o'clock at night. Where was Sinico if he was back from Rotterdam but was not in Dublin that night?

21. Colleen Lamos produces a fascinating analysis of Duffy that concludes that "he stands in a melancholic (non)relation to the world." She therefore rejects the notion that James Duffy mourns for Emily Sinico at all. "Having refused both love and the deprivation of it, Duffy does not mourn; precisely his inability to grieve—his pain*less*ness, as it were—marks him as a melancholic, in Butler's sense of the term" (63).

Works Cited

Beck, Warren. *Joyce's "Dubliners": Substance, Vision, and Art*. Durham: Duke University Press, 1969.

Bew, Paul. *Charles Stewart Parnell*. Dublin: McGill Macmillan, 1991.

Brady, Margery. *The Love Story of Parnell and Katharine O'Shea*. Dublin: Mercier, 1991.

Chambers, Ross. *Room for Maneuver: Reading (the) Oppositional (in) Narrative*. Chicago: University of Chicago Press, 1991.

Connolly, Thomas E. "A Painful Case." In *James Joyce's "Dubliners": Critical Essays*, edited by Clive Hart, 107–21. New York: Viking, 1969.

Corrington, John William. "Isolation as Motif in 'A Painful Case.'" In *James Joyce's "Dubliners": A Critical Handbook*, edited by James R. Baker and Thomas F. Staley, 130–39. Belmont, Calif.: Wadsworth Publishing, 1969.

Gifford, Don. *Notes for "Dubliners" and "A Portrait of the Artist As a Young Man."* 2d ed. Berkeley and Los Angeles: University of California Press, 1982.

Giles, Jana. "The Craft of 'A Painful Case': A Study of Revisions." In *New Perspectives on "Dubliners."* European Joyce Studies 7, edited by Mary Power and Ulrich Schneider, 195–210. Amsterdam: Rodopi, 1997.

Girard, René. *Deceit, Desire, and the Novel: Self and Other in Literary Structure*. 1961. Translated by Yvonne Freccero. Baltimore: Johns Hopkins University Press, 1965.

Henke, Suzette A. *James Joyce and the Politics of Desire*. New York: Routledge, 1990.

Ingersoll, Earl G. *Engendered Trope in Joyce's "Dubliners."* Carbondale: Southern Illinois University Press, 1996.

Jackson, Roberta. "The Open Closet in *Dubliners*: James Duffy's Painful Case." *James Joyce Quarterly* 37, no. 1/2 (fall 1999/winter 2000): 83–97.

Kershner, R. B. *Joyce, Bakhtin, and Popular Literature: Chronicles of Disorder*. Chapel Hill: University of North Carolina Press, 1989.

Lamos, Colleen. "Duffy's Subjectivation: The Psychic Life of 'A Painful Case.'" In *Masculinities in Joyce/Postcolonial Constructions*. European Joyce Studies 10, edited by Christine van Boheemen-Saaf and Colleen Lamos, 59–71. Amsterdam: Rodopi, 2001.

Leonard, Garry M. *Reading "Dubliners" Again: A Lacanian Perspective.* Syracuse: Syracuse University Press, 1993.

Lowe-Evans, Mary. "Who Killed Mrs. Sinico?" *Studies in Short Fiction* 32, no. 3 (summer 1995): 395–402.

Norris, David. "The 'unhappy mania' and Mr. Bloom's Cigar: Homosexuality in the Works of James Joyce." *James Joyce Quarterly* 31, no. 3 (spring 1994): 357–73.

Sedgwick, Eve Kosofsky. *Epistemology of the Closet.* Berkeley and Los Angeles: University of California Press, 1990.

Sloan, Barbara L. "The D'Annunzian Narrator in 'A Painful Case': Silent, Exiled, and Cunning." *James Joyce Quarterly* 9, no. 1 (fall 1971): 26–36.

Tolstoy, Count Leo. *Anna Karenina.* Translated by Constance Garnett. New York: Modern Library, 1950.

Torchiana, Donald T. *Backgrounds for Joyce's "Dubliners."* Boston: Allen and Unwin, 1986.

Valente, Joseph. "Joyce's (Sexual) Choices: A Historical Overview." In *Quare Joyce,* edited by Joseph Valente, 1–16. Ann Arbor: University of Michigan Press, 1998.

Vesala-Verttala, Tanja. *Sympathy and Joyce's "Dubliners": Ethical Probings of Reading, Narrative, and Textuality.* Tampere: Tampere University Press, 1999.

Voelker, Joseph C. "'He Lumped the Emancipates Together': More Analogues for Joyce's Mr. Duffy." *James Joyce Quarterly* 18, no. 1 (fall 1980): 23–34.

Wicht, Wolfgang. "'Eveline,' and/as 'A Painful Case': Paralysis, Desire, Signifiers." *New Perspectives on "Dubliners." European Joyce Studies* 7, edited by Mary Power and Ulrich Schneider, 115–42. Amsterdam: Rodopi, 1997.

Wright, David G. "The Secret Life of Leopold Bloom and Emily Sinico." *James Joyce Quarterly* 37, no. 1/2 (fall 1999/winter 2000): 99–112.

Joyce and the Origins of Modernism

... What Is Not Said in "Telemachus"

Morton P. Levitt

Over the years, I've suggested various, usually imagined moments as the possible starting point of literary modernism, under the principle that since it's impossible to single out an actual historical moment (1900? 1910? 1914? 1918? 1922?) when so rich and diffuse a period began (not to mention when it may or may not have ended), why not imagine a symbolic event that seems best to commemorate the most important cultural development of the twentieth century? The first of my imaginings was the moment when the young James Joyce purportedly threw the manuscript of what we have since come to call *Stephen Hero* into the fire and began work instead on *A Portrait of the Artist as a Young Man*. In broad, rather general terms, this moment continues to work rather nicely, I think, celebrating the leap from the traditional Edwardian *Künstlerroman* to a form not yet fully defined but surely more modern.

For instance, who doesn't recall the scene in *A Portrait* in which Stephen Dedalus, in full view of all of his schoolmates, accosts Emma Clery and thereby invites her rejection? Is that in chapter 2 or chapter 3? Before the hellfire sermon or soon after? No one remembers it? Well, obviously not, since although that scene did escape the probably apocryphal fire, the young author chose to leave it behind in *Stephen Hero*, his first draft, preferring for the finished version of his novel the possibility that poor Emma (who is made to carry through literary history so heavy a load) had indeed betrayed the developing young but still Romantic artist. This uncertainty is far more appropriate to the maturing artist's vision of the world than certainty could possibly have been. And so my imagined moment does make some general sense. It is in this same spirit that Joyce opens *A Portrait* with the child's-eye view of reality through a glass darkly.

Two other such imagined moments work much more precisely, however: the first of them the moment when that same James Joyce decided to turn his first few, isolated published stories into that revolutionary, developing book of stories named for their setting, *Dubliners*; the second at the start of *Ulysses*, when he chose to name his point of view for us in a manner that most readers have missed. These two moments, both of them focused on Joyce's subtly developing, modernist point of view—of what a character may know, of what an author can tell us, of a reflected vision of a changing world—work in concert.

Distracted by the flash and fire that characterize so many of the modernist innovations in fiction, especially in point of view (that presumed "experimentation" which so disturbed F. R. Leavis and C. P. Snow and a later generation of English novelists), we are likely to miss what is perhaps the most revolutionary aspect of that extraordinary literary revolution: what is left out. While it is the encyclopedic Joyce, for example, who most attracts our attention—the Joyce who in *Ulysses* demands the total involvement of his reader and thereby creates both a break with the more leisurely implied contract between Victorian author and audience, and, at the same time, a new kind of attentive reader; or the Joyce who in *Finnegans Wake* provides a glossary of twentieth-century history and culture as an integral part of this comic story of a dysfunctional Dublin Protestant family and thus makes its members (miraculously, it seems) universal—the most daring leap that Joyce ever made, I believe, occurs near the beginning of his literary career, in *Dubliners*.

This is a leap, as it were, in two stages: the first conceptual (and structural), the second in its vision of reality (and of narrative technique as a means to effect that reality). Conceptually, there were no prose fiction models for the kind of interconnected yet independent short stories that Joyce creates in *Dubliners*. The only previous potential models were from poetry, especially such sonnet sequences as George Meredith's *Modern Love* (1862). But even these are connected primarily on the surface level of characterization and plot, whereas the links in *Dubliners* are more nuanced, very nearly subterranean: these fifteen tales are related to one another essentially through image, attitude, tone, theme, and point of view, matter that would become basic to the construction of modernist fictions but that was quite new in 1905, when Joyce at twenty-three began his (re)visionary work, and is even today less readily defined, less easily created and recognized. The conception itself is our first sign of Joyce's creative genius: these stories are more about the place than about its people (although they, too, are vitally realized), more about the forces impacting on their lives than about the facts of those lives themselves.[1]

In an early draft version of "The Sisters"—quite similar to the story originally published in *The Irish Homestead* on August 13, 1904—the young James Joyce wrote, from the point of view of his still younger protagonist:

> Three nights in succession I had found myself in Great Britain Street at that hour, as if by providence. Three nights I had raised my eyes to that lighted square of window and speculated. I seemed to understand that it would occur at night. But in spite of the providence which had led my feet and in spite of the reverent curiosity of my eyes I had discovered nothing. Each night the square was lighted in the same way, faintly and evenly. It was not the light of candles so far as I could see. Therefore it had not occurred yet.
>
> On the fourth night at that hour I was in another part of the city. It may have been the same providence that led me there—a whimsical kind of providence—to take me at a disadvantage. As I went home I wondered was that square of window lighted as before or did it reveal the ceremonious candles in the light of which the Christian must take his last sleep. I was not surprised, then, when at supper I found myself a prophet. Old Cotter and my uncle were talking at the fire, smoking. Old Cotter was a retired distiller who owned a batch of prize setters. He used to be very interesting when I knew him first, talking about *faints* and *worms*, but afterwards he became tedious.
>
> While I was eating my stirabout I heard him say to my uncle:
>
> —Without a doubt. The upper storey (he tapped an unnecessary hand at his forehead) was gone—
>
> —So they said. I never could see much of it. I thought he was sane enough—
>
> —So he was, at times, said old Cotter—
>
> I sniffed the *was* apprehensively and gulped down some stirabout.
>
> —Is he any better, Uncle [and the name "John" is crossed out here]?—
>
> [. . .]
>
> —He's dead—
>
> —O. . . . .—
>
> [. . .]

So old Cotter had got the better of me for all my vigilance of three nights. It is often annoying the way people will blunder on what you have elaborately planned for. I was sure he would die at night.[2]

There is virtually none of this in the version of "The Sisters" that opens *Dubliners* for us today: no name for the uncle and not much presence, no absence in another part of the city for the boy, no questioning of the dead man's sanity ("there was something uncanny about him," old Cotter says now [D 10]), no questions from the boy ("Is he any better, Uncle?") and no explicit comments of his, as he remembers past events ("It is often annoying the way people will blunder on"). What we have instead are those pivotal terms, *simony, gnomon*, the dread *paralysis*, with all of their imagistic and thematic implications for the larger text of *Dubliners*; we also have the clear sense that we are hearing everything in the present, as the boy hears it; as well as the explicit comment that nothing in these events may be made explicit: "I knew that I was under observation," the boy tells us but not his viewers, "so I continued eating as if the news had not interested me" (D 10). The adults in the story coyly avoid offering in front of the boy their own opinions about the dead priest (although they obviously want to elicit his views), and he does not trust them with his thoughts or emotions. Nor, evidently, does he trust us, leaving us, as he does, to fill in the details for ourselves (a sign, it would seem, that the author does indeed trust his reader). And we at least understand enough by this point not to be surprised at the absence of a "whimsical . . . providence." The key to understanding "The Sisters" as we know it today lies in what is not being said and in what we must do as readers to manage the absences.

Similarly, in the pivotal final scene of the story, with the boy's aunt and Father Flynn's sisters, we are in this early version told directly what had gone wrong in the priest's life: "It was his scrupulousness, you see, that affected his mind. The duties of the priesthood were too much for him," says his sister (D 250). No mystery here and no ambiguity either: merely another Dublin story of a spoiled priest, a little daring perhaps for *The Irish Homestead* in 1904, but nothing that would especially shock or surprise its readers. The final words of both early and late versions of the story are almost the same, describing in both the image of the priest's breakdown in the confessional, "Wide-awake and laughing-like to himself" (D 18). In the version that we know today, however, this image "made them think that there was something gone wrong with him" (D 18), where in the early version, "Then they knew something was wrong" (D 252). We know nothing for certain today. And so it is fitting that Joyce chose finally to omit the final words of his early version, "—God rest his soul!—" (D 252).

Victorian omniscience (God in the narrative) is omitted in "The Sisters"; certainty is left out, preparing the way for *Dubliners* as an entity and for every modernist fiction that follows it; the reader's narrative crutches are left standing against the wall, uncalled upon, gathering dust; the Victorian world is left behind where it belongs, in the nineteenth century. The new literary century, which will prove both encyclopedic and demanding, thus begins with a simple, yet revolutionary act of omission.

This is not a simple, familiar matter of Joyce's practice as editor and reviser of his own work to add to and subtract from his texts as he proceeded, always slowly, toward publication. Joycean critics from the start— long before anyone, except perhaps Joyce himself, could imagine the phenomenon of Joyce Studies—have recognized his tendency, his evident need, to add to and occasionally omit from his manuscripts and proofs. Even when such details relate to matters of substance ("love" and "death" the most obvious example), this is a procedural practice on Joyce's part, sign of his compulsive need to get it right for as long as time allows. Can anyone doubt that if he were still alive today he would continue to find possibilities to expand upon in *Finnegans Wake*? If Joyceans can do so, surely Joyce himself could.

But the omissions from "The Sisters" are in themselves substantive, not merely figures of adjustment or nuance: they alter the very nature of the work; it is as if we are witnessing on the page Joyce's vision of the world expand as he omits. What matters about these omissions is their implication for the vision of the world that the novelist is offering his readers, a vision that Joyce is discovering and developing as he omits, a world that half a century afterward, others would come to call modernist.

In the final version of "The Sisters," Joyce sets the young boy who is his protagonist and point of view at the center of a society whose hostility he intuits yet never articulates. The boy, of course, is a projection of what the young Joyce might have been had he had the advantage of greater experience, greater wisdom, a greater sense of isolation: the position of several of the protagonists of the stories in *Dubliners* and the very condition of the Romantic artist in a clearly post-Romantic world. Joyce's sources in "The Sisters," as in the other stories in *Dubliners*, are explicitly post-Romantic: the literary realism of Ibsen, the naturalism of Zola, the narrative innovations of Flaubert. Ibsen's presence in "The Sisters" rests in the social surfaces, the tensions, the personal discoveries of life and death in lower-middle-class Dublin society; the naturalistic presence may be found in the darkening streets outside these closed doors and barely lighted windows, in the seamy subsurface of religious and sexual innuendo as to the dead priest's past (and perhaps his relationship with the boy), and in the sense of fatalism in the face of such forces. And Flaubert's narrative presence, finally, emerges within the boy's limited perspective: limited to what the boy can know, limited by his experience and sensibility, limited in what he will share with his various audiences. What Joyce adds to the mix—the surprising discovery that would prove the key to all of his work, I believe, from the remaining stories of *Dubliners* all the way through to *Finnegans Wake*—is what he does not tell us, what he does not say at all, what he knows well enough even at this early stage of his development to leave out: and thus leave to his reader. The great master of the vast, encyclopedic modernist narrative is distinguished most by what he omits.

The continuity between the boy in "The Sisters" and those in "An Encounter" and "Araby" is evident, somewhat less so that between him/them and those later manifestations, the immature protagonists of "After the Race" and "The Boarding House"; the girls who will never mature to become women in "Eveline" and "A Mother" (Kathleen Kearney the victim of her parent, Eveline ultimately her own victim); as well as the middle-aged men of "A Painful Case" and "The Dead." As Joyce develops all of these figures, they become at once naturalistic victims of circumstance and existential heroes, responsible for their own fates. Of them all, only Bob Doran's fate is made manifest and that, of course, only in *Ulysses*, but it is easy enough to extrapolate from these open-ended stories to recognize where each of them stands in relation to that first boy in *Dubliners'* first story. (I exclude Maria from this chain of character continuity because she lacks the consciousness to be either hero or victim.) And it would be easy enough to stretch the chain to contain most of the other Dubliners whom we encounter through Joyce.

What we notice most of all from this catalogue is that the continuity within *Dubliners* is forged largely by character and theme; where it is also possible to see connections from this book to Joyce's novels, the links that matter most are primarily matters of style and technique, and especially of point of view. Again, arguably, the most vital of them relate not to the author's magnificent (and sometimes mannerist) inventions—those rich and complex additions that may even appear encyclopedic as we view them on the page—but rather to what he leaves out: this is not merely a conceptual matter but one also of narrative technique. (Think of the beginning and the end of "The Dead," as we slide without notice from Lily's to Gabriel's consciousness and from him, silently, to a sense of universality.) As difficult as it may seem at first to accept—for it surely does seem counterintuitive—the great narrative secret of both *Ulysses* and *Finnegans Wake* derives from that first lesson that the young James Joyce taught himself when revising "The Sisters."

As a generality, while this may seem mildly surprising, it is not likely, I think, to be terribly controversial. But its implications, if followed through closely while carefully reading the texts, may prove a bit more difficult for some critics of Joyce to accept, for they are likely to upset some widely accepted assumptions: about narrative technique especially, to be sure, but also about the worldview which emerges from that technique. To assume a consistent development within Joyce's canon, from the first revised story of his quietly revolutionary first book through to his aggressively demanding and encyclopedic last book—among all the works of his canon, that is—is also to assume a consistency of narrative development within each work: even, that is, within *Ulysses*, from the very first scene to the last. And because we have tended to misread that first scene, set atop the tower, we have assumed that there is a more or less conventional beginning to an otherwise revolutionary book. But we are mistaken in that assumption, I am convinced. Viewed within the context of the history of narrative technique, *Ulysses* is radical from its opening words, consistently radical through to its closing words. There is no break—in technique or in theme—between the first and the second parts of the novel. And so the conclusions that follow from that assumption are similarly likely to prove mistaken. And if that is true, it may also prove true that some of our expectations about modernism itself have been wrong.

In what may well be the most influential of the many readings of narrative technique/point of view and its impact on our understanding of Joyce's—and modernism's—most influential novel, Karen Lawrence, discussing what she calls "The Narrative Norm," comments on the "continuity" between the first three chapters of *Ulysses* and *A Portrait of the Artist as a Young Man*, "in particular," as well as their links to "the traditional novel." "[E]ven the reader of *Ulysses* who fails to recognize this continuity will experience a sense of security from the presence of this narrative voice," she assures us.

The staples of the novel—third-person narration, dialogue, and dramatization of a scene—also promise narrative security to the reader who begins *Ulysses*: they act as signposts promising him familiar terrain on the subsequent pages.

Lawrence concludes—and here I am in total agreement with her—that "*Ulysses* begins like a narrative with confidence in the adequacy of the novel form" (38). Where we disagree, however, is in what such confidence consists: what, precisely, is that "adequacy of the novel form"? Since I am convinced that the most basic tradition of the novel—from Defoe, Richardson, Fielding, and Sterne on to the present moment—demands changing narrative patterns in order to realize and manifest the changing times, I see such "adequacy" not in reversion to familiar forms but in their adaptation.

Lawrence and I also agree generally that *Dubliners* is something of an anomaly in regard to "third-person narration," one each of us values. But where I read *Ulysses* as continuing in and developing *Dubliners'* line, she sees it as representing a rupture:

> In the initial conception of *Ulysses*, Joyce departed from the aesthetic of economy and scrupulous choice that had directed the writing of *Dubliners* in favor of an aesthetic of comprehensiveness and minute representation. (39)

The implications of such a break are significant: *Ulysses*, in Lawrence's formulation, is a novel split somewhere in two, the first eleven chapters more or less traditional—marked by "the presence of an identifiable and relatively consistent style of narration"—the final seven chapters far more "radical" (41, 3).

The implications of this reading, now widely accepted, are significant both for Joyce studies and for studies in the modernist novel in general. They lend unwitting support, in retrospect, for the virulent attack by Leavis and Snow on modernist "experimentation" as a departure from the novel's great tradition,[3] as well as, paradoxically, for the subsequent postmodernist (theoretical and fictional) assault on the allegedly too-traditional modernist approach. Lawrence can have anticipated none of this and bears no responsibility for it. But I do believe that her reading misjudges Joycean narrative: the text that she reads as a break from *Dubliners*, I read as its continuation and expansion; the novel that she sees as split between an early bow to tradition and a later "succession of stylistic experiments" (208), I see as consistent from the first words of the opening episode,

"Telemachus," to the final words of "Penelope"; "the recognizable, idiosyncratic narrative voice" that Lawrence hears as *Ulysses* opens—that
"dominant narrative voice," that "third-person narration" and "third-person narrator" (40–41)—is to my ears not a narration at all, with no narrator, no character, no presence in any guise serving as intermediary between
the events and the reader.[4]

My disagreement here is not just with *The Odyssey of Style in
"Ulysses,"* a book that I admire even as I disagree with some of its basic
assumptions and conclusions. For Lawrence's presumed narrator is part of
a widespread and, I believe, careless tendency in recent years. In *Narrative
Contexts in "Ulysses,"* Bernard Benstock traces, with a hint of disapproval,
some of those critics who have posited a narrator for the various chapters
of the novel. Practically every one of the contributors to Clive Hart and
David Hayman's *James Joyce's "Ulysses"* speaks, at some point or other, of
a "narrator."[5] Building on and citing Hart and Hayman, Hugh Kenner in
Ulysses gives us the "Arranger," he of the "difficult personality," who,
"when he deigns to notice our presence," "treats us ... with the sour xenophobic indifference Dublin can turn upon visitors who have lingered long
enough for hospitality's first gleam to tarnish." Noting that Hart has seen
in him "the spirit of Dublin itself" (65), Kenner attempts to explain his
presence and function but in a way that reminds us irresistibly of our old
friend, the "narrator."[6]

It is the rare article or submission on Joyce that I read these days that
does not, somewhere or other, often in passing, mention this narrator:
sometimes in order to account for an unusual and perhaps difficult usage,
more often as a matter of course, unthinkingly. For Lawrence, the "Telemachus" episode especially gives witness to his "naive narrative quality"
(45), naïve, of course, because of what she sees as the essentially traditional
nature of narrative in the first half of Joyce's novel. For the so-called narrator of "Telemachus" relies upon and, in turn, makes possible this reading
of the novel as, at first, traditional and only gradually turning revolutionary, that is to say, modernist. I find it necessary to demur.

The problem is manifested even more forcefully in Kenner's otherwise
elegant reading of Joycean narration in *Joyce's Voices*. Kenner identifies
many of the same issues that I do in Joyce's use of point of view, but he
resolves them rather differently and, I believe, in the end, inconsistently.
For although his "Uncle Charles Principle" states, in a memorable phrase,
that *"the narrative idiom need not be the narrator's"* (18), he nonetheless
seems compelled to find a narrator in Joyce even where his own evidence

and system would seem to deny one. When Kenner declares, "The Uncle Charles Principle entails writing about someone much as that someone would choose to be written about" (21), he is attempting to account for the difference between what he calls the "grammar" of a description and its "idiom": thus, "The grammar of twelve of the stories [of the fifteen in *Dubliners*] is that of third-person narrative, imparting a deceptive look of impersonal truth. The diction frequently tells a different tale" (16). His prime examples are very nearly my own—the beginnings of "The Dead," with its tacit invocation of Lily's point of view and its subtle shift to Gabriel's, and of "Telemachus." Up to this point, Kenner and I are in almost absolute agreement, even if our phrasing is different; but instead of concluding that the diction of the opening scene of the novel is Stephen's, Kenner compounds the confusion by positing a "second narrative voice," a "second narrator" (71), a conclusion that I find cumbersome, unnecessary, even dangerous, for it would seem to emphasize that same omniscient presence that Joyce was endeavoring to avoid.

As I understand it, the verb "to narrate" is a transitive verb, requiring an action that goes across from one source to another: from a narrator, that is, to an audience (if only an implicit audience). We may use the term "narrative" as a synonym for "story" or for "novel," but this is not necessarily the same narrative as told by a narrator. Speaking of "narrative," then, does not automatically entitle us to speak of a "narrator." For this "narrator," even this "Arranger," or putative relative, is, in practice, merely a presumably acceptable way of naming Joyce an omniscient author. No one would dare do so directly, of course, for everyone knows that Joyce exiled that Victorian gentleman from the province of the modernist novel: indeed, we might well define the modernist novel by that very absence, as by the many and intricate means of point of view that Joyce and his followers devised to effect it. But what else does this nonexistent, nonfunctioning narrator manage to do except allow us to attribute omniscience to Joyce without actually labeling him so?

In continuing to leave out all traces of certainty and thereby to lure his reader into the lives of his people, as he had first learned to do in revising "The Sisters," Joyce omits any intervening voice at all at the tower other than those we hear in conversation (those of Buck Mulligan, Stephen Dedalus, the Irishist Englishman Haines and his counterbalance, that unknowing symbol of Ireland, the old milkwoman). There is no need for a narrator when Stephen is present to filter all of this material for us and to relay it to us.

From the first words of "Telemachus" through to its end, Stephen is the sole point of view of the episode, and he is never here (as he will be in "Aeolus" and "Scylla and Charybdis"—and then not especially effectively) a narrator. The evidence is plentiful and, I believe, conclusive. And so, when we ask the question, "Who is it who says the words, 'Stately, plump Buck Mulligan came from the stairhead,'" we are asking the wrong question. For no one recites them. They are not spoken at all, but imagined, and their source is present all the time, the person most likely to provide the ironic tone that the words require, as well as the listener to and observer of all that will follow. The incongruity of "Stately" and "plump"— along with the deflation that follows in their juxtaposition—indicates that the terms are not descriptive after all but rather judgmental, that they are not objective but subjective, that they derive not from some presumably neutral, if imagined, "third-person narrator" but are, in function, first-person. (And what matters in point of view is not appearance but function, so that a third-person pronoun may prove highly subjective and a first-person pronoun may serve—in practice at least—objectively. To be bound in our assessment by the form of a word is to assume that novels are both to be written and read by grammarians.)

The source of this ironic view of young doctor Mulligan—a view never to be shared with its victim because the perpetrator does not quite dare to do so—is not some outsider but his towermate. The question that we should ask is not who says, "Stately, plump Buck Mulligan came from the stairhead" (*U* 1.1) but who hears him and who sees him do so, who visualizes and (on the basis of past, unexpressed experience) judges him.

And in the event that we miss Stephen's presence, Joyce notes it explicitly for us: shaving, cavorting, calling out loudly and blasphemously, Mulligan, we discover, "skipped off the gunrest and looked gravely at *his watcher*" (*U* 1.30; emphasis added), that skeptical and scorned young man of the "absurd name" (*U* 1.34), who is now, finally, identified for us as Stephen Dedalus. And just in case we may have missed the point that it is Stephen's view of Mulligan that is being shared with us, the key term is now repeated, although its form has been changed: "*watching* him still" (*U* 1.37; emphasis added). There is not a comment in "Telemachus" that Stephen cannot hear, not an event that he cannot witness directly or at least visualize, not an observation that he cannot make. For even if he does not ascend to the roof of the tower until some moments after Mulligan, with the performance already in progress, the door remains open, and he can clearly hear (and possibly even see) his sometime friend cavort, and since this performance possesses the air of a ritual, it seems not unlikely that he has witnessed it before this.

Even for those few moments, that is, when he is not physically atop the tower alongside Mulligan, Stephen possesses enough information—from his other sense perceptions, from past knowledge, perhaps even from imagination—to visualize for himself what is occurring there. And since he is not reporting—narrating—these events to anyone, for they take place entirely within his consciousness, he has no obligation to be accurate or truthful. (We will discover, of course, that even when he is narrating to others, as in "Scylla and Charybdis," Stephen feels no imperative to maintain traditional expectations of truthfulness.) This is not Mulligan per se whom we see on the first page of *Ulysses*, but Mulligan as perceived by Dedalus. This is not, then, a simply realistic (or even naturalistic) performance by Joyce, but one tinged with impressionism, Freud, Dublin humor and irony, and the mature novelist's understanding of what it means to leave out the old indicators of narrative certainty: this story is radical from its very first words.[7]

Moreover, the fact that Stephen, like Mulligan and Haines, is at times referred to by name and at times by the pronoun "he" in no way changes the fact that he is the episode's sole point of view throughout. Even the fact that he is sometimes "I," as in the observation that follows, in no way alters this fact: the "him" in this passage is every bit as subjective as the "I" and the "my."

> A cloud began to cover the sun slowly, wholly shadowing the bay in deeper green. It lay beneath him, a bowl of bitter waters. Fergus' song: I sang it alone in the house, holding down the long dark chords. Her door was open: she wanted to hear my music. Silent with awe and pity I went to her bedside. (*U* 1.248–52)

For we are now within Stephen's consciousness, and these are his perceptions (both sensory and ideational) and his memories and feelings.

I would argue that every single word in "Telemachus"—every image heard, seen, smelled, touched or tasted, every thought and every memory, whether presented in the first person or second or third, whether or not accompanied by a name or a pronoun plus a verb, no matter whose name it may be—derives from the point of view of Stephen Dedalus: originates in and/or is filtered through his sense perceptions, memory, consciousness. I challenge any reader to choose any passage in this opening episode—not bound by some functionless convention that "he said," for example (or its absence), is proof of some outside source—and demonstrate that Stephen could not be its source.

Who needs a narrator in "Telemachus" when Stephen Dedalus is present to watch, to listen to, and, even in the moment before he too comes from the stairhead onto the deck of the tower, to imagine or to remember the scene, since he has so likely seen and heard it before this? What Joyce does at the start of *Ulysses* is thus to announce to us that this is not the conventional narrative that we have tried (perhaps inadvertently) to make of it; following the pattern that he had developed in *Dubliners*, he elimi-nates not just the omniscient author but any possible surrogate as well. From the very first scene of *Ulysses*, that is, we are presented with the new (we have since learned to call it modernist) narrative reality that the only possible certainty available to us is uncertainty, for we are limited in what we can know of the world to what our (limited) point of view is able to show us. And since that point of view at the start is Stephen's, and since we should know from the end of *A Portrait* that he is not in all matters reli-able, we must recognize that truth here is relative, that for the objectivity of a narrator or Arranger, as for the "second narrator" of the Uncle Charles Principle, we must substitute—as Joyce has—the subjectivity of a some-what suspect character. To impose a "narrator" on this scene is thus not just to rearrange Joyce's reality—the key, I believe, to his accomplishment as a novelist and of the whole modernist age to follow him—but to deny it. It is the same effect that we reach when we attempt to fill in the narrative gaps—such as what might have happened at the Westland Row Station, no matter how cleverly done—when the whole point is that in life there are inevitable gaps in what we can know of what passes for reality. Not cer-tainty, but ambiguity is the state of affairs under which we must live, as distressing as that may be to true believers.

And so I would offer a principle of reading narrative in *Ulysses*—call it Levitt's Law, if you will; I won't object. As we suspend disbelief as we enter a theater, so we must be willing to forget as we read the pages of a novel that this is a physical object and that someone whose name we happen to know has written these words. For it is not a novel's physical presence that activates us but the world that it creates. And when the creator of such a world has made it clear throughout his career and everywhere in his book that he intends his narrative technique to reflect a particular worldview, we are obligated to interpret that technique in a manner consistent with that worldview. Put simply, when the point of view of a scene in *Ulysses*—such as "Stately, plump"—may be read as either closed or open, as functionally omniscient and Victorian or potentially ambiguous and modernist, as a narrator's or as a character's—Stephen's or Bloom's or Molly's—then we are obliged to read it as the latter. To do otherwise is to substitute our intent for the author's.

There is a postmodernist critical tendency to denigrate the modernist novelists as overly heroic (a paradox). That tendency is furthered by another to elevate the critic above the creator (a tautology). We can avoid both—and let Joyce speak in his own voice—by the simple expedient of not inventing a narrator to tell us about the morning ablutions of a clever blowhard on a fine June morning a century ago and to look at him instead through the narrow, suspicious, intelligent if not wise, but open-to-experience perceptions of his sometime friend. Only if we can appreciate Stephen's beginning at the tower with Mulligan can we comprehend his growth on Eccles Street with Bloom.

What is more, by reading point of view in *Ulysses*, as in *Dubliners* and even in the *Wake*—that last grist for another essayed mill[8]—as being consistent, part of a developing narrative strategy whose origin, in retrospect, can be seen in the early revision of a single story, "The Sisters," we can begin to appreciate just how modernist, through all eighteen episodes, *Ulysses* is. "The narrator" in *Ulysses* is a necessary postmodernist critical invention in order to justify the existence of a postmodernist criticism. For if point of view in the final seven chapters is absolutely consistent with that of the opening eleven—indeed, a development of that initial technique (as proven by the presence of Stephen as "watcher" in the opening scene of "Telemachus")—then it becomes impossible to conclude that this represents the beginning of postmodernism.[9] If there is no split, if the wonderful inventions from "Cyclops" onward are of the same imaginative order as those from "Telemachus" through "Sirens," then all those qualities that some contemporary critics like to label "postmodernist" are, in practice, still modernist, and we may well need to rethink the relationship between modernism and what follows in its wake: perhaps what we have rushed to make postmodernist remains, in fact, modernist; perhaps the novelist, after all, remains more heroic than the critic in our simple scheme of affairs. Perhaps, as Joyce learned to do near the beginning of his career (and he, of course, never did learn to think of himself as even a modernist), we would be wise to learn what to leave out of our own constructions.

It is important for Joyceans, I believe, to remember that for all of his greatness, even his uniqueness, Joyce was not alone in bringing about the revolution in narrative technique and in worldview that we have come to call literary modernism. But he was surely, at least, representative. When we speak, then, of narrative in Joyce, we are likely to be commenting as well on modernist narrative at large. While I have been claiming for the past quarter of a century that the Modernist Age might as fruitfully be labeled the Age of James Joyce, no one can deny that there were others in this, the great age of the novel, who at about the same time were exploring new means of reflecting the new realities around them on the pages of the novel: think of Kafka and Mann and, especially, of Proust and Woolf; and, in the next generation, of Hemingway endeavoring to consolidate these advances in order to accommodate his own more limited vision and Faulkner working to expand them. Following them, there are Graham Greene and William Golding, Claude Simon and Alain Robbe-Grillet, Carlos Fuentes and Gabriel García Márquez, Saul Bellow and Philip Roth, and a vast host of others, all of whom I would call modernist and mean by that that they have worked to explore the possibilities of vision that Joyce had developed on the opening pages of *Ulysses*. The most substantial part of the literary history of the twentieth century, at least as I read it, is tied to narrative, and we risk not only misreading Joyce but denying the modernists if we refuse to acknowledge the full force—and consistency—of his innovation at the start of "Telemachus."

Notes

1. Those story sequences that follow in the literary wake of *Dubliners*—notably William Faulkner's *Go Down, Moses* and John Barth's *Lost in the Funhouse*—are not quite so fiercely focused as is Joyce's work. Yet Yoknapatawpha County, race, and history may comparably link Faulkner's stories (with their own versions of simony/selling out, gnomon/metaphoric readings, and moral paralysis). It may be only coincidental that the central story of *Go Down, Moses,* "The Bear," stands alongside "The Dead" among the most powerful stories of the modernist century. We might almost say the same of "Night-Sea Journey," the opening story of *Lost in the Funhouse.* And where Joyce himself becomes a figure in Barth's title story, the book as a whole is the story more of the development of the artist—Barth's *Portrait,* as it were—than of the import of the place: Stephen Dedalus counts more here than does the Eastern Shore of Maryland. To call any of these books a "collection," of course, would be to miss the point entirely.

2. See "An Early Version of 'The Sisters,'" in Robert Scholes and A. Walton Litz, eds., *James Joyce's "Dubliners": Text, Criticism, and Notes* (D 243–52).

3. Leavis's complaints in *The Great Tradition* about the sacrifice of realism and morality alike in modernist fiction are, in essence, complaints about a point of view that deviates from his omniscient norm. There is no evidence that he had ever read

"The Sisters" in either of its versions, but given his assumptions, he seems quite justified in his suspicions about Joyce.

4. While my reading of point of view and its effects in *Ulysses* is rather obviously at odds with that of Karen Lawrence, I am struck by how close we are in our general interests. Thus, I agree almost totally with her when she writes about the novelist's intentions:

> Simultaneous with Joyce's perceptions of the limitations of both the conventional novel and his own previous fiction was an interest in further developing a method with which to present the workings of consciousness. (48)

Our disagreement lies in the specifics of Joyce's response to that interest. Thus, while Lawrence is able to say of the first three Bloom chapters in *Ulysses* that "As in the 'Telemachiad', one finds in these chapters a sympathy between narrator and character that again involves the borrowing of linguistic habits" (49), she does not make the leap that I do to see in this "sympathy" proof that the point of view is, in practice, the characters'—Stephen's and Bloom's—and not that of some invented narrator.

5. Hart and Hayman, eds., *James Joyce's "Ulysses": Critical Essays.* Throughout his essay on "Telemachus," Benstock too speaks here of a "narrator."

6. Discussing this "arranging presence," Kenner credits David Hayman, "the first critic to dwell on its intrusions," as the coiner of the term (*Ulysses* 65). Hayman writes, in a passage Kenner cites: "I use the term 'arranger' to designate a figure who can be identified neither with the author nor with his narrators, but who exercises an increasing degree of overt control over his increasingly challenging materials" (70). My own inclination is to conclude that even the most challenging of these materials can be attributed to the point of view of some individual or group (as of the community, for example). The very form of Hayman's word "Arranger," I fear, implies a presence outside the story, and all such presences may distract from—in this case— Stephen's. The "Arranger," that is, like the "narrator," would seem inevitably to affirm the author's presence within his narrative, and all such presences may become—in the hands of a reader less skilled than Hayman—surrogates for the omniscient author. The fact that this Arranger may exercise "overt control over his . . . materials" proves, I think, my point. See my "Radical Consistency."

7. If we were to investigate closely each image of this initial description of Buck Mulligan's performance, we could account for every one of them. Thus, Stephen from below can hear him "gurgling in his throat and shaking his head" (*U* 1.12–13, so that the reference to *gemens* and *tremens* is Stephen's and not Mulligan's or Joyce's); he can likely see from below (the entry to the roof is obviously open) the "yellow dressinggown, ungirdled . . . sustained gently behind him on the mild morning air" (*U* 1.3–4, in a scene similar to Kafka's "The Judgment," a work that Joyce cannot possibly have known), as well as the holding aloft of the now-sanctified shaving bowl (we may be inclined here to think of the broken chalice of "The Sisters"). But if he cannot actually see it, he can certainly envision it, for this is probably not the first time that Stephen has witnessed the performance. Moreover, Stephen

may well have been climbing the stairs all this time, for when we first see him, he is "lean[ing] his arms on the top of the staircase" (*U* 1.13–14). If we first see Stephen as Buck sees him ("Then, catching sight of Stephen Dedalus, he bent towards him" [*U* 1.11–12]), we understand easily that this is Stephen seeing Buck seeing Stephen. We require no omniscient voice, no putative narrator, to inform us that the latter is "displeased and sleepy" (*U* 1.13), that he looks "coldly" (*U* 1.14) at the clowning face before him: seen from Stephen's point of view, none of these terms is objective.

8. I make a tentative beginning toward such a reading in my *Rhetoric of Modernist Fiction*.

9. To argue, as some critics do, that this presumed shift is the opening gesture of postmodernism depends on a reading of modernism as inherently traditional (that is, as possessing all of those conservative attributes that thirty years ago we assumed to be Victorian) and of postmodernism as possessing all of those admirable qualities—irony, mythopoesis, innovative points of view and the like—that we used to regard as modernist: indeed, as the very basis of the modernist novel.

Works Cited

Barth, John. *Lost in the Funhouse*. New York: Bantam, 1980.

Benstock, Bernard. *Narrative Con/Texts in "Ulysses."* Urbana: University of Illinois Press, 1991.

Faulkner, William. *Go Down, Moses*. New York: Modern Library/Random House, 1945.

Hart, Clive, and David Hayman, eds. *James Joyce's "Ulysses": Critical Essays.* Berkeley and Los Angeles: University of California Press, 1974.

Hayman, David. *"Ulysses": The Mechanics of Meaning*. Englewood Cliffs, N.J.: Prentice-Hall, 1970.

Kenner, Hugh. *Joyce's Voices*. Berkeley and Los Angeles: University of California Press, 1978.

———. *Ulysses*. Rev. ed. Baltimore: Johns Hopkins University Press, 1987.

Lawrence, Karen. *The Odyssey of Style in "Ulysses."* Princeton: Princeton University Press, 1981.

Leavis, F. R. *The Great Tradition*. New York: New York University Press, 1967.

Levitt, Morton P. "The Radical Consistency of Point of View in *Ulysses*: A Traditional Reading." *James Joyce Quarterly* 26, no. 1 (fall 1988): 67–88; reprinted in *James Joyce and Modernism: Beyond Dublin*. Lewiston, N.Y.: Edwin Mellen, 2000.

———. *The Rhetoric of Modernist Fiction: From a New Point of View*. Lebanon, N.H.: University Press of New England, forthcoming.

Meredith, George. *Modern Love*. London: Constable, 1922.

Scholes, Robert, and J. Walton Litz, eds. *James Joyce's "Dubliners": Text, Criticism, and Notes*. New York: Viking, 1969.

Condoms, Conrad, and Joyce

Thomas Jackson Rice

> [It's] as if he did not, after all, quite want us to understand his story,
> as if he had, not quite conscious of what he was doing, ended by
> throwing up between us and it a fortification of solemn burlesque
> prose—as if he were shy and solicitous about it, and wanted to pro-
> tect it from us.
>
> **Edmund Wilson,** *Axel's Castle*

Early in *Lady Chatterley's Lover,* a novel that earned its notoriety by
speaking frankly and graphically about sex, D. H. Lawrence's spokesperson
of the moment, Tommy Dukes, contends "that sex is just another form of
talk, where you act the words instead of saying them"—"sex is a sort of
communication like speech" (70, 72). But Dukes leaves unspoken the other
half of this equation: sex is talk *because* talk is just another form of sex.
Typically, for him, in *Lady Chatterley's Lover* Lawrence deconstructs the
hierarchies privileging thought over act and oral discourse over sexual intercourse, central to Western philosophical and religious thought, conversely asserting that a sacred communion is imbedded in the profane activity of speech. Lawrence recognizes the hierophany—in Mircea Eliade's
term (11)—already encoded in our language: namely, communication *is*
communion, "intercourse" signifies both verbal and sexual exchange, and
"conversation" means both speech and cohabitation (via the French *con-
verser,* meaning both "to talk with" and "to live with").[1] While this recognition of the spiritual within the mundane is akin to Joyce's conception of
the epiphany, Joyce more immediately exploits an identical double signifi-
cation of "conversation" for his conclusion to "The Dead" when Gabriel
Conroy checks into the Gresham Hotel, expecting "communion" with his
wife, Gretta. Ironically, before he sleeps Gabriel does have intercourse, but
not sex, with Gretta. T. S. Eliot similarly correlates discourse with intercourse throughout *The Waste Land,* associating speechlessness with emas-
culation, the male lamenting "I could not / Speak" in the hyacinth-girl
episode (ll.38–39), for example, or the female imploring her impotent
gentleman caller in "A Game of Chess" to "Stay with me. / Speak to me."

Why do you never speak. Speak" (ll.111–12), just as he associates garru-lousness with promiscuity in the same section's pub scene (ll.139–73). Elsewhere in Eliot, J. Alfred Prufrock's problem seems to be that he cannot converse with his beloved, in either sense of the term. That Prufrock's in-ternal monologue, however, is more eloquent than anything he might say ("Shall I say . . . " [l.70]) should remind us that the internalization of speech in the stream-of-consciousness technique, most clearly in Virginia Woolf, both emphasizes physical isolation and privileges spiritual, bodi-less, telepathic, and definitely nonsexual communication. Clearly, this as-sociation of speech with sexuality—discourse with intercourse—is a com-mon subtext among the writers of the early part of the twentieth century. I want to argue, however, not only that this subtext is pervasive in mod-ernist writing, but also that thwarted communication, both among charac-ters in these works of literature and between their authors and their audi-ence, comes to represent a kind of prophylaxis. Modern writing may necessarily be "*difficult*," as Eliot contends, because it reflects the complex-ity of contemporary life ("The Metaphysical Poets" 1104), but much of this difficulty results from what we might call the *condomization* of the text: with the exception of Lawrence, these writers I have cited seem self-protectively to sheathe their texts, to shield their words from their audi-ence, not so much from the fear that their words might be made flesh as from an anxiety that a more direct conversation with the public body might expose their works to some kind of contamination. They seem to want "to protect [them] from us" (Wilson 217). The Italian anatomist Fallopius, after all, developed the sheath in the sixteenth century as a pro-tection from venereal disease, namely syphilis, not as a means of birth control.[2] Moreover, this figurative condomization of the text approaches the literal in Joseph Conrad's particularly opaque novel *The Secret Agent*, a work that, in turn, exerted an underappreciated influence on Joyce's *Ulysses*.[3]

My principal focus in this essay is the symptom of textual prophylaxis, rather than its many possible causes, which is fortunate because there are no easy answers here. In part, these modernist authors may be withdraw-ing from a mass audience that they believed they were never destined to reach, both in reaction against the enormous growths of general literacy and middle- to low-brow literatures aimed at these new readers through the nineteenth century and in a broader rejection of the bourgeois com-modification of culture. As Andreas Huyssen remarks, "Modernism con-stituted itself through a conscious strategy of exclusion, an *anxiety of con-*

tamination by its other: an increasingly consuming and engulfing mass culture" (vii; emphasis added).[4] Yet in part, these writers may also be determined, in principle, to distance themselves from their audience through impersonality, in response to what appeared to them an excessive self-investment in their works by writers in the immediately preceding generations. In part, too, they may be reflecting—to extend Eliot's argument in "The Metaphysical Poets"—the influence of new theories in psychology, physics, and linguistics at the beginning of the century that intensified their sense of the complexity of both the "new" reality and the task of its representation. Certainly, in part, they are responding to the collapse of various structures of authority in recent cultural history by rejecting the role of the "one who knows"—and tells—in their authorship. Nowhere is this more evident than in the prevalence of the ironic mode in modernist writing, the author's prophylactic suppression of intention, which seems to function as both a strategy of detachment from, and an abdication of responsibility for, the horrors their works represent.

There is no greater irony in Conrad's sustained application of the "ironic method" for *The Secret Agent* than his choice of subtitle for the novel, "A Simple Tale" ("Author's Preface" xxvii). Much as in *Heart of Darkness,* Conrad's particularly dense style in *The Secret Agent* makes his tale far from simple, demanding that its first-time readers decode meanings in a work that itself concerns deciphering the subterfuges of international politics. Further, Conrad's disruption of linear chronology—displacing four chapters in time—deceives the readers into misreading the events of the "bomb outrage in Greenwich Park" (190) and then challenges them to reassemble the temporal order in a work that itself concerns an attack on time. Added to this, the readers contend with initially impenetrable dialogues throughout *The Secret Agent,* most memorably the cross-purpose conversations between Adolph Verloc and Mr. Vladimir, between Comrade Ossipon and the Professor, between Inspector Heat and the Assistant Commissioner—which features an eleven-page expository interruption in the midst of their exchanges, one of the novel's several "sudden holes in space and time" (85) that disrupt the reading process, rather like this insertion in my own sentence—and then between Verloc and his wife, Winnie, and between Winnie and Ossipon, all of which rely on one or both of the characters' ignorance of the full import or the larger context of what the other is saying. Conrad's readers, too, have a right to complain, as the Assistant Commissioner does to Heat, that the author "shouldn't leave me to puzzle things out for myself like this" (124) and that his method "seems to consist in keeping" them "in the dark" (132). Thus Conrad condomizes his text, imposing prophylactic barriers to complete intercourse both within *The Secret Agent* and between this novel and its readership. But beyond coining the term "condomization" for Conrad's techniques, I want to make clear that he is himself exploiting both the condom as a governing symbol and as a significant prop for his tale, and the idea of prophylaxis for his central theme.

Like the historically disreputable condom, an invention the English have traditionally credited to the French (the "French Letter") and the French to the English ("*la capote anglaise*") (Himes 194; Kruck 36–37), Conrad's shady central character, Verloc, has both French and British heritage (22). Conrad, in fact, presents Verloc as a kind of human condom, a "mortal envelope" (37, 263) for protection who "exercise[s] his vocation as a protector of society" by acting as a spy amongst revolutionaries (5), a man who has prophylactically "prevented" terrorist plots from reaching their fulfillment and thus thwarted the contagion of the pestilential anarchists (25):[5] Verloc "surveyed through the park railings the evidences of the town's opulence and luxury with an approving eye. All these people had to be *protected. Protection* is the first necessity of opulence and luxury. They had to be *protected;* and their horses, carriages, houses, servants had to be *protected;* and the source of their wealth had to be *protected* in the heart of the city and the heart of the country; the whole social order favourable to their hygienic idleness had to be *protected* against the shallow enviousness of unhygienic labour" (12; emphases added). More than this, Conrad reinforces his prophylactic symbolism by making Verloc a dealer of condoms, a protector of personal as well as social hygiene. Verloc's "ostensible business" (3), his appropriately *prophylactic* cover for his real trade as a double agent, is a stationery shop in a seedy section of London, which is ironically also a cover, in a second sense, for his trade in sexual goods: the window display of his shop features "photographs of more or less undressed dancing girls" (3), alerting passersby, and Conrad's readers by the third paragraph of the novel, to Verloc's second trade as "a seller of shady wares," unspecified products that prompt Conrad's initial mention of his epithet for Verloc, "a protector of society" (5). We can grasp Conrad's irony here by revisiting the brief episodes that immediately precede his introduction of this motif in the text. Mr. Verloc customarily sells over his counter "some object looking obviously and scandalously not worth the money which passed in the transaction: a small cardboard box with apparently nothing inside" (4–5). When Winnie tends the shop, however, male customers evidently intending to purchase such an object, particularly those "of comparatively tender years[,] would get suddenly disconcerted at having to deal with a woman" and instead buy some ridiculously overpriced stationery goods (5). These transactions strongly suggest that Verloc sells prophylactics—small, virtually weightless, and extremely awkward for a young man to purchase from a female—and Conrad reinforces this deduction later in the novel by noting that Verloc supported his household "on the wages of a secret industry eked out by the sale of more or less secret wares: the poor expedients devised by a mediocre mankind for *preserving* an imperfect society from the dangers of moral and physical corruption, both secret too, of their kind" (258; emphasis added). (One of the standard euphemisms for condoms is "preservatives," dating from the eighteenth century [Himes 195; Youssef 227].) We could easily interpret this last passage as referring to Verloc's sale of information to the police and foreign embassies, which it does on one level, for it is difficult to see how condoms could preserve society from *moral* as well as physical corruption. On the other hand, Inspector Heat's earlier comment that Verloc runs the risk of having his wares, "these packages he gets from Paris and Brussels[,] opened in Dover, with confiscation to follow for certain, and perhaps a prosecution as well," implies that he deals in the always highly valued, imported condom (131). As early as the 1770s, for instance, one Mrs. Philips of "No.5 *Orange-court*, near *Leicester-fields*," was circulating handbills announcing that "She defies any one in *England* to equal her goods, and hath lately had several large orders from *France, Spain, Portugal, Italy,* and other foreign places. Captains of ships, and gentlemen going abroad, may be supplied with any quantity of the best goods on the shortest notice" (quoted in Himes 198). The ultimate irony here, however, is that Conrad seems to have prophylactically obscured the fact of Verloc's condom trade in the novel by muting the explicitness of some of these passages when he revised the serial version of *The Secret Agent*. His description of the object purchased in the transaction I have just quoted, for example, instead of reading "a small cardboard box with apparently nothing inside," was originally more explicit: "a small cardboard box labeled 'Superfine India Rubber'" (Ford, "James Joyce" 8).

Prophylactic imagery proliferates in *The Secret Agent*—coats, cloaks, veils, and most especially Verloc's omnipresent hat—but the more important point is that the novel thematically and structurally reinforces the idea of prophylaxis. The Assistant Commissioner, who like Verloc sees his work in terms of "social protection" (103), decides that the best response for the British government is *no reaction at all* to Mr. Vladimir's scheme for provoking police action and thus prevents Vladimir's plot from having any large national and international consequences. Similarly, Stevie's accidental death, his stumbling with the Greenwich bomb and thereby both blowing himself to bits and absorbing the full impact of the explosion with his body, is an act of prophylactic suppression that also involves the death of the idiot boy, a kind of little man or homunculus.[6] Structurally, Conrad shows the shock of the literally and figuratively abortive terrorist attack climactically moving outward and upward in a series of chapters, until balked by the bulky figure of Sir Ethelred, the Home Secretary. This "great personage['s]" prophylactic decision to suppress an understandable official response (135), in effect, turns the novel and the consequences of the bombing back upon themselves. Correspondingly, after "the police ha[ve] managed to smother so nicely" the affair (309), the balance of the tale traces its rebound shock effects, first on Mr. Vladimir, whose awe of "the miraculous cleverness of the English police" leaves him "slightly sick" (226), then on Verloc, who "is shaken morally to pieces" (230), and then on his wife: shock "waves . . . of the proper length, propagated in accordance with correct mathematical formulas, flowed around all the inanimate things in the room, lapped against Mrs. Verloc's head as if had been a head of stone" (260). These waves then propagate the wife's murder of her husband, the consequent shock of this action upon Winnie, and finally the impact of her suicide upon Comrade Ossipon, within whose hollow interior Conrad leaves the last waves of reaction to reverberate as the novel ends.

Conrad published *The Secret Agent* on September 10, 1907 (Ford, "James Joyce" 6), and Joyce purchased the 1907 Tauchnitz edition for his Trieste library. He probably acquired the novel shortly after its publication, because he apparently used some of the vocabulary in the Verloc-Vladimir conversation in chapter 2 when tutoring his Triestine English students.[7] It is hard to imagine Joyce not being struck, when he read *The Secret Agent*, by the two bedroom encounters between Adolph and Winnie Verloc in Conrad's novel (55–60, 177–81), which resemble his treatment of Gabriel and Gretta Conroy at the Gresham Hotel in the recently written conclusion of "The Dead." (Joyce apparently completed this story, coincidentally, on or about September 10, 1907 [*JJII* 263–64].) In both Verloc scenes, the gas has similarly been turned off, the wife has also preceded her spouse in bed, and the husband likewise looks upon her recumbent form. In the first of these, Verloc observes himself, Gabriel-like, in the "looking glass" (56) and shortly after turns his gaze to the "window-pane" (57). As in the conclusion to "The Dead," the married couple has verbal discourse rather than sexual intercourse in both *Secret Agent* scenes, although with Conrad's pair the conversations are as ineffectual as we gather their sexual relations to be. In each, Verloc fails to confide his problems to Winnie (59, 179) and is too distracted to make any response to his wife's attempts at conversation. Most significantly, however, Conrad describes the quality of Verloc's love for his wife in terms that would have strongly reminded Joyce of Gabriel's proprietary relationship to Gretta: "Mr. Verloc loved his wife as a wife should be loved—that is, maritally, with the regard one has for one's chief possession" (179).

There seems to be no clear evidence for how extensively Joyce might have revised "The Dead," after completing its initial draft simultaneously with Conrad's publication of *The Secret Agent*, so it would seem safer to suggest that he appreciated the novel's treatment of the Verlocs, when he *did* read the book, than to argue that Conrad exerted any direct influence on the final scene of Joyce's story.[8] Nevertheless, *The Secret Agent* must have arrested his attention, and he seems to have kept Conrad's book in mind approximately a dozen years later when he worked on the final stages of *Ulysses*. There is also little doubt that Joyce would have understood and appreciated the motif of prophylaxis in Conrad. Joyce seems to have considered condoms disreputable (Brown 65), and we have no way of knowing whether he used them himself either for protection or for contraception (Lowe-Evans 26), but we do know that he was intensely interested in birth control issues and contraceptive practices when he was writing *Dubliners* and, indeed, throughout his career.[9] He would have recognized the signals Conrad uses to indicate Verloc's condom trade. While the sale of prophylactics was not strictly illegal in England (or the United States, despite the restraints on their trade imposed by the Comstock Laws), as it was in Ireland until only recently, it was always a decidedly shady business, licit or illicit, tainted by the association of condom use with random promiscuity. Bordellos and prostitutes were, logically, chief sources for condoms for much of their history, although not necessarily the only distributors by the beginning of the twentieth century.[10] As James Carens has discovered, Alec Bannon's reference to a "*marchand de capotes,* Monsieur Poyntz" in the "Oxen of the Sun" episode of *Ulysses* is topical (*U* 14.776): apparently young men of comparatively tender years obtained their contraceptives from the "waterproofers and hosiers" S. R. Poyntz & Co. in turn-of-the-century Dublin (346). Leopold Bloom, however, seems to have preferred mail-order prophylactics. In "Ithaca," we learn that he has "purchased by post from Box 32, P.O., Charing Cross, London, W.C.," both "erotic photocards" and "rubber preservatives with reserve pockets" (*U* 17.1805, 1809, 1804), one of which he carries with him as a kind of back-up for his "Potato Preservative against Plague and Pestilence" (*U* 15.1952).

Joyce, in fact, associates Bloom with the condom at a number of places in *Ulysses*. As both he and Molly remark, he carries his "French letter" in his "pocketbook" (*U* 13.877; 18.1235), with two in reserve that Molly doesn't know about in the locked drawer of the sideboard (*U* 17.1804). Although he has liberated the *Photo Bits* nymph from the indignity of coexisting with ads for contraceptives—"Rubber Goods. Neverrip brand as supplied to the aristocracy" (*U* 15.3256)—elsewhere in "Circe" he advocates free distribution to the masses of *"rubber preservatives in sealed envelopes tied with gold thread"* (*U* 15.1571) and is shortly after accused by Theodore Purefoy of "employ[ing] a mechanical device to frustrate the sacred ends of nature" (*U* 15.1741–42). (Yet another eighteenth-century code word for the condom is "machine" [Youssef 227; Kruck 8].)[11] Beyond his personal and perhaps ideological investments in condoms, Bloom's suppression of his habitual "Mister Knowall" (*U* 12.838) opinions through that most prophylactic of the novel's episodes, "Oxen of the Sun," is itself a prophylactic gesture, a form of self-restraint as he, for instance, "enjoin[s] his heart to repress all motions of a rising choler and, by intercepting them with the readiest precaution, foster[s] within his breast [a] plentitude of sufferance" amidst the episode's "tumultuary discussions" (*U* 14.861–63, 849). And I would argue that Joyce's related conception of his own textual prophylaxis in this same episode, his figurative and, as we shall see, *literal* condomization of his text, strongly suggests his unacknowledged debt to Conrad's example in *The Secret Agent*, particularly as he worked on the latest stages of his composition of *Ulysses*.[12]

In the "Ithaca" episode, for instance, Joyce presents Leopold Bloom's response to the "outrage" at 7 Eccles Street (*U* 17.2196–97), his wife's potentially explosive infidelity, in terms very similar to the official reaction to the "bomb outrage in Greenwich Park" in *The Secret Agent* (190). Rather than return to his home and bed as "an estranged avenger, a wreaker of justice on malefactors, a dark crusader, a sleeper awakened" (*U* 17.2020–22), Bloom decides his best response to Molly's revolutionary gesture is *no reaction at all*, nor any immediate act of "retribution" (*U* 17.2200). "Ithaca," furthermore, concludes with condomized intercourse, strictly verbal, between Leopold and his wife, a conversation in which he is as disingenuous as Verloc. If "sex is just another form of talk" (Lawrence 70), and talk is just another form of sex, neither the talk nor the sex is very good for husband and wife in this scene. Appropriately, this is the point in *Ulysses* where Joyce makes clear that Bloom and Molly have not had "complete carnal intercourse" for "10 years, 5 months and 18 days" (*U* 17.2278, 2282), nor have they enjoyed "complete *mental intercourse*" for "9 months and 1 day" (*U* 17.2285, 2289; emphasis added). Like Conrad, in other words, Joyce makes explicit the prophylactic suppression of the "sacred ends" of both sex and speech through the relationship of Bloom and Molly. The Blooms' culminating, cross-purpose conversation, like the dialogues in *The Secret Agent*, challenges both one of its parties, in this case Molly, and of course the readers as well to decipher exactly what her husband has said. (We will never know whether Bloom has "ask[ed] to get his breakfast in bed," as Molly assumes [*U* 18.1–2].) Nevertheless, despite some uncertainties at the end of "Ithaca," the readers of *Ulysses* can naturalize this scene and penetrate the author's stylistic and technical sheaths, as in most of the novel, with modest effort. They know with extraordinary precision who is speaking to whom, more or less what each is saying, and when and where they are conversing (as Joyce, for example, scrupulously describes the Blooms' "posture[s]" in bed, "relatively to themselves and to each other" [*U* 17.2311, 2307]). The same cannot be said, however, for much of "Oxen of the Sun," the episode that most resists these strategies of naturalization and the episode that is centrally concerned with the frustration of the "sacred ends of nature."

The opacity of Joyce's style in "Oxen in the Sun" far exceeds anything found in Conrad. More than this, Joyce takes his predecessor's exercise in imitative form a step further, as I will suggest, to use the condom as yet another of the several structural models for this episode. Mary Lowe-Evans's description of the theme of "Oxen" as "intricate and nearly indecipherable" is only one of the more recent in a long tradition of critical responses to this chapter that seem to echo the complaint of Conrad's Assistant Commissioner: "You shouldn't leave me to puzzle things out for myself like this" (124). Edmund Wilson, for an early example, regrets that "in the maternity hospital, at the climactic scenes of the story, . . . Joyce has bogged us as he has never bogged us before" (216), missing the central point that Joyce has staged, in fact, the prophylactic anticlimax of the narrative thrust of *Ulysses*. Like many readers, Wilson is frustrated by the incomplete intercourse here between author and audience. At the most basic level, Joyce repeatedly thwarts, as he will again throughout *Finne-*

gans Wake, the readers' natural appetite to know who's speaking to whom, what each is saying, what they look like, or even who sits where in the room; contrast this with the conclusion of "Ithaca" or to virtually every other scene in *Ulysses*. "Furthermore, Joyce has here half-buried his story under the virtuosity of his technical devices," Wilson complains. "It is almost as if he had elaborated it so much and worked over it so long that he had forgotten, in the amusement of writing parodies, the drama which he had originally intended to stage." Little realizing, it seems, the intimations of contraception and prophylaxis in what he is saying, Wilson concludes his commentary observing that Joyce defrauds his readers by suppressing the climax of his novel—"we . . . [are] dissatisfied with the flatness . . . of Dedalus's final meeting with Bloom"—as if he wishes to prevent both insemination and contamination, that is, "as if he did not, after all, quite want us to understand his story, as if he had, not quite conscious of what he was doing, ended by throwing up between us and it a *fortification* of solemn burlesque prose—as if he were shy and solicitous about it, and wanted to *protect* it from us" (217; emphases added). If the writer's pen is, indeed, the penis, as *Finnegans Wake* maintains, for "Oxen of the Sun" Joyce's wears a condom.[13]

Benefitting from our access to the author's own intentions for "Oxen of the Sun," unlike Wilson in 1931, we now know that this critic, by feeling defrauded, is responding to the episode exactly as Joyce wished. Among the "Correspondences" on the Gorman-Gilbert schema, Joyce identifies the "Crime" of "Fraud" for this episode (Ellmann, *Ulysses on the Liffey*, appendix), a motif that embraces Stephen's misrepresentation of the source of his earnings, Bloom's "pelican" piety (*U* 14.921), and much else, but also the crime of birth control. (At the turn of the century, "fraud" was "a common name for contraception" [Lowe-Evans 73].) We also have Joyce's much-quoted March 20, 1920, letter to Frank Budgen, written as he worked on "Oxen of the Sun," wherein he identifies his main "idea" as "the crime committed against fecundity by sterilizing the act of coition" and then delightedly outlines, as he then saw it, his exercise in imitative form: the embryological model for the nine stages of the episode's linguistic development (*SL* 251). In *Crimes against Fecundity*, Mary Lowe-Evans excellently surveys the various social, ideological, and ecclesiastical forces that converged to sterilize coition, both literally and figuratively, in early twentieth-century Ireland (53–74), and Robert Janusko thoroughly explores the episode's "Embryological Framework" in his *Sources and Structures of James Joyce's "Oxen"* (39–54). What both overlook, however, is the contradiction between Joyce's main idea of contraception and his purported formal paradigm based upon fecundation.[14] I want to argue that Joyce, while keeping with his plan to structure much of his episode upon the development of the embryo, simultaneously elaborates a patterned association between the episode's progress and the act of sexual intercourse, or more specifically, condomized sex. The pattern begins with the initial penetration of Bloom's entrance into the hospital, intensifies in friction with the episode's debates, has its momentary longueurs in Bloom's reveries, and then climaxes with Stephen's outburst: "Burke's! outflings my lord Stephen, giving the cry" (U 14.1391). The virtue of this suggestion is that it helps us better understand Joyce's purpose for the last several pages of "Oxen of the Sun," which Janusko believes represent a kind of afterbirth—"The tailpiece . . . is probably best considered as the placenta" (53)—whereas I would argue that this swirling mass of ejaculations, fragmentary phrases, and word particles disseminates the unfecundating seeds of conversation, the residue of both verbal and sexual intercourse that remains after the prophylactic sterilization of coition.[15] The artist's pen in "Oxen of the Sun," then, is not condomized by "a stout shield of oxengut" (U 14.465), but by one of those new and improved condoms of the turn of the century, favored by Bloom, that contain the residue of intercourse in its reservoir tip, a "reserve pocket" at its end (U 17.1804).[16]

Joyce's use of a latent (if not yet latex) condom as an objective correlative for the textual prophylaxis of "Oxen of the Sun" not only resembles the thematic and structural strategies of condomization in The Secret Agent but also replicates yet another fundamental irony in Conrad's book: both authors figuratively employ a mass-cultural product as a shield to protect their works from full communication with, and contamination by, mass culture itself. In doing so, Joyce and Conrad engage in what Andreas Huyssen describes as the "compulsive pas de deux" modernism and mass culture have danced "ever since their simultaneous emergence in the mid-19th century" (57). Huyssen's After the Great Divide, as well as Peter Bürger's Theory of the Avant-Garde and, for Joyce studies, Margot Norris's Joyce's Web, have crystallized our awareness of how the "modernist aesthetic" functioned as a prophylactic "reaction formation" to contemporary mass culture: "Only by fortifying its boundaries, by maintaining its purity and autonomy, and by avoiding any contamination with mass culture and with the signifying systems of everyday life can the art work maintain its adversary stance: adversary to the bourgeois culture of everyday life as well as adversary to mass culture and entertainment which are seen as the primary forms of bourgeois cultural articulation" (Huyssen 53–54). Yet, as Norris makes clear and as the dual motifs of contraception and fecundation of "Oxen of the Sun" also suggest, there is a vital difference between Conrad's and Joyce's embrace of this modernist aesthetic: while *The Secret Agent* illustrates the artist's privileging the autonomy of the work of art as "totally separate from the realms of mass culture and everyday life" (Huyssen 53), "Oxen of the Sun" and *Ulysses* as a whole are "dramatization[s] and reenactment[s]" of "the oppressive social function of art and texts" implicit in the aesthetic ideal of autonomy (Norris 147). In other words, Joyce's work both exemplifies and critiques the "autonomy aesthetic" of modernism (Bürger 10), simultaneously embodying "an anxiety of contamination by," and celebrating its conversation with, "its other: an increasingly consuming and engulfing mass culture" (Huyssen vii). While Joyce's condomization of the text of "Oxen of the Sun," then, is consistent with the modernist suppression of direct intercourse with the public sphere, his dissemination of the potentially fecundating seeds of discourse at the episode's conclusion (to bear fruit when released in *Finnegans Wake*), together with his imbedded paradigm of fecundation and gestation, parallel the contemporary protest of what Peter Bürger calls "the historical avant-garde," whose aim was to attack the political impotence of the autonomy aesthetic as a crime against fecundity and thus "reintegrate art into the praxis of life, [by] reveal[ing] the nexus between autonomy and the *absence of any consequences*" (27, 22; emphasis added).

There has been relatively little discussion of Joyce's relationship to such avant-garde movements as Dada or surrealism, even though he lived (and composed much of *Ulysses*) in Zurich contemporaneously with Tristan Tzara, Hans Arp, and others, for reasons well articulated by Margot Norris. The "canonization" of Joyce as the preeminent modernist author and the consequent "equation of Joyce with the aestheticism of modernism" (6)— most notably in T. S. Eliot's praise for his ahistorical "use of Homeric myth in *Ulysses* as 'a step toward making the modern world possible for art'" (5; Eliot, "*Ulysses*" 202)—have totally occluded his investment in the avant-gardist critique of "the detachment of art as a special sphere of human activity from the nexus of the praxis of life" (Bürger 36).[17] And for that matter, there has been no consideration, to my knowledge, of Joseph Conrad's possible response to the turn-of-the-century avant-garde. Nevertheless, I would argue that both *Ulysses* and *The Secret Agent* share one final important similarity, as well as a strong contrast, in their reflection of the avant-gardist attacks on the late nineteenth- and early twentieth-century bourgeois institution of art "as a social realm that is set apart from the means-end rationality of daily bourgeois existence" (Bürger 10). In radical resistance to the idea of autonomy in fin-de-siècle aestheticism and an emergent modernism, the avant-garde sought to reintegrate "art into life praxis," to close "the gap separating art from reality," and thus to "make art productive for social change" (Huyssen 7–8). In short, the avant-garde attempted to conjoin art with political and social revolution (Huyssen 12).

For a renowned political novel, *The Secret Agent* is strangely apolitical in its messages that the best action is inaction and that the masses are well served by remaining in ignorance of the causes and import of the Greenwich bombing. In fact, Conrad's book is equally if not more concerned with the political as a metaphoric substitute for the aesthetic, to make a case for the detachment of art from the public sphere of action. To see this clearly, it helps to recognize that "[t]hroughout the 19th century the idea of the avantgarde [was] linked to political radicalism," finding "its way into socialist anarchism and eventually into substantial segments of the bohemian subcultures of the turn of the century" (Huyssen 5). In this light we can see that Conrad demonizes the Professor both as the "perfect" political anarchist (82) and as an avant-garde artist, "free from everything artificial . . . and all sorts of conventions" (68), much as he presents the equally insidious Mr. Vladimir as a kind of artist in the text: "His wit consisted in discovering droll connections between incongruous ideas" (19). Vladimir descends socially and, in Conrad's terms, aesthetically to the level of the avant-garde by planning a "series of outrages" calculated to "influence the public opinion" (30), beginning with the Greenwich bombing, a quintessential avant-gardist manifestation: "an act of destructive ferocity so absurd as to be incomprehensible, inexplicable, almost unthinkable; in fact, mad" (33). Conrad doubles the Professor and Vladimir with the idiot boy Stevie, who is both a walking bomb and an artist of social protest whose abstract designs of "circles, circles, circles . . . innumerable circles . . . suggested a rendering of cosmic chaos, the symbolism of a mad art attempting the inconceivable" (45), and juxtaposes them all to the only admirable character in *The Secret Agent*, the Assistant Commissioner, the protector of England's social and political institutions (read: the institution of autonomous art), who by virtue of his "miraculous cleverness" (226) thwarts any attempt to make "art productive for social change" (Huyssen 8).

The obvious artist figure in *Ulysses*, of course, is Stephen Dedalus, whose ambition to "forge . . . the uncreated conscience of [his] race" (*P* 253), though hardly yet realized, suggests as much his affinity for the

avant-gardist attempt to reintegrate art and the praxis of life as his aesthetics in both *A Portrait of the Artist as a Young Man* (for example, the
ideal of "esthetic stasis" [*P* 206]), and his discussion of Shakespeare, the
artist as androgynous "only begetter" (*U* 9.838–39), in the "Scylla and
Charybdis" episode of *Ulysses* would suggest his attraction toward the
autonomy aesthetic of modernism. The most important point to stress,
here, is that Joyce's similarly equivocal relationship to the *pas de deux*
between the autonomy aesthetic of modernism and the activism of the
avant-garde not only strongly distinguishes his receptiveness to the
avant-gardist critique of the bourgeois institutionalization of art from
Conrad's endorsement of institutional suppression in *The Secret Agent*
but also acts a major, insufficiently acknowledged, governing tension in
Ulysses. And this tension, most apparent in the contradiction between the
paradigms of prophylaxis and fecundation in "Oxen of the Sun," bears its
ultimate fruit in *Finnegans Wake*: a novel that sustains, as Norris has brilliantly argued, a "dialectical relation" between avant-gardism and Joyce's
"earlier aestheticism" (93).[18] The *Wake*, in its sheer complexity, would
seem the limit case of modernist textual condomization. Conversely, in its
hypercommunicativity—its superabundance of discourse, rather than
thwarted intercourse—*Finnegans Wake* disseminates the seeds of the conclusion of "Oxen of the Sun," there held in reserve, to generate a work that
stands equally as a monument of literary modernism and of the avant-
garde: a socially, politically, and aesthetically revolutionary attempt to
make art possible for the modern world.[19]

Notes

1. The first definition of "conversation" in the *Oxford English Dictionary* is "The
action of living or having one's being *in* a place or *among* persons" (in use as early
as 1340); the *OED*'s earliest citation for "conversation" to denote sexual intercourse
is 1511 (third definition), and the earliest for our current primary usage, "Inter-
change of thoughts and words; familiar discourse or talk," the seventh definition in
the *OED*, is dated 1580. "Intercourse" was similarly innocent of sexual denotation
and connotation until even later, initially signifying trade and "Communication to
and fro between countries" (circa 1494) and only acquiring its current meaning of
sexual relations at the end of the eighteenth century (earliest citation, 1798).

2. See Himes 188, 190. As Janet Brodie observes, advertisers continued to recom-
mend condoms primarily for protection against disease throughout the nineteenth
century, much as they are again recommended in this era of AIDS (205–6). Norman
E. Himes's chapter on the "History of the Condom or Sheath" from ancient times to

their mass production into the 1930s, in his classic *Medical History of Contraception* (1936), remains the standard survey of the subject (186–206). Himes notes some early anticipations of the condom in the penis sheaths Egyptian males wore, either for decoration or for protection against insect bites and tropical diseases, in the myth of Minos and Pasiphae, and perhaps in imperial Rome, and considers Fallopious's claim to have perfected a linen sheath for protection against syphilis (1564), but he suspects the original inventor, long since lost to history, was "a medieval slaughter-house worker" who came up with the idea of using animal membranes to "protect against venereal infection" (191). The value of the sheath for contraception awaited the better understanding of the process of conception, but was well-established by the eighteenth century. Casanova, in particular, appreciated this use of condoms, describing them as "preservatives that the English have invented [*sic*] to put the fair sex under shelter from all fear" (quoted in Himes 195). His contemporary Boswell was also a user of condoms, for self-protection rather than contraception, during his regular meetings with prostitutes. Referring to these encounters euphemistically as "engage[ments] in armour"—using one of many slang terms for the condom in the later eighteenth century—Boswell even recorded his first use of protection "in Saint James's Park" on "Friday 25 March," 1763, in his *London Journal: 1762–1763* (227; see also Kruck 7–8). As Himes notes, "[w]idespread, common use of the condom" followed the development of the vulcanization process for rubber "by Goodyear and Handcock in 1843–44" (201), while the twentieth century introduced the use of "liquid latex" and "automatic machinery" for their mass production (201). By the mid-1930s, just one American manufacturer, the Youngs Rubber Corporation, was producing 20 million condoms per year (201).

The etymology of the name "condom" has itself perplexed both historians and linguists. In his *Looking for Dr. Condom*, William E. Kruck identifies the first appearance of this term for the sheath, in the English language, in 1705 (2), but his study thoroughly discredits the legend that the article was invented by a Restoration-era physician in attendance on Charles II, named Condom or Condon: "The man and his act of invention . . . are a myth" (57).

The always circumspect *Oxford English Dictionary* first acknowledged the word "condom" in the first volume of its *Supplement: A–G*, published in 1972 (Kruck 20).

3. Jane Ford has provided the only substantial discussion to date on the relations between *Ulysses* and *The Secret Agent* in her "James Joyce and the Conrad Connection."

4. Most appropriately for my argument, Huyssen not only implies a metaphor of prophylaxis in describing the modernists' relations to mass culture as affected by an "anxiety of contamination," here and throughout his *After the Great Divide*, but also describes the persistent gendering of "Modernism's Other" as *female*; see "Mass Culture as Woman" 44–62.

5. Conrad equates the Professor in *The Secret Agent*, for instance, to a disease, probably venereal: he is a "moral agent," an "unwholesome-looking little agent of destruction" who "passe[s] on unsuspected and deadly, like a pest in the street full of

men" (81, 83, 311); see also Haltresht 101–5. In a long list of euphemisms for the condom, Brodie mentions "membraneous [sic] envelopes," "apex envelopes," and "fibrous envelopes," but not *mortal* envelopes (207).

6. Joyce's anti-euphemism for the condom, "Killchild" (*U* 14.467), seems to be his own coinage.

7. Although Joyce left the Berlitz school in Trieste in the summer of 1907, he continued privately tutoring students in English (*JJII* 262–63; "Introduction" xii–xv). For Joyce's probable use of *The Secret Agent* as an instructional text, see Gillespie 77, and for a description of his notations on his copies of Conrad's fiction, see Ford, "James Joyce's Trieste Library" 145–56. Although Joyce might have bought the book simply because of his interest in Conrad, or for the novel's treatment of anarchists, revolutionaries, and spies, he may also have known that Conrad modeled two of its characters, Michaelis and the Professor, on later-nineteenth-century Fenians: Michael Davitt and Luke "Dynamite" Dillon; see Sherry 260–69, 283–85.

8. Robert Scholes does not speculate about the date of the earliest surviving fragments of the holograph manuscript of "The Dead," which the printer used to set the aborted 1910 Maunsel edition of *Dubliners*, in his study of the story's textual history (192–94).

9. Raised when, where, and how he was, as Richard Brown observes, Joyce "could not but have had a strong awareness of the birth-control issue" (63). The standard study of Joyce's career-long preoccupation with the question of population control is Mary Lowe-Evans's *Crimes against Fecundity*. For Joyce's use of prophylactic imagery throughout *Dubliners*, see also Bowen 257–73.

10. "Condoms had been associated only with the brothel, and many [at the end of the nineteenth century] saw their use within marriage as defiling the marriage bed. . . . As important as condoms were quickly to become in family limitation, they never quite lost their disreputability. They remained tainted by the old association with prostitution and venereal diseases and disreputable because they were often sold in shops that also carried pornography and erotica in the seamier areas of . . . cities" (Brodie 206). To counter the condom's ill-repute, in the 1920s in the United States, Merrill Youngs, "an astute marketer," decided to capitalize on the "health aspect" of the sheath as a prophylactic against disease, selling his product "exclusively to druggists": "The natural outlet for their sale was the pharmacy." Consequently, Youngs's brand, "Trojans[,] bec[ame] synonymous with condoms for many Americans" (Murphy 11). Himes describes the development of similar marketing strategies in England (326–29).

In the United States, the "Comstock Laws," "passed in 1873 at the insistence of Anthony Comstock, leader of the Society for the Prevention of Vice, . . . included sweeping prohibitions against mailing, interstate transporting, or importing 'obscene, lewd, or lascivious' articles. . . . The Comstock statutes did not forbid the manufacture or sale of contraceptives but did ban interstate commerce in these products" (Murphy 9). The situation in England was, apparently, comparable to that in the United States at the turn of the century. In Ireland, however, the sale of condoms, which "were banned in a papal bull of 1826" (Kruck 23), remained illegal until the 1980s (Duffy 211).

11. "Mildly erotic magazines like *Photo Bits* . . . were indeed among the most common popular sources for contraceptive information and for the purchase of contraceptives" (Brown 66). Despite Theodore Purefoy's charge, Bloom apparently does not use condoms for contraception with Molly and believes he has kept his possession of "rubber preservatives" a secret from her. That he and Molly have had sex, at least on occasion, over the past ten-plus years is clear; Joyce simply qualifies the nature of their relations: "carnal intercourse had been incomplete, without ejaculation of semen within the natural female organ" (*U* 17.2283–84). As David Hayman notes, this "statement does not preclude coitus interruptus, cunnilingus . . . , or manual stimulation . . ., to say nothing of the nightly buttock kiss" (115); see also Brown 67.

12. Jane Ford, who finds several "parallels in character configuration and similarities in imagery and tone" between *Ulysses* and *The Secret Agent* ("James Joyce" 9), notes a number of late additions Joyce made to the text of *Ulysses* that suggest he was covertly acknowledging some debts his book owes to Conrad.

13. Although the topic is beyond the scope of the present essay, *Finnegans Wake* is obviously the limit case of textual prophylaxis in modern literature. As a narrative and linguistic experiment, moreover, the *Wake* seems to emerge, as many have noted, out of Joyce's composition of the "Oxen of the Sun" chapter of *Ulysses*, especially the tailpiece of the episode, discussed below. For discussions of the motifs of "immaculate contraceptives" (*FW* 45.14) and birth control in the *Wake*, see Lowe-Evans 75–99, and Brown 63–78.

14. Although he, too, fails to find a contradiction in Joyce's intentions, Harry Levin, in another early response to "Oxen of the Sun," registers both frustration with a "narrative . . . clotted with Shandyan digression and inflated with sheer linguistic exuberance" and exasperation with a structural "principle of embryonic growth," which "reduce[s] Joyce's cult of imitative form to a final absurdity" (95).

15. Richard Ellmann sees the conclusion of "Oxen of the Sun" as both "placental outpouring" and "ejaculative spray": "*coitus interruptus* becomes a verbal more than a genital matter in the episode's last pages, which are made up of a series of random ejaculations, a spray of words in all directions" (*Ulysses on the Liffey* 136, 135).

16. "The earliest teat-ended products which hold ejaculate appeared for sale in 1901" (Youssef 227).

17. Ellmann merely notes, in passing, Joyce's exposure to an "atmosphere of literary experimentation" in Zurich (*JJII* 409); Norris considers Ellmann's biography, together with the common identification of Stephen's aesthetic in *A Portrait of the Artist as a Young Man* as Joyce's, as the chief sources for "the powerful mythology of Joyce as modernist artist" in literary studies: "the Ellmann biography's blatant patronization of the way Joyce negotiated his material circumstances . . . serves to firmly demarcate and valorize the separation of his art from his material and

domestic life. Perhaps more than other literary biographies, the Ellmann biography reinforces the ideology of artistic autonomy by trivializing and denigrating what falls outside Joyce's art, including . . . Joyce's socialist and other political tendencies" (8).

18. Differing with Peter Bürger, like Norris, Astradur Eysteinssohn cogently argues that sharp distinctions between the avant-garde and modernism break down when dealing with many of the major works of the period. Although acknowledging that "one way to radicalize modernism fruitfully is to read 'modernist' works from the perspective of the avant-garde," Eysteinssohn concludes that "rather than enforce a rigid separation, I find it a good deal more critically stimulating and historically challenging to work on the assumption that while texts such as *Ulysses, Der Prozeß, Nightwood,* and *The Cantos* are modernist works, they are also avant-garde in their nontraditional structure and their radicalized correlations of form and content, and that while the avant-garde movements are historical phenomena in their own right, they are also salient motors of modernism" (177–78).

19. Margot Norris makes a strong case for reading *Finnegans Wake* as an avant-garde work, particularly in her analysis of "Shem the Penman" (*FW* 169–95) as Joyce's unraveling of Stephen's privileging of aesthetic autonomy in *A Portrait of the Artist as a Young Man,* via the intermediary modifications of his Shakespeare commentary in *Ulysses,* in which Stephen emphasizes the artist's significant relation to the "material world" (77). Seeing Shem as the *"Bête Noire* of Modernism" (82), Norris persuasively "explor[es] 'Shem the Penman' as an avant-garde self-criticism of art" (73).

Works Cited

Boswell, James. *Boswell's London Journal, 1762–63.* Edited by Frederick A. Pottle. New Haven: Yale University Press, 1950.

Bowen, Zack. "Joyce's Prophylactic Paralysis: Exposure in *Dubliners.*" *James Joyce Quarterly* 19, no. 3 (1982): 257–73.

Brodie, Janet Farrell. *Contraception and Abortion in Nineteenth-Century America.* Ithaca, N.Y.: Cornell University Press, 1994.

Brown, Richard. *James Joyce and Sexuality.* Cambridge: Cambridge University Press, 1985.

Bürger, Peter. *Theory of the Avant-Garde.* Translated by Michael Shaw. Minneapolis: University of Minnesota Press, 1984.

Carens, James F. "Some Points on Poyntz and Related Matters." *James Joyce Quarterly* 16, no. 3 (1979): 344–46.

Conrad, Joseph. *The Secret Agent.* Edited by Norman Sherry. London: Dent, 1974.

Duffy, Enda. "Interesting States: Birthing and the Nation in 'Oxen of the Sun.'" In *"Ulysses"—En-Gendered Perspectives,* edited by Kimberly J. Devlin and Marilyn Reizbaum, 210–28. Columbia: University of South Carolina Press, 1999.

Eliade, Mircea. *The Sacred and the Profane: The Nature of Religion*. Translated by Willard R. Trask. San Diego: Harcourt Brace, 1959.

Eliot, T. S. *The Complete Poems and Plays, 1909–1950*. New York: Harcourt, Brace, and World, 1962.

———"The Metaphysical Poets." In *The Norton Anthology of Theory and Criticism*, edited by Vincent B. Leitch et al., 1098–105. New York: Norton, 2001.

———"*Ulysses*, Order, and Myth." In *James Joyce: Two Decades of Criticism*, 2d ed., edited by Seon Givens, 198–202. New York: Vanguard Press, 1963.

Ellmann, Richard. Introduction to *Giacomo Joyce*, by James Joyce. New York: Viking, 1968.

———*Ulysses on the Liffey*. New York: Oxford University Press, 1972.

Eysteinssohn, Astradur. *The Concept of Modernism*. Ithaca, N.Y.: Cornell University Press, 1990.

Ford, Jane M. "James Joyce and the Conrad Connection: The Anxiety of Influence." *Conradiana* 17, no. 1 (1985): 3–18.

———"James Joyce's Trieste Library: Some Notes on Its Use." In *Joyce at Texas: Essays on the James Joyce Materials at the Humanities Research Center*, edited by Dave Oliphant and Thomas Zigal, 141–57. Austin: Humanities Research Center, 1983.

Gifford, Don. "*Ulysses*" *Annotated: Notes for James Joyce's "Ulysses."* Rev. ed. Berkeley and Los Angeles: University of California Press, 1988.

Gillespie, Michael Patrick, ed. *James Joyce's Trieste Library: A Catalogue of Materials at the Harry Ransom Humanities Research Center, The University of Texas at Austin*. Austin: Humanities Research Center, 1986.

Haltresht, Michael. "Disease Imagery in Conrad's *The Secret Agent*." *Literature and Psychology* 21 (1971): 101–5.

Hayman, David. "The Empirical Molly." In *Approaches to "Ulysses": Ten Essays*, edited by Thomas F. Staley and Bernard Benstock, 103–35. Pittsburgh: University of Pittsburgh Press, 1970.

Himes, Norman E. *Medical History of Contraception*. New York: Schocken, 1970.

Huyssen, Andreas. *After the Great Divide: Modernism, Mass Culture, Postmodernism*. Bloomington: Indiana University Press 1986.

Janusko, Robert. *The Sources and Structures of James Joyce's "Oxen."* Ann Arbor, Mich.: UMI Research, 1983.

Kruck, William E. *Looking for Dr. Condom*. Publication of the American Dialect Society. No. 66. Tuscaloosa: University of Alabama Press, 1981.

Lawrence, D. H. *Lady Chatterley's Lover*. New York: Grove, 1957.

Levin, Harry. *James Joyce: A Critical Introduction*. 2d ed. New York: New Directions, 1960.

Lowe-Evans, Mary. *Crimes against Fecundity: Joyce and Population Control*. Syracuse, N.Y.: Syracuse University Press, 1989.

Murphy, James S. *The Condom Industry in the United States*. Jefferson, N.C.: McFarland, 1990.

Norris, Margot. *Joyce's Web: The Social Unraveling of Modernism.* Austin: University of Texas Press, 1992.

The Oxford English Dictionary. <http://dictionary.oed.com/entrance.dtl>

Scholes, Robert. "Some Observations on the Text of *Dubliners:* 'The Dead.'" *Studies in Bibliography* 15 (1962): 191–205.

Sherry, Norman. *Conrad's Western World.* Cambridge: Cambridge University Press, 1971.

Wilson, Edmund. *Axel's Castle: A Study in the Imaginative Literature of 1870–1930.* New York: Scribner's, 1931.

Youssef, H. "The History of the Condom." *Journal of the Royal Society of Medicine* 86 (April 1993): 226–28.

Plausibility and Epimorphs

Fritz Senn

This probe into narrative trust and stratification in *Ulysses* takes its origin from the naïve question of whether, in the library chapter, Stephen Dedalus, or for that matter anyone else, could—or ever would—speak exactly in the manner in which the dialogue is presented, or whether epic retouches come in. Not a question to arouse everyone's interest, perhaps, yet possibly relevant for those who still believe in such distinctions. It is still expedient to simplify that *Ulysses* moves from a more (often extravagantly) realistic mode to one that questions the applicability of realism, or from direct to indirect presentation, from What happens to How it is being told. Allowing for epistemological quibbles, in reading practice the early chapters do create an illusion as though acts and spoken words (thoughts insofar as they ever can be verbalized) were taken straight from what is imaginable in "real life." Joyce once referred to an "initial style" from which the book then increasingly departs. Though no one perhaps will ever be able to define "realism," its presence is evidenced by the mere possibility of walking tours in Dublin or the existence of, even need for, maps or topographical guides. What people say has the ring of Dublin idiom or, as the case may be, of refined diction, pomposity, or live irony. In other words, many of the descriptions and perhaps all of the dialogue in the early episodes could be treated as a script for stage or film, but that is not the case with most of the later chapters, and not at all in "Oxen of the Sun," and hardly for "Ithaca."

The initial chapters are closer to literal verisimilitude than the later ones. Where *Ulysses* changes tracks is not simple to determine. Neat schematizations simply do not apply. It is not a matter of a first half (nine episodes) and a second, with a break in the schematic center, that would be between episodes 9 and 10. But episode 10, "Wandering Rocks," is in many ways far less complex than episode 9, "Scylla and Charybdis." The autonomous headlines/captions in "Aeolus," added, as we know, in a later process of revision, transcend the predominantly psychorealistic progress of the first half.

For my present purposes, the point of departure is the discussion in the National Library. "Scylla and Charybdis" continues the tripartite mode of the initial chapters, a pliable fusion of narrative, dialogue, and interior monologue. A striking novel feature is a fanciful saturation of the narrative parts that up to this point were relatively pragmatic. There is a marked transition from the end of "Lestrygonians"—"His hand looking for the where did I put found in his hip pocket soap lotion have to call tepid paper stuck" (U 8.1191–92)—to a typical capricious amalgamation in the library, where two exceptional words sidetrack our attention: "Twicreakingly analysis he corantoed off" (U 9.12). Both sentences conflate a substratum of objective depiction with either fleeting thoughts (Bloom) or echoes of preceding phrases ("on neatsleather creaking . . . True in the larger analysis" [U 9.5, 11]). There is some probability that Stephen mentally transforms a simple, but somehow affected way of walking into Shakespearean verbiage. It is characteristic of "Scylla and Charybdis" that the third-person statements (generally attributed to a hypothetical "narrator") are suffused by literary echoes. This salient deviation from the earlier chapters, so many readers might agree, may be one result of what is called Stephen's "fantastical humour" (U 9.950). Other accounts are no doubt possible, but a Stephenesque slant in the whole episode seems well in evidence.

The difference is not just the one between Bloom's and Stephen's minds or vocabularies but also one of degree. The mode of the chapter, its concern with literature, overtones, resonances, and verbal high jinks, seems to leave almost nothing untouched, quite in the manner of the second half of the book. The episode that deals with literature calls up its literary tradition. Even names are tampered with and lose their habitual integrity ("Eglintonus Chronolologos," "Cuck Mulligan" [U 9.811, 1025]).

"As One Hears in Real Life"?

Is Stephen's part of the dialogue realistically plausible—plausible within the framework that the earlier chapters set up? Could or would anyone sustain such a high level of allusive sophistication? One quick answer is, Certainly, everything could in fact be said. But Joyce had a good ear for what any character in fiction might be able to formulate in free speech, and Stephen's almost perfectly phrased tour de force may appear to be above even his amazing capacity and, therefore, beyond probability. Yet how to determine such an issue, always assuming it is worth investigating?

In A Portrait, Stephen Dedalus was already holding forth on aesthetics to a somewhat irreverent audience of one, Lynch, and there it looked as though the views had been mentally almost ready for instant publication. So there is a precedent, with significant shifts. The opinions offered in the library deviate from the earlier tenet of an artist's invisibility in a dramatic work. Above all the prose in the library is resonant at almost every ingenious turn (and, consequently, in drastic need of scrupulous annotation).

But first, a conventional departure from realism has to be dealt with. Like practically all writers, Joyce does not aim at acoustic verisimilitude in ordinary polylogue, that is, when two or more people talk together. For the sake of clarification, in books speakers usually take neat turns, waiting for the others to finish before they raise their own impatient voice; in real life we more often interrupt each other in mid-speech in a jarring blend of voices. Interruptions can be simulated by ellipses ("—Saint Thomas, Stephen began ... /*Ora pro nobis,* Monk Mulligan groaned") followed by resumption: ("—Saint Thomas, Stephen smiling said ..." [*U* 9.772–78]). Multiple voices generally defy linear presentation. Lines separated on a printed page may be taken to occur simultaneously: Bob Doran's interference ("—Who's dead?") in the conversation about Dignam's death would hardly be spaced discreetly between Alf Bergan's "Sure I'm after seeing him ..." and Joe Hynes's "You saw his ghost then" (*U* 12.323–26). Linearity cannot accommodate aural polyphony or marginal noise. In the medley of utterances that accompanies Russell's departure (U 9.316), the unidentified voices are presented in orderly sequence. The end of "Oxen" presents the same problem: an exuberant group of animated young men on the way from Holles Street to Burke's pub would hardly comply with parliamentary procedures. In such cases, orderly textual *nacheinander* streamlines messy vocal *nebeneinander*. Type on a printed page is usually more distinct than what the ear picks up empirically from a welter of voices. In other words, even the most true-to-life dialogue in fiction is rendered in qualified realism according to conventional norms.

"Just Mix Up a Mixture of Theolologicophilolological"

Yet on the whole, Joyce's dialogue appears plausible, in tune with the characters, whether they are witty, trite, pretentious, or fumbling. This plausibility seems to apply still to "Scylla and Charybdis." The intellectuals in residence are voluble, articulate, erudite (in distinct contrast to the less than eloquent Bloom as we have come to know him).[1] Stephen's performance, however, may appear almost too impeccable (the emphasis here is not on what he says, his line of argument, but the phrasing, *how* he puts it). All his sentences are complete, well poised, printable without any need for editing. Few speakers can move on such a high level, especially with such a plenitude of historical particulars and Elizabethan period flavor, echoes, and quotations.

We know Stephen generally has little concern for his audience; self-confident virtuosity overrides a feeble urge to communicate. Even the intellectuals in the library—or any contemporary professor of literature—would hardly be able to follow Stephen or remotely pick up most of his allusions.[2] Stephen produces considerable oral waste; most of his transient implications would be thrown away. He preens himself, moreover, in front of a very small audience of five people at the utmost, generally fewer.

There is something written and artificial about Stephen's longish speeches. The librarian Best is a good foil for comparison: "But *Hamlet* is so personal, isn't it? Mr Best pleaded. I mean, a kind of private paper, don't you know, of his private life. I mean, I don't care a button, don't you know, who is killed or who is guilty . . ." (*U* 9.362–64). No such diffidence mars the supple flow of Stephen's much more elaborate periods, like the polished one at the end of a very long speech, such as:

The playwright who wrote the folio of this world and wrote it badly (He gave us light first and the sun two days later), the lord of things as they are whom the most Roman of catholics call *dio boia*, hangman god, is doubtless all in all in all of us, ostler and butcher, and would be bawd and cuckold too but that in the economy of heaven, foretold by Hamlet, there are no more marriages, glorified man, an androgynous angel, being a wife unto himself. (*U* 9.1047–52)

The structure can be seen as quite on a par with the rhetorical sample pieces that were aired in the newspaper office. When Stephen was exposed to exemplary speeches (of Seymour Bushe and John F. Taylor), he expected further "[n]oble words coming" and asked himself, "Could you try your hand at it yourself?" (*U* 7.836–37). Trying one's hands refers to writing,[3] possibly revising at leisure;[4] an off-the-cuff presentation is quite another challenge. Few of us would be able to bring off such an impromptu performance; even the most academically cultivated scholars, to the delight of every audience, prefer to read their own carefully preformulated prose, and many of us have had the sobering experience of listening on tape to what we said when we believed we were articulate and coherent at the time.

That Stephen's flaunted periods are more artistic, more formally perfect, or more lexically embroidered may be a matter of judgment, but they are, at any rate, demonstrably longer. A quick survey reveals that Stephen's spoken sentences average eighteen words (markedly longer than in his interior monologue throughout), but those of Eglinton, Best, or Lyster about eleven (theirs can usually be uttered in one breath). In the earlier episodes, Stephen usually spoke in fairly short sentences. In "Aeolus," he presents no rhetorical sparkle; his contributions are pointedly unostentatious.

After a particularly elegant run, Stephen reflects, "Drummond of Hawthornden helped you at that stile" (U 9.386). He has echoed a thought of that writer,[5] but the homophone "style" asserts itself behind the surface. Stephen speaks the sort of poised prose that authors before him have composed in writing. Somehow at the back a proverbial phrase—"helping a lame dog over a stile"—seems to be lurking.[6] The focus of this essay is on the lame prose of everyday conversation as against Dedalian eloquence.

Is Stephen's "best French polish" (U 9.315) due to inspiration on the spur of a moment? Although many unforeseen moments spur him on, Stephen no doubt has pored over his views and articulated them in his mind; much of the ingenuity may have been rehearsed and is now ready, memory permitting, for instant retrieval. Some passages obviously are already in Stephen's mind. Some ruminations on trinitarian doctrines in the morning—"the subtle African heresiarch Sabellius who held that the Father was Himself His own Son" (U 1.659–60)—will be integrated and expanded: "Sabellius, the African, subtlest heresiarch of all the beasts of the field, held that the Father was Himself His Own Son. The bulldog of Aquin, with whom no word shall be impossible, refutes him" (9.862–64). Otherwise there are few indications of any rehearsal in the course of the morning, oddly enough none of them in the extended musings in "Proteus." In "Aeolus," a reference to Homer's "poor Penelope" calls up "Penelope Rich" (U 7.1039–40); she is transferred as "Penelope Rich, a clean quality woman" to the argumentation (U 9.639).

Stephen has certainly shared some of his ideas with others; Haines, a recent visitor, already knows of their existence. At their mere mention, Buck Mulligan offers his by now well-known parody, "I'm not equal to Thomas Aquinas and the fiftyfive reasons he has made to prop it up. ... He proves by algebra that Hamlet's grandson is Shakespeare's grandfather and that he himself is the ghost of his own father" (U 1.546–57). The concise distortion shows that Mulligan has been exposed to a substantial part

of the theory, which indeed features a ghost, algebraic equations, (grand)-
fathers and sons, as well as issues of identity. Above all, it features Thomas Aquinas. But strangely enough, in the library Saint Thomas does
not become the cornerstone or argumentative grid that Buck Mulligan
proclaimed in amusing exaggeration ("fiftyfive reasons"). Aquinas re-
futing Sabellius, as quoted above (U 9.862), is fairly peripheral. The second
reference appears to be triggered by Eglinton's "Prove that [Shakespeare]
was a jew" (U 9.763) and may not even have been part of the original
thesis:

> —Saint Thomas . . . whose gorbellied works I enjoy reading in the
> original,[7] writing of incest from a standpoint different from that of
> the new Viennese school Mr Magee spoke of, likens it in his wise and
> curious way to an avarice of the emotions. He means that the love so
> given to one near in blood is covetously withheld from some stranger
> who, it may be, hungers for it. Jews, whom christians tax with avarice,
> are of all races the most given to intermarriage. (U 9.778–84)

The episode's version as we know it from the Rosenbach manuscripts did
contain some garbled Aquinas in Latin ("*Amor vero aliquid alicui bonum
vult unde et ea quae concupiscimus*" [U 9.430]), but whether it was taken
out by Joyce in an undocumented revision or else got lost in transcription
by an oversight, it does not have much bearing on the theory itself. If
Stephen were repeating himself verbatim, the satirical Buck would probably interject a few punchy comments.

It seems that a lecture on Shakespeare was not part of Stephen's agenda
for the day. Frank Budgen surmised that Stephen "has a rendezvous at the
National Library, at any rate intends going there, and it is there that he
will expound it" (Budgen 109). But nothing in "Nestor," "Proteus," or
"Aeolus" indicates that Stephen is about to deliver a lecture later in the
day; it is Deasy's letter that directs him to the library. The Shakespeare
discussion opens *in medias res;* we do not know how it originated. When
Haines left, uninterested, it must already have been underway (U 9.91–
95).

Again on a practical level, could Stephen construe on the spot or sum-
mon to mind all these intricate periods? One hundred years ago people
might well have had more effective memories than we, aided by technol-
ogy, can now muster. Memorizing speeches was also taught in school. Even
so, when poetic inspiration strikes Stephen on the beach, he gropes for a
piece of paper to record it:

Here. Put a pin in that chap, will you? My tablets.
. . . Paper. The banknotes, blast them. Old Deasy's letter. . . . That's
twice I forgot to take slips from the library counter. (*U* 3.399–407)

A poem after all, because of its rhythm and rhyme, would be far easier to
memorize than a lengthy, convoluted literary treatise. Stephen, in this respect the equivalent of his author (whose extant notebooks now preoccupy
a score of scholars), depends on paper to jot down fleeting ideas: "That's
twice I forgot to take slips from the library counter"; "Take some slips
from the counter going out" (*U* 3.407, 9.1058). Somewhat incongruously,
therefore, the Shakespeare lecture is delivered and cleverly expanded
without a single slip.

Even so Stephen *might* have internalized his ideas on Shakespeare,
down to minute formulations, and stored them on his mental hard drive
for instant download and adaptation to new material or probing questions,
improbable as it may appear. However, he does not only deliver a lecture
but ingeniously parries interjections in exactly the same vein. There are
indications that Stephen spurs himself on as he goes along: "Work in all
you know. Make them accomplices," and again: "Composition of place.
Ignatius Loyola, make haste to help me!" (*U* 9.158, 163). Some time later
he pats himself on the back: "I think you're getting on very nicely. Just mix
up a mixture of theolologicophilolological. *Mingo, minxi, mictum, min-
gere*" (*U* 9.761–62). This phrasing suggests that Stephen is still mentally
composing, not recalling something pre-articulated; the pieces may already be in his mind (including a point he did not remember: "Forgot: any
more than he forgot the whipping lousy Lucy gave him" [*U* 9.1134]), but
their composition calls for impromptu skills that Stephen, against plausibility, seems to manage almost without effort, never groping for the right
word.

When challenged, Stephen comes up with quick cunning retorts, and he
skillfully adapts items that were gathered during the day. In the newspaper
office, MacHugh had compared Stephen to a Greek philosopher: "—You
remind me of Antisthenes, the professor said, a disciple of Gorgias, the
sophist. . . . he wrote a book in which he took away the palm of beauty from
Argive Helen and handed it to poor Penelope" (*U* 7.1035–39). When
Eglinton compares Anne Hathaway to "a Penelope stay-at-home,"
Stephen picks up the cue and cleverly twists it into a classical footnote: "—
Antisthenes, pupil of Gorgias, Stephen said, took the palm of beauty from
Kyrios Menelaus' brooddam, Argive Helen, the wooden mare of Troy in

whom a score of heroes slept, and handed it to poor Penelope" (*U* 9.621–23). Within the given matrix he elaborates on Helen, as the wife of Menelaus (on whom he bestows an entirely non-Homeric honorific *kyrios*, a word held up for inspection within a different context, in "Aeolus" [*U* 7.562–64]); with strong misogynous emphasis he disparages her as "brooddam" (her notoriety was not in breeding) and makes her more promiscuous than the sources warrant; his supplementary "in whom a score of heroes slept" deftly mixes a Homeric scene of her outside the wooden horse and endangering the lives of the hidden Greek heroes (*Od.* 4:271–89) with exaggerated unfaithfulness; the "mare" echoes the back-kicking "nightmare of history" from "Nestor" (*U* 2.377): the slur "dam" derives from lines by a colonialist Swinburne poem that flashed through Stephen's mind not too long ago (*"Whelps and dams of murderous foes"* [*U* 9.137]). All of this Stephen conjures up spontaneously and fits into the given frame, quite an exploit of compressive ingenuity: so different from Joyce himself, who did not make up the intricacies in one brilliant stroke but substantially revised the sentence between late 1918 and autumn 1921.[8]

In "Oxen of the Sun," Stephen has similar virtuoso runs; but there Stephen's (like almost everybody else's) words can hardly be extricated from their period furnishings. The question that is pursued here amounts to whether the mannerism of the later episode, from mimicry to parody, has possibly rubbed off on the earlier one, both dealing, in their own way, with Literature.

"If My Memory Serves Me"

The speech by John F. Taylor that is quoted by MacHugh in "Aeolus" warrants a digression to a related improbability. Taylor himself, if we trust the information, was capable of producing "the finest display of oratory" off the cuff: "That he had prepared his speech I do not believe" (*U* 7.792, 814–15). Taylor's rhetorical dexterity looks astonishing, but not less so the fact that MacHugh would remember it letter perfect. He could not have read it, for "there was not even one shorthandwriter in the hall," and he throws in a cautious prefatory note: "as well as I can bring them to mind" (*U* 7.815–16, 824). Are we as readers to suppose that, within the fiction, the speech we read, memorable as it is, is a reliable, verbatim record of what was spoken? The actual speech has not survived, so Joyce at least in part must have made it up. The question here is whether the recital could be trusted on a simple level of reality or whether this speech already, like Stephen's performance, is more due to narrative artificiality. "Aeolus," after all, is the first chapter that points toward its fictional contrivances, an event in print: it also has an editor presiding who determines what goes in.

In "Scylla and Charybdis," Stephen can effortlessly generate polished periods. Indirect acknowledgment of the written nature of his argument emerges in Stephen's response to the editor of *Dana*—"For a guinea . . . you can publish this interview" (*U* 9.1085). Flippant as the response is, what Stephen has said might be transferred to print with little adaptation.

If, however, a true-to-life Stephen is holding forth, then Joyce forged an *alter ego* of superior rhetorical skills. There is no record that Joyce himself ever was a dazzling orator (he did appear to need notes for his Trieste lectures on Shakespeare). The age-old question of whether Stephen would ever become a Joyce and write *Ulysses* takes on another slant: in speaking performance, fictional Stephen Dedalus surpasses his own creator. Stephen, brilliant verbal artificer, for once is verbally living up to his mythical namesake, the builder of a labyrinth. In his own estimation, however, Stephen feels less a soaring Daedalus than a drowning Icarus, "Lapwing . . . fallen, weltering" (*U* 9.953–54). Most of his aspirations may in fact have failed up to now, but then it is all the more incongruous that verbally he is flying far above average competence. In the Daedalian prose there is no trace of weltering. The artful, urbane, resonating diction does not contain any fumbles.

Stephen realizes how much he is putting on an act: "Speech, speech. But act. Act speech. They mock to try you. Act. Be acted on" (*U* 9.978–79).[9] He does in fact "act speech," and the act is not entirely his own, just as Shakespeare's "boywomen are the women of a boy. Their life, thought, speech are lent them by males" (*U* 9.254–55). Stephen's speech is lent by artifice, or a supervising and carefully revising author. His speech too is "always turned elsewhere" (in rich overlovely English: see *U* 9.471–72). In the library, as in the maternity chapter, Stephen boasts he can call "the past" and literary "phantoms . . . into life across the waters of Lethe" (*U* 14.1112–14). The chapter's mode in turn affects his utterances. The narrative parts look partly manipulated, transformed in Stephen's mind. The thematic mode of the episode, Literature, infuses what Stephen says, in the form of refined essay style.

Sequential Bulliness

Narrative plausibility will be suspended in the chapters to follow. Yet on occasion it may trouble some traditionalist readers. In "Oxen," the literary, imitative mode is responsible for the wording that occludes the actual conversations, so the focus cannot be on what may actually be spoken. In the manner of Swift, an unattested historical event—how Pope Adrian IV gave Ireland away to Henry II—is transposed to an elaborate yet somewhat blurry allegory of "a bull that's Irish" (*U* 14.578–648). The problem aired here is not what precisely anyone is saying but the oddity that several speakers take turns and serially concoct a fairly complex tale. It appears that, on a cue from Stephen, "Mr Vincent" (Lynch) gets it on the road and is ably assisted by "Mr Dixon"; the two of them share the burden, but soon "Another then put[s] in his word" and continues without hesitation, to be succeeded by a different "another"; the tale is finally wound up by Stephen. This is quite a feat of five speakers improvising and embroidering a fable without any noticeable inconsistency. Of course a prototype of such a tale might have been in circulation at the time as a point of reference. Are we to assume, at this fairly late stage, that a group of five young men, animated by Bass's ale, could seamlessly fabricate such an extended, wayward Irish bull? There is also the disproportion of five yarn-spinners within a group of hardly more than eight, so that the tellers outnumber the audience. Or is my consideration perhaps the kind of simpleminded (Bloomian?) attitude that the book helps us to grow out of? If the Tale of a Bull sequence is felt to be relatively univocal in tone and phrasing, as it is in my impression, it would be a strange inversion of the episode's stylistic bias, which translates the articulations of the men present into varying styles according to the given stage of literary development; in contrast, the Irish Bull performance streamlines (presumably) individual expressions into the same mold of Swiftian features. An episode that patently favors variety, usually from paragraph to paragraph, often even within a single one, may conversely merge a series of different voices into dubious homogeneity.

In the same vein, would the group in the hospital on their way to the pub be able to play the collective game of the inspired vernacular variations of the final passages, the "afterbirth" (or "Coda") paragraphs (*U* 14.1440–1591)? As in the Irish Bull series, such dexterous speaking in tongues is more likely to occur in literature than in most of our lives. Reduced to its bare bones, the issue is just how much artifice is insinuated on that pedestrian level that the chapter mode tends to occlude.

"A Certain Analogy There Somehow Was" ("Eumaeus")

Literature dominates "Scylla and Charybdis"; in the "Eumaeus" episode, Bloom airs literary pretensions and attempts to speak above his customary level, and he commands a more ambitious, though stereotyped, vocabulary and more elaborate phrasing. This also applies to his reflections, as they are reported, but the distinct chapter tinge, a mixture of as-you-go-along associations and secondhand literary diction, seems to mastermind those passages. As Bloom aspires to impress his new associate in resilient rhetorical efforts, he becomes unusually figurative, redundant. But even so, aided by second-wind, Aeolian, inspiration, would he be capable of phrases such as the ones I italicize here for demonstration?: "—No, Mr Bloom repeated again, I wouldn't *personally repose much trust in that boon companion* of yours who *contributes the humorous element,* Dr Mulligan, *as a guide, philosopher and friend* if I were in your shoes" (*U* 16.279–81).[10] In many effusive Eumaean paragraphs it is impossible to distinguish whether Bloom is merely ordering some thoughts, rehearsing a possible speech, or actually speaking. Many paragraphs might well be modifications of an interior monologue or a stylized version of what has been put into words. A long internal ramble, touching on the Invincibles and Ireland's precarious relations with England in general, moves from obvious rumination to unmarked indirect speech toward the end: "Then as for the other he had heard not so long before the same identical lingo as he told Stephen how he simply but effectually silenced the offender" (*U* 16.1078–80). The sequence denotes clearly that Bloom began to speak aloud before the text indicates it: "—He took umbrage at something or other, that muchinjured but on the whole eventempered person declared, I let slip" (*U* 16.1081). The antecedent to "He" or "the offender," the Citizen, must have been introduced at some stage. We cannot determine what exactly of Bloom's musings has been put into speech, let alone what his words would have been. The distinctions between the narrative report and actual speech become blurred and cease to be of prime significance.

If phrases like "repose much trust in" or "a guide, philosopher and friend" are not Bloom's own words taken down verbatim, it means that, as conceivably in the library episode, we can also not repose much trust in the dashes that, all along, have heralded direct speech. A typographical certainty has evaporated along the way. This would fit a chapter of prevailing doubt, rumors, uncertainty, and pretense. What Bloom says in his more inspired moments seems to be imbued by the episode's stylistic features. The narrative mode of "Eumaeus" affects Bloom's words just as the literary bias of the library episode animates Stephen. The idiosyncrasies of the respective episodes—literary scintillation or the sparkle of figurative embellishment—have encroached on the (semblance of) actual spoken words.

A circular technique can be seen at work in the two episodes that have been linked in regard to the plausibility of some dialogue passages. In both episodes, features of the central character are pushed beyond realism. Stephen's obsession with literature and a turn of mind that tends to frame incipient thoughts into almost finished sentences help shape the texture of "Scylla and Charybdis." In analogy the verbal convolutions of "Eumaeus" in large part draw on a Bloomian endeavour to imbue his opinions with rhetorical sparkle.

A symptomatic passage contrasts Stephen's mind, which almost automatically connects a specific place with a literary model (echoing a passage in A Portrait—"Stephen thought to think of Ibsen, associated with Baird's the stonecutter's in his mind somehow in Talbot place"), with Bloom's, who, homme sensuel, turns to a physical stimulus ("while the other . . . inhaled with internal satisfaction the smell of James Rourke's city bakery, situated quite close to where they were"). But instantly he thinks of expressions that might transmute the daily actual bread of experience into memorable phrases: "Bread, the staff of life, earn your bread, O tell me where is fancy bread, at Rourke's the baker's it is said" (U 16.52–59). If Stephen can twist Shakespearean quotations into a new mold, Bloom is at least able to remember (which is probably what is happening) a Byronian line brought down to a Dublin witticism.

Transformations are taken for granted in all those parts of Ulysses that are dominated by manifest artistry or a mood of parody or imitation. In all of "Oxen," where Stephen also has very inspired runs, we can only speculate, in imaginative translation, about the characters' exact wording; the speaking parts in the "Cyclops" interpolations are not taken at face value. At some (indefinite) point, a salient (for some early readers, disgusting) realism and an apparent norm (which Joyce labeled as "initial style") begins to hide in the folds of narrative caprice.

Epimorphs

I have been belaboring a questionable but expedient contrast, between the Scylla of hard rock "realism" and the Charybdis of a whirlpool of literary, stylistic transposition—concretely the step from "That bee or bluebottle here" to "a horrible and dreadful dragon was smitten him" (U 4.483–84, 14.129–30). With increasing stridency, each episode puts its distinct stamp (or "signature") on the events it deals with, and the texture of each one seems to be at the mercy of the author or some deputy manager (personified intermediaries like "narrator," "arranger," "demiurgos," or whatever). I do not think these impositions, which for some readers still appear whimsically gratuitous and distractive, have been labeled. I propose "epimorph" as a term for the deviations away from, or superimposition on, an initial realistic mode. The ad hoc term "epimorph" serves as a label for the particular colorings that seem to be imposed, thrust upon, as it were from above (therefore epi), on the chapter's shape (morphe). A Greek verb epimorphazein meant to fashion, or to simulate, feign. Episodes are noticeably fashioned. "Oxen of the Sun," for one, is a series of simulations or forgeries, perhaps the most thoroughly epimorphed of all chapters.[11] Mythologically speaking, Joyce puts much of his tale into "the arms of Morpheus" (U 16.947–48), the Greek, or Ovidian, auxiliary god who imitates shapes and assumes any given form.[12] He is a master of illusions; an illusion (in-lusio) to start with was to bring play or game (ludus) into reality and thereby change it. The nonconforming chapters of Ulysses are illusive.[13]

The effect itself is commonplace: thematic concerns encroach on and modify the language, at times so forcefully that some erstwhile admirers raised objections. The typographical layouts of "Aeolus," "Circe," "Ithaca," and "Penelope" show differences even at a superficial glance. In "Circe," an apparent psychodrama escalates into metafictional textuality; toward the end distanced, objective, precise stock-taking asserts itself and falls short. What actually happens beneath the textual surface may come to be extracted or translated back into something like "normal" English. What at first might have impressed as a norm is challenged and undercut. In old-fashioned diction, which Joyce helps to overcome, content and form seem to follow their separate paths.

The term "epimorph" is merely a descriptive convenience, a coloring pencil, a new bottle label for old wine. It should assist us in distinctions, as one way of pinpointing an orchestration like "All most too new call is lost in all" in "Sirens" (*U* 11.634). Epimorphic throughout is the Homeric overlay, tucked on, or intermingled with, the plot and surface, not primarily operative (so it can be overlooked). So are all other symbolic or tangential correlations. The chapter colorings assert themselves in a prevalence of words or figurative uses that reinforce a dominant theme. Overtones or connotations of death tinge "Hades"; musical elements shape and in part distort the phrasing in "Sirens." Parodic, imitative, representation takes over. Epimorphic elements become more intrusive; Aeolian headlines/captions are the first overt signs, a blatant new device, emanating from a narrative agency outside a subjective consciousness. Similarly the opening of "Sirens" is something unheard of, both in *Ulysses* and in literature before, and has to be accounted for (musical comparisons are at hand: "overture, prelude, tuning up"). The Cyclopean interpolations are not just parodic exaggerations; they disrupt the even flow of narrative. In practical terms, or in the day-to-day experience of a classroom, epimorphic excrescences require explicit justifications.

All Joycean texts tend to be hybrid (there is always something else), and within the compounds some admixtures are easier to isolate than others. In a Circean direction (*"Bloom with his hand assuralooms Corny Kelleher that he is reassuraloomtay"* [*U* 15.4918–19]), the song refrain can be removed and the surface meaning is purged; names like Eglinton Johannes, Bloowhose, Senhor Enrique Flor, St. Owen Caniculus, and so on, can be translated to their proper forms; when an "anticipated diamond jubilee" is followed by a "posticipated opening" (*U* 17.429–30), Ithacan pedantry is linked to a binary reflex. The emphasis here is not so much on the obvious, monstrous (Aeolian, operatic, obstetric, and so on) extravagances but on the more low-key presences. On closer looks, glaring necessary distinctions have a way of evaporating. "The voices blend and fuse."

Epimorphs can be latent, as in most early chapters, where they do not ruffle the surface, or else, in rapid escalation, blatantly manifest. In "Lestrygonians," Bloom sets out in front of the windows of Graham Lemon's (8.6); the location is factual, a confectioner's shop in O'Connell Street. That the name happens to contain edible ingredients need not sidetrack any reader at all but happens to be part of the latent schematic order. Manifest epimorphic energy, however, turns an empty biscuit tin's feeble though possibly noisy impact on a street into a cataclysmic earthquake (*U* 12.1858), whose causes are historic echoes, Dublin municipal details, a technique of grotesque exaggeration and Homer's Poseidon, the shaker of the earth and father of Polyphemos, and many overhead items.

Hardly anyone would claim that the "normal," "realistic" elements could authentically be separated from (what is here labeled) epimorphic infusion. Several features can be accounted for either way. Two sentences in "Aeolus" depict what can be a sequence of perception *and* an oratorical overlay: "Grossbooted draymen rolled barrels dullthudding out of Prince's stores and bumped them up on the brewery float. On the brewery float bumped dullthudding barrels rolled by grossbooted draymen out of Prince's stores" (*U* 7.21–24). An impression of barrels rolled noisily from one place to another fits into a street scene of working life. The process can be viewed from a store to a float, or in reverse direction, as though by a movie camera. The onomatopoetic echoes may already draw attention to themselves, but the near-chiasmic arrangement looks more like a thematic device in accordance with the chapter's focus on rhetorical figures. Plain naturalism or else contrived artifice.

When Bloom has been snubbed by John Henry Menton near the exit of the cemetery in "Hades," we see him "chapfallen" (6.1027), certainly not a word of his own lexical range, but one supplied by the narrative context. It can take us to another, famous cemetery scene, Hamlet holding the skull of "poor Yorick . . . quite chapfallen" (often "chop-fall'n" [*Ham.* 5.1.184– 92]).[14] Minutes before Bloom has thought of "Gravediggers in *Hamlet*" (*U* 6.792). The choice adjective is a case of intertextual "Underground communication" (*U* 6.991).

Naturally the presentation of some epimorphs superimposed on basic real events is misleading, as though it were a matter of addition rather than a fusion or interpenetration. It is a process similar to distillation or transubstantiation (in which the basic substances are never quite refined out of existence). In practice, distinctions have to be made even if all eventually dwindle into invalidity. As was expatiated here, epimorphs intrude after the initial chapters, patently in "Aeolus," and at some indeterminate point tend to take over. But there is a kind of retroaction; they occur right from the start, with initial words like "Stately," "crossed," "ungirdled." Especially that conspicuous one-word sentence "Chrysostomos" (*U* 1.26) might qualify; I used to take it as possibly the first instance of Stephen's interior monologue, and still do, but for all we know it might be a premonitory inkling of an overarching commentary. The interior monologue is introduced gently, yet it gradually grows in proportion and already usurps most of "Proteus." At the end of "Telemachus," we find it extended when Haines cross-examines Stephen's beliefs:

The proud potent titles clanged over Stephen's memory the triumph of their brazen bells: *et unam sanctam catholicam et apostolicam ecclesiam*: the slow growth and change of rite and dogma like his own rare thoughts, a chemistry of stars. Symbol of the apostles in the mass for pope Marcellus, the voices blended, singing alone loud in affirmation: and behind their chant the vigilant angel of the church militant disarmed and menaced her heresiarchs. A horde of heresies fleeing with mitres awry: Photius and the brood of mockers of whom Mulligan was one, and Arius, warring his life long upon the consubstantiality of the Son with the Father, and Valentine, spurning Christ's terrene body, and the subtle African heresiarch Sabellius who held that the Father was Himself His own Son. Words Mulligan had spoken a moment since in mockery to the stranger. Idle mockery. The void awaits surely all them that weave the wind: a menace, a disarming and a worsting from those embattled angels of the church, Michael's host, who defend her ever in the hour of conflict with their lances and their shields.

Hear, hear! Prolonged applause. *Zut! Nom de Dieu!* (U 1.650–65)

Stephen might conceivably think all this up—it is quite in his line—but the fairly long run of almost two hundred words would take up appreciable time, more than Haines can be supposed to pass in patient silence, until Stephen finally attends to him again. The impression is rather that Haines moves almost immediately from "It seems history is to blame," just before the monologue, to "—Of course I'm a Britisher" (U 1.649, 666) right afterward. A conventional epic device, to stop time for asides, or some artificial extension ("prolonged") may be overriding customary dialogue pauses, as later on they will in the extended and often autonomous stage directions in "Circe" where clock time is generally suspended.[15] All of this indicates that the later *Ulyssean* exorbitances (literally what leaves a conventional track) are germinally operative right from the start.

In the nonliterary sense of imposing designs on reality, the mind is by nature epimorphic. It modifies perceptions and impressions according to its built-in patterns. Everything is adapted to our own frame of mind. This is one of the peculiarities to interior monologue. Stephen transposes the bells of Saint George into "*Liliata rutilantium*" (U 17.1230). Molly metamorphoses a printed word "metempsychosis" into her own range, "Met him pike hoses"; she re-forms the sounds "in plain words" and again assimilates Bloom's technicality "reincarnation" into a more familiar, Christian, "the incarnation" (U 8.112, 4.343, 18.566). Bloom emphatically endows Stephen with a female companion: "Ferguson, I think I caught. A girl. Some girl. Best thing could happen him" (U 15.4950–51). Ulysses highlights subjective adaptations and bases its eighteen subsections into equivalent matrixes. Everyone, we may learn from the library episode, creates his or her own Shakespeare; and we all epimorph the exuberance of Ulysses according to our own parallactic lights. Interpretations are epimorphic conversions.

History is "Fabled by the daughters of memory" (U 2.7). Memory transforms, distorts, selects, embellishes. Above all, language itself is epimorphic, words do multiple duty and accrete meaning or become historical repositories. Joyce can purposefully even turn simple words like "nice" (in A Portrait) or "home" into motifs. In Ulysses, "jingle" jingles menacingly, and so do innocuous phrases like "at four" or "for him." Lexical accumulation in accordance with a theme characterizes the episodes ("eye," "blind," and so on, in "Cyclops"). Perhaps we are just playing a game we have been infected with when we associate a string like "bar" with a place in "Proteus" ("Dublin bar"), a street in "Wandering Rocks" ("Temple bar"), music in "Sirens," and the law in "Cyclops"—and of course always with a pub. The memory of a prostitute "under her fustian shawl" refers to cloth, but in a chapter foregrounding oratory ("Aeolus" [U 7.928]) "fustian" secondarily functions as "bombastic speech"; the word occurs between various rhetorical set pieces and Stephen's own lapidary story about two women, which—by hindsight only—acquires meaningful and suggestive titles, "Pisgah Sight" and "Parable."

"Affecting in the Extreme"

As usual, Joyce is extreme in any direction, on the one hand more realistic, which incites archaeological rummaging[16] (so much so that, whenever a Dublin detail from Ulysses gives way to urban development, there is a sense of sacrilege), but then he turns with equal abandon toward the egregiously counterfeit. A style of "scrupulous meanness" was once defended "with the conviction that he is a very bold man who dares to alter in the presentment, still more to deform, whatever he has seen and heard" (5 May 1906, SL 83). The author, as he went along, became bolder and bolder

256   Fritz Senn

in his inventive deformations. An ecstatic Stephen Dedalus, prompted no doubt by his inventor, once thought of "transmuting the daily bread of experience into the radiant body of everliving life" (*P* 221); in the course of rapid stylistic evolution, this transmuted body's life became more and more autonomously radiant. Daedalus, who was suitably introduced to the literary world through a work called *Metamorphoses*, could imitate nature, fashioning a creditable wooden cow, but he could also construct a labyrinth for which presumably there was no precedent—fabulous artificer indeed.

Notes

1. "—Just this ad, Mr Bloom said, pushing through towards the steps, puffing, and taking the cutting from his pocket. I spoke with Mr Keyes just now. He'll give a renewal for two months, he says. After he'll see. But he wants a par to call attention in the *Telegraph* too, the Saturday pink. And he wants it copied if it's not too late I told councillor Nannetti from the *Kilkenny People*. I can have access to it in the national library. House of keys, don't you see? His name is Keyes. It's a play on the name. But he practically promised he'd give the renewal. But he wants just a little puff. What will I tell him, Mr Crawford?" (*U* 7.971–79).

2. In decades of scholarship we have not even caught up collectively, as annotators, to follow all the bypaths.

3. "—Are you going to write it?" Stephen is asked by Mr. Best (*U* 9.1068).

4. Contrary to possible expectation, Joyce did not heavily revise the passage quoted in its structure, which was set up early in Rosenbach. The changes were mainly word substitutions ("dramatist" > "playwright," "also" > "doubtless," "coupler" > "bawd"), and some additions ("the folio," "foretold by Hamlet," "an androgynous angel"), but substantial nevertheless. For details, see Gabler's *Critical and Synoptic Edition* 458.

5. As to what is echoed, Gifford (*Annotations* 218) supplements a note of William M. Schutte (318–19).

6. Stevenson's *Book of Quotations* lists "Help the lame dog over the stile. . . . Lame dogs over stiles, Help your lame dog o'er a stile" (893).

7. The phrase "whose works I enjoy reading in the original" is presumably an intentional stab at Mulligan's "the Greeks. . . . You must read them in the original" (*U* 1.79–80). Both phrases were added in the same phase of revision, June and August 1921. See Senn, "In the Original."

8. He first had "Antisthenes, pupil of Gorgias, Stephen said, took the palm of beauty from Kyrios Menelaus' broodmare, Argive Helen, and handed it to poor Penelope" (Rosenbach, and typescript, *JJA* 12: 360; "broodmare" was put in as an

afterthought). On a placard he added "the wooden mare of Troy in whom a score of heroes slept," then in the next set the redundant "-mare" was replaced by "-dam" (*JJA* 18: 182, 190). The process can also be extricated from the synoptic page of Gabler's critical edition (vol. 1, 430). Stephen uses the disparaging word "dam" again in the Maternity Hospital: "that earthly mother which was but a dam to bear beastly" (*U* 14.249–50)—given the likely assumption he does actually say it.

9. This may contain a possible Shakespearean echo: "*Hamlet*: Give us a taste of our quality, come, a passionate speech. / *First Player*: What speech, my good lord? / *Hamlet*: I heard thee speak me a speech once, but it was never acted on" (*Hamlet* 2.2.460).

10. Ironically the part that sounds most like Bloom, "if I were in your shoes," is particularly off target: Stephen is not in his own shoes, but those of Buck Mulligan.

11. *Fiction* is something *feigned*, originally the shaping of material like *dough* (which is a cognate of *feign, figure, fiction*); as readers of *A Portrait* have been made aware, to *forge* (from *fabricare*) denotes both a creative and a duplicative act.

12. In an echo Joyce ironically transposes Ovid's impersonator Morpheus (*Metamorphoses* 11:633ff.) back into a common Irish name: "in the arms of Murphy" (*U* 16:1727). Within the distinctions overstated here, Murphy and Morpheus, both creators of illusions, would be the realistic and respectively epimorphic exponents.

13. In Latin, the verb *illudere* also meant to mock, ridicule, and again to maltreat. It is Buck Mulligan who sets the pace for that aspect. The formal vagaries of *Ulysses* could be described by an increasing current of Mulliganesque parody.

14. As it happens, Glasnevin Cemetery contains a statue of a famous Irish actor, Barry Sullivan (died 1894), precisely in the arch-stereotype pose of Prince Hamlet, skull in hand. If this coincidence is of any relevance (take it or leave it), it is within the marginal realistic enmeshment.

15. As it happens *"Prolonged applause"* reappears in "Circe" right after one of Bloom's political speeches, and the applause is indeed prolonged to include a huge procession of dignitaries, bands, craft guilds, and aristocracy (*U* 15.1398ff.). The observation that the passage in "Telemachus" may pave the way for Circean amplifications was first made, as so often, by Hugh Kenner, in conversation long ago.

16. From one of Bloom's drawers, an "indistinct daguerreotype of Rudolf Virag and his father Leopold Virag executed in the year 1852 in the portrait atelier of . . . Stefan Virag of Szesfehervar, Hungary" is listed (*U* 17.1875–77). Whether something like this ever existed or not is esthetically immaterial, but it so happens that an advertisement for "Virág Sándor, Fényképészeti Müterme, Székesfehérvár" has been dug up (Endre 87). This may be a marginal source rather than an improbable coincidence. Joyce seems to have replaced a Sándor by a Stefan, closer to home, and misspelled "Székesfehérvár" ("Fényképészeti Müterme" would translate into "Photographic Studio").

Works Cited

Budgen, Frank. *James Joyce and the Making of "Ulysses."* London: Grayson and Grayson, 1934.

Endre, Tóth. "Leopold Bloom származása: egy fiktív családfa." *Vasi Honismereti és Helytörténeti Közlemények* (2001/2): 87.

Gabler, Hans Walter. *Critical and Synoptic Edition of "Ulysses."* Vol. 1. New York: Garland, 1984.

Gifford, Don, with Robert J. Seidman, *"Ulysses" Annotated: Notes for James Joyce's "Ulysses."* Second ed., rev. Don Gifford. Berkeley and Los Angeles: University of California Press, 1988.

Schutte, William M. "Allusions in 'Scylla and Charybdis': A Supplement to Weldon Thornton's List." *James Joyce Quarterly* 7 (summer 1970): 315–25.

Senn, Fritz. "'In the Original': Buck Mulligan and Stephen Dedalus." *Arion: A Journal of the Humanities and the Classics* 2, no. 1 (winter 1992): 215–17.

Stevenson, Burton Egbert. *Book of Quotations.* London: Cassell, 1967.

Theoretical Bloom

Zack Bowen

I sought a theme and sought for it in vain
I sought it daily for six weeks or so.
Maybe at last, being but a broken man,
I must be satisfied with critical theory, although
Winter and summer till old age began
My explications were all on show,
Those tuneful tropes, that burnished Bloomusalem,
Scatology, and blasphemy and the Lord knows what.

In the twenty-first century one can hardly proclaim to be a professional Joycean, much less an informed reader of modern literature, without cognizance of the theoretical tools of the profession. Increasingly theory has come to assume precedence over the sanctity of textual explication for its own New Critical sake. This essay will lay the cornerstones of a New Critical Bowenusalem for the coming century of Joyce criticism by resolving the differences between those contemporary critics who cite Joyce in order to substantiate their favorite literary theory and others who apply literary theory merely to illuminate their favorite Joyce text. The difference between their methods is hardly trivial, and now, thank Joyce, we should be able in the following essay to resolve any academically political difficulties into a sort of harmonious retrospective arrangement that cannot help but please everybody by drawing its critical/theoretical stance as well as its subject matter from the evolving literary/aesthetic theories of Stephen and Bloom as they appear in *Portrait* and *Ulysses*. My thesis is that Stephen's youthfully tormented aesthetic theories in both *Portrait* and *Ulysses* appear in direct contradistinction to Bloom's comic sense of reality regarding the ends of art, and that the combination of the two indicates a maturation of Joyce's own artistic sensibility.

In the largely self-portrait of the artist as a young man, Joyce seasons Stephen's somewhat contradictory aesthetic theories with large grains of ironic salt, so that we are warned not to digest them fully before making up our minds whether his ideas are as convincing as they appear to be. On first reading, *Portrait* is a fairly straightforward Künstlerroman providing a cultural orientation for the emerging theoretical positions of its protagonist through a succession of scenes and ideas that produce an artwork, the villanelle, within the book itself. The poem is the result of Stephen's emerging aesthetic philosophy, as spelled out in his episodes with the Dean and Lynch in the last chapter. The proximity of Stephen's enculturation process and Joyce's own strongly suggests an identification between Joyce and young Dedalus without necessarily admitting any intellectual congruence between the two; however, we are invited to read the book autobiographically, if ironically. Through the first four chapters of *Portrait*, Stephen amasses a tangled web of self-identifications with martyrs, saints, tortured lovers, suffering servants, and great writers. From these come his idea of transforming himself into a work of art in the villanelle, acting as both priest and sacrifice through the transubstantiation of his sacrificial life into his poetry—in short, by making himself the subject of his own art. Most of Stephen's preparation for embarking on the aesthetic rationale behind his poem is the product of the Roman Catholicism in his background, combined with a little creative chutzpah. While the rationale for his art appears to be his own sex life blended with his priestly ambition, his aesthetic basis for writing his poem is precipitated by several theoretical/philosophic conversations preceding the villanelle in chapter 5.

The first is with the Dean, who pontificates on the liberal arts and the useful (didactic) arts and in the process reflects only a skewed, superficial knowledge of what Augustine (the originator of the terminology of liberal and useful arts) was talking about in *The City of God*. Augustine, who found it difficult to forget his old life in Carthage, was enamored of the beauty of its (liberal) arts and didn't want them to be excluded from the newly envisioned religious life for man. So Augustine proposed that artists and poets convert their liberal pagan arts into didactic "useful arts," exemplifying the spirit and substance of the new Christian religion. His idea became the source of the pervasive iconography of the Middle Ages, where nearly all art was created in the service of God and His church. The Dean, himself a follower of Cardinal Newman, who in turn had used Augustine's ideas to bolster his defection from the Anglican Church during the Oxford movement, is preoccupied by making the fire in the lecture hall, and refers to his humble contribution as a "useful art," hardly the kind that Stephen would spend his life creating. For Stephen, didacticism was beginning to get a bad name.

The second conversation, with the peace-petition crowd, involves becoming one of the boys, instead of going his solitary intellectual/artistic way, and the third, with Davin, is about Stephen's duty to dedicate his art to the glorification of his race/nation.

Stephen's aesthetic pronouncements to Lynch reflect elements of these earlier talks. The ideas that his work should be didactic—that he should write for his would-be peers, and that he should write to glorify an idyllic Ireland—are all issues responded to in his aesthetic theory, which equates propagandistic didacticism with kinetic or improper art; which concentrates on beauty instead of truth; and which eschews personal identification/involvement as the lowest (lyric) form of art. At the same time, Stephen establishes the highest (dramatic) form as one in which the author is behind the work, "refined out of existence, indifferent, paring his fingernails" (P 215). I don't think it is completely coincidental that these are also tenets of New Criticism. In separating the basket from everything that surrounds it, Stephen isolates the art work from anything that is extraneous to it (integritas). In New Critical terminology this means reading literature as separate from its politics, its setting, its intended message. Stephen's second step is to come to terms by dissecting the complex structure of the isolated art work itself (consonantia), a New Critical version of what we now call deconstruction. And having done that the critic/reader comes to an insight (claritas) regarding its meaning by way of its artistic beauty. Thus the viewer/reader/listener achieves an apolitical insight, later more commonly known as an epiphany. It's standard Brooks and Warren New Criticism.

The problem is, of course, the use to which the epiphany is put. Is it simply aesthetic knowledge for its own sake? Few of us (post-Foucault) really believe that anything exists in an intellectual or moral vacuum, divorced from culture, power, politics, and so on, but instead, epiphanies seem to many to affirm readers' preconceptions mainly because we have been conditioned to receive them as such. One is tempted to doubt the efficacy of the villanelle's beauty or universal truth when we know that its composition was preceded by a wet dream and a long speculative reminiscence about EC's chummy relation to that "priested peasant," Father Moran, while Stephen, the young "priest of eternal imagination," has to content himself with a mentally masturbatory transmutation of "the daily bread of experience into the radiant body of everliving life" (P 221). In a sense Stephen's own egocentric and jealous thoughts in chapter 5 undercut the rationale he develops for his aesthetics because he creates a work in the lyric (lowest/personal) mode, and fails to divorce the subject matter of the villanelle from its relation to its author.

In the famous penultimate diary entry (26 April), Stephen universalizes the personal impetus of his biographical experiences, by offering "to encounter for the millionth time the reality of experience," and thereby "to forge [read—transmute] in the smithy of . . . [his] soul [now a public arena] the uncreated conscience of [his] race" (P 252–53). This hyperbole runs counter to the New Criticism's antididactic purpose. As in the life history of that other major suffering servant, Jesus, there is something of a moral lesson in this process-of-artistic-creation narrative, at least for every Irishman. Joyce, on reaching early middle age, must have realized that Stephen's soul was not big enough for this scheme, so he took on another middle-aged, uniquely common soul, Leopold Bloom's, as co-transmutor.

Bloom's theories are mostly practical: tramlines to the cemetery, stipends to all infants left to compound over the years into tidy sums, and so on. And his aesthetic values, many of which are conceived on the outhouse stool, run more to the mundane than the spiritual or theological, just as his gustatory tastes run to the nutty inner organs of beasts and fowls, in particular grilled mutton kidneys, which give to his "palate a fine tang of faintly scented urine" (U 4.4–5). To pick up where I left off fifteen years ago ("Ulysses" as a Comic Novel 93–97), Bloom's Sancho Panza is the complement of Stephen's Don Quixote in aesthetic as well as economic, religious, and political terms. While Stephen resents being "a servant of two masters . . . The imperial British State . . . and the holy Roman catholic and apostolic church" (U 1.638–44) and an unspecified third, presumably Ireland, Bloom would welcome almost any literary tasks that paid the going rate. He is an advertising man, someone who creates ideas or copies them from the Kilkenny People in order to sell things. He is a sort of creative prostitute, pandering to the aesthetic tastes of tea, wine, and spirit merchants like Keyes, or anyone else who'll buy advertising space. I don't need to regloss the critical history of Bloom as an advertising man, except to distinguish its dialogic opposition to Stephen's own raison d'être for his art. Bloom's commercial grubbiness is one of his most endearing qualities, of course, because it bespeaks a popular-cultural, anti- or semi-intellectualism. Bloom's vision is not confined to gatherings in library offices, or literary sessions in Dawson chambers, but plastered on such egalitarian settings as the walls of public urinals, like Dr. Hy Franks's admired advertisement for clap treatment, posted where acute need meets remedy.

Bloom's sources of artistic inspiration are heavily involved with the alimentary system, as an inspired Lindsey Tucker twenty years ago so splendidly informed us. Preparatory to nearly everything else, Bloom encounters his first ad—one that will stick with him the rest of the day—in Dlugacz's porkbutcher's shop, where he picks up the Agendath Netaim newspaper advertisement heralding the chance of a little bit of heaven for Bloom in the exotic East. He has been preconditioned for the ad by his walk to the shop in the sun, bringing back memories, right out of Said's postcolonialist *Orientalism,* of an exotic journey walking . . .

> along a strand, strange land, come to a city gate, sentry there, old ranker too, old Tweedy's big moustaches, leaning on a long kind of spear. Wander through awned streets. Turbaned faces going by. Dark caves of carpet shops, big man, Turko the terrible, seated crosslegged, smoking a coiled pipe. Cries of sellers in the streets. . . . I pass on. Fading gold sky. A mother watches me from her doorway. She calls her children home in their dark language. High wall: beyond strings twanged. Night sky, moon, violet, colour of Molly's new garters. Strings. Listen. A girl playing one of those instruments what do you call them: dulcimers. I pass. (*U* 4.86–98)

The exoticism of the East, associated with Molly and her father, will blossom in the book to major proportions as a nirvana not only with overtones of eroticism but also abetted by commercialism in the income from the produce of the eucalyptus trees and fruit produced by the planters' company at Agendath: a paying game if there ever was one, as vast sandy tracks are turned to profit by the advertisement. The fantasy will culminate in the plump mellow yellow smellow melons of Molly's behind late that night.

Bloom's most perceptive aesthetic cogitations are, however, raised after breakfast in the atmosphere of the outhouse. The intervening literary/aesthetic conversation between the Blooms involved a question of immortality regarding the word "metempsychosis," the issue arising from Molly's critical reading of *Ruby: The Pride of the Ring.* Even in soft porn there are hints of imperishable artistry, as the scene is presided over by *The Bath of the Nymph* over the bed. The picture, "Given away with the Easter number of *Photo Bits,*" is described as a "splendid masterpiece [that is, deathless, commemorating Easter] in art colours" (*U* 4.369–70).

Immortality still hangs heavily on Bloom, as do his bowels, as he enters the outhouse, there to read Philip Beaufoy's prize titbit, *Matcham's*

Masterstroke, a three-and-a-half-column story, written for payment of a guinea per column. Bloom is ready to produce his own artistically conceived, natural, ultimately immortal contribution even as he contemplates writing another column at the going rate. Perhaps Bloom's written artwork will, like Beaufoy's column, begin and end morally, "Invent a story for some proverb" (*U* 4.518–19). If Stephen sees the didactic as the lowest form of art, Bloom aspires to nothing higher than a moral story, proverbial and therefore deathless in nature. However, his turd of the moment is art for art's sake, produced quickly and neatly so as not to occasion piles, and admittedly accomplished with the aid of a tabloid of cascara sagrada. It is "just right" (*U* 4.510). As Bloom luxuriates in his current production, he speculates on what a cooperative authorship of ensuing articles might mean. He would make literature out of Molly's sayings, the scenes in which she starred, and perhaps, it is hinted, even a mini-*Ulysses.*

The literary/critical perspective on the scene is later, in "Circe," to come from the critic Beaufoy himself when he accuses Bloom of misapplying "a specimen of [his] maturer work disfigured by the hallmark of the beast" (*U* 15.844–45). Bloom wipes his behind with the prize titbit both literally and *metaphorically,* raising the story to an undreamed of literary immorality in his very act of interfacing it (to borrow from the hybrid language of critical theory) with his behind and depositing it along with the perfect turd on the cuckstool floor in an aesthetic wedding of the higher and lower Bakhtinian moieties.

I have already discussed elsewhere how Bloom's beach scene with Gerty MacDowell recapitulates Stephen's epiphanic encounter with the girl on the beach at the end of chapter 4 of *Portrait* (Bowen, "*Ulysses*" 505). The *Portrait* scene draws its metaphysical "ecstasy" from John Donne's poem of the same name, and Stephen has a spiritual orgasm. This is contrasted with Bloom's literal masturbatory ecstasy and orgasm in "Nausicaa." The point I would like to make here concerns the aesthetic concept of the epiphany. Stephen's bird-girl's gaze may produce an ornithological epiphany of inspiration, but we never know what the bird-girl may be thinking, whether the idea of Stephen's silent communion is the product of an overstimulated imagination on the young poet's part, or whether his "Heavenly God!" cry, made silently from his soul, ever made any impression on her at all. After all, it was epiphanically delivered in "the holy silence of his ecstasy" (*P* 171, 172). However, in "Nausicaa" we do know what both Gerty and Bloom are thinking, and that Bloom's orgasm is literal, if self-manipulated. His soggy shirt tails prove that. The intriguing

thing about Bloom's insight into Gerty's mind is that, while it is as speculative as Stephen's epiphany, it is also fairly accurate. Bloom provides the
key to a lot of Gerty's thoughts when, with his first observation of her
condition after she gets off the rock, he notes that she is lame. That intuition alone explains her reluctance to play with the kids, her jealousy of
Cissy, and her preoccupation with advertisements and literature related to
romantic situations and her own body and its adornments. Gerty is not
simply another pubescent girl thinking girlish things. Her thoughts are
animated by what she considers, but never overtly admits, to be a pervasive
physical handicap. In a stroke of Bloom's insight we see her as an individu-
alized, suffering human being, operating in a realistic environment in
which deformity is demeaning, and trying to erect her imaginative de-
fenses against the real world. When Bloom finally comes, he does it thinking not of Gerty, but of Molly with Boylan. The epiphany of imperfection
in "Nausicaa" lies closer to reality than Stephen's ecstatic projections of
the bird-girl. Perhaps that is why Joyce rewrote the scene in the first place.

Another difference between Bloom's and Stephen's aesthetic sensibilities is their regard for the aesthetic values of the Roman Catholic Church.
Beside hearing the confessions of horny women, Stephen sees little to attract him to the priesthood other than the aesthetic value of its mimetic
reproduction of reality: "He had seen himself, a young and silentmannered
priest, entering a confessional swiftly, ascending the altarsteps, incensing,
genuflecting, accomplishing the vague acts of the priesthood which
pleased him *by reason of their semblance of reality and of their distance
from it*" (*P* 158; emphasis added). I take this to mean that the aesthetic
representational symbolism of the church and Stephen's participation in
its activities attract him by the distance they hold from reality rather than
any association with it.

For Bloom, on the other hand, the ecclesiastical rites have much more
mundane purposes. Stopping by All Hallows, he enters a chancel full of
female worshipers: "Something going on: some sodality. . . . Nice discreet
place to be next some girl. Who is my neighbour? Jammed by the hour to
slow music. That woman at midnight mass. Seventh heaven" (U 5.340–
42). As the priest passes out the communion wafers, Bloom, who obviously
has never been close to them, wonders if they are in water. When he hears
a snippet of the priest's incantation, things fall into pattern: "What? *Corpus*: body. Corpse. Good idea the Latin. Stupefies them first. . . . Rum idea:
eating bits of a corpse. Why the cannibals cotton to it": "Lollipop" (*U*
5.350–52, 360). Bloom intuits a demystified mass, but in his own way

again gets the realistic, historically accurate message of internalizing the holy spirit by eating the body of Christ. After erroneously speculating on the letters on the priest's robe, Bloom resumes the worship/sex conjunction that Stephen had originally speculated on in *Portrait*.

Religion plus sex inevitably involve Molly, as Bloom subconsciously shifts gears at the end of the mass to lament the lack of music, his only real familiarity with the ritual and one provided by his wife. Hurrying out to avoid the collection plate ("Better be shoving along. . . . Pay your Easter duty" [*U* 5.450–51]), Bloom discovers a couple of open button holes on his waistcoat, and decides "Good job it wasn't farther south" (*U* 5.456). Bloom's performance-art aesthetics are colored by a complete desacralization of the ritual, including the symbolism, the costume, the intent, and the performance itself. He offers a sexual interpretation to the whole business, informed again by a privileging of monetary considerations. The activities of the priesthood, like those of creative writers, are, for the ad salesman, all part of profit-oriented enterprises. Symbolism for its own sake goes by the board in Bloom's aesthetic of the literal.

Still, Bloom, like Stephen, is given to a variety of aesthetic abstractions. In "Lestrygonians," Bloom remembers his most romantic encounter with Molly, high on Ben Howth, suffused with rhododendrons. After a satisfying glass of wine, Bloom looks around Davy Byrne's, equating the assembled tins of food with the thoughts and moods that their contents generate through their alimentary digestion. The temptation of tinned fruit is associated with the orange groves of Agendath Netaim, which need artificial irrigation to be succulent, and oysters' "Effect on the sexual" (*U* 8.867), associated with Boylan and his impending affair later in the afternoon with Molly.

Exoticism and the more mundane plight of two flies stuck on the window pane combine with the effects of the wine to produce the poignant memory of Molly's kiss during which the holy seedcake communion took place. Unlike the commercialism of the earlier scene in All Hallows, the Howth imagery in Bloom's mind is associated with nanny goat currants and the buzzing of stuck flies. Mundane as Bloom's thoughts may be, they stem as much from reality as from purely disembodied aesthetic speculation. Nevertheless, Bloom's level of aesthetic apprehension is heightened as he regards "the silent veining of the oaken [bar] slab. Beauty: it curves: curves are beauty. Shapely goddesses, Venus, Juno: curves the world admires" (*U* 8.919–21). Here again, however, Bloom wants to translate such abstraction to its source in the lower moiety: "Lovely forms of women sculped Junonian. Immortal lovely. And we stuffing food in one hole and out behind: food, chyle, blood, dung, earth, food: have to feed it like stoking an engine. They have no. Never looked. I'll look today. Keeper won't see. Bend down let something drop. See if she" (*U* 8.928–32). The last thought is no idle aesthetic fancy. Bloom will later be spotted by Mulligan checking out goddess orifices in the National Museum. But there are more immediate matters in Byrne's. Still ruminating on the sexual activities of goddesses with mortal men, Bloom responds to the call of his bladder (itself presumably moved by his aesthetic speculation) with a trip to the yard. We never learn what his thoughts are during this eliminative exercise but have to content ourselves with Nosey Flynn's description of the Bloom household goddess: "She's well nourished, I tell you. Plovers on toast" (*U* 8.952), an aesthetic expression which might be a popularized form of Pre-Raphaelite sensibility.

When Bloom follows Stephen and Lynch into the brothel district in "Circe," their activities reflect unconscious manifestations that include aesthetic as well as libidinous reflections. One of Bloom's prime accusers in the first of his trials is Beaufoy, who, before his culminating ass-wiping accusation, first accuses Bloom of plagiarism: "A plagiarist. A soapy sneak masquerading as a *littérateur*. It's perfectly obvious that with the most inherent baseness he has cribbed some of my bestselling copy, really gorgeous stuff, a perfect gem, the love passages in which are beneath suspicion. The Beaufoy books of love and great possessions, with which your lordship is doubtless familiar, are a household word throughout the kingdom" (*U* 15.822–27). While Beaufoy may be right that Bloom during the day has more than once replicated an idea or even line or two that appeared in Beaufoy's three and a half columns, the point to be taken here is that most popular writers, like literary critics, make their living on appropriated (in the harshest sense, read plagiarized) language. If you have any doubts of the conjunction, consult any of Stephen Joyce's public pronouncements on Joyce criticism. Beaufoy's own anything-for-money moral philosophy undercuts his elevated response to aesthetic violation, when he requests witnesses' fees for himself and his agent, J. B. Pinker, for their testimony.

Most of Bloom's real or imagined malefactions seem to me to be more misdemeanors than felonies, and his accusers a group of Kenneth Starrs looking to hang some seriocomic infractions on him. Prosecutory types usually seem to be forces of intolerance and bigotry. As the Clinton/

Lewinski polls indicated, a majority of the world loves a good, masochistic, womanly man, whose suffering may be acute for the moment, but harmless enough and even funny in the long run (no pun intended).

That the accusations against Bloom are probably self-induced from his own conscience does not alter their comic and thus nullifying potential. Bloom's aesthetic cogitations, like the rest of his mental projections in "Circe," seem only realistically to burlesque his already well-established sense of self, while Stephen's sublimated projections of his guilty relationship with his mother come back to haunt him literally as well as figuratively. One liminal projection of Stephen, involving music, does, however, have prophetic as well as aesthetic currency. Seated at the piano, Stephen speculates on the eight-note scale. He situates the foundation tone, the tonic (or the doh on the so/fa scale) in opposition to the dominant or fifth (sol), the note furthest removed from the tonic in the scale. Stephen's point is that the dominant or furthest removed usually anticipates a return to the tonic in normal circumstances. He likens the progression to divisions of character types, inferring for the reader that the vast difference between Bloom and himself may harbinger an eventual amalgamation of the two. I do not think it coincidental that in the middle of this speculation, "The Holy City"—Bloom's theme song of the New Bloomusalem (the idyllic Dublin / Ireland under his own aegis)—"*begins to blare*" (*U* 15.2115). Stephen asks, "*(abruptly)* What went forth to the ends of the world to traverse not itself, God, the sun, Shakespeare, a commercial traveller, having itself traversed in reality itself becomes that self. . . . Self which it itself was ineluctably preconditioned to become. *Ecco!*" (*U* 15.2117–22). Like a chord resolving itself, Stephen and Bloom, drawn together in "Eumaeus" on the only ground on which they have much in common, music, may have found the source of commonality to forge the uncreated conscience of their race.

They attempt to explore that source of commonality in "Ithaca," comparing the Irish and Hebrew music and languages. They begin with Stephen singing "Suil Arun" for Bloom, and Bloom singing one of the Songs of Solomon for Stephen. They continue to trace possible combinations of Irish and Hebrew characters and phonics, leading Bloom to sing the "Hatikvah" or Hope for the Israeli nation, which Stephen counters with a rendition of the ever-perplexing anti-Semitic traditional ballad "Little Harry Hughes," reminiscent of Chaucer's "Prioress's Tale."

While Stephen's motives for offering this seemingly insulting song remain opaque even after his textual explication, the saving grace in the scene is Bloom's failure to take permanent offense. At this point whether he was conscious of any insidious metaphoric intent, or because he was so literal-minded he was merely oblivious to what most people would take as an insult, remains in doubt. Bloom is happy his window is not broken like the Jew's in the song, but he greets with mixed feelings the potential identification of Milly as the Jew's homicidal daughter. Stephen's subsequent commentary does little to clear up who the "victim predestined" might be, although Bloom identifies with both "victim predestined" and "secret infidel," and in his typically tangential way, begins to look at the social aspects of the story: "He weighed the possible evidences for and against ritual murder: the incitations of the hierarchy, the superstition of the populace," and so on, and so on (*U* 17.833–45).

The songfest, the communal cocoa, and Stephen's refusal of Bloom's invitation to spend the night do little to affirm or nullify the possible importance of their backyard penumbra urination, marked by stars, signs, and portents, including Molly's cave-wall reflection backed by an interior candle against the upstairs window shade. Their lives have momentarily crossed like the trajectories of their urinations, in a ceremony marked with potential mystery and realism that reflect the dual nature of the protagonists' theoretical approaches to life and the aesthetics of their literary understanding.

Finally, I would like to suggest that the question/answer narrative format of "Ithaca" is a sort of culmination to two divergent aesthetic theories: the literalist and the metaphoric/speculative. While the literal predominates the prose, the metaphoric struggles for interpretation. Just as Stephen early on sets the traditional, if complex, tone of the book, with its complexities of theme such as father-son manifestations cross-referenced with Shakespeare, the Holy Trinity, Odysseus and Telemachus, and a host of other situations, Bloom's literalism comes, when we get to "Ithaca," to prevail in the narrative of such mundane matters as the mortgage payment schedule on Bloom's prospective new house, through more than we ever want to know about the elaborate numerical difference in their ages, to the budget for June 16, as Joyce's readers struggle to make thematic or metaphoric sense of whatever they can in the welter of detail. The narrative of "Ithaca" is dictated by an aesthetic different from the hyperbolically comic lists of "Cyclops," or the obfuscatory turgidity of the evolving prose of "Oxen"; but, absorbed with a Sisyphusian patience, the quieter rewards of a close reading of "Ithaca" are just as comic as informational. In "Penelope," although we still have to work to unravel the unpunctuated syntax and pronoun references, the literal becomes once again accessible, and we think once more that we can grasp the meaning of Molly's thoughts through our understanding of her priorities. I'm not sure that is possible. The critical battles over Molly's integrity, morality, and literality have subsided slightly during the last few years, but if they prove anything about the truth, it is about what is in the eye of the beholder/reader, where it always was. Joyce's complicated literary/theoretical games are in a sense as much of a Rorschach for their critical interpreters as they are an insight into the pleasure we take from literature itself.

Works Cited

Bowen, Zack. "*Ulysses*" as a Comic Novel. Syracuse: Syracuse University Press, 1989.

———. "*Ulysses*." In *A Companion to Joyce Studies*, edited by Zack Bowen and James Carens. Westport, Conn.: Greenwood, 1984.

Tucker, Lindsey. *Stephen and Bloom at Life's Feast: Alimentary Symbolism and the Creative Process in James Joyce's "Ulysses."* Columbus: Ohio State University Press, 1984.

Contributors

Keri Elizabeth Ames received her Ph.D. from the Committee on Social Thought at the University of Chicago, where she studied Greek with David Grene. Her dissertation examined the convergence between Homer's *Odyssey* and Joyce's *Ulysses*. She taught at Connecticut College and in the Graham School of General Studies at the University of Chicago and is currently teaching at Yale University. She has been published in the *James Joyce Literary Supplement* and the *Joyce Studies Annual*.

Morris Beja is professor emeritus at Ohio State University and has been a visiting professor at the University of Thessaloniki, Greece, and University College Dublin, Ireland. A Guggenheim Fellow, he has also held two Fulbright lectureships. His books include *Epiphany in the Modern Novel* (1971), *Film and Literature* (1979), and *James Joyce: A Literary Life* (1992). He has edited a scholarly edition of Virginia Woolf's *Mrs. Dalloway* (1996), as well as volumes of essays on Joyce, Virginia Woolf, Samuel Beckett, and Orson Welles. Beja founded the International Virginia Woolf Society and is executive secretary and past president of the International James Joyce Foundation. He is co-coordinator of the academic program for Bloomsday 100, the International James Joyce Symposium in Dublin, June 2004.

Zack Bowen teaches at the University of Miami, where he was chair of the Department of English. His books on Joyce include *Musical Allusions in the Works of James Joyce* (1974), *"Ulysses" as a Comic Novel* (1989), and *Bloom's Old Sweet Song: Essays on Joyce and Music* (1995); he also coedited *A Companion to Joyce Studies* (1984). His other books include *Padraic Colum: A Critical Biographical Introduction* (1970), *Mary Lavin* (1975), and *A Reader's Guide to John Barth* (1993). He has produced a series of recorded interpretations of *Ulysses*, in dramatic form with music, reissued by the Smithsonian Institution in 1993. He is editor of Critical Essays on British Literature at Twayne Publishers, the James Joyce Series at the University Press of Florida, and the *James Joyce Literary Supplement*. Bowen has served as president of both the James Joyce Society of New York and the International James Joyce Foundation.

Richard Brown is a Reader in Modern Literature in the School of English at the University of Leeds, where he is one of the directors of the James Joyce Research Group. He is the author of *James Joyce and Sexuality* (1985), *James Joyce* (1992), and a volume of poetry, *Transparencies* (1987). He has edited Joyce's *A Portrait of the Artist as a Young Man* for Everyman's Library (1991). He cofounded and coedits the *James Joyce Broadsheet*. Brown has been a Cline Fellow at the Harry Ransom Humanities Research Center at the University of Texas at Austin.

Anne Fogarty is a lecturer in the Department of English, University College, Dublin, and is director of the James Joyce Summer School. She has published widely on the connections between gender and genre in twentieth-century Irish women's writing and on Renaissance literature. She was guest editor of the June 2000 special issue of the *Colby Quarterly* on Irish women novelists 1800–1940 and is completing a study of Edmund Spenser and early modern colonial representations of Ireland. Fogarty is general editor of the *Irish University Review*. She is co-coordinator of the academic program for Bloomsday 100, the International James Joyce Symposium in Dublin, June 2004.

Ellen Carol Jones has taught as associate professor of English and International Studies at Saint Louis University. She has edited *Joyce: Feminism/Post/Colonialism* (1998) and four special volumes of *MFS: Feminist Readings of Joyce* (1989), *Virginia Woolf* (1992), *The Politics of Modernism* (1992), and *Feminism and Modern Fiction* (1988). She is the author of numerous essays on Joyce and on Virginia Woolf; "Empty Shoes," on iconic representations of the Holocaust, was published in *Footnotes: On Shoes* (2001).

Sebastian D. G. Knowles is professor of English at Ohio State University. He is the author of *A Purgatorial Flame: Seven British Writers in the Second World War* (1990) and *The Dublin Helix: The Life of Language in James Joyce's "Ulysses"* (2001), the coauthor of *An Annotated Bibliography of a Decade of T. S. Eliot Criticism: 1977–1986* (1992), and the editor of *Bronze by Gold: The Music of Joyce* (1999). He is a member of the board of trustees of the International James Joyce Foundation and of the board of editors of the *James Joyce Quarterly*.

Morton P. Levitt has long been interested in the matter of Joyce's presence—his aura—among modern novelists, as evident in books such as *Modernist Survivors: The Contemporary Novel in England, the United States, France, and Latin America* (1987), *James Joyce and Modernism: Beyond Dublin* (2000), *The Modernist Masters: Studies in the Novel* (2002), and *The Rhetoric of Modernist Fiction: From a New Point of View*, (2004). He has been editor of the *Journal of Modern Literature* since 1986.

Mary Lowe-Evans is chair of the Department of English and Foreign Languages at the University of West Florida. She has written *Crimes against Fecundity: Joyce and Population Control* (1989) and *Frankenstein: Mary Shelley's Wedding Guest* (1993), and edited *Critical Essays on Mary Wollstonecraft Shelley* (1998). She has also contributed numerous articles to scholarly journals and collections, including *Gender in Joyce* and *The Comic Tradition in Irish Women Writers*.

Margot Norris is professor of English and comparative literature at the University of California at Irvine. Her books on Joyce include *The Decentered Universe of Finnegans Wake: A Structuralist Analysis* (1976), *Joyce's Web: The Social Unraveling of Modernism* (1992) and *Suspicious Readings of Joyce's Dubliners* (2003); she has also edited *A Companion to James Joyce's "Ulysses"* (1998) and coedited *Joycean Cultures, Culturing Joyces* (1998). Other books include *Beasts of the Modern Imagination: Darwin, Nietzsche, Kafka, Ernst and Lawrence* (1985) and *Writing War in the Twentieth Century* (2000). She is vice president of the International James Joyce Foundation.

Mark Osteen is professor of English and director of film studies at Loyola College in Maryland. He is the author of *The Economy of "Ulysses": Making Both Ends Meet* (1995) and *American Magic and Dread: Don DeLillo's Dialogue with Culture* (2000), coeditor of *The New Economic Criticism* (1999), and editor of *The Question of the Gift: Essays across Disciplines* (2002).

Thomas Jackson Rice is professor of English at the University of South Carolina. He is the author of eight books, including *Joyce, Chaos, and Complexity* (1997), *James Joyce: A Guide to Research* (1982), and *James*

Joyce: Life, Work, and Criticism (1985) as well as being the author of more than one hundred essays and papers, chiefly on nineteenth- and twenti-eth-century British fiction.

John Rocco is assistant professor of humanities at the Maritime College of the State University of New York. He has published several books of rock criticism, including *The Doors Companion* (1997), *The Nirvana Companion* (1998), *Dead Reckonings: The Life and Times of the Grateful Dead* (1999), and *The Beastie Boys Companion* (2000). He is at work on a study of Joyce and modernist vision.

Fritz Senn took part in the inception of the International James Joyce Symposia (1967) and *A Wake Newslitter* and has written many essays and notes. Some are collected in *Joyce's Dislocutions: Essays on Reading as Translation* (1984), *Inductive Scrutinies: Focus on Joyce* (1995), *Nichts gegen Joyce: Joyce versus Nothing* (1983), and *Nicht nur Nichts gegen Joyce* (1999). He has been director of the Zürich James Joyce Foundation since 1985.

Jolanta Wawrzycka is professor of English at Radford University, Virginia, and director of the study abroad program European Literary Trails. She has published chapters in books on James Joyce, Milan Kundera, and Roland Barthes; essays on Joyce and translation; and translations from Polish. She is coeditor of *Gender in Joyce* (1997).

Index

The Florida James Joyce Series
Edited by Zack Bowen

James Joyce's "Fraudstuff," by Kimberly J. Devlin (2002)

Rite of Passage in the Narratives of Dante and Joyce, by Jennifer Margaret Fraser (2002)

Joyce and the Scene of Modernity, by David Spurr (2002)

Joyce and the Early Freudians: A Synchronic Dialogue of Texts, by Jean Kimball (2003)

Twenty-First Joyce, edited by Ellen Carol Jones and Morris Beja (2004)